I0754233

THE WORKS OF

WILLIAM SHAKESPEARE

THE PLAYS EDITED FROM THE FOLIO OF MDCXXIII, WITH VARIOUS READINGS FROM ALL THE EDITIONS AND ALL THE COMMENTATORS, NOTES, INTRODUCTORY REMARKS, A HISTORICAL SKETCH OF THE TEXT, AN ACCOUNT OF THE RISE AND PROGRESS OF THE ENGLISH DRAMA, A MEMOIR OF THE POET, AND AN ESSAY UPON HIS GENIUS

By RICHARD GRANT WHITE

VOL. I.

BOSTON
LITTLE BROWN AND COMPANY
1871

Cambridge: Printed by John Wilson and Son.

TO

THOMAS P. BARTON, Esquire,

THIS EDITION

OF THE POET WHOSE WORKS HE HAS STUDIED SO PROFOUNDLY

AND COMPREHENDS SO THOROUGHLY,

AND FOR THE ILLUSTRATION OF WHICH HE HAS ACCUMULATED

AND SYSTEMATICALLY ARRANGED,

WITH AN INTELLIGENT PURPOSE RARELY BROUGHT TO THE TASK,

A MASS OF MATERIAL UNEQUALLED IN THIS COUNTRY,

AND HARDLY SURPASSED IN THE WORLD,

IS DEDICATED,

IN RECOGNITION OF HIS ATTAINMENTS IN SHAKESPEARIAN LETTERS,

AND IN ACKNOWLEDGMENT OF AID WITHOUT WHICH

IT COULD NOT HAVE BEEN COMPLETED,

BY HIS OBLIGED FRIEND AND FELLOW-STUDENT,

R. G. W.

Richter del. Angus sculp.

Published as the Act directs by Bellamy & Roberts June 20, 1791

PREFACE.

GOOD reasons only can justify the addition of a new book to the enormous mass with which the world is cumbered. This is particularly true of a new edition of Shakespeare's works, which, in its main purpose, only professes to be a better presentation of that which has been presented tolerably well before. Therefore these words of preliminary explanation.

The first object sought in the preparation of this edition has been a text as nearly pure as possible, and the reduction of the field of doubt and conjecture in all directions to the narrowest attainable limits; the second, and last, to place the reader as nearly as possible in the position of those for whom these plays were written, and to give all accessible information concerning their origin, and the circumstances under which, and the manner in which, they were produced. The vicissitudes through which the text has passed, and the time which has elapsed since it was written, make the performance of these offices necessary. The most perfect understanding and the most satisfactory enjoyment of any author's writings, especially of a poet's, are attained by direct communication with the author's mind. An unnecessary intermediary is always an intruder: a note thrust between a poet and his reader which is not required for the full comprehension of the poet's meaning is always an offence. At best, an editor, like a physician or a lawyer, is a necessary evil. Had Shakespeare superintended the publication of his own plays, it is clear that the office of their modern editor would have been limited to the explanation of a few obsolete words and phrases, the illustration of passages alluding to by-gone manners and customs, and perhaps an attempt at the literary history of each composition. But the text of these plays was published with such corruption in all the early copies that not one of them is continuously readable until it has undergone some emendation and regulation; and in the case of certain plays, such are the variations between those early copies, that the text of no one of them can be accepted as sound and satisfactory. In all the early texts, quarto and folio, some entire scenes are found in the utmost confusion,—a confusion which has not yet in all cases been reduced to order. It is this deplorable condition of the authentic and *quasi* authentic texts of Shakespeare's plays that has made extended editorial labor upon them necessary, and has given opportunity for it when it is not necessary; so that a careful editor finds that it is his duty not only to restore, but — such temptation is there on the one hand, and such temerity on the other — to defend what has been restored, and to protect against the hand of sophisticating innovation that which needs no restoration.

Failing an authentic text of Shakespeare's plays from his own hand, the authority which goes with authenticity pertains to the folio edition published in 1623 by the care and labor of his friends and fellow-theatrical proprietors John Heminge and Henry Condell. They were his literary executors — self-appointed, it is true, and not so faithful and painstaking as it behooved them to be; but having some right to, and (as play-publishing went in those days) no little fitness for, the office which they assumed. Their edition is, indeed, so very far from being perfect, that the demand, which has been made in some quarters, that its text should be published without change for tho use of the general reader, could only have been made by persons entirely ignorant of its real condition. In very many passages it is absolutely unintelligible; and, beside, it lacks some of the finest passages of Shakespeare's poetry. But corruption, although it impairs authority, cannot defeat authenticity; and the incompleteness of the folio text, being often manifestly the result of adaptation to stage purposes, is evidence of some weight in favor of the genuineness of what is given. For sixteen of the thirty-seven plays in this collection, the folio of 1623 is the only authority. It is also important to state that every kind of corruption which is found in the folio is found in a greater degree in the quartos.

For the reasons above given, the text of the present edition is founded exclusively upon that of the first folio, and has been prepared, in the first instance, as if no other edition of authority had appeared since that was published, although afterward the readings of every edition, ancient and modern, and the suggestions of every commentator, have been carefully examined, adopted when they appeared admissible, and recorded when they were deemed worthy of preservation. The text of the first folio alone having the stamp of authenticity, some better reason than the editor's mere opinion or his preference has been deemed necessary to justify any essential deviation from that text in favor of the readings of editions of either an earlier or a later date. Evident corruption of that text, with at least highly probable restoration of what mere accident destroyed, and the recovery of what had been omitted, for stage purposes, from the copy furnished to the printer, are the only reasons which have been regarded as sufficient for such deviation. The superior antiquity of the quarto texts of some of these plays is not unfrequently brought to the attention of the critical reader of Shakespeare in support of a reading taken from some one of those texts: — as if the age of a surreptitiously printed edition could supply its lack of authenticity! But in many cases, at least, "the oldest authority" seems to rival "the oldest inhabitant" in foisting feeble nonsense upon credulity, and to rival in trustworthiness that much-vaunted oracle. I am, however, no champion of the readings of the first folio, as such. It seems to me plain, indeed, that the circumstances of its publication require us to assume that its text is correct, except where it is manifestly corrupt or imperfect. But in those cases it is to be corrected boldly, and with none of the hesitation produced by that superstitious reverence of mere antiquity which is called conservatism.

It is not uncommon to hear true lovers of Shakespeare, men of intelligence and no little acquaintance with literature, remark with gravity that it is dangerous to disturb the text. *The* text! what text? That of the folio, which, in scores of passages, is absolutely unintelligible, and in others deficient? That of the quartos, of which the same is true, though in a greater degree, of all those plays which first appeared in that form? The text of the Variorum of 1821, and read, for instance, as people read for twenty-five years, "So much un*cu*rable her garboils," instead of, "So much un*curb*able her garboils"? Every reader will reply, that, of course, he wishes the corrupted passages of the folio and the quartos, and such as that just quoted from Malone's Variorum, to be restored; and it will be found that when men talk apprehensively about disturbing the text, and of their veneration for the old text, they mean merely the text of the edition which they have been accustomed to use, the peculiar oldness of which may not reach to half a century, or the care in its printing equal that taken in the office of a country newspaper. I have seen an intelligent man, unacquainted with any other text of Shakespeare than that of a London trade impression bearing the names of Johnson and Steevens on its title-page, — which he possessed in a miserable reprint with smudgy, careless press-work upon spongy, whity-brown paper, — as conservative about that text as if the proof-sheets of his copy had been read by Shakespeare himself; the reason of his solicitude being an attachment to that text, the consequence merely of his familiarity with it and his lack of acquaintance with any other, and also his utter ignorance of the earliest form of the text and its subsequent vicissitudes. It does not take many years to root error in minds inclined to this kind of conservatism. The old priest of whom Camden tells us, who read *Mumpsimus*, *Domine*, rejected the proposal to read

Sumpsimus, &c., because he "had used *Mumpsimus* thirty years, and would not leave his old *Mumpsimus* for their new *Sumpsimus*." Most of the texts which some people are anxious to conserve are not more venerable, or worthier of veneration.

The truth is, that in deciding upon the purity of the texts of the old copies, and in the restoration of their corrupted and defective passages, there is occasion for all the knowledge, the judgment, the taste, the imagination, and the sympathetic appreciation of the author that can be brought to this task by the most gifted and accomplished editor. Constant vigilance, also, on the part of competent scholars, repeated collation with the text of the old copies, and examination of the reasons assigned by modern editors for the changes which they have made in that text, are necessary to the preservation of Shakespeare's writings in a state nearly approaching that in which they came from his hand. The mere accidents of the best printing-offices — to say nothing of the oversights of editors — are such that no edition is worthy of confidence, or, indeed, to be called an edition, the text of which has not been compared, word by word, with that of the folio of 1623 and the precedent quarto copies. It was very smart in Steevens to sneer at "the Nimrods of *ifs* and *ands*;" but we all know that the absence or presence of a particle or a point will change the meaning of a sentence. The thief strikes only three letters out of the eighth commandment.

For the reasons above given, a notice of even the slightest deviation from the text of 1623 in this edition has been deemed obligatory; but a like respect has been paid to older or more modern texts only when, in the former case, the deviation is of some importance, or, in the latter, the rejected reading has been approved by some distinguished editor. Very many instances of variation from the text of the folio of 1623 are characterized as almost unworthy of mention in the very notes in which they are brought to the reader's attention. A large proportion of these may be justly regarded, indeed, as quite unworthy of notice, if we consider their actual or their relative importance. But as a guarantee of accuracy the indication of these trifling variations has its value. A merchant notices the discrepancy of one cent in the balance-sheet of an account of millions, not for the value of the sum in error, but for the importance of exactness. If the error of a unit has passed the accountant's eye there is no surety against the oversight of an error of thousands.

Careful literal conformity to the old text, except in its corruptions and irregularities, has, however, a greater value than this of being a guarantee of exactness. For instance, in these passages in *Hamlet*, —

" —— yet once methought
It lifted up *it* head, and did address
It self to motion" (Act I. Sc. 2);

" This doth betoken
The corse they follow did with desperate hand
Fordo *it* own life" (Act V. Sc. 2);

and in this in *Lear*, —

" The hedge-sparrow fed the cuckoo so long,
That it had *it* head bit off by *it* young," —

the use of 'it' in the possessive sense is not only a trait of the time, but, even if there were no other evidence, is enough to show that *Hamlet* and *Lear* were written before *The Winter's Tale*, in which we find "*it's* folly and *it's* tenderness," and before *Henry the Eighth*, in the first scene of which we have, "made former wonders *its*." The last passage affords the earliest instance known, I believe, of the use of the neuter possessive pronoun without the apostrophe. And yet until the appearance of the present edition of Shakespeare's works 'its' was given indiscriminately throughout the text of all editions.* The editors probably thought that in printing *its* they were merely correcting a typographical error; whereas they were destroying evidence of a change in the language which took place during Shakespeare's career as a dramatist, and which the printers of the folio of 1623, with all their negligence in other respects, carefully preserved.

A certain class of merely typographical errors in the old copies must, however, be passed over, of necessity, by even the most punctilious editor; such, for instance, as that in the following line in *Julius Cæsar*, which appears thus in the folio: —

"Then to answere euery man directly and breefely."

Here the unpractised eye will hardly detect *breesely*, printed for *briefly*, due to the mistake by the compositor of an old-fashioned long *s* (ſ) for an *f*, or perhaps to the mere accidental mutilation of the latter. When such accidents affect the sense, even in the slightest degree, and thus make a new reading, they have

* See the Notes on the passages above cited.

always been noticed in this edition; but otherwise they have been passed over.

In the preparation of the text herewith presented great care has been taken to give Shakespeare's words as nearly as possible with syllabic faithfulness to the form in which they were used by him and by his contemporaries. Only by a preservation of this form can the rhythm of either Shakespeare's verse or prose be preserved. Faithful conformity in this respect, however, does not require, it need hardly be said, the preservation of the irregular spelling of the Elizabethan era, except in those extremely rare instances in which that spelling preserves an old form of a word, or, in some cases, the rhythm of a verse. The following are, I believe, all the words in which the old spelling has been retained: *libbard* (leopard), *squire* (square), *pill* (peel), *spet* (spat), *misconsters* (misconstrues), *commandement*, *module* (model), *wrack* (wreck), *murther* (murder), *fadom* (fathom), *egal* (equal), *paiock* (peacock), *porpentine* (porcupine), with certain plurals and possessive cases in *es*, as *owles*, *moones*, and *Jewes*. It will be seen that these are not, except perhaps in the case of *pill*, mere instances of irregular orthography, that is, not different modes of expressing the same sounds which are expressed by the modern orthography of the words which convey the same ideas.

In continuation of this subject it may be remarked that too little attention has heretofore been paid to the old usage in regard to the full or the contracted forms of the past participle in *ed*, the second person singular of the present tense in *est*, the fusion of words, and other traits of like character. The bad effect of a disregard of the practice of Shakespeare's day in these particulars may be gathered from the examination of a few examples. The following line —

> "Th' unstain*ed* sword that you have used to bear,"
> 2 *Henry IV.*, V. 2 —

is printed in all other editions, I believe, "*The* unstained sword," &c., or "*The unstain'd . . . ,*" &c., (the pronunciation in either case "*unstaind*,") and similar contractions have been generally, if not universally, disregarded. But this loses the accent which Shakespeare intended; requiring "The *un*stain'd," &c., instead of "Th' un*stain*-ed," &c. Shakespeare might have written "The unstain'd;" but, in accordance with the usage of his time, he preferred to preserve the participial termination, and throw the accent upon the radical syllable. So in *Hamlet*, Act II. Sc. 2, he writes "Th' unnerv*ed* father flies," and not "*The* un*nerv'd* father," &c; and in *Henry the Fourth*, —

> "Then let him not be sland'*red* with revolt,"
> I. 3, —

where all modern editions but this give "Then let him not be slan*der'd*," &c., thus disregarding a characteristic though minute trait of the pronunciation and the prosody of the Elizabethan period. Numberless like instances occur in these plays, a few of which are remarked in the notes to this edition. The prosodic importance of the participial termination is very manifest in the following lines from a speech in *Romeo and Juliet*: —

> "Beguil'd, divorced, wronged, spited, slain."
>
> "Despis'd, distressed, hated, martyr'd, kill'd."

Here a disregard of the contractions, and the printing of these lines thus, —

"Beguiled, divorced, wronged, spited, slain,"

"Despised, distressed, hated, martyred, killed," —

would either destroy the rhythm or put the reader at fault in that regard until he had examined them. And in *Love's Labour's Lost*, Act IV. Sc. 2, how out of character it would be for the pedant *Holofernes* to speak in our modern clipped way of *Dull's* exhibition of his "undress'd, unpolish'd, uneducated, unprun'd, untrain'd, or rather, unletter'd, or ratherest, unconfirm'd fashion," instead of "his undress*ed*, unpolish*ed*, uneducated, unprun*ed*, untrain*ed*, or rather, unletter*ed*, or ratherest, unconfirm*ed* fashion"! The passage is prose; but it is worthy of special remark that the old copy makes these distinctions no less carefully in prose than in verse, and that the folio is most carefully printed in this respect. So in *Troilus and Cressida*, Act II. Sc. 3, where *Thersites* says, according to the old copy, "If I could have remembered a guilt counterfeit thou *would'st* not have *slipt* out of my contemplation," we may be sure that it is not by mere accident that we do not find 'remem*bred*,' or 'remem*ber'd*,' 'would*est*,' and 'slip*ped*.' Yet the indications of the old copies in this instance, as in almost all of like character in prose passages, have hitherto been disregarded. And what is worse than a uniform disregard, they have been observed in some instances and disregarded in others, even in the same passage. Thus in *Julius Cæsar*, Act I. Sc. 2, the first part of one of *Casca's* speeches is printed thus in the folio: "Marry, before he fell downe, when he perceiv'd the common Heard was glad he refus'd the Crowne, he pluckt me open his doublet, and offer'd them his Throat to cut." Here the contraction of 'perceived' is observed in the Variorum of 1821, and by Mr. Collier, but the others are disregarded, which is more confusing than the disregard of all in other editions.

The contraction of *ed* when it follows a vowel, as in 'sued' and 'died,' has, I believe, been hitherto disregarded. But it was not disregarded in Shakespeare's time, or even by the careless printers of dramatic poetry in his day. And with good reason, as will be seen by the following examples: —

> "But he's a tri*ed* and a valiant soldier."
> *Julius Cæsar*, Act IV. Sc. 1.

> "by which account
> Our business valu*ed* some twelve months hence."
> 1 *Henry the Fourth*, Act III. Sc. 2.

> "Lord Bassianus lies embru*ed* here."
> *Titus Andronicus*, Act II. Sc. 4.

In these passages, unless 'tried,' 'valued,' and 'embrued' have their full participial pronunciation, the first as a dissyllable, the last two as trisyllables, the verse becomes prose. The particularity with which this contraction was observed is shown in a passage in *Othello*, where 'learned,' which to this day we pronounce, when it is a participial adjective, as a dissyllable, even colloquially, was contracted by Shakespeare, for the nonce, into a monosyllable: —

> "And knows all qualities with a learn'd spirit."

This, I believe, is the only instance of Shakespeare's use of this word as a monosyllable; and yet, although the folio misprints "qualities" "*quantities*" in the same line, the contraction is marked, with a carefulness which has not been imitated by modern editors.

Quite as important as the contraction of syllables is the elision of final and initial letters, by which two words are compressed into one; and yet this has been almost as generally disregarded as the other. When Shakespeare wrote in one line of *Macbeth*, —

"Boil thou first *i' th'* charmed pot;"

and in another, —

"In *the* cauldron boil and bubble;"

in a prose passage, "fold it, write *upon't*, read it, afterwards seal it;" in *Lear*, in two contiguous lines, —

"O Regan, wilt thou take her *by the* hand ?
Why not *by th'* hand, sir? How have I offended?"

and in *Hamlet*, —

"Sith not *th'* exterior nor *the* inward man," —

he meant something by these distinctions. Yet they are almost, if not quite, universally ignored by editors. No one of these cases is in itself of much importance; but the sum of all the cases of similar neglect in these plays is of great importance. Perfect accuracy in this respect is attainable only, if attainable at all, by the minutest attention on the part of the editor. It will not do to adopt a printing-office rule in this matter; for Shakespeare used contractions and elisions more and more freely as he grew older; and thus they are one of our guides in determining the dates at which his plays were written.

The question has been seriously mooted whether the peculiar and irregular grammatical forms of the old text should be preserved. But it seems to me that there is no good ground of doubt upon this subject. I can see no reason for printing Shakespeare's text, either in this respect or in any other, as if it were written yesterday. The variations of that text from our present syntactical standard are minute and comparatively few; but such as they are, they are characteristic of the time when these plays were produced. The very incongruities of the old text in this respect are a trait of the period, indicating generally a transition stage in certain syntactical forms. Thus we have in the Lord's Prayer, and in many other passages of our English Bible, "Our Father *which* art in heaven," but elsewhere, for instance, "Hannah said unto Eli, I am the woman *who* stood by thee here, praying unto the Lord." And here the latter pronoun was consciously introduced; for Coverdale and the Genevan Bible both have "the woman *that*," &c. Now, the attempt to secure conformity to the prevailing syntax by reading, "Our Father *who* art," or uniformity, by reading, "I am the woman *which* stood," would be unjustifiable. Such peculiarities are subject to the same rule which applies to the individual irregularities of a writer, which are as much a trait of his mental character as any other peculiarity of style, and are therefore to be carefully preserved. An editor's function is to think, not for, but with, his author. Therefore such passages as the following have not been regulated according to a modern, or even a uniform, standard in this edition: — "Is crown'd so soon, and broke his solemn oath;" "His scandal of retire;" "is set him down to sleep;" "those powers . . . have arriv'd our coast;" "the wind who woos," "my armed knees who bowed;" "Earth hath swallowed all my hopes but she;" "All debts are cleared between you and I;" "That fair for which love groaned for;" "In what enormity is Marcus poor in?" "Shall's [shall us] to the Capitol?" "What he is, more suits you to conceive than I to speak of." Such syntactical irregularities as these are too thickly strewn through the literature of the Elizabethan period to be slips of the pen, or printer's errors.

The evils which may result from one editor's trusting to another in matters of authority are great; because, however careful, we are all liable to error. Examples might be pointed out in the work of even the most competent editors. Therefore all readings and quotations in this edition, with exceedingly rare exceptions, have been given not at second hand, — as I have found is too frequently the case, — but from the originals; the excepted cases being passages in two of the earlier quartos and two or three extremely rare books, copies of which have not yet floated over to us, in which recourse has been had to the next best authority, the careful reprints of these volumes under the eyes of the most eminent Elizabethan scholars of England, compared with such collations as those of Capell and Mr. Dyce. The copy of the folio of 1623 which I have constantly used is that in the Astor Library, which is the well-known copy formerly in the collection of the Duke of Buckingham at Stowe. But I have also, whenever it seemed desirable, had the privilege of examining the admirable copy of the first folio, now in the noble Shakespearian library of Mr. Thomas P. Barton of New York, which entire collection, indeed, has at all times been open to me for consultation when the limits of my own humbler shelves were reached. But the kindness which I have received from this distinguished collector and thorough and accomplished student of Shakespeare, I have endeavored elsewhere more worthily to acknowledge. To Mr. James Lenox my readers as well as myself also owe much for the very generous and unreserved manner in which he placed his collection of the early quartos — the value of which is hardly known except to the best informed bibliographers — entirely at my service.

In the notes upon the regulation of the text, I have endeavored to assign each restoration of a corrupted passage to its author; for I do not understand how gentlemen and scholars can claim an edition as their own, and then take no small proportion of their text and of their notes from other editors without a word of acknowledgment. A similar course has been pursued with regard to quotations made in support of conjecture or in elucidation of obscurity; and these, including conjectural emendations thought worthy of notice, but not of a place in the text, being generally given in the order of time, a concise history of every restored or doubtful passage is presented. The reader of a critical edition of a great author's works has the right to know upon what authority any reading, gloss, or critical judgment is adopted. In every case, I believe, where no such credit is given for a restoration, I am responsible for it; and as much prominence need not be given to claims of this sort, in those cases it is merely remarked that hitherto the text has stood otherwise. On revising my labors I find that the number of such instances in these volumes is sufficiently large to give me some solicitude, even although I am conscious of the reverent spirit in which the corrections have been made, and the logical conditions to which I held myself bound, even after perception and judgment had done their work. The tables of restored and of corrupted readings indicate the textual points and those relating to the history of the several plays in which this edition differs from those which have preceded it in the present century. They are given for the purpose of presenting in a compact form, easy of reference, a view of the principal peculiarities of the edition in these respects. In the course of my work I have often wished that previous editors had given such a synopsis of their dealings with the text. It would have saved their successors much trouble. This comparative view is limited by the present century, not only because the acquaintance of the large majority of even the more critical readers of Shakespeare with the individual labors of his editors and commentators is confined to that period, but because the first quarter of the century is marked by the appearance of a new spirit of criticism upon these plays, and the introduction of new methods of editing them. The efforts of the last century culminated in the Boswell-Malone Variorum of 1821; and Mr. Singer's Chiswick edition of 1826 is imbued with the spirit of the eighteenth century, and is, in fact, but an abridgment of the 1821 Variorum.

The causes of the great corruption of the old texts of Shakespeare's plays are probably all included in the following enumeration: incorrectness in the copies made for stage purposes; hasty and surreptitious procurement of copies by short-hand writers at the performances; careless proof-reading, or none at all; printing by the ear;* sophistication, i. e., the introduction by copyist, compositor, or editor of what he supposed was the author's word in a sound passage which he regarded as corrupt because he did not apprehend its meaning; and finally, carelessness, or even some obscurity of thought, on the part of the poet himself. In the regulation of the text of this edition it has not been assumed that Shakespeare, writing as a playwright for the stage only, and not as a poet for the press, always attained, or even strove to attain, faultless perspicuity of expression and clear syntactical coherence, or that he did not knowingly leave some verses imperfect. The whole body of the dramatic literature of his time

* Some persons are incredulous as to the possibility of misprints by the ear, or the representation of the sound which the compositor has in his mind instead of the form of the letters which are before his eyes. But a few somewhat peculiar examples will illustrate this strange cause of error. In *Romeo and Juliet*, Act I. Sc. 4, the quartos of 1598 and 1609, and the folio of 1623, all have the collocation of letters *philom*, which form no English word, and which are unknown to the language except as a contraction of 'Philomath.' Yet when we read, in *Mercutio's* description of Queen Mab's equipage, "the lash of philom," we see that the compositor merely put in type a mispronunciation of 'film,' *fillum*, sometimes heard nowadays. The printing in the folio (*Troilus and Cressida*, v. 2) of "*that test* of eyes and ears," for "*th' attest* of eyes and ears," is too plainly a putting of sound instead of form into type to be doubted by any intelligent reader. This mistake also shows that where 'the' and an ensuing syllable were made to fill the place of one syllable, it was done not by a quick, light pronunciation of the two, according to modern custom, but by dropping the vowel from the article, as the typography of the day indicates. In the French scene of *Henry the Fifth* "il est appelle" is twice printed with the character & for *est*, showing that the copy was written by the ear, 'est' being taken for 'et.' A like instance of phonography appears in Act IV. Sc. 4 of the same play, where "a cette heure" is printed "*asture*." I know also of an instance in which *Falstaff's* exclamation in *Henry the Fourth*, Part I. Act II. Sc. 4, "ecce signum" appeared in the second proof "*esse* signum," although it was put in type from correct printed copy. The compositor saw *ecce*, but read the word in his mind with the first *c*, as well as the second, soft; which same mistake was made in proof-reading by the copy-holder, who read aloud. It is difficult to account for some errors of another kind. I have known 'objurgation,' written in letters as plain as those upon this page, appear in a second proof as "*civilization*." Yet candid men of

shows that, had his plays been complete in the last respect, they would have been as singular in that as they are preëminent in all others. But assuming that there may be obscurity and imperfection in these works, which are due to the manner in which and the purpose for which they were written, and to the facility and copiousness of word and thought noticed in their author by his contemporaries, and which therefore cannot, with safety, even if with propriety, be corrected, every means at command has been used for the restoration of corruptions attributable to the other causes above named. I have endeavored to guide myself by fixed but not inflexible principles; to weigh

letters will confess that their own oversights are often corrected by the care and attention of the printing-office. I gladly confess my obligations in this respect. It is sometimes objected to the corrections of Shakespeare's text that they are based upon the supposition of typographical errors, transpositions, and the like, which are too ingeniously conjectured and too subtly unravelled: for instance, Theobald's famous change of "a table of green fields" to "'a *babbled* of green fields." But a modern instance from a carefully and tastefully printed book, the proofs of which had the benefit of the author's own perusal, will illustrate and justify almost any correction of this nature. In Mr. George William Curtis's *Nile Notes of a Howadji*, which are less notes than revelations of the poetic feeling roused in their accomplished writer by the ruined civilization of the past and sensuous luxuriance of the present in Egypt, a "love-drunken poet" is represented as bursting into song over the sumptuous, alluring South; and these are the first lines of his song: —

"I muse, as a traniuce, whene'er
The languors of thy love-deep eyes
Float on me." — p. 225.

Doubtless many a reader has puzzled himself in vain to discover the significance of that Eastern phrase "a traniuce." But if the *iu* be taken out of the mysterious word, and the *u* turned over, we shall have *in;* and by placing this before the article we shall have, —

"I muse, as *in a trance*, whene'er," &c.,

which I am as sure as if I had asked him is what was written by the Howadji; and I here present him with the conjectural emendation without fee or hope of reward.

carefully all the evidence, and every authority which bears upon each doubtful passage; to keep constantly in mind the customs, the manners, the cast of thought, and the idioms peculiar to the poet's time; to trace through the chirography and the printing of the Elizabethan era the course of probable corruption; and above all, to place myself, as nearly as possible, in the position of a reader of Shakespeare's day, whose mind was brought by Shakespeare's power into sympathetic action with that of the great master. Having come to my task in this spirit, and pursued it in this manner, I have at times not hesitated to make bold changes. Should I therefore be charged with presumption and temerity, I interpose between me and my censor this shield furnished me by the greatest of modern critics and editors — Porson. "Who shall decide what reading is indubitably certain? The decision must be in a great measure left to the discretion of the editor. 'What! are we to give to every man who sets up for a critic an unlimited right of correcting ancient books at his pleasure?' Not at his pleasure, but in conformity to certain laws well known and established by the general consent of the learned. He may transgress or misapply those laws, but without disowning their authority. No critic in his senses ever yet declared his resolution to put into the text what he at the time thought to be a wrong reading; and if a man, after perusing the works of his author perhaps ten times as often as the generality of his readers, — after diligently comparing MSS. and editions, — after examining what others have written relative to him professedly or accidentally, — after a constant perusal of other authors with a special view to the elucidation of his own,—if, after all this, he must not be trusted with a discretionary power over the text, he never could be qualified to be an editor at all. Whatever editor (one, we mean, who aspires to that title) republishes a book from an old edition, when the text might be improved from subsequent discoveries, while he hopes to show his modesty and religion, only exposes his indolence, his ignorance, or his superstition."* This bulwark is strong enough for my protection. My right to stand behind it can only be established by the ensuing pages.

The edition being designed to meet the wants of all readers, from those who open Shakespeare merely for a moment's pleasure to those who wish to study his text critically, on the one hand comment has been made upon many phrases and words which need no elucidation to the well-read English scholar, and on the other all old readings, i.e., variations of text which involve a difference of meaning, whether from the early quartos or the later folios, and all readings from modern editors and commentators, deemed, upon a very catholic judgment, worthy of attention, have been given in the notes, together with such comments upon corrupted or obscure passages as were included by a similar latitude of choice. Thus ample means are afforded for the critical study of the text to all readers whose purpose does not impel them to the laborious collation of original editions.

In the preparation of the Notes and Essays the possession of ordinary intelligence and knowledge of our language and literature by the reader has been as-

* *Tracts and Miscellaneous Criticisms*, p. 89.

sumed, but no special knowledge, or what may be called purely literary acquirement. If there be no note upon any passage, it is because it was supposed to be perfectly clear to any person possessing such a degree of intelligence and knowledge as has just been mentioned. On the other hand, a definition is sometimes given, or an illustrative passage quoted, not with the notion of presenting a novel view or displaying recondite reading, but with an eye to the pleasure, and perhaps the instruction, of readers (and I trust they will be many) who have not at hand even such books as Nares's Glossary, or Halliwell's and Wright's Archaic Dictionaries. Some notes have also been written and some quotations made in support of readings which are quite able to stand alone, because, comment upon these plays being free to all, it seems desirable to do whatever can be done within moderate compass to prevent and meet beforehand foolish and feeble perversions, and doubts as to clear passages, which, being broached and bandied about, win the attention of presuming half-knowledge, and make thankless and irritating labor for the after-coming scholar.

It has been a point in the preparation of this work to give results rather than processes, except when a knowledge of the process is necessary to an appreciation of the result; to make the notes as few and as concise as possible, consistently with the attainment of the end in view — the formation and maintenance of a sound text, and the explanation of obsolete phrases and customs; and to resist all temptations to expressions of individual admiration and to esthetic criticism. Neither the Antony nor the Brutus of my hero, I come neither to bury nor to praise him. Therefore, except in the first volume, I have confined my labors to the text and to subjects directly connected with it. When, to the best of my ability and to the extent of my acquaintance with the literature and the customs of Shakespeare's time, I had furnished the reader with the words of my author, and if it seemed necessary, with an explanation of those words, and in the Introductory Remarks, with all the information within my reach as to the origin, the history, and the textual condition of each play, I deemed that my legitimate labors were at an end. For like reasons, also, I did not feel justified in obtruding upon the reader mere laudatory comment from the works of any of Shakespeare's critics, however eminent — a department of Shakespearian literature, by the way, with which my acquaintance is merely casual, and very limited. In the purely editorial part of his work, it is, in my judgment, an editor's business simply to enable the reader to possess and understand his author. Nevertheless esthetics and psychology are sometimes constrained to do handmaid's service to verbal criticism.

In the following pages there will be found, I think, nothing at all of a certain kind of annotation which has filled a large space in many editions of this author, the object of which is to explain Shakespeare's poetry or to justify his use of language. No exercise of the editorial function seems to me so superfluous, I will say so impertinent. That a recent commentator should complain, as one, learned if not appreciative, has complained, that in these passages —

"No; let the candied tongue lick absurd pomp,
And crook the pregnant hinges of the knee
Where thrift may follow fawning;"

> "and his poor self
> A dedicated beggar to the air;"
>
> "The grief is fine, full, perfect, that I taste,
> And violenteth in a sense as strong
> As that which causeth it"—

the commentators have not "justified," by authority and argument, Shakespeare's use of 'candied,' 'pregnant,' 'dedicated,' and 'violenteth,' is, to me, simply amazing. So it is that another should tell us that Cæsar's exclamation, "Wilt thou lift up Olympus?" means, wilt thou attempt an impossibility? and that another should explain "broad-fronted Cæsar," and explain it, too, as having reference "to Cæsar's baldness"! and tell us that when *Helena* says *Parolles* is "solely a coward," she means that he is "*altogether* a coward, without the admixture of the opposite quality," and even give us a definition of "ill-nurtured." Others dispute the propriety of *Boyet's* most expressive and almost colloquial phrase, "O, I am stabb'd with laughter;" and many spend time, and ink, and paper, in assuring us that in *Claudio's* song, "Done to death by slanderous tongues," means killed by slanderous tongues, and that Shakespeare was "justified" in using the phrase because it had been used long before his time. Why, if it had never been used before this day, what justification or what explanation would it require if it were to appear to-morrow in a poem or a leading article? The extreme of this mode of annotation is reached by one editor, who gravely assures the reader that when *Antony* says that at *Cæsar's* assassination Pompey's statue "all the while ran blood," it "is not intended to imply that the statue of Pompey shed blood in miraculous sympathy with Cæsar, *as Cæsar was his bitter enemy*, but that the blood of Cæsar spurted out upon the statue and trickled down it." Whoever cannot understand, without explanation, such a use of language as that of which these passages are examples, had better lay down Shakespeare, or any true poet, as a sealed book. To explain such phrases is to insult the reader by implying his incapacity of poetic apprehension; while to go about justifying them is to assume the right of depriving the poet of part of his power as a "maker." Yet poets themselves sometimes, in timidity, thus blot their own pages. In Miss Barrett's *Drama of Exile*, Eve, gazing at night upon the heavens and scanning the constellations, says,—

> "But look off to those small humanities,
> Which draw me tenderly across my fear,—
> Lesser and fainter than my womanhood,
> Or yet thy manhood,—with strange innocence
> Set in the misty lines of head and hand
> They lean together!"

The maiden poetess thereupon deliberately takes the life of the child of her own imagination, by adding a note in which she explains Eve's speech by saying that "Her maternal instinct is excited by Gemini." And Rogers, in his little poem "On a Tear," destroys the effect of the last pretty stanza, which almost redeems the prim platitude and tiewig-time sensibility of its five predecessors, by deliberately informing his reader that when he says that the very law which moulds a tear and causes it to fall, is the same which preserves the earth a sphere and guides the planets, he means "the law of gravitation"!

My text has, I believe, been punctuated with great care; and I suspect that this is the first time that that by no means trifling task has ever been thoroughly performed for these works, except with regard to passages which have been discussed as obscure, or which are entirely deformed by the punctuation of the first folio. Through all others, commas and colons appear to have been scattered, at some remote period, with indiscriminating hand, and not to have been disturbed till now.

What I have here done is not the fruit of malice aforethought. The studies of which this work is one result, were begun, and were continued for some years, only for the pleasure they afforded, and without any ultimate purpose; as such studies, I am sure, are pursued, to a certain degree, by hundreds in Europe and America to whom Shakespeare's writings are a dearly prized inheritance. But, with a closer acquaintance, if not a more thorough understanding, of Shakespeare, and a wider knowledge of the literature of his time and the labors of his editors and commentators, came a conviction that, with all the learning and all the critical ability that had been brought to the regulation and the illustration of his dramas, they had never yet been edited upon just those principles, or presented in exactly that form, which would satisfy the greater number of his loving and intelligent readers. Then the baleful temptation to undertake the supplying of this want presented itself insidiously upon every occasion of dissatisfaction with existing editions. How many of my fellow-students must have been similarly tempted! Happy they whose occupations, whose foresight, or whose indolence deterred them from the task! However extended and thorough his knowledge of English literature, however intimate his acquaintance with the text of Shakespeare in all its shapes, no man can form any thing like a just estimate of the time and labor which must be given to the conscientious preparation of a thorough critical edition of Shakespeare's plays, until after he has performed the task himself. And thus, with a very clear perception of the ideal at which I was aiming, but with a very imperfect conception of the difficulties which lay in the way of attaining it, I began the work of which the result is now presented to the reader. Favorably as the bulk of it has already been received, it would be unreasonable to hope that others will find less fault with it than I do myself. It has, at least, I trust, taught me charity toward my fellow-editors. The man who honestly, and with some capacity for his task, undertakes to reform abuses and to rectify errors, will generally end by apologizing for some of the very faults which, at first, he most strongly condemned.

And now, the labors ended which have taxed others' patience as well as mine, I lay down from a weary hand the pen taken up blithely, and perhaps too confidently, seven years ago. I can truly say that my task has been performed as thoroughly as I expected to perform it, and even more minutely, if not so perfectly or so easily. The very proofs have required more time than I expected to give to the whole work. My place must be among those who have not attained the height of their endeavor, or even perhaps the extreme of their capacity, because they found their endeavor limited by circumstances unforeseen. Shakespearian pursuits have not been, as some of my generous critics and kind correspondents seem to have supposed they were, my principal or even my continued occupation. This work, whatever may be its value, is the fruit of hours stolen from sleep, from recreation, from the society of friends, and from nearer and dearer companionship. Begun when our country was strong and happy in long-continued peace and prosperity, it was interrupted, near its close, by a bloody struggle which has tried and proved that strength as no other nation's strength was ever tried or proved, which threatened, though but for a brief period, to shake that prosperity to its foundations, and which, involving us all in its excitement, absorbed the best energies of every generous soul; — it is finished as that strength seems to be renewed and established more firmly than before, and under the glad auguries of a peace and a prosperity which we may reasonably hope will never again be so interrupted.

Here is my peace-offering.

R. G. W.

New York, April 23, 1865.

SUPPLEMENTARY NOTES AND CORRECTIONS.

VOL. II.

The Tempest.

[In some copies the corrections proposed in these Supplementary Notes have been already made.]

p. 11. "—— and as leaky as an *unstanch'd* wench": — What is the meaning of 'unstanched' here? Not, it would seem, except in way of pun, that undiscussible one which is the most obvious. See,

"For who can lesse than smile that sees *unstanch* and riveled *faces*
To shelter coylie underneath Fannes, Tifnies, Masks, Bongraces."
Albion's England, Chap. 101, p. 400, ed. 1606.

p. 19. "From the still vex'd *Bermoothes.*" See Vol. XII. p. 437.

p. 26. "*Courtsi'd when you have,* and *kiss'd*": — The dashes at the end of this line and the next should be removed. "The wild waves whist" is not parenthetical. As the Cambridge editors have remarked, *Ferdinand* says, —

"This music crept by me upon the waters,
Allaying both *their fury* and my passion."

p. 36. "Of *its* own kind": — Read, "Of *it* own kind." So the folio. See the Note on "it's folly, it's tenderness," &c. *Winter's Tale,* Act I. Sc. 2.

p. 41. "—— to keep *them* living": — I now think that Malone was right in his conjectural reading, "to keep *thee* living."

p. 70. "And do the *murther* first": — The assertion in the Note on this passage that *murther* was the uniform mode of spelling this word was incautiously and forgetfully made.

Two Gentlemen of Verona.

p. 108. "*Nod-ay? why, that's noddy*": — In support of my reading and explanation of this much mooted passage, which have been silently adopted by the Cambridge editors, see the following dialogue from *The Woman turned Bully*, 1675: —

"*Good.* Come hither, sirrah. Can you go to Mr. Docket's and come again presently, and not play at chuck farthing by the way?
Boy. [*bowing*] Yes, forsooth, Madam.
Good. Yet it's no matter neither. — Is Truepenny about the house?
Boy. [*bowing*] Yes, Madam.
Good. Go, send him to me quickly.
Boy. [*bowing*] Yes, Madam."
Act III. Sc. 2, p. 44.

p. 125. "O, that *shoe* could speak now like *an old* woman": — Is it at all probable that Theobald's reading, "a *wood* woman," which appears in almost every subsequent edition, gives the true text? For 'would' could not be a misprint by the ear for *wood;* because in 'would' the *l* was pronounced.

p. 131. "Yet let her be a *principality*": — The Note on this passage was written with too little consideration of the subject; and a critic in the *Atlantic* magazine (Feb. 1859) corrects me by saying "there were three orders of angels above the principalities, the highest being the Seraphim." It is difficult to find an authoritative marshalling of the celestial hierarchy, and perhaps not less difficult to discover exactly what was meant by principalities or by powers in that order. But I wonder at my mistake; for before making it I had read this passage in Drayton's *Man in the Moone:* —

"Those Hierarchies that Jove's great will supply,
Whose orders formed in triplicitie,
Holding their places by the treble trine,
Make up that holy theologike nine:
Thrones, Cherubin and Seraphin that rise,
As the first three; when Principalities,
With Dominations, Potestates are plac'd
The second: and the Ephionian last,
Which Vertues, Angels, and Archangels bee.

p. 150. "She is not *to be fasting* in respect of her breath": — It must be admitted that Rowe's reading "to be *kissed* fasting" is more than plausible. For, "to be fasting," though it has a plain and appropriate meaning, is a very awkward phrase. *Launce's* caution is of ancient date. It occurs in Ovid's *Art of Love*, in a passage thus translated by Congreve: —

"And you whose breath is touched this caution take,
Nor fasting, nor too near another speak."
Book III.

p. 162. "By my *halidom*": — In the Note on this passage read, "from the Anglo-Saxon *halig* = sacred, and *dom* = doom."

p. 163. "*Madam, I pity much your grievances*": — This passage is probably corrupt by omission of a line, or perhaps by a misprint in 'plac'd.'

The Merry Wives of Windsor.

p. 215. "—— *goot* words": — The folio has "*good* words," and the like often. But should such irregularity in so incorrectly printed a book as the first folio cause us to doubt a moment that Shakespeare made *Sir Hugh's* Welsh-English consistent throughout?

p. 218. "—— he's a justice of peace in his *country*": — There can be no doubt as to the correctness of 'country' in this passage. It is used in like manner in New England to this day.

p. 221. "—— there's pippins and *cheese*," &c. Read "and *seese*," as elsewhere.

" "—— bully *rock*." This cant phrase has been hitherto spelled "bully *rook*," and explained, "sharper, one who lives by his wits," which makes it a very unfit and unlikely epithet for the *Host* to apply to *Falstaff*, his "Emperor. Cæsar, Keisar, and Pheazar," a guest who sits "at ten pounds [about $300 with us now] a week," and afterward to *Mr. Justice Shallow*. That the true signification of the term is, a brave, dashing, overbearing fellow, seems to me to be decided by these lines from the Prologue to Sedley's *Bellamira*, 4to, 1687, which I have met with since the proofs of this play were corrected:

"What c.... y' have met with, and what punks are sound,
Who are the *Bully-rocks*, and who *gives ground*."

The contrast here is evident. The bully rock is the man who does not give ground, who, in our slang phrase, "faces the music." This interpretation seems to be entirely sustained by the following passages: —

"What do we fight for? — For pay, for pay, my *bull rocks*." Shirley's *Honoria and Memnon*, 1659.

"And devillishly are they us'd when they meddle with a guard man or any of *the Bully Rocks indeed*."

The Feign'd Astrologer, 1668.

"He, poor soul, must be hectored till he likes 'em, while *the more stubborn bully-rock* damms and is safe."

Shadwell's *Sullen Lovers*, 1668.

"Thou art mine own sweet *Bully*."

Thomas of Reading, ed. 1618. E 3.

In Rabelais, Book V. Chap. 7, Urquhart translates "*Dieu de Battailes*," "that bully-rock Mars." This use of 'bully' has never entirely passed away in this country. Of late it is much heard among the boys, who use it just as it is used in the passages above quoted. The spelling 'bully *rook*,' a mere phonographic irregularity, doubtless led to the supposition that there was some connection between this word and 'rook' = sharper, cheat.

p. 230. "What, have *I* 'scap'd love letters?" — The folio omits *I*.

" "—— for though love use reason for his *precisian*":— Dr. Johnson's conjecture that we should read "his *physician*" probably hits the truth. See the following line in Sonnet 147: —

"My reason, the physician to my love."

p. 238. "I, *ay*, I myself." So in Seneca's *Ten Tragedies*, —

"And sith that I, I Caitife, I, abridged have thy life,"

(ed. 1581, fol. 73 b,) —

where we plainly should read, "I, ay, caitiff, I."

p. 259. "—— *if Fortune thy foe were not*, — *Nature thy friend*": — i. e., Nature being thy friend, and having given thee beauty which would grace higher fortunes. *Falstaff* probably quotes here the burthen of an old song: "It plays Fortune my foe as distinctly as may be." *Lingua*, Sig. F 2, ed. 1607. And see the following lines from Lilly's *Woman in the Moone*, Act I.: —

"Use all these well, and Nature is thy friend;
But use them ill, and Nature is thy foe."

" "—— the reek of a lime *kill*": — Although both folio and 4to read "lime-*kill*," *kiln* is given in all modern editions — the very Cambridge edition itself. See in Withal's *Short Dictionarie*, 15–, "A lyme-kyll — *Fornax calcaria*," and in Seneca's *Ten Tragedies*, —

"When up he [Hercules] stept on Œta mount, and gazed on his *kill*,
Being layd aloft he brake the block, so heavy was he still."
Ed. 1581, fol. 213.

p. 269. "—— a *posset* of sack" : — See Supplementary Note on "A good sherris sack." *King Henry Fourth*, Part II.

p. 275. "—— and the numbers of *the* genders" : — I have no doubt that Shakespeare wrote "*thy* genders."

" "—— you must be *preeches*" : — We should read, "be *preeched.*" Parson *Evans's* faults are not in grammar. The text of the folio is probably the result of a mistake of the final *s*.

p. 286. "—— and in that *trim*" : — Read "that *tire*," as the Note on the passage plainly indicates.

VOL. III.

Measure for Measure.

p. 37. "He hath *offended but as* in a dream" : — I am not sure that, strange and contradictory as the original reading, "He hath *but as offended*," &c., seems to us, it is not warranted by the idiom of Shakespeare's day.

p. 38. "—— to fine the *fault*" : — The folio, "*faults.*"

p. 49. "*Of the all-holding law*" : — The critical canon referred to in the Note on this passage is Tyrwhitt's, not Theobald's.

" "—— *I've* been sick for" : — Read, "*'have* been sick for." The folio has, "that longing *have* been sick for," there being an elision of the pronoun, which was not uncommon in Shakespeare's day.

p. 84. "One of our *convent*" : — Read, "our *covent.*" So the folio. This is an old form of the word, still preserved in "Covent Garden."

Comedy of Errors.

p. 147. "Who *falling* there to find his fellow forth" : — Read, without a doubt, "Who *failing* there," &c. The two drops are "in the ocean," and one seeks the other. It does not fall into the ocean.

p. 160. I learn from Mr. Halliwell's folio Shakespeare that my conjectural correction, "*forced* fallacy," is found on the margins of the Dent folio.

p. 182. "—— expect spoon meat, *and* bespeak a long spoon" : — Read, with Capell, "*so* bespeak," &c.

p. 184. "—— by my long *ears*" : — i. e., my long 'years.' Even at the present day we hear so many Englishmen from the old country, of even higher grade than *Dromio's*, pronounce 'ears' *years*, that there can be no doubt that Shakespeare intended the pun which the Cambridge editors first indicated.

Much Ado about Nothing.

p. 258. "*Into, Hey nonny, nonny*" *:* — For the hitherto unsuspected significance of this strange burthen see Florio's *New World of Words*, ed. 1611: "*Fossa*, a grave, a pit, a trench. . . . Used also for a woman's pleasure-pit, *nony-nony*, or palace of pleasure."

p. 296. "*Let them be, in the hands of coxcomb*" *:* — When the Note on this passage was written, I had forgotten, or had not observed, that Theobald made the same distribution of the text. He, however, gave no reasons for his decision.

Love's Labour's Lost.

p. 353. "—— *against gentility*" *:* — I am of opinion that we should read, "A dangerous law; — against gentility."

p. 359. "—— until then, *Sit down, Sorrow*" *:* — Read, "Sit *thee* down," &c.

p. 361. "—— for she had a green *wit*" *:* — i. e., a green *withe*, *th* having been pronounced as *t*, and a punning allusion (hitherto unnoticed because of the ignorance of the pronunciation of *th*) being made to the green withes with which Delilah bound Samson. See Vol. XII. p. 431.

p. 380. "Of trotting *paritors*" *:* — i. e., apparitors, who were officers of a bishop's court.

p. 390. "Master *Person* — quasi *pers*-on" : — As to the pronunciation of 'person,' see Vol. XII. p. 423.

p. 394. "*In love I hope*" *:* — The folio assigns this speech to *Longaville*, with manifest error.

p. 397. "*Thou* for whom Jove would swear" : — The author of the criticism on this edition in the *Atlantic* magazine, denying by implication that the quantity and accent proper here to 'thou' make any addition to this line superfluous, says that, if read as it is printed, "the effect would be something of this kind: 'Thou-ou for whom Jove would swear,' which would be like the 'bow-wow-wow before the Lord' of the country choirs." Enjoying the laugh at my own expense quite as heartily as my critic did, I do not see that his joke is fatal to my prosody. He must know that the vowel sound in 'thou' is a junction of *ah* and *oo*, the Italian *a* and *u*, and that the least prolongation of this sound will, at a poet's need, make the diphthong in 'thou' fill the place of a dissylable just as manifestly as it does in the following lines:—

"For in his male he had a pilwebere,
Which (as he said) was *our* Lady's veil."
Chaucer's *Canterbury Tales*. Prol. l. 696.

p. 398. "Not you *to* me," &c. I neglected to remark that the folio has, "Not you *by* me, but I betray'd *to* you," and that the transposition, imperatively required, was suggested by Monck Mason.

p. 402. "—— of their sweet complexion *crack:*"—'Crack' here means not speak of, talk, but boast; in which sense it is commonly enough used with us in the phrase 'crack up.' Its use to mean 'gossip' is Lowland Scotch, as in "a crack wi' Monkbarns." *The Antiquary*. As to the use of 'sweet' here, instead of 'white' or 'fair,' it is to be noticed that in Shakespeare's day and afterward complexion meant, not the tint of the skin, but (See Vol. XI. 169, 197) the whole physical being, what we call now the organization; and that it was to the repulsiveness of this in the Ethiopian, and not to his color only, that Shakespeare makes the King allude.

p. 403. "*For when would you, my lord,*" &c.:—The most casual reader must be struck by the repetitions and want of logical sequence in this speech; and it is more than probable that we have in the old copies both what Shakespeare intended to strike out from the speech, as originally written, and what he substituted. But as there is no guide, except individual judgment, to determine which is the old and which the new matter, the course pursued by Capell and Mr. Dyce, who omit six lines from "For when would you, my Lord," &c., and nine from "For where is any author," &c., seems very unsafe, if not unwarrantable.

p. 409. "—— *remember thy courtesy*":—Mr. Howard Staunton is of opinion that 'remember thy courtesy' was a conventional phrase for 'pray you put on your hat.' To sustain this interpretation he quotes three passages, of which, upon examining the context of each, it seems to me that only the following one is in point: "To me, sir! What do you mean?—Pray you, *remember your court'sy*. [Reads.] 'To his most selected friend Master Edward Knowell.' What might the gentleman's name be, sir, that sent it? Nay, *pray you be cover'd.*" *Every Man in his Humour*. Act I. Sc. 1. It may be that this gives the correct interpretation of the passage which is the occasion of the present Note; and that also when *Hamlet* (Act V. Sc. 2) says to *Osric*, "But, I beseech you, remember —" and moves him to put on his hat, he was about to add, "your courtesy." But by what mental process such a phrase came to have such a significance is past my conjecture; for, beyond a doubt, taking off the hat was a courtesy two hundred and fifty years ago, as it is now. "Let us make a lawe that no man put off his hat or cap, &c., &c. This is a kind of courtesy or ceremony rather to be avoided than otherwise *at table*," &c., &c. Florio's *Second Fruites*. 1591. Again, in Greene's *Tu Quoque*, *Staines*, who is teaching an Englishman Italian manners, says, "Only, sir, this I must condition you off: in your affront or salute never to move your Hatte: But here, here is your courtesie."

p. 410. "—— shall *pass Pompey* the Great": — So the old copies. The Cambridge editors conjecture, "shall pass *as* Pompey," &c.

p. 437. "—— my griefs are *dull*": — Read, with the old copies, "my griefs are *double*," i. e., heavy, strong. So, —

"a voice potential,
As *double* as the Duke's."

Othello, Act I. Sc. 1.

p. 459. "—— which to *annotanize*." From Mr. Halliwell's folio edition I have learned that Mr. Knight has made this correction. I was first directed to it by remarking the pronunciation of *th* as *t*. See Introduction to *Much Ado about Nothing* (*Noting*).

VOL. IV.

A Midsummer-Night's Dream.

p. 25. "[*Hermia*,] for aught," &c.: — Read, with the 4to, "*Ay me*, for aught," &c.

" "—— the choice of *merit*": — Read, with the 4to, "the choice of *friends*." My defence of the folio text is over subtle.

p. 35. "Or *on* the beached margent of the sea": — Read, "Or *in* the beached margent," &c., with the old copies. 'In' has been too frequently changed to 'on' in these plays. It was used as we use 'on:' it is the Latin *in* = upon. Christ's great exposition of his doctrine is "The Sermon *in* the Mount."

p. 36. "The human mortals *want*," &c.: — To whom I am indebted for the suggestion, "The human mortals *chant*," &c., I do not remember. In any case, I cannot regard it as having even the least plausibility.

p. 40. "I know a bank *where* the wild thyme blows": — I am now much inclined to doubt that Shakespeare could use 'where' to fill the place of two syllables, the *second* of which would be accented. 'Whereon' might be well received into the text.

p. 41. "Lull'd in these *bowers*": — I yielded too readily to the plausibility of the reading found in Mr. Collier's folio of 1632. Read, with the old copies, "Lull'd in these *flowers*;" 'in' having, of course, the sense of upon.

p. 49. "—— *and* let him hold his fingers," &c.: — The folio, "*or* let," &c.

p. 53. "I desire you *of* more acquaintance, good Master Mustard-seed": — Mr. Dyce, in his recent edition, first pointed out that the old copies accidentally omit 'of' in this speech. See *Bottom's* two preceding speeches. A trifling change in the plate enables me to profit by this suggestion.

p. 57. "—— against she *doth* appear": — The reading, "she *do*," &c., is from the 4tos.

p. 71. "So doth the *woodbine*," &c.: — There can be no doubt that the names woodbine and honeysuckle were applied in Shakespeare's time, if indeed they are not now applied, to the same vine. But there are two kinds of honeysuckle, very distinct, mentioned by Dodoens in his *Herbal*, a translation of which was published in 1578. Perhaps one was called, or has since come to be called, 'woodbine,' and the other, 'honeysuckle.' I certainly have heard country folk thus distinguish them.

p. 76. "And *he did bid* us follow": — The folio and Roberts's 4to omit 'he,' as well as 'did.'

p. 80. "—— what *abridgment* have you?" — The suggestion that here 'abridgment' means brief, though plausible, is not sound. In *Hamlet*, Act II. Sc. 2, the prince calls the players his 'abridgment.' We have evidently lost the meaning with this use of the word.

p. 86. "Now is the *moral* down": — The Note upon this passage assumes too subtle a meaning. *Mural* is probably right; or perhaps 'moral' is a misprint for '*wall*.'

The Merchant of Venice.

p. 158. "—— *land*-thieves and *water*-thieves": — By an oversight, I neglected to quote "Notable pirate, thou salt water thief," (*Twelfth Night*, Act V. Sc. 1,) in support of the transposition made here, which I have since discovered in the "List" of the corrections in Mr. Collier's folio of 1632.

p. 175. "Will be worth a *Jewes* eye": — In support of this reading, add to the Note the following passages: —

"And so did bastard Astrey, too, whose mother was *a Jew*." *Golding's Ovid*, Book V. fol. 57 b. 1612.

"And after certain days, when Felix came with his wife Drusilla, which was *a Jew*."

Acts xxiv. 24. Authorized translation, ed. 1611.

p. 203. "—— an *equal* yoke of love": — Read, "an *egal* yoke," &c.

As You Like It.

p. 315. "Atalanta's *better part*": — Some doubt has been expressed as to the interpretation of this passage given in the Note upon it. But there should be none. Atalanta's legs are meant. The word 'parts' was specially applied to the lower limbs of women.

"And last of all (though couered) stretched out her round cleane foote,
Supporter of that building brave, of beautious forme the roote.
The rest (and *better part*) lay hid. Yet what was to be seene
To make one lose his liberty enough and more had beene."

Honour's Academy, 1610, Part III. p. 97.

I have at hand a dozen more such examples in point.

p. 354. "—— which are *your* only prologues," &c.: — Read, with the old copies, "which are *the* only prologues," &c. The old idiom was "*the* only" where we now say "only the."

The Taming of the Shrew.

p. 393. "Go by, *St. Jeronimy*": — Mr. Keightley proposes to read, "*Sr.* or *Signior* Jeronimy." There can hardly be a doubt that this is the correct reading.

p. 440. "—— like to *mose in the chine*": — Good reason why I could not understand this phrase. It is corrupt. Read, "*mourn* in the chine." See Urquhart's translation of Rabelais: "In our Abbey we never study for fear of the mumps, which disease in horses is called *mourning in the chine*." Book I. Chap. 39.

VOL. V.

All's Well that Ends Well.

p. 13. "You shall find *of the* King a husband": — This can hardly be distinguished as a French construction. 'Of' was used two or three centuries ago very much in this manner by many English writers. In the Note, read, "*Vous trouverez de* par *le Roi*," &c.

p. 22. "*This* his good melancholy," &c.: —Read, —

"Let me not live —
Thus his good melancholy oft began," &c.

And perhaps, as Mr. Staunton suggests, in the next line below, "When *wit* was out."

p. 50. "*War* is no strife": — Read, "*Wars* is," &c. See "is there not wars?" *Second Part Henry IV.*, Act I. Sc. 2.

p. 79. "—— *make rope's in such a scarre*": — Since the Note on this line (in which Mr. Dyce reads, "make *hopes* in such a *case*") was stereotyped, I have met with an important passage which confirms me in the opinion that the text should not be disturbed, although it cannot be explained. In the old play, *Lingua, or the Combat of the Tongue*, in the first edition, Act I. Sc. 6, Sig. B, *Tactus*, having found *Lingua's* crown and robe, which she lays in his way, puts them on, assumes them as his due, and with them royal airs; and he says, —

"Peasants I'le curb your head-strong impudence,
And make you tremble when the Lyon roares,
Yea [ye] earth-bred wormes, O for a looking glasse:
Poets will write whole volumes of this *scarre*."

Now, here we have the same word, with exactly the same spelling; and in both passages the word refers to a startling event or emergency. It seems quite impossible that exactly the same arrangement of types should have been fortuitous in both instances. In Mr. Collier's edition of Dodsley's Old Plays, 1825, the line is printed, "Poets will write whole volumes of this *change*," with a note by him to the effect that, "'Poets will write whole volumes of this *scar*' was the reading of the edition of this work in 1780; but it is mere nonsense: the true word has been supplied from the old copies. C." Which "old copies" furnished this reading does not appear: the original edition, which only I possess, we have seen, was not among them; and I cannot believe that had Mr. Collier consulted the first edition, and remembered the obscure passage in *All's Well that Ends Well*, he would have been so confident as to his 'change,' which is, besides, not very well suited to the context. If 'scarre' must be accepted in the sense of emergency, or a similar sense, the change of 'rope's to 'hopes' is more than plausible.

p. 80. "—— he *has* sworn to marry me": — The original reads, "he *had* sworn," &c. — an error of the press hitherto unnoticed. *Bertram* says, earlier in the Scene, "How *have* I sworn;" and note in this speech *Diana's* declaration, "therefore I *will* lie," &c.

p. 106. "*Find him, and bring him hither*": — After this order from the King, there should be a stage direction, *Exit an attendant*, which Mr. Dyce has added.

Twelfth Night.

p. 198. "—— I'll get them all three *all ready*": — Mr. Dyce says, with great plausibility, "read 'all three *ready*.'" The folio has, "all three *already;*" and it is quite probable, though not, I think, sufficiently certain for a change in the text, that the latter 'all,' or 'al,' is a mere repetition of the first.

p. 206. "*My* yellow stockings": — The folio has, "*Thy* yellow stockings." The emendation, which is Mr. W. N. Lettsom's, appears imperative. For not only has *Olivia* "no idea that Malvolio is quoting the letter," as Mr. Lettsom remarks, but she is *entirely ignorant that he has received any letter*, and the pronoun in the second person addressed to her, can *to her* mean only herself; and therefore, when *Malvolio* quotes, "Go to, thou art made," &c., she replies, "Am *I* made?" And then, too, the humor of the Scene, which with the old misprint depends only on *Malvolio's* conceit, becomes stupendous by this logical bringing in of the Countess's supposition that her steward talks to her about *her* stockings and *her* garters!

p. 211. "—— too unchary *on't*": — Read, with Theobald, "too unchary *out*." *Olivia* might lay her love, but not her honor, upon a heart of stone. The misprint is an easy one to be made.

p. 222. "Nay, I am *for all waters*": — There have been various comments upon this passage, none of which have been accepted as satisfactory. The *Clown's* meaning is plain enough, without comment; but is not his allusion to the 'Waterologers,' who were the sovereign quacks in the reigns of Elizabeth and James, and later, although their absurd pretensions were made the subject of constant ridicule? See the following passage in the Satire on the People's Physitian in Whitlock's *Zootomia, or Observations on the Present Manners of the English.* London, 1654: "— or at most, if his English Library can furnish him with but the confused Notions of some Diseases, and he can but discourse them *to fit all Waters*, their Patient is ready to admire and cry," &c. P. 64.

The Winter's Tale.

p. 294. "By all their *influences*": — I think it more than probable that the true text is, "By all their *influence*." The rhythm demands but three syllables, and the addition of a superfluous *s* was common enough. See the Note on "Servile to all the skyey *influences*." *Measure for Measure*, Act III. Sc. 1.

p. 300. "I'll *keep* my *stables*," &c.: — Mr. Staunton explains this passage, "I'll fasten, bar up my stables," saying that the allusion is to the unnatural passions of Semiramis. The suggestion is very ingenious and plausible, but I think over subtle and far-fetched. Would Shakespeare have made so remote an allusion so obscurely? I am inclined to doubt that he would. But 'keep' may well be used in the sense of bar, defend; and in that case is not the allusion rather to these passages of Jeremiah? — "They were fed as horses in the morning: every one neighed after his neighbor's wife." Chap. v. 8. "I have seen thy adulteries and thy neighings." I doubt if Shakespeare knew the whole story of Semiramis.

p. 316. "With what *encounter so uncurrent*," &c.: — 'Uncurrent' is the only difficult word in this passage. May it not be a misprint for '*occurrent*'? "Another ridiculous foole of Venice thought his shoulders and buttocks were made of glasse, wherefore he shunned all *occurrents*, and never did sit downe to meat," &c. *Optic Glasse of Humors*, p. 139. Bacon used '*occurrent*' in the sense of incident. See Webster's *Dictionary*.

p. 325. "—— a *god* or a child": — Steevens's definition of 'child' = a girl, has been adopted in two or three recently published glossaries; but the authors of these works have cited in support of that gloss always and only this very passage! I offer them instead the following lines, which furnish the only instance known to me in which 'child' may possibly mean girl distinctively: —

"The gentlemen whose titles you have bought
Lose all their fathers toil within a day,

While Hob, your son, and Sib [Isabella], your nut browne *child*
Are gentlefolks, and gentles are beguil'd."
Greene's *James the Fourth*, p. 146, ed. Dyce.

But notice here the rhyme needed for 'beguil'd,' and see in the passage quoted below, from *King Lear*, son and child both used to mean a man child, *filius*. In regard to my reading in this passage, the Honorable Charles Daly, Chief Justice of the Superior Court of New York, a careful and discriminating student of Shakespeare, said to me, in support of the old reading, that he had been told by a Warwickshire man that in that county 'child' was used to mean a girl. But see that Greene, a Warwickshire man, in the tale makes the seeking for the pap and crying — acts common, of course, to babes of both sexes — unmistakable signs that this one was "a childe;" and Warwickshire Shakespeare, in *King Lear*, Act I. Sc. 2, has this passage: "This villain of mine comes under the prediction; there's *son* against father: the king falls from bias of nature; there's father against *child*." 'Child,' too, is used in this play by this very Shepherd, both before and after the passage in question, in the general sense of infant. Would Shakespeare, after having put the word in this sense in the mouth of the peasant, have used it afterward in another and a distinctive sense, when 'girl' or 'wench' would have answered the purpose just as well, and when Greene, in the passage which he was dramatizing, and which he had before him, used it merely to mean an infant, a human child, *as opposed* to "a little god"? In the *Promptorium Parvulorum*, 'child' is defined, *puer*, *infans*. And finally, in Wise's *Glossary of Words still used in Warwickshire to be found in Shakspere*, London, 1861, Child = girl, does not appear, although Childing = to bring forth a child, does. It would seem that Steevens's hearsay and the Warwickshire man's testimony must yield to Shakespeare, to Greene's novel which Shakespeare was using, Wise's Warwickshire *Glossary*, and to the usage of all the ballad writers.

p. 334. "—— *sworn*, I think, to shew myself a glass": — Mr. Dyce remarks, that the passage, with the reading 'sworn,' cannot possibly mean that *Perdita* thinks *Florizel*, in donning a swain's costume, to have sworn to show her a reflex of her own condition, because "the word '*myself*' at once refutes it." I cannot but think that my honored friend Mr. Dyce forgot, when he wrote this note, that 'myself' was and is continually used only as a strong 'me.'

p. 341. "—— break a foul *jape*": — The Note upon this passage is inexact in saying that 'jape' did *not* mean a jest.

It was used in that sense, but was by no means confined thereto. It was coarse slang of a very wide signification. See Florio's *Dictionary* in v. *Fottere*.

p. 355. "—— and admiring the *nothing* of it": — i. e., the *noting*, &c., such having been the pronunciation of 'nothing,' and a pun being intended here, as in the name of *Much Ado about Nothing*.

p. 377. "—— thou art no *tall fellow of thy hands*": — In this phrase, so common among our early writers, I am now convinced that my first impression was right, and that 'hands' is put metaphorically for bodily strength.

VOL. VI.

King John.

p. 45. "This *widow'd* lady": — When I wrote the Note upon this passage I forgot the story of the "widow woman" and her cruse of oil, told in the seventeenth chapter of the first book of *Kings*. The old reading must stand.

King Richard the Second.

I should have remarked that certain unimportant variations of the 4to of 1615 are not mentioned in the Notes on this play.

p. 210. "We at time of *year*": — I am inclined to think that the true reading is "at time of *vere;*" vere being *ver* = spring. See Skelton's verses on Time: —

"The rotys take theyr sap *in time of vere;*
In time of somer, flowers fresh and grene;
In time of harvest men their corne shere;
In time of winter the north wynde waxeth kene,
So bytterly bytynge the flowres be not sene."

But see the following passage in Andrew Borde's *Boke of the Introduction of Knowledge:* "In the Forest of St. Leonardes in Southsex there dothe never sing Nightingale, although the Foreste rounde about in *time of yeare* is replenyshed with Nightingales." But might not the same easy misprint have been made here?

King Henry the Fourth. Part I.

p. 368. "Nor *moody* beggars": — The 4tos of 1598 and 1599 have, "Nor *muddy* beggars," which may be the true text. 'Moody' and 'muddy' were pronounced alike.

King Henry the Fourth. Part II.

p. 431. " —— I would I might never *spit white* again": — The following passage from Urquhart's translation of Rabelais seems to show that 'to spit white,' meant to be thirsty; a very appropriate sense here: " — for every man found himself so altered and a-dry with drinking these flat wines, that they did nothing but spit, and that as dry as Maltha cotton; saying, We have of the Pantagruel, and our throats are salted." Book II. Chap. 7.

p. 454. "Sneak's *noise*": — i. e., Sneak's band of music. 'Noise' was commonly used in this sense.

p. 496. "*A good sherris sack*": — The following decision in the Court of King's Bench was made A. D. 1648, a period quite near enough to Shakespeare's day for the settlement of the question as to what sack was. Parmenter *v.* Cresy, Trinity Term, 23 Car. I. Defendant promised to deliver to plaintiff so many pipes of sack which he had then lying in a cellar. Decided, *inter alia*, that defendant must show plaintiff the wine in the cellar, "to the intent that he might make his choice, *which is not to be of the species of Sack*, viz., *whether Canary or Sherry, etcetera*, for then indeed the Plaintiff should [i. e., would] have made his choice before he could have requested delivery, but of the goodness of it." Aleyn's *Select Cases in Banco Regis*, 22, 23, 24 Car. I. fol. London, 1681. Plainly, therefore, sack was not a "brewage," but any kind of dry wine, and was kept in pipes in cellars; and, consequently, *Falstaff* could not have requested *Bardolph* to "*brew*" him a pottle (or measure) of sack. 'Sack,' although strictly applicable to any kind of dry wine, seems to have been generally applied only to sherry; just as 'corn,' which is a generic word applicable to wheat, rye, barley, or maize, is applied in Great Britain specially to wheat, the principal grain there; but in the United States to maize, the grain which is most important to the people there in their daily life.

VOL. VII.

King Henry the Fifth.

p. 107. "Pass our *accept* and peremptory answer": — There can be no doubt that this, the old, reading is correct. See in Browne's *Pastorals*, —

> "Things worthy their *accept*, our offering." II. 5.

King Henry the Sixth. Part I.

p. 152. "He ne'er *lift* up his hand but conquered": — Perhaps it should have been noticed that this form of the preterite was in common use in the Elizabethan era. "When Jesus then *lift* up his eyes." John vi. 5; and so the earlier translations.

King Henry the Sixth. Part II.

p. 281. "—— our supplications *in the quill*": — A correspondent of the London *Athenæum* of February 27, 1864, suggests that "in the quill" means together, *ex compacto agere;* and supports his gloss by a reference to Ainsworth's *Latin Dictionary*, ed. 1773.

p. 377. "*So lie thou there,*" &c.: — The 4to of 1619 has, "So lie thou there, and *tumble in thy blood.*"

VOL. VIII.

King Richard the Third.

p. 180. "*Of you, and you, Lord Rivers, and of Dorset*": — Read, according to the suggestion in the Note, "Of you, Lord Rivers, and, Dorset, of you."

King Henry the Eighth.

p. 326. "Must fetch him in *he papers*": — This, the old, reading is the true text.

> "Set is the soveraigne Sunne did shine when *paper'd* last our penne."
>
> *Albion's England*, Chap. 80, ed. 1606.

VOL. IX.

Coriolanus.

p. 175. "—— the store-house and *the shop*": — As to the true meaning of 'shop,' see these lines from Juliana Berners' Boke of St. Albans, —

> "Our Lorde that *shope* both sonne and mone
> 'Lend us spending in our purse." Sig. e. 5.

'Workshop' is a pleonasm.

p. 244. "*Tent* in my cheeks": — The following passage from a poet of the Elizabethan period, whose name I do not remember, (it has been torn off the bottom of my memorandum,) strongly supports the text and the explanation of it given in the Note: —

> "—— doting sires
> Carped and cared to have them lettered;
> But their kind college from the teat did *tent*,
> And forced them walk before they weaned were."

Here 'tent' plainly means take.

p. 275. "—— *but he has a merit*": — Two half lines or more seem to have been lost before these words.

" "Hath not *a tomb so evident as a chair*," &c.: — The greater part of the Note upon this passage is superfluous. The passage is far from being so obscure as it appeared to me when looked at through a cloud of commentary. *Aufidius* is impressing upon his hearers the consequences of *Coriolanus's* inflexible, impracticable nature. He tells them that our virtue lies in the interpretation of the time, that is, we must be rated according to the disposition of those around us; as *Rosaline* says that "a jest's prosperity lies in the ear of him that hears it, never in the tongue of him that makes it." He then adds, as a corollary, that power, self-sufficient and self-complacent, has not so sure, so manifest, a grave as the very seat of authority to which its deeds have raised it, and which its over-weening egotism is likely to use in such a manner as to alienate those to whom it owes its elevation.

VOL. XI.

King Lear.

I have thought it desirable to notice more of the various readings of the first two quarto copies of this play (both published in the same year) than are mentioned in the Notes. A careful collation of the originals with each other and with the folio has led me to suspect that no other editor has had the opportunity or taken the trouble of performing this laborious but interesting task with thoroughness. The variations are very numerous, and most of them are not very important. In the large majority of instances they are unimportant; and the readings peculiar to the quartos are almost invariably inferior to those of the folio. Only those are mentioned which are of some real significance. The 4to which has no place of sale mentioned upon the title page is called the second.

p. 207. "—— for *qualities* are so weighed": — The 4tos, "for *equalities*," &c.

p. 209. "Where *nature* doth *with merit* challenge": — The 4tos, "Where *merit* doth *most* challenge *it*."

" "[*Sir*] I am made of *that self* metal as my sister": — The folio omits '*Sir*.' The 4tos have, "of *the* self *same* metal that my sister *is*."

p. 210. "Than that *conferr'd* on Goneril": — The 4tos, "Than that *confirmed*," &c.

p. 212. "*O*, vassal *miscreant*": — The 4tos, "vassal *recreant*."

p. 213. "Revoke thy *gift*": — The 4tos, "Revoke thy *doom*."

" "*Five* days we do allot thee": — The 4tos, "*Four* days," &c.; and in the next line, "on the *fift*."

" "*Freedom* lives hence": — The 4tos, "*Friendship* lives hence;" and in the next line, "The gods to their *protection*."

p. 215. "When it is mingled with *regards*," &c.: — The 4tos, "When it is mingled with *respects*."

p. 220. "—— and fathers *declin'd*, *the* father": — The 4tos, "and fathers *declining*, *his* father."

p. 222. "*That's my fear*": — The 4tos, "That's my fear, *brother*."

p. 223. "To hold *my course*": — The 4tos, perfecting the verse, "To hold my *very course*."

p. 230. "—— if I had a monopoly out, they would have part on't, and *loads* too": — Read, "and *ladies* too." This is the reading of the first 4to, and gives the true text, as the whole context shows. Ladies were as fond of speculating in monopolies in England in Shakespeare's time as in South Sea stock in John Law's, or as nowadays they are said to be of taking shares in blockade runners. Besides, see the last word in the sentence. This passage is not in the folio; and editors say that "the old copies give *loads* and *lodes*;" Mr. Collier censuring those who read *ladies* "without the slightest authority, . . . when the old copies have not a word about ladies." But of Mr. Lenox's copies of the two editions of 1608, the one with the place of sale named in the imprint has, "and Ladies too;" the other, "and lodes too."

p. 235. "*Let it be so: I have another* daughter": — The 4tos, "*Yea, is't come to this? Yet I have left a* daughter."

p. 241. "—— the *revenging* gods": — The 4tos have "the *revengive* gods."

" "Bringing the murtherous *coward*": — The 4tos, "murtherous *caitiff*."

" "—— *would* the *reposal*": — The 4tos, "*could* the *reposure*."

p. 242. "To have the *expense* and *waste* of his revenues": — The first 4to has, "the *waste* and *spoyl*," &c. The second 4to, "To have *these* — and waste of *this* his revenues."

p. 244. "Good *dawning* to thee, friend": — The 4tos, "Good *even*," &c.

p. 248. "When he, *compact*": — The 4tos, "When he, *conjunct*."

p. 253. "*That, sir*, which seeks," &c.: — Read, "*That sir* which seeks," &c., without the commas.

p. 254. "*They are* sick? *they are* weary?" — Read, with the 4tos, "*They're* sick? *they're* weary?"

" "*Fiery? what* quality?" — The 4tos, "*What fiery* quality?"

p. 310. "I fear I am not *in my perfect mind*": — The 4tos, "*perfect in my mind*."

p. 317. "More than in your *addition*": — The 4tos, "in your *advancement*."

p. 322. "Never (O *fault!*) revealed myself": — The 4tos, "Never (O *father!*)" &c., which may well be the true text, and which has a tenderness not found in the reading of the folio.

VOL. XII.

Antony and Cleopatra.

p. 36. "And made their bends *adornings*": — Read, of course, "And make their bends, *adoring*," as the Note requires.

p. 115. "—— how *honourable*": — Read, "how *honourably*."

MEMOIRS.

MEMOIRS OF

WILLIAM SHAKESPEARE.

ALTHOUGH William Shakespeare was a popular actor and author, and the friend of many persons of distinction in his day, few particulars of his personal life have come down to posterity. Tradition and the allusions of his contemporaries furnish us with little information in regard to him ; and much of that little we owe to the reverential care of another actor, Thomas Betterton, who visited Shakespeare's native place, probably between 1670 and 1675, for the express purpose of gathering materials for his biography. All that he learned was probably embodied by Nicholas Rowe in the account of the poet's life which appeared in Rowe's edition, published in 1709. The laborious investigations of Malone and others during the succeeding century and a half have added to our little stock of knowledge upon this interesting subject. But what we know, what is probable, and the poet's own works, may enable us to trace, at least, the general course of his life's uneventful story.

Warwickshire, in Old England, seems to have been the favorite haunt, if it were not the ancestral soil, of a family whose name more than any other in our tongue sounds of battle and tells of knightly origin. It is possible, indeed, that *Shakespeare* is a corruption of some name of more peaceful meaning, and therefore mayhap (so bloody was ambition's very lowest step of old) of humbler derivation; for in the irregular, phonographic spelling of antiquity it appears sometimes as *Chacksper* and *Shaxpur*. But upon such an uncertain foundation it is hardly safe even to base a doubt; and as the martial accents come down to us from the verge of the fourteenth century, we may safely assume that a name thus spoken in chivalric days was not without chivalric significance.*

The Shakespeares, however, seem never to have risen to the rank of heraldic gentry, or to have established themselves firmly among the landholders of the county. An old register of the Guild of Saint Anne of Knolle in Warwickshire, which goes back to 1407, shows that among many Shakespeares, in whose eternal welfare the brothers and sisters were led to concern themselves,

* The manner in which the name is spelled in the old records varies almost to the extreme capacity of various letters to produce a sound approximating to that of the name as we pronounce it. It appears as Chacksper, Shaxpur, Shaxper, Schaksper, Schakesper, Schakspere, Schakespeire. Schakespeyr, Shagspere, Saxpere, Shaxpere, Shaxpeare, Shaxsper, Shaxspere, Shaxespere, Shakspere, Shakspear, Shakspeere, Schakspear, Shackspeare, Shackespeare, Shackespere, Shakspeyr, Shaksper, Shakespere, Shakyspere, Shakeseper, Shakespire, Shakespeire, Shakespear, Shakespeare, Shakaspeare; and there are even other varieties of its orthography.

But Shakespeare himself, and his careful friend Ben Jonson, when they printed the name, spelled it *Shake-speare*, the hyphen being often used; and in this form it is found in almost every book of their time in which it appeared. The final *e* is mere superfluity, and might with propriety be dropped; but then we should also drop it from Greene. Marlowe, Peele, and other names in which it appears. There seems, therefore, to be no good reason for deviating from the orthography to which Shakespeare and his contemporaries gave a kind of formal recognition. As to the superior martial significance of this name to all others, we have, indeed, Breakspeare, Winspeare, Shakeshaft, Shakelance, Briselance, Drawswerde, Curtlemace, and some others of that sort; but in this regard they all must yield to that which was an attribute of Mars himself as long ago as Homer —

"Μαίνετο δ', ὡς ὅτ' Ἄρης ἐγχέσπαλος."

Iliad, O. 605.

there was a Prioress Isabella, whose soul was prayed for in 1505 (did player William know it when he wrote *Measure for Measure*?), and a Lady ("Domina") Joan, who seems to have been living in 1527; but these trifling distinctions are the highest which have been discovered in connection with the name.

Little need we care, however, what was the condition of those Shakespeares who were mouldering in the earth before he without whom they would never have been heard of appeared upon it. Who his paternal grandfather was, we do not surely know; but there is little doubt that he was one Richard Shakespeare, farmer, of Snitterfield, a village near Stratford on Avon. This Richard Shakespeare was a tenant of Robert Arden, a gentleman of ancient family but moderate estate, who lived at Wilmecote, three miles from Stratford, and who tilled a part of his patrimonial fields, and let a part to humbler husbandmen. The Ardens had been high among the gentry of Warwickshire since a time long before the Conquest, at which period Turchill de Arden was military governor, *vice-comes* (or viscount, then not an hereditary dignity) of Warwick Castle. The family took its name from the wooded country, called Arden or Ardern, which lay in the northern and western part of that county, of which at one time they had no small part in their possession.* Robert Arden's branch of this family held lands in Snitterfield as far back, at least, as the early part of the fifteenth century; and he inherited his property there in direct succession. Two of the family had held places of some honor and responsibility in the household of King Henry VII.: Sir John

* The name Ardern, or Wood, was given at first to a forest-covered tract, which extended from the Avon to the Trent on the north, and the Severn on the west; but it was retained at a very early period only by that part which lay within Warwickshire.

Arden, who was squire of the body, and his nephew Robert, who was page of the bed-chamber, to that shrewd and thrifty monarch, in whose service they both prospered.

Robert Arden, the page of the bed-chamber, was grandfather to the Robert Arden who let his land to Richard Shakespeare — a fact in which we may be sure that landlord and tenant took some pride, because, as we shall see, it was so well remembered by their grandson. Of the family affairs and fortunes of Richard Shakespeare, nothing of interest is known; but among the Shakespeares of Snitterfield were two, John and Henry, who were of the age which his sons might be, and who were brothers. There appears to have been but one family of the name in the place, and there is hardly room for doubt that they called him father. Henry Shakespeare's name will come up again; but our concern is with the fortunes of his brother John, who appears to have been a man of thrift and capacity, and withal, as such men are apt to be, somewhat ambitious. Robert Arden had no son to inherit his name, his property, and his bed-chamber honors; but he had seven daughters. The youngest of these, Mary, who seems to have been her father's favorite, John Shakespeare won to look on him with liking; and so he married into the landlord's family, and allied his blood to that of the Ardens, with their high old English pedigree, stretching past the Conqueror away beyond the reign of the Confessor. And to us of English race it is a matter of some interest to know that Shakespeare came of pure English blood, and not upon his mother's side of Norman, as some have concluded because of her gentle and ancient lineage, and because to use the words of one of them, Arden "sounds like a Norman name." But *Ardern*, which became Arden, is Celtic, and the name was given to the northern part of Warwickshire by the ancient Britons. And as there has been even a book written to show that Shakespeare was a Celt, it may be well to say here, that the Turchill* de Arden who is above mentioned was the first of his family who assumed a surname. His father's name was Alwin, which, like his own, was common enough of old among the English. He called himself Turchill de Ardern; but the Normans called him Turchill de Warwick, because of the office which he held under Edward the Confessor, and which the Conqueror allowed him to retain in spite of his English blood, because, like many other powerful Englishmen, he had not helped Harold, and did not oppose Duke William's title. For it should always be remembered that, according to the loose dynastic notions of that day, the Norman bastard had some claim to the throne of England, and that it was the land of a divided people that he successfully invaded. From this people, who swallowed up their conquerors (like themselves, of Teutonic race), and imposed upon them their language, their customs, and their very mental traits, came the man in whose origin we have so great an interest; and, to all intents and purposes, from this people only, even on the mother's side; for the Ardens, in spite of their position, seem to have intermarried almost altogether with English families.†

But, to return to the humbler members of the Arden family, with whom we have more immediate concern. Whether Robert Arden consented to the marriage of the daughter who has given him a consequence in the eyes of posterity that he little dreamed of, or whether the pedigree and the charms of the fair Mary were the only

* The *ch* is hard in this name, which was often written *Turkill*.
† See Dugdale's *Antiquities of Warwickshire*, passim.

motives of John Shakespeare's choice, we cannot tell; because the wedding did not take place until after, and probably not until a full year after, the death of the young lady's father, by which event she became the inheritress of a pretty fortune in possession and in reversion. Her father had bequeathed her a farm, of between fifty and sixty acres, in Wilmecote, called Ashbies, with a crop upon the ground, and £6 13*s*. 4*d*. in money, beside her share in what was left after legacies were paid; and she had also a reversionary interest of far greater value than Ashbies in a step-mother's dower estate at Snitterfield, and in some other land at Wilmecote. The small sum of money set down to the young heiress (though in the end she doubtless had much more) may excite a smile, until we remember that money had then nearly six times its present value, and also how very little of actual money is got, or in fact needed, by agricultural people, even of comparatively large possessions. Robert Arden died about the 1st of December, 1556, and the first child of John Shakespeare and Mary Arden was baptized on September 15th, 1558. Joan Shakespeare received her name in the Church of the Holy Trinity, the parish church of Stratford on Avon, where her father had for some years been settled, and had become a prosperous and rising man. When he went thither we do not know; but he was there, and a householder in Henley Street, in 1552. His chief occupation seems to have been that of a glover; for he is so styled in a law document issued in June, 1556. But he was also engaged in husbandry, and in company with another person; for, on the 19th of November in the same year, he brought a suit against Henry Field, who unjustly kept from him eighteen quarters of barley. John Shakespeare's private and public fortunes advanced steadily and rapidly for twenty years from the time when he first appears in Stratford. It is true that he could not write his name; but that was no disgrace, and little impediment, at a time when men much above him in social position were equally incapable. In 1556 he purchased the copyhold of two houses, one with a garden and croft, and one — that in Henley Street — with a garden only. In the course of the next year he acquired other property (how considerable for a man in his station, we have already seen) by his marriage. In this year he was regarded as of sufficient substance and importance to be marked as one of the jury of the court-leet, upon which he served soon afterward; and at this date he was also appointed ale-taster — an office of which, in spite of its humble name, the mighty consumption of that fluid in old England must have made the duties arduous, though pleasant, and the perquisites acceptable. He must have given the burgesses of Stratford cause to speak well of him over the liquor that they loved; for in 1557 they elected him one of their number, and they were only fourteen. The next year saw him a constable, and also the father of the girl who was called after him; and in 1559 he was reëlected one of the keepers of the Queen's peace in Stratford. About this time he appears to have dropped his glover's trade. It was, indeed, quite inconsistent with the notions of propriety in that day that the husband of an Arden and an heiress should be an artisan; and this consideration could not but have had its weight with the young burgess, now that he had land and beeves. The year 1561 saw him made an affeeror in the spring, and before the leaves began to fall, elected chamberlain. It was the duty of an affeeror to impose fines upon offenders who were punishable arbitrarily for misdemeanors to which no express penalty was attached by statute — an office only to be filled by a man of discretion and integrity; and as John Shakespeare, according to the date when he is with good reason believed to have been born, was at this time but thirty or thirty-one years old, his appointment to this office by the court indicates, not only soundness of character on his part, but somewhat unusual ripeness of judgment. He served as chamberlain two years, in the second of which another daughter was born to him, who was called Margaret. But Mary Arden's little family did not thrive like her husband's business. A few months lightened the young mother's arms to lay a load upon her heart. Margaret as well as Joan died in early infancy.

To the now childless couple there came consolation and a welcome care in their first-born son, whom, on the 26th of April, 1564, they christened and called William. The Reverend (or, as he was then called, Sir) John Breechgirdle probably performed that office. Of the day of William Shakespeare's birth there exists, and probably there was made, no record. Why should it have been otherwise? He was only the son of a Warwickshire yeoman, a burgess of a little rural town. And there were two score at least of children born that year in Stratford, who, in the eyes of their parents and of the good towns folk, were of just as much importance, and of whose appearance in the world no other note was taken than such as tells us of his advent — the entry of their christening in the parish register. As yet it was not the custom to record upon the blank leaves of the Bible the dates of life and death in humble families; and had John Shakespeare owned a Bible, neither he nor even his higher born wife could have written the words to read which, if they had endured, men would have made a pilgrimage. All unsuspecting what he was whom she had borne and whom she cherished in her bosom, the mother of William Shakespeare could have looked on him only as the probable inheritor of his father's little wealth, the possible recipient of his father's little honors, or mayhap, in some moment of high hope, the occupant of a position like that of his

maternal grandfather. And had he become a peer instead of a player, the day of his birth might have been no less uncertain. Tradition says it was the 23d of April; and the old custom of christening on the third day after birth, though it was far from universal, if it did not give rumor a hint, gives tradition some support.

A court roll tells us that in 1552 John Shakespeare

lived in Henley Street, and another that he bought the copyhold of a house in that street in 1556: tradition points out a house in Henley Street, which we know belonged to John Shakespeare, as the birthplace of his illustrious son, who himself became its owner; and the probability of the truth of this tradition amounts, to all intents and purposes, to certainty. Neglect, subdivision, and base uses had reduced this house at the beginning of the present century to a very forlorn and unsightly condition. But as late as 1769 it preserved enough of its original form to show that William Shakespeare was born and passed his childhood and his adolescent years in a home which was not only pretty and picturesque, but very comfortable and unusually commodious for a man in his father's station in the middle of the sixteenth century. For in the reign of Elizabeth domestic architecture was in its infancy. Something had been done for the household comfort of noblemen and gentlemen of large estates; but almost nothing for the homes of that large class, composed, in the words of Agar, of those who have neither poverty nor riches, but food convenient for them, and which now gives the architect his chief employment. Old abbeys, priories, and granges, recently sequestered, and newly-built halls, were taking the place of the cold, crumbling castles as dwellings for the rich; and between these and the humble farm-house or village cot, often built, as the haughty Spaniard wrote in the reign of Elizabeth's sister, "of sticks and dirt," there was no middle structure. People corresponding in position to those whose means and tastes would now insure them as much comfort in their homes as a king has in his palace, and even simple elegance beside, then lived in houses which in their best estate would seem at the present day rude, cheerless, and confined, to any man not bred in poverty. In 1847 the Shakespeare house passed into the hands of an association under whose care it has been renovated; but unfortunately, like some of the Shakespeare poetry, not restored to a close resemblance to its first condition; though that was perhaps impossible. Whether it was in this house that John Shakespeare and his wife, with their only precious child, staid out the plague, which visited Stratford in

1564, or whether they fled to some uninfected place, we do not know. But families did not move freely in those days, or easily find house-room; and on the 30th of August in that year John Shakespeare, as the Stratford register tells, was at a hall or meeting, held in a garden, probably for fear of infection. On this occasion he gave twelve pence for the relief of poor sufferers. The highest sum given was seven shillings and four pence, the lowest, six pence; and there were but two burgesses who gave more than twelve pence. In September he gave six pence more, and in October eighteen pence. It may be assumed as quite certain, then, that the Shakespeares remained at Stratford during the plague, thus leaving William, like any other child, in peril of the pestilence. They passed through a period of fearful trial. The scourge made Stratford desolate. In six months one sixth of their neighbors were buried. But although around them there was hardly a house in which there was not one dead, there was a charm upon their threshold, and William Shakespeare lived.

In the next year the father was chosen one of the fourteen aldermen of the town; and in 1568 he was made high bailiff, which office he filled one year. He continued to prosper, and in 1570 he took under his cultivation yet other lands, a farm called Ington, at the then goodly rent of £8. The year 1571 saw him chief alderman; and in 1575 he bought two freehold houses in Henley Street, with gardens and orchards. William Shakespeare, therefore, at ten years of age was the son of one of the most substantial and respected men of Stratford, who was one of its fourteen burgesses, and who had rapidly attained, step by step, the highest honors in the gift of his townsmen. He was styled *Master* Shakespeare — a designation the manly style of which we have belittled into *Mister*, voiding it at the same time of its honorable significance. As high bailiff and chief alderman he sat as justice of the peace, and thus even became 'worshipful.' There has been much dispute as to what was his occupation at this time; his glover's trade having been before abandoned. Rowe, on Betterton's authority, says that he was "a considerable dealer in wool." John Aubrey the antiquary, or rather *quid-tunc*, says that he was a butcher: in a deed dated 1579, and in another seventeen years later, he is called a yeoman; and his name appears in a list of the gentlemen and freeholders of Barlichway hundred in 1580. One of his fellow-aldermen, who was his predecessor in the office of bailiff, was a butcher; but with our knowledge of his landed possessions and his consequent agricultural occupation, we may be pretty sure that his nearest approach to that useful business was in having his own cattle killed on his own premises. Wool he might well have sold from the backs of his own flocks without being properly a wool-dealer. But what was his distinctive occupation is a matter of very little consequence, except as it may have affected the early occupation of his son, and of not much, even in that regard. He was plainly in a condition of life which secured that son the means of a healthy physical and moral development, and which, if he had lived in New England a century or a century and a half later, would have made him regarded, if a well-mannered man, as fit company for the squire and the parson and the best people of the township, and emboldened him perhaps to aspire to a seat in the General Court of the Colony. But the first that we hear of John Shakespeare is, that in 1552 he and a certain Humphrey Reynolds and Adrian Quiney made a muck-heap in Henley Street, against the order of the Court; for which dirty piece of business they were punished by a fine, as they well deserved. Yet next year John Shakespeare and Adrian Quiney repeated the unsavory offence, and this time in company with the bailiff himself. It is plain that William Shakespeare's father was not singular in the uncleanliness of his habits in this respect. Stratford on Avon was a dirty village; yet not dirtier, perhaps, than most villages were three hundred years ago. Out-door cleanliness and order are among the modern improvements upon former ways of living; and even at the period referred to, the apartments in noblemen's houses and in palaces were so neglected that they became offensive to the senses, and perfumes were burned in them, a substitute — a very poor one — for the use of broom, and soap, and water. Stratford, also, like most country villages three centuries ago, was composed chiefly of thatched cottages and small farm-houses, the meaner of which were without chimneys and glazed windows, and most of which would

be pronounced uninhabitable nowadays by people of the means and condition of those by whom they were then inhabited. But, after the fashion of those times, in the midst of these hovels were a few fine mansions, and a large and beautiful stone church; and over the fertile, gently rolling country round were scattered the stately country houses of the gentry. A fine stone bridge of fourteen arches had been built here across the Avon by Sir Hugh Clopton, who also built the Great House, a mansion afterward called New Place, and in which the readers of these Memoirs are interested.

II.

What was the education of William Shakespeare were a question indeed of interest to all reasonable creatures, and, to those who think that education makes great men, of singular importance. But of his teachers we know nothing, save of one — his father. What were his mother's traits of character, and whether by maternity and training she had transmitted any of them to her son, we cannot tell. In which ignorance there is a kind of bliss to those people who have taken up the novel notion of the day, that men of mark derive their mental and their moral gifts, not from the father, but the mother.

Mary Arden may have been such a woman as it would please us to imagine the mother of William Shakespeare; but the limits of our knowledge oblige us to look upon him during childhood only under the tutelage of the father, whose good sense and strong character are shown by his rapid and steady rise of fortune and advancement among his townsmen. His son was taught, we may be sure, to fear God and honor the King,* and in the words of the Catechism, to learn and labor truly to get his own living, and do his duty in that state of life to which it had pleased God to call him; for that was the sum and substance of the home-teaching of our forefathers. For book instruction, there was the Free Grammar School of Stratford, well endowed by Thomas Jolyffe in the reign of Edward IV., — forever therefore let his name be honored! — where, unless it differed from all others of its kind, he could have learned Latin and some Greek. Some English, too; but not much; for English was held in scorn by

* "*Moriamur pro rege nostro;*" as applicable to Elizabeth of England as to Maria Theresa of Hungary.

the scholars of those days, and long after. The only qualifications for admission to this school were residence in the town, seven years of age, and ability to read. That the sons of the chief alderman of Stratford went there, there could have hardly been a doubt, even had not Betterton learned the tradition that William had been bred there for some time. The masters of the school between 1572 and 1580 were Thomas Hunt, the parson of the neighboring village of Luddington, and Thomas Jenkins. Had either the Englishman or the Welshman known when they breeched Shakespeare *primus* that he would have his revenge in making the one sit for his portrait as *Holofernes*, and the other as *Sir Hugh Evans*, they would doubtless have taken out their satisfaction grievously in advance upon the spot. Could any one have told them, with power of conviction upon his tongue, what he was whom they were flogging, they would have dropped the birch and fled the school in awe unspeakable. There is better discipline, even for a dull or a vicious boy, than beating; but, aside from question of the kind of training to which he was subjected, it was well perhaps for William Shakespeare that his masters knew only what he then was. Insight of the future would not always bring good fortune.

At school Shakespeare acquired some knowledge of Latin and of Greek. For not only does Ben Jonson tell us that he had a little of the former and less of the latter, but his very frequent use of Latin derivatives in their radical sense shows a somewhat thoughtful and observant study of that language; and although he has left fewer traces of his personal feelings and experience upon his works than any modern writer, he wrote one passage bearing upon this subject, and telling a plain story. *Warwick*, pleading to *King Henry IV.* in extenuation of the fondness of *Prince Hal* for wild associates, says, —

"My gracious lord, you look beyond him quite.
The prince but studies his companions,
Like a strange tongue; wherein, to gain the language,
'Tis needful that the most immodest word
Be looked upon and learn'd; which once attain'd,
Your highness knows, comes to no farther use,
But to be known and hated."
Second Part of King Henry IV., Act IV. Sc. 4.

Genius does not teach facts; and every man who has himself been through the curriculum will see that the writer of that passage had surely gone, at least, part through the same course before the days of expurgated classics. Jonson's phrase, "small Latin and less Greek," has been generally taken as meaning a mere smattering of the first, and nothing at all of the second; but without sufficient reason, in my opinion. So does Edward Bathurst, B. D., in his memoir of his friend Arthur Wilson, the author of *The Inconstant Ladie*, written before 1646, say that "He had little skill in the Latin tongue and less in the Greek, a good readiness in the French and some smattering in the Dutch;"* and yet, according to the same authority, Wilson had been a fellow-commoner of Trinity College, Oxford, where he had been regular and studious; and by his own account he could, at a pinch, speak Latin.† Little and much are comparative terms, the value of which can be determined only when we know the standard according to which they are used. Jonson's scholarship, though not profound or various, seems to

* "Character of Wilson," &c., in the Appendix to "*The Inconstant Ladie.*" Ed. 1814, p. 156.

† "Observations of God's Providence in the Tract of my Life." *Ibid.* p. 128

have been very thorough and exact, and Bathurst was probably a man entirely given up to study. Both, we may be sure, would speak very lightly of the Latin and Greek of many men now-a-days who have well earned their degree of Master of Arts, and who can make good use of their academical acquirements. From report and from the evidence of his works we may reasonably conclude that William Shakespeare read, as boys read, the easier classical Latin authors at Stratford Grammar School, and added to them the favorite of that day, old Baptista Mantuan, whom he quotes in *Love's Labour's Lost*, and that he retained enough of what he learned to have thereby a finer insight and more thorough mastery of English, if not to enjoy Virgil and Terence in the original. It is true, as Farmer has shown, that his works furnish evidence undeniable that in preparing himself to write upon Greek and Roman subjects he used the existing translations of the classics. But how many who for years have spent a part of every day in the study of Greek and Latin do the same, when college exercises are driven out of mind by the duties and labors for which college studies are but discipline, and turn laboriously from translation to original only when they wish to examine some particular passage closely! When, in *The Taming of the Shrew*, *Tranio* quotes a passage from Terence, he is inaccurate, and gives it not as it appears in the text of the Latin dramatist, but as it is misquoted in the Latin Grammar of William Lilly, whose accidence was in common use among our forefathers when Shakespeare was a boy.* But, even if this showed that Shakespeare had not read Terence, which

* "Quid agas? nisi ut te redimas captum quam queas Minimo." *Eunuchus*, Act I. Sc. 1.

"Redime te captum quam queas minimo."
The Taming of the Shrew, Act I. Sc. 1

it does not, it surely does show that he had studied Master Lilly's book, which, be it remembered, is itself, not in English, but in Latin, after the strange, pedantic fashion of the times when it was written. The scene between *Sir Hugh* and *William*, in *The Merry Wives of Windsor*, is as surely evidence of the writer's knowledge of the Latin grammar. "*Singulariter, nominativo hic, hæc, hoc*," does not lie very far over the threshold of that elementary book; but the question which elicits the declension, "What is he, William, that does lend articles?" by which the pragmatic parson tries to trip the poor boy up, shows an intelligent acquaintance with the rudiments of the Latin language.

Italian and French were not taught, we may be sure, at Stratford Grammar School; but this is the most convenient occasion on which to say that Shakespeare appears to have learned something of them before he became too busy a man to study. It was probably in his earlier London years. Both these languages, and especially the former, were much in vogue among the cultivated people of that period. Shakespeare was likely to be thrown into the society of those who taught them; and their instructions he might well requite, if he were sparing of money, by orders of admission to the theatre, which have been held to pay many a larger debt in later times. He has left several traces of a knowledge of Italian, which might be great or small, scattered through his plays; but in two passages, there are indications of an acquaintance with two Italian poets, which, though hitherto passed by, cannot, I think, be mistaken. When *Othello*, in the dawning of his jealousy, chides *Desdemona* for being without the handkerchief, his first love-token, he tells her, —

"There's magic in the web of it.
A sibyl, that had number'd in the world

The sun to course two hundred compasses,
In her prophetic fury, sewed the work."

The phrase "prophetic fury" is so striking, so picturesque, and so peculiar, that in itself it excites remark, and remains upon the memory as the key-note of the passage; but when we regard it as applied to mood in which a web was woven or embroidered, all these characteristics are much enhanced. Now, in the *Orlando Furioso* there is the following passage about a tent which Cassandra gave to Hector, and which descended through Cleopatra to Constantine, who gave it to Melissa: —

"Eran de gli anni appresso che due milia
Che fu quel ricco padiglion trapunto.
Una donzella de la terra d' Ilia
Ch' avea il furor profetico congiunto,
Con studio di gran tempo e con vigilia,
Lo fece di sua man, di tutto punto." *
Canto XLVI. St. 80.

Here we have the identical thought, and, in their Italian form, the identical words, *furor profetico*, used in the description of a woman, sibyl-like, if not a sibyl, weaving a cloth of magic virtues. There is, too, in both passages the idea of a great lapse of time, though in one it is applied to the weaver and in the other to the thing woven. It would seem impossible that this striking coincidence of thought, of incident, and of language could be merely accidental; and there was no other translation of the *Orlando Furioso* into Eng-

* Thus rendered by Rose: —

"Two thousand tedious years were nigh complete,
Since this fair work was fashioned by the lore
Of Trojan maid, warmed with prophetic heat;
Who 'mid long labor, and 'mid vigil sore,
With her own fingers all the storied sheet
Of the pavilion had embroidered o'er."

lish in Shakespeare's time than Sir John Harrington's, published in 1591, and in that the phrase "prophetic fury," or any one like it, does not occur.*

Again, when *Iago*, distilling his poison into *Othello's* ears, utters the often quoted lines, —

"Who steals my purse, steals trash; 'tis something, nothing;
'Twas mine, 'tis his, and has been slave to thousands
But he that filches from me my good name
Robs me of that which not enriches him,
And makes me poor indeed," —

he but repeats with little variation this stanza of Berni's *Orlando Innamorato*, of which poem, to this day, there is no English version: —

"Chi ruba un corno un cavallo un anello,
E simil cose, ha qualche discrezione,
E potrebbe chiamarsi ladroncello;
Ma quel che ruba la reputazione,
E de l' altrui fatiche si fa bello,
Si puo chiamare assassino e ladrone;
E tanto più odio e pena è degno
Quanto più del dover trapassa il segno."†
Canto LI. St. 1.

Now, when we consider that the faculty and habit

* See Harrington's *Orlando Furioso in English.* Canto XLVI. St. 64. Ed. 1591.

† As no English translation has been made of the *Orlando Innamorato*, I must ask the reader who cannot command the original to be content with this rendering of the above stanza: —

The man who steals a horn, a horse, a ring,
Or such a trifle, thieves with moderation,
And may be justly called a robberling;
But he who takes away a reputation,
And pranks in feathers from another's wing,
His deed is robbery, assassination,
And merits punishment so much the greater
As he to right and truth is more a traitor.

of assimilating what he read was one of Shakespeare's mental traits, and that both these passages of his, so identical in thought and in expression with others in two Italian poets who wrote on kindred subjects, occur in a play founded upon an Italian novel which had not been rendered into our language in his day, can we reasonably doubt that he was sufficiently an Italian scholar to read Ariosto, Berni, and Giraldi Cinthio in the original? * The consideration of this subject has diverted us from the course of Shakespeare's life, and has given us an anticipatory glance of one of its few landmarks; which, however, are so well known, that I have not sought and shall not seek solicitously to show them only in due order.

John Shakespeare's prosperity hardly lasted to his eldest son's adolescence. Betterton heard a tradition that the narrowness of his circumstances and the need of his son's assistance at home forced him to withdraw William from school; and the evidence of town registers and of court records corroborates the story In 1578, when the young poet was but fourteen years old, his father mortgaged the farm at Ashbies for forty pounds to Edmund Lambert. That this step was taken not to raise money for a venture in trade or for a new

* See the Introduction to *Othello*, Vol. XI. p. 361 of this work. Mr. Halliwell in his Life of William Shakespeare, p. 190, quotes from a MS. entitled *The New Metamorphosis*, which was written "by J. M. Gent. 1600," the following lines, which he. not having Berni's stanza in mind, naturally regards as an imitation of the passage of *Othello* in question, and therefore, of course, as evidence that that play was written before the date of the MS.: —

"The highwayman that robs one of his purse
Is not soe bad; nay, these are ten times worse!
For these doe rob men of their pretious name,
And in exchange give obloquy and shame."

But J. M.'s lines are, on the contrary, a manifest imitation of Berni's, rather than Shakespeare's; and if they have any bearing at all upon the question of the date of *Othello*, (which, in my opinion, they have not,) they show that it was written after 1600.

purchase, but on account of serious embarrassment, is shown by a concurrence of significant events, all pointing in the latter direction. In the same year when his fellow-aldermen assessed themselves 6 *s.* 8 *d.* each towards the equipment of pikemen, billmen, and an archer, he is set down as to pay only 3 *s.* 4 *d.* Again in that year when the other aldermen paid 4 *d.* each a week for the relief of the poor, it was ordered that John Shakespeare should not be taxed to pay any thing. In March, $157\frac{8}{9}$, the inhabitants of Stratford having been assessed for the purchase of arms, he failed to contribute his quota. In October, 1579, he sold his wife's share in the Snitterfield property, and in 1580 a reversionary interest in the same, the latter for forty pounds. Six years afterwards his little wealth had found such wings that a distraint having been issued against him, the return made upon it was, that he had nothing upon which to distrain; whereupon a writ of *capias* was issued against his person; he who as high bailiff had but a short time before issued such writs against others.* He seems even to have been in hiding about this time; for the town records show that in 1586 he was deprived of his alderman's office, the reason given being that "Mr. Shaxpere dothe not come to the halles when they be warned, nor hathe not done of longe tyme;" and it appears, on the same authority, that he had thus absented himself for seven years. But before March of the next year he had been arrested, and was imprisoned or in custody, doubtless for debt, according to the cruel and foolish practice of which our brethren in the mother country have not yet rid themselves. This we know by his suing out a writ of *habeas corpus* in the Stratford Court of Record. Per-

* The Shakespeare Society of London was in possession of two such writs.

haps he suffered this indignity on account of his kindness to his brother Henry, before mentioned, who had much money trouble, and for whom he became surety to one Nicholas Lane for ten pounds. Henry not having duly paid this sum, Lane sued John Shakespeare for it in February, 1587. To follow his sad fortunes yet farther, in 1592 a commission, upon which were Sir Thomas Lucy and Sir Fulke Greville with six others, which had been appointed to inquire into the conformity of the people of Warwickshire to the established religion, with a special eye to Jesuits, priests, and recusants, reported many persons "for not comming monethlie to the churche, according to hir Majestie's lawes;" and among them was John Shakespeare. But the commissioners specially note as to him and eight others, that "it is sayd that these last nine coom not to churche for fear of processe for debtte."

Thus low in fortune and estate had sunk the once prosperous high bailiff of Stratford, in the veins of whose children ran the blood of men who had owned half the county through which he skulked, a bailiff-hunted debtor. Those very children added largely to his anxiety and his cares. For since Margaret's death six had been born to him: William; Gilbert, born in 1566; a second Joan, in 1569; Anne, in 1571; Richard, in $157\frac{3}{4}$; and Edmund, in 1580. Rowe, upon Betterton's authority, says that John Shakespeare had "ten children in all." But Betterton only reported tradition; and the Stratford parish register, better authority on such a point, records the baptism of no more than eight, two of whom, as we have seen, died before their father reached the height of his prosperity; and Anne died at the beginning of his troubles. At her burial there were both pall and bell, for which it has been discovered that viii *d.* were paid, while other children buried in the same year (1579) were honored with only half the ceremony, the bell, at half the price; which has been accepted as evidence that John Shakespeare had money to spare. So regarded he meant that it should be; and he deceived even posterity. As long as funeral ceremonies are deemed important, they will be the last as to which poverty will compel retrenchment. In 1579 John Shakespeare had not abandoned the struggle to keep up appearances. Had his purse been fuller, or his position lower, he might have been willing to save the four pence. But a few years later five little mouths to feed, five little backs to clothe, were quite enough to harass the poor man who could not keep his own body out of a debtor's prison, and to cause him to abandon any ambitious projects which he might have formed for his eldest son, and call him from his studies to contribute something to his own support, and perhaps to that of the family. The traditions of the townsfolk upon this subject were surely therefore in the main well founded, though in their particulars they were discordant. Rowe, speaking for Betterton, says, that "upon his leaving school he seems to have given entirely into that way of living which his father proposed to him," which, according to the same authority, was that of a dealer in wool. Gossiping John Aubrey, who says that John Shakespeare was a butcher, adds, "I have been told heretofore by some of the neighbors that when he was a boy he exercised his father's trade; but when he kill'd a calfe he wold doe it in a high style, and make a speeche." Aubrey, who died about 1700, probably received this precious information from the same source through which an old parish clerk of Stratford, who was living in 1693, and was then more than eighty years old, derived a similar story, that Shakespeare had been "bound apprentice to a butcher." Aubrey also records, on the authority of an unknown Mr. Beeston, that William Shakespeare "understode Latin pretty well, for he had been many years a schoolmaster in the country." The only point upon which these loose traditions are of importance, is that upon which they are unanimous, that William Shakespeare was obliged to leave school early and earn his living. Isolated passages of the poet's works have been gathered together and gravely brought forward to sustain each of these traditions as to his early occupation,—surely a wise and penetrative method of getting at the truth in such a matter. There is hardly a calling, from that of bishop or general to that of pimp or serving-man, which could not be fastened upon him by this process. Utterly ruined, however, as John Shakespeare was, he seems never to have been driven out of his house in Henley Street, or to have lost his property in it; though how this could be in the case of a man as to whom the return upon an execution was "no effects," it is not easy to conjecture.

But what was William Shakespeare doing in all those years through which his father was descending into the vale of poverty, whither we have followed him to the lowest depth? We have passed over thereby some events of great importance to the son, whom his father's trials seem not to have chastened into sobriety. In estimating Shakespeare's character, the fact that he left among his neighbors the reputation of having been somewhat irregular in his youth cannot be lightly set aside. Nor is it at all strange that such a reputation should have been attained in the early years of a man of his lively fancy, healthy organization, and breadth of moral sympathy. It is from tradition that we learn that during his father's misfortunes he was occasionally engaged in stealing deer; but we know on good evidence that about that time he also got himself married in no very creditable fashion. While he was sowing his wild oats in the fields round Stratford, he naturally visited the cottage of Richard Hathaway, a substantial yeoman of Shottery, who seems to have been on terms of friendship with John Shakespeare. This Richard Hathaway had, among other children, a daughter named Anne, who might have dandled William Shakespeare in his infancy upon her knee; for she was eight years old when he was born, in 1564. Whether or no Anne Hathaway had a fair face and a winning way which spontaneously captivated William Shakespeare, or whether he yielded to arts to which his inexperience made him an easy victim, we cannot surely tell. But we do know that she, though not vestally inclined, as we shall see, remained unmarried until 1582, and that then the woman of twenty-six took to husband the boy of eighteen. They were married upon once asking of the banns; and the bond given to the Bishop of Worcester for his security in licensing this departure from custom, was given in that year, on the 28th day of November.*

* "Noverint universi per præsentes nos ffulconem Sandells de Stratford in comitatu Warwici, agricolam, et Johannem Rychardson ibidem agricolam, teneri et firmiter obligari Ricardo Cosin generoso, et Roberto Warmstry notario publico, in quadraginta libris bonæ et legalis monetæ Angliæ, solvend. eisdem Ricardo et Roberto, hæred. execut. vel assignat. suis, ad quam quidem solucionem bene et fideliter faciend. obligamus nos et utrumque nostrum per se pro toto et in solid. hæred. executor. et administrator. nostros firmiter per præsentes sigillis nostris sigillat. Dat. 28 die Novem. anno regni dominæ nostræ Eliz. Dei gratia Angliæ, Franc. et Hiberniæ reginæ, fidei defensor, &c. 25.

"The condicion of this obligacion ys suche, that if herafter there shall not appere any lawfull lett or impediment, by reason of any precontract, consangui[ni]tie, affinitie, or by any other lawfull meanes whatsoever, but that William Shagspere one thone partie, and Anne Hathwey of Stratford in the dioces of Worcester, maiden, may lawfully solennize matrimony together, and in the same afterwardes remaine and continew like man and wiffe, according unto the lawes in that behalf provided: and moreover, if there be not at this present time any action, sute, quarrell, or demaund, moved or depending before any judge ecclesiasticall or temporall, for and concerning any suche lawfull lett or

About those days there was great need that Anne Hathaway should provide herself with a husband of some sort, and that speedily; for in less than five months after she obtained one she was delivered of a daughter. The parish register shows that Susanna, the daughter of William and Anne Shakespeare, was baptized May 26th, 1583.

There have been attempts to turn aside the obvious bearing of these facts upon the character of Anne Hathaway. But it is a stubborn and unwise idolatry which resists such evidence as this, — an idolatry which would exempt Shakespeare, and not only him, but all with whom he became connected, from human passion and human frailty. That temperament is cruel, and that morality pharisaic, which treats all cases of this kind with inexorable and indiscriminating severity, and that judgment outrageously unjust which visits all the sin upon the weaker and already suffering party. Yet if in the present instance it must be that one of this couple seduced the other into error, perhaps where a woman of twenty-six is involved with a boy of eighteen, for the honor of her sex the less that is said about the matter the better. Besides, Anne Hathaway rests under the implied reproach of both the men whose good opinion was to her of gravest moment. Her father,

impediment: and moreover, if the said William Shagspere do not proceed to solemnizacion of mariadg with the said Anne Hathwey without the consent of hir frindes: and also, if the said William do, upon his owne proper costes and expences, defend and save harmles the right reverend Father in God, Lord John Bushop of Worcester, and his offycers, for licensing them the said William and Anne to be maried together with once asking of the bannes of matrimony betweene them, and for all other causes which may ensue by reason or occasion thereof, that then the said obligacion to be voyd and of none effect, or els to stand and abide in full force and vertue."

To this instrument are attached the rude marks of Sandells and Richardson, and a seal which bears two letters, R, and another, imperfect, which seems to be an H. This seal is conjectured to be that of the bride's father, who at the execution of the bond had been dead five months.

like Mary Arden's, had died about a year before her marriage; but while Mary Arden had special legacies, and was assigned to the honorable position of executrix by her father's will, Anne Hathaway was passed over even without mention by her father, who yet carefully and minutely remembered all but one of his other children. And to look forward again, — which we well may do, for Shakespeare's wife will soon pass entirely from our sight, — when her husband was giving instructions for his will he left her only his second-best

bed, the one that probably she slept upon. It is true, as Mr. Knight has pointed out, that she was entitled to dower, and that so her livelihood was well provided for; it is true also that a bed with its furniture was in those days no uncommon bequest. But William Shakespeare's will was one of great particularity, making little legacies to nephews and nieces, and leaving swords and rings as mementos to friends and acquaintance; and yet his wife's name is omitted from the document in its original form, and only appears by an after-thought in an interlineation, as if his attention had been called to the omission, and for decency's sake he would not have the mother of his children unnoticed altogether. The lack of any other bequest than the furniture of her chamber is of small moment in comparison with the slight shown by that interlineation. A second-best bed might be passed over; but what can be done with second-best thoughts? And second best, if good at all, seem to have been all the thoughts which Shakespeare gave her; for there is not a line of his writing known which can be regarded as addressed to her as maid or matron. Did ever poet thus slight the woman that he loved, and that, too, during years of separation?

The cottage in which Anne Hathaway lived is still pointed out in Shottery. It is a timber and plaster house, like John Shakespeare's, standing on a bank, with a roughly paved terrace in front. The parlor is wainscoted high in oak, and in the principal chamber is an enormous and heavily carved bedstead. Though a rustic and even rude habitation when measured by our standard, it was evidently a comfortable home for a substantial yeoman in the time of Queen Elizabeth, and is picturesque enough for the cradle of a poet's love. But it can never be looked upon without sadness by those who rightly estimate the sorrow and the shame which there were born to William Shakespeare — sorrow and shame which not all the varied successes of his after-life could heal and obliterate, and his sufferings from which find frequent expression both in his plays and sonnets. True, he was of all poets the most dramatic, and therefore the most self-forgetful; but this trouble he did not forget. His works are full of passages, to write which, if he had loved his wife and honored her, would have been gall and wormwood to his soul; nay, which, if he had loved and honored her, he could not have written. But did the "flax-wench" whom he uses for the most degrading of all comparisons do more "before her troth-plight" than the woman who bore his name and whom his children called mother?* It is not a question whether his judgment was justifiable, but of what he thought and felt.

And even if Anne Hathaway's fair fame, if indeed it was ever fair, remained untarnished, the marriage at eighteen of such a man as her boy husband proved is one of the saddest social events that can be contemplated. Not because it was singular in all its circumstances or its consequences; for, alas! in most of them it is too common. A youth whose person, whose manner, and whose mental gifts have made him the admired favorite of some rural neighborhood, captivated ere he is well a man by some rustic beauty, or often by his own imagination, married and a father before he should be well beyond a father's care, or bound as much in honor, according to the matrimonial code, as if he were married, developing into a man of mark and culture, attaining social position and distinction which would make him the welcome suitor of the fairest and most accomplished woman of the circle into which he has risen by right of worth and intellect, yet tied to one who is inferior to him in all respects, except perhaps in simple truthfulness, and who does not — poor creature, who cannot if she would — keep pace with him; and all this the consequence of a boyish passion, which opposition might have confirmed, but which tact and a little time — so little! — might easily have dissipated: this case, so pitiable! so pitiable for both

* *The Winter's Tale*, Act I. Sc. 2.

parties, even most pitiable for her, we see too often. But add to all this that the man was William Shakespeare, and that he met his fate at only eighteen years of age, and that the woman who came to him with a stain upon her name was eight years his senior, and could we but think of their life and leave out the world's interest in him, should we not wish that one of them, even if it were he, had died before that ill-starred marriage? But chiefly for him we grieve; for a woman of her age, who could so connect herself with a boy of his, was either too dull by nature or too callous by experience to share his feelings at their false, unnatural position. Who can believe that the well-known counsel upon this subject which he put into the *Duke Orsino's* mouth in *Twelfth Night* was not a stifled cry of anguish from his tormented, over-burdened soul, though he had left his torment and his burden so far behind him? It is impossible that he could have written it without thinking of his own experience; the more, that the seeming lad to whom it is addressed is about his years, and the man who utters it about Anne Hathaway's, at the time when they were married.*

* "*Duke.* Thou dost speak masterly:
My life upon't, young though thou art, thine eye
Hath stay'd upon some favour that it loves;
Hath it not, boy?
Vio. A little, by your favour.
Duke. What kind of woman is't?
Vio. Of your complexion.
Duke. She is not worth thee then. What years, i' faith?
Vio. About your years, my lord.
Duke. Too old, by Heaven! Let still the woman take
An elder than herself; so wears she to him,
So sways she level in her husband's heart.
For, boy, however we do praise ourselves,
Our fancies are more giddy and unfirm,
More longing, wavering, sooner lost and worn,
Than women's are.
Vio. I think it well, my lord.
Duke. Then let thy love be younger than thyself,
Or thy affection cannot hold the bent."
Twelfth Night, Act II. Sc. 4

After considering all that has been said, which is quite all that can reasonably be said, about the custom of troth-plight in mitigation of the circumstances of Shakespeare's marriage, I cannot regard the case as materially bettered. It has been urged that Shakespeare put a plea for his wife into the mouth of the *Priest* in *Twelfth Night*, where the holy man says to *Olivia* that there had passed between her and *Sebastian*

"A contract of eternal bond of love,
Confirm'd by mutual joinder of your hands,
Attested by the holy close of lips,
Strengthen'd by interchangement of your rings;
And all the ceremony of this compact
Seal'd in my function, by my testimony."
Act V. Sc. 1.

But what this was is shown by *Olivia's* language at the time when it took place, in a passage which the apologists leave out of sight.

"Blame not this haste of mine: If you mean well,
Now go with me, and with this holy man,
Into the chantry by: there, before him,
And underneath that consecrated roof,
Plight me the full assurance of your faith;
That my most jealous and too doubtful soul
May live at peace: He shall conceal it,
Whiles you are willing it shall come to note;
What time we will our celebration keep
According to my birth. — What do you say?"
Act IV. Sc. 3.

This plainly was a private marriage, in church and by a priest; indissoluble and perfect, except that it lacked consummation, and celebration according to the lady's oirth. As to troth-plight, its import depends entirely upon that to which troth is plighted. The closing words of the binding declaration in the marriage ceremony of the Church of England are, "and thereto I plight thee my troth."

The marriage between William Shakespeare and Anne Hathaway took place in December, 1582. The ceremony was not performed in Stratford; and no record of it has been discovered. But there is a tradition in Luddington, a little village not far off, that it took place there; and the story derives some support from the fact that Thomas Hunt, Shakespeare's schoolmaster, was curate of that parish. Susanna, the first child born in this wedlock, was baptized May 26th, 1583; and Hamnet and Judith, twins, were baptized February 2d, 158$\frac{4}{5}$. William Shakespeare and his wife had no other children; and soon after the latter event their household married life was interrupted for many years by the departure of the youthful husband from Stratford. The eldest son of a ruined man just degraded from office, having four brothers and sisters younger than himself, and a wife and three children upon his hands before he was twenty-one, there were reasons enough for him to go, as he did, to London, if he could get money there more rapidly than at Stratford. But tradition assigns a particular occasion and other motive for his leaving home. Betterton heard, and Rowe tells us, that he fell into bad company, and that some of his wild companions, who made a frequent practice of deer-stealing, drew him into the robbery of a park belonging to Sir Thomas Lucy, of Charlecote. For this, according to Rowe's story, he was prosecuted by the knight, and in revenge lampooned him in a ballad so bitter that the prosecution became a persecution of such severity that he was obliged to flee the country, and shelter himself in London. There is what may perhaps be accepted as independent authority for the existence of this tradition. The Reverend William Fulman, an antiquary, who died in 1688, bequeathed his manuscript biographical memorandums to the Reverend Richard Davies, rector of Sapperton in Gloucestershire, and archdeacon of Lichfield, who died in 1708. To a note of Fulman's, which barely records Shakespeare's birth, death, and occupation, Davies made brief additions, the principal of which is, that William Shakespeare was "much given to all unluckinesse in stealing venison and rabbits, particularly from S^r —— Lucy, who had him oft whipt and sometimes imprisoned, and at last made him fly his native country, to his great advancement: but his revenge was so great that he is his Justice Clodpate, and calls him a great man, and that in allusion to his name bore three louses rampant for his arms." Davies may have heard this story in Stratford; but considering the date of his death, 1708, and that of Betterton's visit to Warwickshire, 1675, and Rowe's publication of his edition of Shakespeare's Works, 1709, it is not at all improbable, to say the least, that the story had reached the archdeacon directly or indirectly through the actor. But Capell tells us* that a Mr. Thomas Jones, who lived at Tarbick, a few miles from Stratford, and who died there in 1703, more than ninety years of age, remembered having heard from old people at Stratford the story of Shakespeare's robbing Sir Thomas Lucy's park. According to Mr. Jones their story agreed with that told by Rowe, with this addition — that the lampoon was stuck upon the park gate, and that this insult, added to the injury of the deer-stealing, provoked the prosecution. Mr. Jones had written

* Notes and Various Readings, &c., Vol. II. p. 75.

down the first stanza of this ballad, and it reached Capell through his own grandfather, a contemporary of Jones. A similar account of a very old man living near Stratford, and remembering the deer-stealing story and the ballad, is given by Oldys, the antiquarian, in his manuscript notes. Oldys and Capell plainly derived their information from the same source, though possibly through different channels; and the stanza of the ballad is given by both of them in the same words, with the exception of a single syllable. These are the lines according to Oldys, with the addition of "O" in the last line, which appears in Capell's copy, and which plainly belongs there: —

"A parliemente member, a justice of peace,
At home a poor scare-crowe, at London an asse,
If lowsie is Lucy, as some volke miscalle it,
Then Lucy is lowsie whatever befall it:
He thinks himself greate,
Yet an asse in his state
We allowe by his ears but with asses to mate.
If Lucy is lowsie, as some volke miscalle it,
Sing O lowsie Lucy, whatever befall it."

This story enriches with a rare touch of real life our faint and meagre memorials of Shakespeare. Not sufficiently well established to be beyond the assaults of those who think it scorn that the author of *King Lear* and *Hamlet* should have stolen deer and written coarse lampoons, it yet may well be cherished, and its credibility maintained, by those who prize a trait of character and a glimpse of personal experience above all question of propriety. In Queen Bess's time deer-stealing did not rank with sheep-stealing; and he who wrote, and was praised for writing, *The Comedy of Errors* and *Troilus and Cressida* when he was a man, may well be believed.

without any abatement of his dignity, to have written the Lucy ballad in his boyhood. Malone thought that he had exploded the tradition by showing that Sir Thomas Lucy had no park, and therefore could have no deer to be stolen; and the lampoon has been set aside as a fabrication by some writers, and regarded by all with suspicion. But it appears that, whether the knight had an enclosure with formal park privileges or not, the family certainly had deer on their estate, which fulfils the only condition requisite for the truth of the story in that regard.* I think that there is a solution to the question somewhat different from any that has yet been brought forward, and much more probable.

The first Scene of *The Merry Wives of Windsor* certainly gives strong support to the tradition; so strong, in fact, that it has been supposed, with some reason, to have been its origin. In that Scene Shakespeare makes Justice *Shallow* (who, in the words of Davies, is his clodpate, or, as we should say, his clownish or loutish justice) bear a dozen white luces, or pikes, in his coat of arms, which bearing gives the Welsh parson the opportunity for his punning jest that "the dozen white louses do become an old coat well." † The Lucys bore punning coat-armor, three luces, *hariant;* and the allusion is unmistakable. In that Scene, too, the country gentleman who is so proud of the luces in his old coat,

* Sir Thomas Lucy, son of Shakespeare's victim, sent a buck as a present to Harehill when Sir Thomas Egerton entertained Queen Elizabeth there in August, 1602. *Egerton Papers*, pp. 350, 355.

† Some critics have attributed the transformation of *luces* to *louses*, to *Sir Hugh's* incapacity of English speech; but this is to rob the Welshman of his wit. The pronunciation of *u* as *ow* is no trick of a Welsh tongue, or of any other, I believe; but "louse" was prononnced like "luce" or "loose" by many people. So the ballad tells us that "lousy is Lucy as some volke miscall it." There is a similar variation as to the name Toucey, which some pronounce *Toosey*, giving the first syllable the vowel sound of *too* and *you*, others *Towsey*, with the sound of *how*, *thou*.

bursts upon the stage, furious at Falstaff for having killed his deer. Now, in Shakespeare's day, as well as long before, killing a gentleman's deer was as common a sport among wild young men as robbing a farmer's orchard among boys. Indeed, it was looked upon as a sign of that poor semblance of manliness sometimes called spirit, and was rather a gentleman's misdemeanor than a yeoman's; one which a peasant would not have presumed to commit, except, indeed, at risk of his ears, for poaching at once upon the game- and the sin-preserves of his betters. Noblemen engaged in it; and in days gone by the very first Prince of Wales had been a deer-stealer. Among multitudinous passages illustrative of this trait of manners, a story preserved by Wood in his *Athenæ Oxonienses* fixes unmistakably the grade of the offence. It is there told, on the authority of Simon Forman, that his patrons, Robert Pinkney and John Thornborough, the latter of whom was admitted a member of Magdalen College in 1570, and became Bishop of Bristol and Worcester, "seldom studied or gave themselves to their books, but spent their time in fencing schools and dancing schools, in stealing deer and conies, in hunting the hare and wooing girls." * In fact, deer-stealing then supplied to the young members of the privileged classes in Old England an excitement of a higher kind than that afforded by beating watchmen and tearing off knockers and bell-pulls to the generation but just passed away. A passage of *Titus Andronicus*, written soon after Shakespeare reached London, is here in point. *Prince Demetrius* exclaims, —

"What, hast thou not full often struck a doe,
And cleanly borne her past the keeper's nose?"

* *Athenæ Oxonienses*, Vol. I. p. 371.

But he with the "three louses rampant" on his coat makes much more than this of *Falstaff's* affair. He will bring it before the Council, he will make a Star-chamber matter of it, and pronounces it a riot. And, in fact, according to his account, *Sir John* was not content with stealing his deer, but broke open his lodge and beat his men. It seems then, that in writing this passage, Shakespeare had in mind not only an actual occurrence in which Sir Thomas Lucy was concerned, but one of greater gravity than a mere deer-stealing affair; that having been made the occasion of more serious outrage.

Now, Sir Thomas Lucy was a man of much consideration in Warwickshire, where he had come to a fine estate in 1551, at only nineteen years of age. He was a member of parliament twice; first in 1571, and next from November, 1584, to March of the following year; just before the very time when, according to all indications, Shakespeare left Stratford. Sir Thomas was a somewhat prominent member of the puritanical party, as appears by what is known of his parliamentary course. For instance, during his first term he was one of a committee appointed upon "defections" in religious matters, one object of the movers of which was "to purge the Common Prayer Book, and free it from certain superstitious ceremonies, as using the sign of the cross in baptism, &c." He was, on the other hand, active in the enforcement and preservation of the game privileges of the nobility and gentry, and served on a committee to which a bill for this purpose was referred, of which he appears to have been chairman. This took place in his last term, 1584 to 1585 — the time of his alleged persecution of William Shakespeare for poaching. Charlecote, his seat, being only three miles from Stratford, and he being a man of such weight and position in the county, he would naturally have somewhat close public relations with the towns-people and their authorities. That such was the case the records of the town and of the county furnish ample evidence. Whenever there was a commission appointed in relation to affairs in that neighborhood he was sure to be on it; and the Chamberlain's accounts, as set forth by Mr. Halliwell, show expenses at divers times to provide Sir Thomas with sack and sugar, to expedite or smooth his intercourse with the corporation. But in spite of mollifying drinks, the relations of the Lucy family with the Stratford folk were not always amicable. Mr. Halliwell's investigations have shown that they were not unfrequently engaged in disputes with the corporation of that town. Records of one about common of pasture in Henry VIII.'s time are still preserved in the Chapter House at London; and among the papers at the Rolls' House is one containing "the names of them that made the ryot uppon Master Thomas Lucy, esquier."

Here are all the conditions of a very pretty parish quarrel. A puritanical knight, fussy about his family pretensions and his game, having hereditary disagreement with the Stratford people about rights of common, — a subject on which they were, like all of English race, sure to be tenacious, — after having been left out of parliament for eleven years, is reëlected, and immediately sets to work at securing that privilege so dearly prized by his class, and so odious to all below it — the game laws. The anti-puritan party and those who stand up stoutly for rights of common vent their indignation to the best of their ability; one of their number writes a lampoon upon him, and a body of them, too strong to be successfully withstood, break riotously into his grounds, kill his deer, beat his men, and carry off their booty in triumph. The affair is an outbreak of rude parish politics, a popular demonstration against an unpopular man; and who so likely to take part in it as the son of the former high bailiff, who, we know, was no puritan, and whose father, ambitious, and, as we shall see, even pretending to a coat of arms, had most probably had personal and official disagreements with, and received personal slights and rebuffs from his rich, powerful, arrogant neighbor; or who so likely to write the lampoon as young Will Shakespeare? There could hardly have been two in Stratford who could have written that stanza, the rhythm of which shows no common clodpole's ear, and which, though coarse in its satire, is bitter and well suited to the occasion. That it is a genuine production — that is, part of a ballad written at the time for the purpose of lampooning Sir Thomas Lucy, I think there can be no doubt: it carries its genuineness upon its face and in its spirit. That Shakespeare wrote it, I am inclined to believe. But even were he not its author, if he had taken any part in a demonstration against Sir Thomas Lucy, and soon after was driven, by whatever circumstances, to leave Stratford for London, where he rose to distinction as a poet, rumor would be sure soon to attribute the ballad to him, and to assign the occasion on which it was written as that which caused his departure; and rumor would soon become tradition.* That Shakespeare meant to pay off a Stratford debt to Sir Thomas

* The stanza given above is plainly one, and not the first, of several. Others have been brought forward as the remainder of the lampoon; but they are too plainly spurious to be worthy of notice. The story of the deer-stealing is said by Mr. Fullom, in his *History of William Shakespeare*, to be confirmed by a note, entered, about 1750, in a manuscript pedigree of the Lucy family, by an old man named Ward, who derived his information from family papers then in his hands. But this date is nearly fifty years after the publication of the story in Rowe's Life, and so is of little or no value. According to the same authority Sir Thomas Lucy ceased his prosecution of Shakespeare, and released him, at the intercession of the Earl of Leicester.

Lucy in that first Scene of *The Merry Wives*, and that he did it with the memory of the riotous trespass upon that gentleman's grounds, seem equally manifest. That he had taken part in the event which he commemorated, there is not evidence which would be sufficient in a court of law, but quite enough for those who are satisfied with the concurrence of probability and tradition; and I confess that I am of that number.

From 1584, when Shakespeare's twin children — Hamnet and Judith — were baptized, until 1592, when we know that he was rising rapidly to distinction as a play-wright in London, no record of his life has been discovered; nor has tradition contributed any thing of importance to fill the gap, except the story of the deer-stealing and its consequences. What was he doing in all those eight years? and what before the former date? For he was not born to wealth and privilege, and so could not, like the future Bishop of Bristol and Worcester, spend all his time in stealing deer and wooing girls. Malone, noticing the frequency with which he uses law terms, conjectured that he had passed some of his adolescent years in an attorney's office. In support of his conjecture, Malone, himself a barrister, cited twenty-four passages distinguished by the presence of law phrases; and to these he might have added many more. But the use of such phrases is by no means peculiar to Shakespeare. The writings of the poets and play-wrights of his period, Spenser, Drayton, Greene, Beaumont and Fletcher, Middleton, Donne, and many others of less note, are thickly sprinkled with them. In fact, the application of legal language to the ordinary affairs of life was more common two hundred and fifty years ago than it is now; though even now-a-days the usage is far from uncommon in the rural districts. There law shares with agriculture the function of providing those phrases of common conversation which, used figuratively at first, and often with poetic feeling, soon pass into mere thought-saving formulas of speech.

There are reasons, however, for believing that Shakespeare had more than a layman's knowledge of the law. Play-going was the chief intellectual recreation of his day, and there was, consequently, an incessant demand for new plays — a demand which young men of education and familiarity with the pen were naturally tempted to supply. To play-writing, therefore, the needy and gifted young lawyer turned his hand at that day, as he does now to journalism; and of those who had been successful in their dramatic efforts how inevitable it was that many would give themselves up to play-writing, and that thus the language of the plays of that time should show such a remarkable infusion of law phrases! To what, then, must we attribute the fact that of all the plays that have survived of those written between 1580 and 1620 Shakespeare's are most noteworthy in this respect? For no dramatist of the time, not even Beaumont, who was a younger son of a Judge of the Common Pleas, and who, after studying in the Inns of Court, abandoned law for the drama, used legal phrases with Shakespeare's readiness and exactness. And the significance of this fact is heightened by another, — that it is only to the language of the law that he exhibits this inclination. The phrases peculiar to other occupations serve him on rare occasions by way of description, comparison, or illustration, generally when something in the scene suggests them; but legal phrases flow from his pen as part of his vocabulary and parcel of his thought. The word "purchase," for instance, which in ordinary use meant, as now it means, to acquire by giving value, applies in law to all legal modes of obtaining property, except inheritance or descent. And in this peculiar sense the word occurs five times in Shakespeare's thirty-four plays, but only in a single passage in the fifty-four plays of Beaumont and Fletcher. And in the first scene of the *Midsummer Night's Dream* the father of *Hermia* begs the ancient privilege of Athens, that he may dispose of his daughter either to *Demetrius* or to death, —

> "according to our law
> Immediately provided in that case."

He pleads the statute; and the words run off his tongue in heroic verse as if he were reading them from a paper.

As the courts of law in Shakespeare's time occupied public attention much more than they do now — their terms having regulated "the season" of London society,* it has been suggested that it was in attendance upon them that he picked up his legal vocabulary. But this supposition not only fails to account for Shakespeare's peculiar freedom and exactness in the use of that phraseology, — it does not even place him in the way of learning those terms his use of which is most remarkable; which are not such as he would have heard at ordinary proceedings at *nisi prius*, but such as refer to the tenure or transfer of real property — "fine and recovery," "statutes merchant," "purchase," "indenture," "tenure," "double voucher," "fee simple," "fee farm," "remainder," "reversion," "forfeiture," &c. This conveyancer's jargon could not have been picked up by hanging round the courts of law in London two hundred and fifty years ago, when suits as to the title to real property were comparatively so rare. And beside,

* Falstaff, for instance, speaks of "the wearing out of six fashions, which is four terms or two actions."

Shakespeare uses his law just as freely in his early plays, written in his first London years, as in those produced at a later period.* Just as exactly too; for the correctness and propriety with which these terms are introduced have compelled the admiration of a Chief Justice and a Lord Chancellor.† Again, bearing in mind that genius, although it reveals general truth, and facilitates all acquirement, does not impart facts or acquaintance with technical terms, how can we account for the fact that in an age when it was the common practice for young lawyers to write plays, one play-wright left upon his plays a stronger, sharper legal stamp, than appears upon those of any of his contemporaries, and that the characters of this stamp are those of the complicated law of real property? Must we believe that this man was thus distinguished among a crowd of play-writing lawyers, not only by his genius, but by a *lack* of special knowledge of the law? Or shall we rather believe that the son of the late high bailiff of Stratford, a somewhat clever lad, and ambitious withal, was allowed to commence his studies for a profession for which his cleverness fitted him, and by which he might reasonably

* Thus, in *Henry the Sixth*, Part II., *Jack Cade* says, "Men shall hold of me *in capite:* and we charge and command that wives be *as free as heart can wish or tongue can tell*" — words which indicate acquaintance with very ancient and uncommon tenures of land. In the *Comedy of Errors*, when *Dromio* of Syracuse says, "There's no time for a man to recover his hair that grows bald by nature," (Hear, O Rowland! and give ear, O Phalon!) his master replies, "May he not do it by *fine and recovery?*" Fine and recovery was a process by which, through a fictitious suit, a transfer was made of the title in an entailed estate. In *Love's Labour's Lost*, almost without a doubt the first comedy that Shakespeare wrote, on *Boyet's* offering to kiss *Maria*, (Act II. Sc. 1,) she declines the salute, and says, "My lips are no common, though several they be." *Maria's* allusion is plainly to tenancy in common by several (i. e. divided, distinct) title. See the Note upon this passage.

† These are Lord Campbell's words: "While novelists and dramatists are constantly making mistakes as to the law of marriage, of wills, and of inheritance, to Shakespeare's law, lavishly as he propounds it, there can neither be demurrer, nor bill of exceptions, nor writ of error"

hope to rise at least to moderate wealth and distinction, and that he continued these studies until his father's misfortunes, aided, perhaps, by some of those acts of youthful indiscretion which clever lads as well as dull ones sometimes will commit, threw him upon his own resources, — and that then, law failing to supply his pressing need, he turned to the stage, on which he had townsmen and friends? One of these conclusions is in the face of reason, fact, and probability; the other, in accordance with them all.

But the bare fact that Shakespeare was an attorney's clerk, even if indisputably established, though of some interest, is of little real importance. It teaches us nothing about the man, of what he did for himself, thought for himself, how he joyed, how he suffered, what he was in his mere manhood. It has but a naked material relation to the other fact, that he uses legal phrases oftener, more freely, and more exactly than any other poet.

III.

Somewhere, then, within the years 1585 and 1586, Shakespeare went from Stratford to London, where we next hear of him as an actor and a mender of old plays. That he went with the intention of becoming an actor, has been universally assumed; but perhaps too hastily. For he had social ambition and high self-esteem; and in his day to become an actor was to cast the one of these sentiments aside, and to tread the other under foot. Betterton's story, told through Rowe, is, that Shakespeare was "obliged to leave his business and family for some time, and shelter himself in London." In so far as this may be relied upon, it shows that Shakespeare had business in Stratford, and that he sought only a temporary refuge in the metropolis. Probably it was with no very definite purpose that he left his native place. Poverty, persecution, and perhaps a third Fury, made Stratford too hot to hold him ; and he might well flee, vaguely seeking relief for the present and provision for the future. He would naturally hope to live in London by the business which he had followed at Stratford. Such is the way of ambitious young men who go from rural districts to a metropolis. And, until every other means of livelihood had failed him, it was not in this high-minded, sensitive, aspiring youth to assume voluntarily a profession then scorned of all men. We may be sure that if he sought business as an attorney in London, he did not at once obtain it. Shakespeare although he was, no such miracle could be wrought for him; nay, the less would it be wrought because of his being Shakespeare. He doubtless in these first days hoped for a publisher ; and not improbably this purpose was among those which led him up to London. Let who will believe that he went that journey without a manuscript in his pocket. For to suppose that a man of poetic power lives until his twenty-first year without writing a poem, which he then rates higher than he ever afterward will rate any of his work, is to set aside the history of poetry, and to silence those years which are most affluent of fancy and most eager for expression.

With *Venus and Adonis* written, if nothing else, — but I think it not unlikely a play, — Shakespeare went to London and sought a patron. For in those days a poet needed a patron even more than a publisher; as without the former he rarely or never got the latter. Shakespeare found a patron; but not so soon, we may be sure, as he had expected. Meantime, while he waited, the stage door stood ajar invitingly, and he was both tempted and impelled to enter. For that natural inclination to poetry and acting which Aubrey tells us he possessed had been stimulated by the frequent visits of companies of players to Stratford, at whose performances he could not have failed to be a delighted and thoughtful spectator. Indeed, as it was the custom for the mayor or bailiff of a town visited by a travelling company to bespeak the play at their first exhibition, to reward them for it himself, and to admit the audience gratis, it may safely be assumed that the first theatrical performance in Stratford, of which there is any record, had John Shakespeare for its patron. For it was given in 1569, the year in which he was high bailiff; and the bailiff's son, although he was then only five years old, we may be sure was present. Between 1569 and 1586 hardly a year passed without several performances by one or more companies at Stratford. But natural inclination and straitened means of living were not the only influences which led Shakespeare to the theatre. Other Stratford boys had gone up to London, and some of them had become players. Thomas Greene, one of the most eminent actors of the Elizabethan period, he who gave his name to *The City Gallant*, which was known and published as "Greene's *Tu Quoque*," was in 1586 a member of the company known as "The Lord Chamberlain's Servants," to which Shakespeare became permanently attached. Greene was of a respectable family at Stratford, one of which was an attorney, who had professional connections in London, and who was Shakespeare's kinsman. Burbadge, Sly, Heminge, and Pope, who all bore Warwickshire names, were on the London stage at the time of Shakespeare's arrival at the metropolis.* If Shakespeare went to London relying upon the

* See the Remarks on the Preliminary Matter to the Folio, Vol. II. pp. xxxvi., xlvii., xlviii. of this work.

good offices of friends, we may be sure that he looked more to his townsman, Greene the attorney, than to his other townsman, Greene the actor. But in that case, considering how shy attorneys are apt to be of the sort of young man who steals deer and writes verses, it is not at all surprising that the player proved to be the more serviceable acquaintance.

Many circumstances combine to show that it was in 1586 that William Shakespeare became connected with the London stage; a few months' variation — and there cannot be more — in the date, one way or the other, is of small importance. Betterton heard that "he was received into the company at first in a very mean rank," and the octogenarian parish clerk of Stratford, before mentioned, told Dowdall, in 1693, that he "was received into the play-house as a servitore." These stories have an air of truth. What claim had this raw Stratford stripling to put his foot higher than the first round of the ladder? In those days that round was apprenticeship to some well-established actor; and as such a servitor William Shakespeare probably began his theatrical career. There is a story that his first occupation in London was holding horses at the play-house door; but it was not heard of until the middle of the last century, and is unworthy of serious attention. The river was the usual thoroughfare in those days from one part of London to the other, and, besides, gentlemen would hardly leave their horses in the care of boys during a whole afternoon's performance. Shakespeare, too, was, as we have seen, not without means of access to employment *inside* the theatre.

Tradition and the custom of the time concur in assuring us that Shakespeare's first connection with the stage was as an actor; and an actor he continued to be for twenty years or more. But although Aubrey tells us that "he did act exceeding well," he seems never to have risen high in this profession. Betterton, or perhaps Rowe, heard that the top of his performance was the *Ghost* in his own *Hamlet;* and Oldys tells a story that one of his younger brothers, who lived to a great age, being questioned as to William, said that he remembered having seen him act the part, in one of his own comedies, of a long-bearded, decrepit old man, who was supported by another person to a table, where they sat among other company, one of whom sang a song. If this were true, Shakespeare played *Adam* in *As You Like It.* And it is consistent with all that we know of him that he should play such parts as this and the *Ghost*, which required judgment and intelligent reading rather than passion and lively simulation. It is not probable that Shakespeare, when he had found that he could labor profitably in a less public walk of his calling, ever strove for distinction or much employment as an actor. We know from one of his sonnets how bitter the consciousness of his position was to him, and that he cursed the fortune which had consigned him to a public life.* If he ever had comfort on the stage it must have been in playing kingly parts, which are assigned to him in the lines of Davies.†

But although Shakespeare began his London life as a player, it was impossible that he should long remain without writing for the stage; and so it happened. With what company he became first connected, there is no direct evidence; but his earliest dramatic employment seems to have been as a co-worker with Greene, Marlowe, and Peele for the Earl of Pembroke's players. There are good reasons for believing that, in conjunction

* Sonnet CXI.

† See page lxxxi.

with one or more of these play-wrights, he labored on *The First Part of the Contention betwixt the Two Famous Houses of York and Lancaster*, *The True Tragedy of Richard Duke of York*, *A Pleasant Conceited History of the Taming of a Shrew*, *Titus Andronicus*, an early form of *Romeo and Juliet*, of which there are some remains in the quarto edition of 1597, and probably some other pieces which have been lost.* It would have been strange, indeed almost unprecedented, if a young adventurer going up to London had immediately found his true place, and taken firm root therein. But little as we know of Shakespeare's period of trial and vicissitude, we do know that it was brief, and that within about three years from the time when he left his native place he attached himself to the Lord Chamberlain Hunsdon's company (previously known as the Earl of Leicester's), of which the Burbadges, father and son, were prominent members, and that he became a shareholder in this company, and remained an active member of it until he finally retired to Stratford.

Shakespeare immediately showed that unmistakable trait of a man organized for success in life, which is so frequently lacking in men who are both gifted and industrious, — the ability to find his work, and to settle down quickly to it, and take hold of it in earnest. He worked hard, did every thing that he could turn his hand to, — acted, wrote, helped others to write, — and seeing through men and things as he did at a glance, he was in those early years somewhat over-free of his criticism and his advice, and, what was less endurable by his rivals, too ready to illustrate his principles of art successfully in practice. He came soon to be

* See the Essay on the Authorship of *King Henry the Sixth*, Vol. VII., and the Introduction to *Titus Andronicus*, Vol. IX., *The Taming of the Shrew*, Vol. IV., and *Romeo and Juliet*, Vol. X.

regarded, by those who liked and needed him, as a most useful and excellent fellow, a very factotum, and a man of great promise; while those who disliked him and found him in their way, and whose ears were wounded by his praises, set him down as an officious and conceited upstart. Elation at his success, and a perception of the coarseness and inflated feebleness of the dramas then in vogue, seem to have tempted him into a little good-natured ridicule, of which we find traces in his works. This could not but have envenomed the jealousy of his rivals. But in any case he was doomed to suffer the resentment always visited upon those who offend by unexpected excellence.

That such was Shakespeare's lot we are not left to conjecture, hardly to infer. One of the play-wrights whom he found in high favor when he reached London, and with whom, as a youthful assistant, he began his dramatic labors, stretched out his hand from beyond the grave to leave a record of his hate for the man who had supplanted him, and who, he saw, would supplant his companions, as a writer for the stage. The drunken debauchee, Robert Greene, dying in dishonorable need, left behind him a pamphlet written on his death-bed, and published after his burial. It was called *A Groats-worth of Wit bought with a Million of Repentance*, and was better named than its author or its editor, Henry Chettle, probably supposed. But Greene, though repentant, with the repentance of sordid souls when they are cast down, was not so changed in heart that he could resist the temptation of discharging from his stiffening hand a Parthian shaft, barbed with envy and malice, and winged with little wit, against young Shakespeare. In the pretended interests of truth and friendship, he warned his companions and co-workers, Marlowe, Lodge, and Peele, that the players who had all been beholding to them, as well as to him, would forsake them for a certain upstart crow, beautified with their feathers, who supposed that he was able to write blank verse with the best of them, and who, being in truth a Johannes Factotum, was in his own conceit the only Shake-scene in the country.* Greene was right, as his surviving friends ere long discovered. Their sun had set; and it was well for them that they all died soon after. They could not forgive Shakespeare his superiority; but he forgave one of them at least his envy; for when, a few years after, he wrote *As You Like It*, he made *Phebe* say of Marlowe, quoting a line from *Hero and Leander*, —

"Dead Shepherd, now I find thy saw of might,
'Who ever lov'd that lov'd not at first sight?'"

Greene sank into his grave, his soul eaten up with envy as his body with disease; but he was spared the added pang of foreseeing that his own name would be preserved in the world's memory only because of his indirect connection with the man at whom he sneered, and that he would be chiefly known as his slanderer. Had he lived to see his book published, he would have enjoyed such base and pitiful satisfaction as can be given by revenge. His little arrow reached its mark, and the wound smarted. As the venom of a sting often inflicts more temporary anguish than the laceration of a fatal hurt, such wounds always smart, but rarely injure; and few men are wise and strong enough to bear their suffering in dignity and silence. Whether, if Greene had been alive, Shakespeare would have publicly noticed his attack, can only be conjectured; but I feel sure that

* See the passage in question, given verbatim and in full, and its significance with regard to Shakespeare's early labors set forth, in the Essay on the Authorship of *King Henry the Sixth*, Vol. VII. pp. 408-412.

he would have been kept from open wrangle with such an assailant by his reticence and self-respect. Yet, although he was above petty malice and recrimination, he was sore and indignant; and he, and others for him, protested against the wrong which had been done him in Greene's pamphlet. He did not protest in vain; for Chettle, Greene's editor, although he treated with great contempt a like complaint of disrespect on the part of Marlowe, whom Greene had also slurred, apologized to Shakespeare in a tract called *The Kind Heart's Dream*, which he published immediately afterward, saying that although he was personally guiltless of the wrong, he was as sorry as if the original fault had been his own, to have offended a man so courteous, so gifted, and one who, by his worth and his ability, had risen high in the esteem of many of his superiors in rank and station.* Greene died in the autumn of 1592, and his pamphlet and Chettle's were both published in the same year. Thus Shakespeare, within six or seven years of his departure from Stratford a fugitive adventurer, had won admiration from the public, respect from his superiors, and the consequent hate of some, and, what is so much harder of attainment, the regard of others, among those who were his equals, except in his surpassing genius.

These two pregnant passages, which we owe to the malice of a disappointed rival, are the first public notice of Shakespeare, and our earliest authentic record of his presence in London.† By this time he had produced, in

* See Chettle's apology in full and verbatim in the Essay on the Authorship of *King Henry the Sixth*, Vol. VII. p. 410.

† In 1835 Mr. John Payne Collier published a small volume entitled *New Facts regarding the Life of Shakespeare*, in which he brought to notice six documents as having been found at Bridgewater House among the papers of Lord Ellesmere, who was Chancellor in the reigns of Elizabeth and James I. One of these documents was an unsigned certificate or memorandum, intended ap-

addition to his contributions to partnership plays and to old ones partly rewritten, *The Comedy of Errors*, *Love's*

parently for the Privy Council, exculpating the players at the Black-friars Theatre from a charge of having meddled in matters of state and religion, which had been brought against the theatres generally in 1589. Among the names of the players mentioned in this paper as sharers in the theatre appears that of William Shakespeare, which stands twelfth on the list. The document is as follows: —

"These are to sertifie yor right honorable Ll., that her Mat[s] pooro playeres James Burbidge Richard Burbidge John Laneham Thomas Greene Robert Wilson John Taylor Anth. Wadeson Thomas Pope George Peele Augustine Phillippes Nicholas Towley William Shakespeare William Kempe William Johnson Baptiste Goodale and Robert Armyn being all of them sharers in the blacke Fryers playehouse haue neuer given cause of displeasure, in that they haue brought into their playes maters of state and Religion, vnfitt to be handled by them or to be presented before lewde spectators neither hath anie complainte in that kinde ever beene preferrde against them, or anie of them Wherefore, they trust most humblie in yor Lls consideracion of their former good behauiour being at all tymes readie and willing to yeelde obedience to any comaund whatsoever yor Ll in yor wisdome may thinke in such case meete, &c.

"Nov. 1589."

Until recently this memorandum was received as genuine; and were it so, it would show us that, within three years after his arrival at London, William Shakespeare had advanced from the position of servitor, apprentice, or hired man in the Lord Chamberlain's company to that of a sharer in the receipts of the company, not that of a proprietor of the theatre. But suspicion of the genuineness of the documents brought forward by Mr. Collier having been excited, this, among the others, was carefully examined by the most eminent palæographists in London, some of them holding high official positions, and all pronounced it a forgery. The facts in regard to the investigation of the character of these documents will be found in Mr. N. E. S. A. Hamilton's *Inquiry*, &c., 4to., London, 1860, Dr. Mansfield Ingleby's *Complete View of the Shakespeare Controversy*, London, 1861, Mr. Duffus Hardy's *Review of the Present State of the Shakespearian Controversy*, London, 1860, and in *The Shakespeare Mystery*, in the *Atlantic Monthly*, Sept., 1861. It is possible, though very improbable, that the judgment pronounced by such high palæographic authorities may be incorrect; but the documents are put by this decision out of question as evidence of the bare and meagre facts in Shakespeare's life which they profess to establish.

In Spenser's *Teares of the Muses*, printed in 1591, a passage beginning with the lines —

"And he the man whom Nature selfe had made
To mock her selfe, and Truth to imitate,
With kindly counter under mimick shade,
Our pleasant Willy, ah, is dead of late" —

has been held to refer to Shakespeare; chiefly, it would seem, because of the name, Willy. But that, like "shepherd," was not uncommonly used merely to mean a poet, and was distinctly applied to Sir Philip Sidney in an Eclogue preserved in Davidson's *Poetical Rhapsody*, published in 1602. And the *Teares of the Muses* had certainly been written before 1590, when Shakespeare could

Labour's Lost, and *The Two Gentlemen of Verona*, his earliest original productions. He was already thriving, with prosperity in prospect. But he had literary ambition which play-writing did not satisfy, (for that he did as a conveyancer draws deeds, — as business;) and he had a poem written; so he still looked about for a patron. Now, there was at this time in London a nobleman of high rank and large wealth, Henry Wriothesley, Earl of Southampton, who had a genuine love of letters, and who was just upon the threshold of a lordly life. As yet he had not exhibited in any marked degree the high spirit, the fine capacity of appreciation, the graciousness and the generosity which made him afterward admired and loved of all men at the court of Queen Elizabeth. For at the publication of Greene's pamphlet he was but nineteen years old, and Shakespeare was nine years his senior. Loving literature and the society of men of letters, he had a special fondness for the drama, and being a constant attendant upon the theatre, he saw much of Shakespeare and his plays; and there can be no doubt that he was one of those "divers of worship" whose respect for the poet's "uprightness of dealing" and admiration of his "facetious grace in writing" Chettle assigns as one reason for his apology to a man whom, it is very easy to see, he did not think it prudent to offend.* Shakespeare must have

not have risen to the position assigned by the first poet of the age to the subject of this passage, and probably in 1580, when Shakespeare was a boy of sixteen in Stratford. Indeed the notion that Spenser had him in mind would not merit even this attention, were it not that my readers might suppose that I had passed it by through inadvertence. All that ingenuity and persistent faith can urge in support of it the reader will find in Mr. Knight's and Mr. Collier's biographies of the poet.

* The meaning of the word "facetious" in this well-known passage has been very generally misunderstood, and by none more completely than by Miss Bacon, who rested her misapprehension of Shakespeare's rank among his contemporaries much on Chettle's use of this epithet, upon which she rung a never-ending change of sneers. But "facetious" here has no reference to that light

had some acquaintance with Southampton at this time, and have felt that he was in his lordship's favor. For to him he determined to dedicate his *Venus and Adonis*, although he had not asked permission to do so, as the dedication shows; and in those days, and long after, without some knowledge of his man and some opportunity of judging how he would receive the compliment, a player would not have ventured to take such a liberty with the name of a nobleman. In the next year (1593) the closing of the London theatres on account of the plague afforded a favorable occasion for the publication of the poem, and it was printed by Richard Field, a Stratford man. It immediately won its author a high literary reputation. Before a year had passed a new edition was called for; a third was published in 1596, and two others within nine years of its first appearance. Southampton must have been a churl not to be gratified at the homage of such a poet; and being a man whose rank was the mere pedestal, and whose wealth the mere adornment, of his real nobility, he acknowledged Shakespeare's compliment in a manner both munificent and considerate. Tradition tells us the former; a second dedication, the latter. In dedicating the *Venus and Adonis*, — and we must not forget that Shakespeare regarded this as his first appearance as an author, — he expressed a fear that he might offend the young Earl by connecting his name with the first heir of his invention; but he promised that, if his patron were only pleased, he would devote all the time that he

comic vein of speech to which it is now exclusively applied. It was used in Shakespeare's time as we now use "felicitous" or "happy" in regard to style. Thus Thomas Sackville, Earl of Dorset, a grave statesman as well as an accomplished man of letters, who in his youth wrote only serious and sententious works, is said by Naunton to have been "so facete and choice in his phrase and style" when drafting state papers, that his secretaries could rarely please him.

could steal from his business of playing and play-writing to some graver labor in his honor. Such a work, we may be sure, he then already had in mind; for in the very next year appeared the *Lucrece*, a grave and even tragic poem, showing much greater maturity of thought and style than its predecessor, and dedicated also to Southampton. But the tone of the poet toward the patron is now very different from what it was a year before; although it is still tainted with that deference of simple manhood to privilege, which, in the time of Elizabeth, English men of Shakespeare's rank, no matter what their age, their ability, or their character, must needs pay to English lads of Southampton's. How is it now, except among those Englishmen who have never bowed again under the yoke of privilege which their ancestors cast off in the days when Milton was our mouthpiece and Cromwell our leader?

It is evident from this dedication that the Earl had done something more than seem pleased with its predecessor. Shakespeare speaks in it of a warrant which he had of his patron's honorable disposition that makes him sure of acceptance, and adds, "What I have done is yours; what I have to do is yours; being part in all I have, devoted yours." This is not flattery, or even deference: words of acknowledgment could not be stronger. On this evidence alone it is plain that something had passed between Shakespeare and the Earl which had bound the former entirely to the latter by lasting ties of gratitude. Again circumstance and tradition strengthen and eke out each other. A story reached Rowe through Davenant (would that so excellent a thing had been preserved in a cleaner vessel!) that Southampton gave Shakespeare a thousand pounds to make a purchase of importance. Now, it so happened that in 1594 the Globe Theatre was built by the company to which Shakespeare belonged, in all the property of which we know that he became a large owner. The sum which the Earl is said to have given to Shakespeare is so very large — being equal to thirty thousand dollars at our present rate of value, that while the world has willingly believed the substance of the story, many have doubted the correctness of its details. And yet, remembering the customs of those times, the more we consider how splendid a fellow young Southampton was, how munificent to men of letters, how whole-hearted to his friends, the more we shall be ready to receive the story of his generosity to Shakespeare without abatement.

Between 1592 and 1596 Shakespeare produced, in addition to his *Lucrece*, *King Richard the Third*, *A Midsummer-Night's Dream*, *The Merchant of Venice*, *King Richard the Second*, and some of his Sonnets, probably also *Romeo and Juliet* and (with the name "Love's Labour's Won") *All's Well That Ends Well*, in earlier forms than those in which they have come down to us; — works which, although none of them exhibited his genius in its full height and power, effectually established his supremacy among his contemporaries as a poet and a dramatist. England now began to ring with his praises. His brother dramatists made their lovers long for his *Venus and Adonis* by which to court their mistresses; other poets made their chaste heroines compare themselves to the Lucretia whom he had "revived to live another age"; they sung of his "hony-flowing vein," and that he had given new immortality even to the goddess of love and beauty; and some of them paid him the unequivocal compliment of plagiarism.* Even

* See Willoughby's *Avisa*, 1594; Drayton's *Matilda*, 1594; Barnefield's *Poems in Divers Humors*, 1598; Heywood's *Fair Maid of the Exchange*, 1607, but written some years before; *Phillis and Flora*, by R. S., 1598; and Nichol-

Spenser, then at the height of his fame and his court favor, having in mind Shakespeare's two martial histories and his name, generously paid the young poet this pretty compliment in *Colin Clout's come Home again*, written in 1594 : —

> " And there, though last not least, is Ætion ;
> A gentler Shepheard may no where be found ;
> Whose muse full of high thought's invention
> Doth, like himselfe, heroically sound." *

Nay, in this interval Colin Clout's mistress, the imperial Elizabeth herself, distinguished him by her favor, won, or acknowledged, by the exquisite compliment in *A Midsummer-Night's Dream.* For we know upon Ben Jonson's and Henry Chettle's testimony, and from tradition, that she did delight in him ; and it is not in mortal woman, least of all was it in Elizabeth, to know of such a compliment, and not to hear it and be captivated.†

son's *Acolastus his Afterwitte*, 1600. In " A Letter from England to her three Daughters," reprinted in the *British Bibliographer*, (Vol. I. p. 274–285,) and which forms the second part of a book called *Polimanteia*, published in 1595, there is a marginal note, " All praise worthy Lucrecia Sweete Shakespeare."

* It may be worth while to say that if Shakespeare's name had been Shaksper or Shakspere, as some would have it, this compliment would have been impossible.

† These well-known lines are from Jonson's verses in memory of Shakespeare, which were published in the folio of 1623 : —

> " Sweet Swan of Avon, what a sight it were
> To see thee in our waters yet appeare,
> And make those flights upon the banks of Thames,
> That so did take Eliza and our James."

On the death of Queen Elizabeth, Chettle, in his *England's Mourning Garment* thus reproached Shakespeare that his verse had not bewailed his own and England's loss : —

> " Nor doth the silver-tonged Melicert
> Drop from his honied Muse one sable tear,
> To mourne her death that graced his desert,
> And to his lines opened her royal eare.
> Shepheard remember our Elizabeth,
> And sing her rape done by that Tarquin, Death."

Having this evidence of his reputation, and other of an equally pleasing and satisfactory character as to his increase in wealth, we can afford to be very indifferent in regard to the trustworthiness of a document about which there has been much ado, and the only interest of which consists in the fact that it enumerates Shakespeare among the owners of the Black-friars Theatre, and names him fifth among eight; but which, after a life of thirty years of antiquarian glory, has been "done to death by envious tongues" as spurious.* A like

* This document exists in the State Paper Office at Westminster. (London.) It was brought to public notice by Mr. Collier in his *History of English Dramatic Poetry*, &c., 1831, (Vol. I. p. 297.) It professes to be an answer to a remonstrance by thirty inhabitants of the Liberty of the Black-friars, "some of them of honour," against the repairing of the Black-friars Theatre. The remonstrance was said by Mr. Collier to be "preserved in the State Paper Office;" but it is not to be found there. This reply is so genuine in appearance that it was given in fac-simile even by Mr. Halliwell, in his great folio edition of Shakespeare's Works, although that gentleman was one of the first to pronounce many of the Collier Shakespeare MSS. spurious. It is as follows: —

"To the right honorable the Lords of her Mat[ies] most honorable privie Counsell.

"The humble petition of Thomas Pope Richard Burbadge John Hemings Augustine Phillips Willm Shaksepeare Willim Kempe Willim Slye Nicholas Tooley and others, seruaunts to the right honorable the L. Chamberlaine to her Ma[tie].

"Sheweth most humbly that yor petitioners are owners and players of the priuate house or theater in the precinct and libertie of the Blackfriers, wch hath beene for manie yearse vsed and occupied for the playing of tragedies commedies histories enterludes and playes. That the same by reason of hauing beene soe long built hath falne into great decaye and that besides the reparation thereof it hath beene found necessarie to make the same more conuenient for the entertainement of auditories comming thereto. That to this end yor petitioners haue all and eche of them putt downe sommes of money according to their shares in the saide theater and whch they haue justly and honestlie gained by the exercise of their qualitie of Stage-players but that certaine persons (some of them of honour) inhabitants of the said precinct and libertie of the Blackfriers have as yor petitioners are enfourmed besought yor honorable Lps not to permitt the saide priuate house anie longer to remaine open but hereafter to be shut vpp and closed to the manifest and great injurie of yor petitioners who have no other meanes whereby to maintaine their wiues and families but by the exercise of their qualitie as they have heretofore done. Furthermore that in the summer season yor petitioners are able to playe at their newe built house on the Bankside calldo the Globe but that in the winter they are compelled to come to the Blackfriers and if yor honorable Lps giue consent vnto that whch is prayde against yor petitioners thay will not onely

fate has befallen a memorandum which would otherwise show us that at this time Shakespeare lived in the part of London called Southwark. Malone speaks of a certain paper which was before him as he wrote, which belonged to Edward Alleyn, the player, and from which it appeared that in 1596 Shakespeare lived in Southwark, near the Bear Garden. Malone makes this statement in his *Inquiry into the Authenticity of Certain Papers*, which were forged by that scapegrace William Ireland; and eminent palæographers and Shakespearian scholars will have it that there was contamination in the subject, and that the following brief memorandum,

while the winter endureth loose the meanes whereby they nowe support them selues and their families but be vnable to practise them selues in anie playes or enterluds when calde upon to performe for the recreation and solace of her Matie and her honorable Court, as they have beene heretofore accustomed. The humble prayer of yor petitioners therefore is that your honble Lps will graunt permission to finishe the reparations and alterations they have begunne and as your petitioners have hitherto been well ordred in their behauiour and just in their dealinges that yor honorable Lps will not inhibit them from acting at their aboue named priuate house in the precinct and libertie of the Blackfriers and your petitioners as in dutie most bounden will ever praye for the increasing honour and happinesse of yor honorable Lps."

This document being in a public office, upon a grave suspicion of its genuineness, Sir John Romilly, Master of the Rolls, ordered a palæographic examination of it to be made; and there is now appended to it the following certificate: —

"We, the undersigned, at the desire of the Master of the Rolls, have carefully examined the document hereunto annexed, purporting to be a petition to the Lords of her Majesty's Privy Council, from Thomas Pope, Richard Burbadge, John Hemings, Augustine Phillips, William Shakespeare, William Kempe, William Slye, Nicholas Tooley, and others, in answer to a petition from the inhabitants of the Liberty of the Black-friars; and we are of opinion that the document in question is spurious.

30th January, 1860.

FRA. PALGRAVE, K. H., Deputy Keeper of H. M. Public Records.
FREDERIC MADDEN, K. H., Keeper of the MSS., British Museum.
J. S. BREWER, M. A., Reader at the Rolls.
T. DUFFUS HARDY, Assistant Keeper of Records.
N. E. S. A. HAMILTON, Assistant, Dep. of MSS., British Museum."

See Vol. II. p. xxxvii., for a professed copy of a letter from the Earl of Southampton concerning Shakespeare, now pronounced spurious with an equal weight of authority.

which Mr. Collier brought forward as the paper to which Malone referred, is also spurious.

"Inhabitantes of Sowtherk as have complaned
this —— [o]f Jully, 1596.
Mr. Markis
Mr. Tuppin
Mr. Langorth
Wilson the pyper
Mr. Barett
Mr. Shaksper
Phellipes
Tomson
Mother Golden the baude
Nagges
Fillpott and no more and soe well ended."

It may be that this is a delusion, deliberately contrived. If it be, the rogue has baited his trap so well that he shall have me a willing prey. I cannot easily believe that such a genuine-seeming glimpse of real life is artificial; and I am loath to lose those neighbors of William Shakespeare upon whom his calm and searching glances fell, and who watched with curiosity the handsome player-poet as he went in and out on his way to and from the Black-friars. I sympathize too heartily with the writer as he shuts his ears against Wilson the piper, who had the real Lincolnshire drone — I have *Falstaff's* word for it — and as he tosses off Fillpot with such a round Amen of thankfulness. I mourn the vanishing Nagges, whom I think of as a humble kind of *Silence*, or perhaps Goodman *Verges*, and am injured at the assertion that Mother Golden — *Mrs. Quickly* in the flesh, and plenty of it — is a myth; than which nothing could be more deplorable, except, indeed, that she were virtuous.

The last five years of the sixteenth century are among the most interesting and important in the history of

Shakespeare's life. He was then rapidly attaining the independent position which he coveted, and for which he labored; while growth, culture, and experience were uniting in the development of those transcendent powers which reached their grand perfection in the next decade. To those years may be confidently assigned the production of *Romeo and Juliet* in its second and final form, *King John*, the two Parts of *King Henry the Fourth*, the first sketch of *The Merry Wives of Windsor*, *Much Ado about Nothing*, *Twelfth Night*, *King Henry the Fifth*, *As You Like It*, and *Hamlet*. They were probably produced in this order, the first in 1596, the last in 1600.* The man who could put those plays upon the stage at a time when play-going was the favorite amusement of all the better and brighter part of the London public, gentle and simple, was sure to grow rich, if he were but prudent; and Shakespeare was prudent, and even thrifty. He knew the full worth of money. And he saw that pecuniary independence is absolutely necessary to him who is seeking, as he sought, a social position higher than that to which he was born. Therefore he looked much more carefully after his material interests than his literary reputation. The whole tenor of his life shows that he labored as a play-wright solely that he might obtain the means of going back to Stratford to live the life of an independent gentleman. His income now began to be considerable; and there are yet remaining records of the care with which he invested his money, and his willingness to take legal measures to protect himself against small losses. It is not pleasant to think of the author of *The Merchant of Venice* going to law to compel the payment of a few pounds sterling: it would be revolting, if the debtor's failure were

* The grounds on which these and other of Shakespeare's works are assigned to certain years, are given in the essays introductory to them.

because of poverty. But as we have to face the fact, we may find comfort in the certainty that a man of that sweetness of disposition could not have been litigious, and in the probability that he knew too much of human nature and of the law to commence a suit, unless to protect himself against fraud, or to decide a legal liability. He who so pitilessly painted *Shylock* could not but have felt the truth of the maxim, *Summum jus, summa injuria.*

Filial piety unhappily is not always a sign of generosity of soul; for hard masters, cruel creditors, and selfish friends are sometimes devoted sons; but it is pleasant, in remarking upon Shakespeare's thrift, to record that one of the earliest uses of his prosperity seems to have been the relief of his father from the consequences of misfortune. The little estate of Ashbies, part of Mary Arden's inheritance, which had been mortgaged to Edmund Lambert in 1578, should have been released by the conditions of the mortgage on the repayment of the mortgage money on or before the 29th of September, 1580. The mortgagors tendered the money, forty pounds; but they owed Lambert more; and he, having possession, and knowing John Shakespeare's inability to incur law expenses, refused to release Ashbies unless the other debt, for which it was not given as security, was discharged also. But in 1597, John Shakespeare and his wife ventured upon that most trying and expensive of all legal proceedings, a chancery suit, to compel John Lambert, the son and heir of Edmund, to restore the estate. There can be no reasonable doubt that the money necessary to this proceeding, and the prompting to undertake it, came from William Shakespeare, incited by filial love and attachment to ancestral fields.

Previous to this date,—how long we do not know, but it was certainly some months before October, 1596,—

John Shakespeare applied to the Herald's College (and, if we are to believe the records, not for the first time) for a grant of coat-armor, by which he, then a yeoman, might become a gentleman. Such applications were then customarily made by men who deemed themselves of sufficient importance to enter the pale of gentry. The arms, if granted, were of value; for they were an official and universally recognized certificate of a certain social standing, which those to whom they were granted were required to show that they were in condition creditably to support. It has been conjectured that John Shakespeare made this application at the instigation and with the means — for the honor cost money — of his now prosperous son. And William Shakespeare himself was doubtless the real mover in this matter. To John Shakespeare, a man past middle life, and without property or position, such a distinction would not have been worth what it cost in mere pounds sterling. But to his prosperous and celebrated son the possession of the rights of gentry, and still more their inheritance, would have brought a certain consideration which had its value. Therefore, probably, it was that the grant was applied for in the name of the father, instead of that of the player son; whose profession, it must also be remembered, would have been against him in the Heralds' College. Shakespeare knew well enough, as any reader of *The Winter's Tale* may see,* the factitious value of heraldic gentry. But it brought with it more or less social consideration; and it was for this social consideration that he toiled and schemed; that he, the Stratford fugitive, might return to his native place and meet Sir Thomas Lucy as a prosperous gentleman.

* Act III. Sc. 6.

IV.

Shakespeare was now able to take an important step toward establishing himself handsomely in his native place. In 1597 he bought the Great House, or New Place, as it was called in Stratford, built by Sir Hugh Clopton, the benefactor of the town. It cost Shakespeare sixty pounds sterling (equal to about $1500); a small outlay for the dwelling of a man of its new possessor's means and capacity of enjoyment. But we know from the fine levied at the sale that the premises included the Great House itself, two barns, two gardens, and two orchards. No representation of the house as it was in Shakespeare's time is known to exist, it having been altered after his death; yet its size was not enlarged; and an existing representation of it in its last condition shows that it was a goodly mansion. But its new master took possession bereaved and disappointed. The death of his only son, Hamnet, in the twelfth year of his age, 1596, left him without a descendant to whom he might transmit, with his name, the houses and lands and the arms which he had obtained by such untiring labor. Shakespeare having money to invest, of course there was no lack of applicants for the pleasure of placing it for him to his advantage. Of these was one Master Abraham Sturley, a Puritan of the first water. He begins a long letter, written at Stratford, January 24th, 1559, to a friend in London, (probably Richard Quiney, whose son afterward married Shakespeare's daughter,) with a pious ejaculation, and then passes promptly to business, urging his correspondent to quicken an intention which Shakespeare was known to have to lay out some of his superfluous money in Stratford property, and especially to recommend to him a purchase of the tithes of Stratford and three other parishes, as profitable to himself, beneficial to the town, and likely to gain him many friends.* The recommendation, as we shall hereafter see, appears to have had some effect. There is another letter of this time, written also to Richard Quiney, which contains an obscure mention of a money transaction with Shakespeare.† And the fact is somewhat striking in the life of a great poet, that the only letter directly addressed to Shakespeare which is known to exist, is one which asks a loan of £30. It is from Richard Quiney, who at the writing was in London, and is as follows; for this money transaction belongs in full to Shakespeare's history.

"Loveinge Contreyman, I am bolde of yo^{w}, as of a ffrende, craveinge yo^{wr} helpe wth xxx^{li}, uppon Mr Bushells & my securytee, or Mr Myttens with me. Mr Rosswell is nott come to London as yeate, & I have especiall cawse. Yo^{w} shall ffrende me muche in helpeinge me out of all the debtts I owe in London, I thanck god, and muche quiet my mynde wch wolde not be indebeted. I am now towardes the Cowrte, in hope of answer for the dispatche of my Buysenes. Yo^{w} shall nether loose creddytt nor monney by me, the Lorde wyllinge; & nowe butt perswade yo^{wr} selfe soe, as I hope, & yo^{w} shall nott need to feare; butt with all hartie thanckfullnes I wyll holde my tyme & content yo^{wr} frend, & yf we Bargaine farther, yo^{w} shall be the

* "Most loveinge and belovedd in the Lord. In plaine Englishe we remember u in the Lord, & ourselves unto u. I would write nothinge unto u nowe, but come home. I prai God send u comfortabli home. This is one speciall remembrance ffrom ur ffather's motion. It semeth bi him that our countriman, Mr. Shakspere, is willinge to disburse some monei upon some od yarde land or other att Shottri or neare about us; he thinketh it a veri fitt patterne to move him to deale in the matter of our tithes. Bi the instructions u can geve him theareof, & by the frendes he can make therefore, we thinke it a faire marke for him to shoote att, & not impossible to hitt. It obtained would advance him in deede, and would do us much good. Hoc movere, et quantum in te est permovere, ne necligas, hoc enim et sibi et nobis maximi erit momenti. Hic labor, hoc opus esset eximiae et gloriae et laudis sibi." &c., &c.

† "Yff yow bargen with Wm. Sh——— or receve money therefor, brynge your money home that yow maye."

paie m^{r} yo^{wr} selfe. My tyme biddes me to hasten to an ende, & soe I comitt thys [to] yo^{wr} care & hope of yo^{wr} helpe. I feare I shall nott be backe this night ffrom the Cowrte. haste. the Lorde be wth yo^{w} & wth us all. amen. From the Bell in Carter Lane, the 25 october 1598.

"Yo^{wrs} in all kyndenes,

"RYC. QUYNEY."

This letter is folded and addressed as is shown in the following fac-simile; the address being "To my loveing good ffrend and countreyman Mr. Wm. Shackespere delr thees."

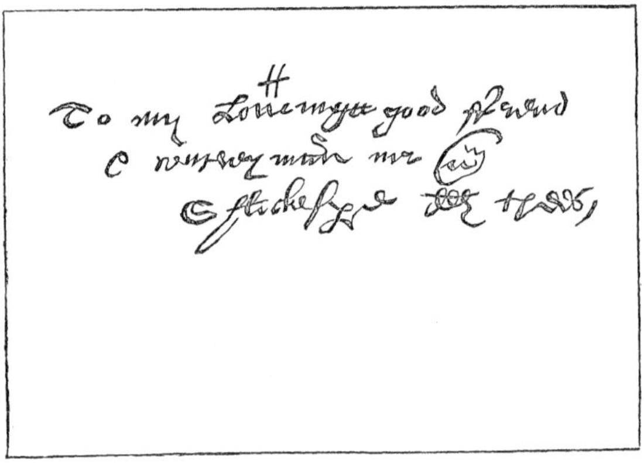

It is impossible to disguise the fact that Quiney offers an approved indorsed note to the author of *Hamlet;* but it is gratifying to observe that he applies to him as a friend. The motive which he touches is not interest, but the helping him out of trouble; and though the sum was a respectable one, — half the price of New Place, — he plainly feels that Shakespeare had both the ability and the willingness to spare it. There is another letter of this period, dated November 4th, 1598, addressed to the same Richard Quiney by Abraham Sturley again. The first part, with which only we have concern, begins, "All health happiness of suites and wellfare be multiplied unto u and ur labours in God our ffather by Christ our Lord," and ends with no less fervor, "O howe can you make dowbt of monei who will not bear xxx-tie or xl. s towardes sutch a match!" But its chief interest to us is, that the writer of these beatitudes has heard that "our countriman Mr. Wm. Shak. would procure us monei, wc. I will like of." It is pleasant thus to see that Shakespeare's townsmen, even the staid and sober men among them, respected and looked up to him, and leaned confidently upon the support of his influence and his purse. And this marvellous "Mr. Wm. Shak." then had real property in London, as well as in Stratford, besides his theatrical possessions; for in October of 1598 he was assessed on property in the parish of St. Helen's, Bishopsgate, £5 13*s.* 4*d.*

In 1598 Ben Jonson's first and best comedy, *Every Man in his Humour*, was produced at the Black-friars, and the author of *King Henry the Fourth* and *Romeo and Juliet* might have been seen for two pence by any London prentice who could command the coin, playing an inferior part, probably that of *Knowell*, in the new play. But, according to tradition, Shakespeare not only played in Jonson's comedy, — he obtained Ben his first hearing before a London audience. The play had been thrown aside at the Black-friars with little consideration, as the production of an unknown writer; but Shakespeare's attention having been drawn to it, he read it through, admired and recommended it, and then and thereafter took pains to bring the author's works before the public. Jonson's honest love for Shakespeare may well have had its spring in gratitude for this great service, which having been performed by one dramatic author to another, who was his junior, indicates both kindness and magnanimity of disposition.

The year 1598 was one of great professional triumph to Shakespeare. In that year, we may be sure, he was honored with a command from Queen Elizabeth to let her see his *Falstaff* in love, which he obeyed by producing in a fortnight *The Merry Wives of Windsor* in its earliest form.* In that year, too, the greatness and universality of his genius received formal recognition at the hands of literary criticism. Francis Meres published in 1598 a book called *Palladis Tamia, Wits Treasury*, which was a collection of sententious comparisons, chiefly upon morals, manners, and religion. But one division or chapter is "A comparative discourse of our English Poets with the Greeke, Latine, and Italian Poets." Meres was a Master of Arts in both Universities, a theological writer, and the author of poetry which has been lost. His comparative discourse makes no pretence to analysis or esthetic judgment. Indeed, according to the modern standard, it can hardly be regarded as criticism; but it may be accepted as a record of the estimation in which Shakespeare was held by intelligent and cultivated people when he was thirty-four years old, and before he had written his best plays. In this book Shakespeare is awarded the highest place in English poetical and dramatic literature, and is ranked with the great authors of the classic days of Greece and Rome. It is

* See this tradition, and the facts which bear upon it, discussed in the Introduction to *The Merry Wives of Windsor*.

true that other poets and dramatists are compared by Meres to Pindar, Æschylus, and Aristophanes, to Ovid, Plautus, and Horace, and that, like all who have judged their contemporaries, he bestows high praise upon men whose works and names have perished from the world's memory. But in his comprehensive eulogy Shakespeare has this distinction, that while he shares equally all other praise, it is said of him, that "as Plautus and Seneca are accounted the best for comedy and tragedy among the Latins, so Shakespeare among the English is the most excellent in both kinds for the stage." *

* The following are all the passages of this chapter of the *Palladis Tama* in which Shakespeare's name appears. They have never been all reprinted before.

"As the Greekes tongue is made famous and eloquent by Homer, Hesiod, Euripedes, Æschylus, Sophocles, Pindarus, Phylocledes, and Aristophanes; and the Latine tongue by Virgile, Ouid, Horace, Sicilius Italius, Lucanus, Lucretius, Ausonius, and Claudianus, so the English tongue is mightily enriched and gorgeously invested in rare ornaments by sir Philip Sidney, Spencer, Daniel, Drayton, Warner, Shakespeare, Marlow, and Chapman."

"As the soule of Euphorbus was thought to liue in Pythagoras, so the sweete wittie soule of Ouid liues in mellifluous and hony-tongued Shakespeare; witnes his *Venus and Adonis*, his *Lucrece*, his sugred sonnets among his priuate friends, &c."

"As Plautus and Seneca are accounted the best for Comedy and Tragedy among the Latines: so Shakespeare among yᵉ English is the most excellent in both kinds for the stage; for Comedy, witnes his *Gētlemē of Verona*, his *Er rors*, his *Loue labors lost*, his *Loue labours wonne*, his *Midsummers night dreame*, & his *Merchant of Venice*: for Tragedy his *Richard the* 2. *Richard the* 3. *Henry the* 4. *King Iohn*, *Titus Andronicus* and his *Romeo and Iuliet*."

"As Epius Stolo said, the Muses would speake with Plautus tongue, if they would speak Latin; so I say the Muses would speak with Shakespeare's fine-filed phrase, if they would speak English."

"And as Horace saith of his, Exegi monumentū ære perennius, Regaliq; situ pyramidum altius; Quod non imber edax; Non Aquilo impotens possit diruere, aut innumerabilis annorum series et fuga temporum; so say I severally of Sir Philip Sidneys, Spencers, Daniels, Draytons, Shakespeares, and Warner's workes."

"As Pindarus, Anacreon, and Callimachus among the Greekes, and Horace and Catullus among the Latines, are the best lyrick poets; so in this faculty the best amōg our poets are Spencer (who excelleth in all kinds), Daniel, Drayton, Shakespeare, Brettō."

"As these tragicke poets flourished in Greece, Æschylus, Euripedes, Sophocles, Alexander Aetolus, Achæus Erithriæus, Astydamas Atheniēsis, Apollodorus Tarsensis, Nicomachus Phrygius, Thespis Atticus, and Timon Apollo-

There is ample evidence that this appreciation of Shakespeare was general, and that although his contemporaries could hardly have suspected that his genius would overshadow all others in our literature, they regarded him as a poet and a dramatist beyond comparison among his countrymen. Shakespeare's plays filled the theatre to overflowing when even Jonson's would hardly pay expenses.* It was not until the moral and literary decadence of the Restoration and the establish-

niates; and these among the Latines, Accius, M. Attilius, Pomponius Secundus and Seneca; so these are our best for tragedie; the Lord Buckhurst, Doctor Leg of Cambridge, Dr. Edes of Oxford, Maister Edward Ferris, the Authour of the *Mirrour for Magistrates*, Marlow, Peele, Watson, Kid, Shakespeare, Drayton, Chapman, Decker, and Beniamin Iohnson."

"The best poets for comedy among the Greeks are these: Menander, Aristophanes, Eupolis Atheniensis Alexis, Terius, Nicostratus, Amipsias Atheniensis, Anaxādrides Rhodius, Aristonymus, Archippus Atheniēsis, and Callias Atheniensis; and among the Latines, Plautus, Terence, Næuius, Sext. Turpilius, Licinius Imbrex, and Virgilius Romanus; so the best for comedy amongst us bee Edward Earle of Oxforde, Doctor Gager of Oxforde, Maister Rowley, once a rare scholler of learned Pembrooke Hall in Cambridge, Maister Edwardes, one of her Maiesties Chappell, eloquent and wittie John Lilly, Lodge, Gascoyne, Greene, Shakespeare, Thomas Nash, Thomas Heywood, Anthony Mundye, our best plotter, Chapman, Porter, Wilson, Hathway, and Henry Chettle."

"As these are famous among the Greeks for elegie, Melanthus, Mymnerus Colophonius, Olympius Mysius, Parthenius Nicæus, Philetas Cous, Theogenes Megarensis, and Pigres Halicarnasœus; and these among the Latines, Mecænas, Ouid, Tibullus, Propertius, T. Valgius, Cassius Seuerus, and Clodius Sabinus; so these are the most passionate among us to bewaile and bemoane the perplexities of loue; Henrie Howard Earle of Surrey, sir Thomas Wyat the elder, sir Francis Brian, sir Philip Sidney, sir Walter Rawley, sir Edward Dyer, Spencer, Daniel, Drayton, Shakespeare, Whetstone, Gascoyne, Samuell Page sometimes fellowe of *Corpus Christi* Colledge in Oxford, Churchyard, Bretton."

* See the verses of Leonard Digges, Vol. II. p. xxxiv. of this work.

In *The Return from Parnassus*, a comedy acted certainly before the death of Queen Elizabeth by the students of St. John's College, Cambridge, but the earliest known copy of which was printed in 1606, there is this tribute to the native superiority of Shakespeare: —

"*Kemp*. Few of the vniuersity pen plaies well; they smell too much of that writer Ovid, and that writer Metamorphosis, and talke too much of Proserpina and Jupiter. Why, heres our fellow Shakespeare puts them all downe; I and Ben Jonson too. O, that Ben Jonson is a pestilent fellow: he brought up Horace giuing the poets a pill: but our fellow Shakespeare hath giuen him a purge that made him beray his credit."

ment of the exotic and artificial standards of the so-called Augustan age of English literature that he was thought to have equals, and even superiors. In spite of Shakespeare's manifest and generally acknowledged superiority, under which Jonson, conscious both of larger learning and higher elaboration, fretted a little, there was warm friendship between the two men, which lasted through Shakespeare's life, and the memory of which inspired and softened gruff Ben when his friend had passed away. There was never more generous or more glowing eulogy of one man by another than that in Jonson's verses which appeared among the preliminary matter to the first folio,* and in the well-known passage in his *Discoveries*, written in his latter years, the crusty critic, though he must carp at the poet, breaks out into a hearty expression of admiration and cherished love of the man.†

In 1599 Shakespeare received a not very welcome tribute to his poetic eminence. A bookseller named Jaggard, who, even in those days of extremest license in his craft, was distinguished by his disregard of the

* See Vol. II. p. xiii. of this work.

† "I remember the Players have often mentioned it as an honour to Shakespeare, that in his writing (whatsoever he penn'd) he never blotted out line. My answer hath beene, would he had blotted a thousand. Which they thought a malevolent speech. I had not told posterity this, but for their ignorance, who choose that circumstance to commend their friend by, wherein he most faulted. And to justifie mine own candor, (for I lov'd the man, and doe honour his memory (on this side idolatry) as much as any.) Hee was (indeed) honest, and of an open and free nature: had an excellent phantsie, brave notions, and gentle expressions: wherein he flow'd with that facility, that sometime it was necessary he should be stop'd. *Sufflaminandus erat*, as Augustus said of Haterius. His wit was in his owne power, would the rule of it had beene so too. Many times he fell into those things, could not escape laughter: As when he said in the person of Cæsar one speaking to him, *Cæsar thou dost me wrong.* Hee replyed: *Cæsar did never wrong but with just cause;* and such like; which were ridiculous. But hee redeemed his vices, with his virtues. There was euer more in him to be praysed, than to be pardoned." *Discoveries. Horace his Arte of Poetry*, &c. fol. 1640. p. 97.

rights of literary property and literary reputation, printed a volume of verses under the unmeaning title *The Passionate Pilgrim*, upon the title-page of which he impudently placed Shakespeare's name, although but a part of its meagre contents were from his pen, and that part had been surreptitiously obtained. Shakespeare was much offended that Jaggard made so bold with his name. This we know on the testimony of Heywood, who in a second edition saw two of his own compositions also attributed to the favorite of the hour, and who publicly claimed his own.* Shakespeare, although offended at the personal liberty, seems to have been careless of any possible injury to his reputation. No evidence of any public denial on his part is known to exist; and it was not until after the publication of the third edition of the volume, in 1612, that his name was taken from the title-page. In 1600 he was made for a time to father *Sir John Oldcastle;* but the publisher appears to have been speedily undeceived or compelled to do justice; for Shakespeare's name was omitted from some part of the impression. We know from Henslow's Diary that *Sir John Oldcastle* was written by Munday, Drayton, Wilson, and Hathway, jointly. The removal of Shakespeare's name from the title page was more probably owing to their pride and jealousy than to Shakespeare's. An edition of *King Henry the Fifth* was published in this year, which shows from internal evidence that the bookseller was so eager to put this work of Shakespeare's before the public that he used a version obtained by surreptitious means, and so mangled as to be almost without connec-

* These were two poetic epistles, from Paris to Helen and from Helen to Paris. See the postscript to Heywood's *Apology for Actors*, 1612. *The Passionate Pilgrim* was printed only on one side of each leaf, to eke out the volume

tion from page to page.* A misfortune more seriously regarded by Shakespeare than any liberty with his reputation fell upon him also in this year, through the plot which cost Essex his head, and his friend and Shakespeare's patron, Southampton, his liberty during the remainder of Elizabeth's reign.

The latter years of John Shakespeare's checkered life seem to have been passed in tranquil though humble ease, through the filial care of his distinguished son. He died in September, 1601, as we know by the record of his burial on the 8th of that month; being then, if we set him down as twenty-one or twenty-two years old when we first hear of him at Stratford, somewhat more than seventy years of age. His house in Henley Street, and probably such other real property as he may have owned at the time of his death, descended to William, who, though the possessor and occupier of the Great House, which had doubtless impressed his youthful imagination by its magnitude and its village preëminence, clung to the memories of his humbler home, and always kept it in his possession. During the next year he added to his landed estate one hundred and seven acres of land in the parish of Old Stratford, which he bought from the brothers William and John a Combe. He also bought a cottage in Henley Street from Walter Gettey; and from Hercules Underhill, a messuage with two barns, two orchards, and two gardens. He was not in Stratford at the time of the completion of the first of these purchases, in which he was represented by his brother Gilbert. In this year, while he was thus rapidly acquiring that landed interest in his native county without which no man in his day could maintain a respectable position as a gen-

* See the Introduction to *King Henry the Fifth*, Vol. VII.

tleman of family, the burgesses of Stratford passed an ordinance forbidding the exhibition of plays of any kind in the chamber, the guildhall, or any part of the house or court — a proscription which was made more rigid in 1612. Is it strange that under these circumstances Shakespeare did not show much solicitude about the careful publication of his dramas and the perpetuation of his fame as a playwright?

The death of Elizabeth, in 1603, which gave our fathers, instead of a royal family that tyrannized firmly and sagaciously, one that was at once tyrannical, feeble, and vacillating, and whose monstrous outrages upon the rights of Englishmen contributed mainly to the founding of an English nation upon this continent, produced a change in Shakespeare's professional position, traces of which remain in the mother country until this day. One of King James's earliest warrants under the privy seal of England made the company of which Shakespeare was a member "His Majesty's servants;" a designation which has since always pertained to the performers at the leading theatre of London. In this warrant Shakespeare's name appears second, Laurence Fletcher's being first.* And in this year, too, if

* It is, verbatim et literatim, thus: —

By The King.

"Right trusty and welbeloved Counsellor, we greete you well, and will and commaund you, that under our privie Seale in your custody for the time being, you cause our letters to be derected to the keeper of our greate seale of England, commaunding him under our said greate Seale, he cause our letters to be made patents in forme following. James, by the grace of God, King of England, Scotland, Fraunce, and Irland, defendor of the faith, &c. To all Justices, Maiors, Sheriffs, Constables, Headboroughes, and other our officers and loving subjects greeting. Know ye, that we of our speciall grace, certaine knowledge, and meere motion have licenced and authorized, and by these presentes doe licence and authorize, these our servants, Lawrence Fletcher, William Shakespeare, Richard Burbage, Augustine Phillippes, John Hemmings, Henrie Con-

we could believe in the authenticity of a letter professing to be written by the poet Daniel to Sir Thomas Egerton, and which Mr. Collier brought to light in 1835,* Shakespeare applied for the office of Master of the Queen's Revels, which, through Sir Thomas Egerton's influence, was given to Daniel. The genuineness of this letter, in which the allusion to Shakespeare is slight and incidental, has been disputed on purely palæographical grounds; but it may also be questioned whether Shakespeare would have applied at this time for such an office as that of Master of the Queen's Revels, which would have occupied much of his time and attention; for he was now at the height of his reputation, and was gathering a profit from his professional labors for the loss of which the position of Master of the Queen's Revels would not have been a recompense. If indeed he did apply for it, the world has reason to be thankful at

dell, William Sly, Robert Armyn, Richard Cowlye, and the rest of their associats, freely to use & exercise the arte and faculty of playing Comedies, Tragedies, Histories, Enterludes, Moralls, Pastoralls, Stage plaies, and such other like, as that thei have already studied or hereafter shall use or studie, aswell for the recreation of our loving subjects, as for our solace and pleasure, when we shall thinke good to see them, during our pleasure. And the said Comedies, Tragedies, Histories, Enterludes, Moralls, Pastoralls, Stage plaies, and such like, to shew & exercise publiquely to their best commoditie, when the infection of the plague shall decrease, as well within theire now usuall howse called the Globe, within our county of Surrey, as also within anie towne halls, or mout halls, or other convenient places within the liberties & freedome of any other citie, universitie, towne, or borough whatsoever within our said realmes and dominions. Willing and commaunding you, and every of you, as you tender our pleasure, not only to permit and suffer them heerin, without any your letts, hinderances, or molestations, during our said pleasure, but also to be ayding or assisting to them, yf any wrong be to them offered. And to allowe them such former courtesies, as hathe bene given to men of their place and qualitie: and also what further favour you shall shew to these our servants for our sake, we shall take kindly at your hands. And these our letters shall be your sufficient warrant and discharge in this behalfe. Given under our Signet at our mannor of Greenewiche, the seaventeenth day of May in the first yere of our raigne of England, France, and Ireland, & of Scotland the six & thirtieth.

Ex per Lake."

* *New Facts regarding the Life of Shakespeare.*

his disappointment. For it is to the first ten years of the seventeenth century that we owe the great tragedies, *Troilus and Cressida*, *Othello*, *King Lear*, *Timon of Athens*, *Macbeth*, *Julius Cæsar*, *Antony and Cleopatra*, and *Coriolanus*, with *Cymbeline*, *All's Well that Ends Well*, *Measure for Measure*, and Shakespeare's part in *Pericles* and *The Taming of the Shrew*, of which all but *Pericles* and *The Taming of the Shrew* were quite surely written after 1603.

In that year Ben Jonson's *Sejanus* was produced at the Black-friars, and the author of *Hamlet* might have been seen playing a subordinate part in it. But about this time he appears to have retired from the stage, where, as we have seen, he had gained but little distinction at much sacrifice of feeling, and to have confined his labors for the theatre to the more congenial occupation of play-writing. Chettle, it is true, says that Shakespeare was excellent in the quality he professed; but in that commendation 'quality' may refer to play-writing as well as to play acting; and mayhap it refers with some vagueness to both. According to some contemporary verses of Davies (in *The Scourge of Folly*), which have been previously mentioned, Shakespeare played kingly parts; and in so doing offended his new master, and marred his fortunes. The verses are not clear, as the reader will see.

"*To our English Terence, Mr. Will Shakespeare.*

"Some say, good Will, which I in sport do sing,
Had'st thou not plaid some kingly parts in sport,
Thou had'st bin a companion for a king,
And beene a king among the meaner sort.

"Some others raile; but raile as they thinke fit,
Thou hast no rayling, but a raigning wit:
And honesty thou sow'st, which they do reape,
So to increase their stocke, which they do keepe."

It cannot be that Shakespeare in playing kingly parts ventured to take off "God's vicegerent upon earth." The temptation to do so must have been great; but he was too prudent to indulge in sport so expensive and so dangerous. It is difficult to see how the mere decorous performance of kingly parts could have offended James; and yet we must remember that he was as petty and capricious as he was tyrannical.* There is a story which was first printed in Lintot's edition of Shakespeare's Poems, published in 1710, that King James wrote with his own hand an amicable letter to Shakespeare, which was once in the hands of Davenant, as a creditable person then living could testify; and conjecture, ever ready, has made *Macbeth's* prophetic vision of kings the occasion of the compliment. It is well to have a more credible person than Davenant to corroborate such a story; and Oldys, in a manuscript note to his copy of Fuller's *Worthies*, says that the Duke of Buckingham told Lintot that he had seen this letter in Davenant's possession. If Oldys meant the last Duke of Buckingham, which is possible, he added not much to our security for the mere existence of such a letter; but if he meant the first Duke of Buckinghamshire, which is also possible, we can the more readily believe that Davenant produced such a letter as that in question, although even then we lack

* Yet James was attacked through the players; of which the following very direct evidence has been found in a treatise on hunting preserved among the Sloane MSS. The writer, having censured the players for lack of decorum, thus continues: "What madnesse is it, I saye, that possesseth them under faigned persons to be censureing of their soveraigne: surely though these poets for many years have, for the most part, lefte foles and devills out of their playes, yet nowe on the suddayne they make them all playe the foles most notoriouslye and impudently in medlinge with him (in waye of taxacion) by whome they live and have in manner there very being." In this grovelling and blasphemous style it was the fashion to speak of a man who was about as mean and sordid a creature as ever lived.

satisfactory evidence of its genuineness. Davenant is the poorest possible authority for any story about Shakespeare. This one, however, is more probable than another which places Shakespeare in royal company. It was unheard of till late in the eighteenth century, and is to the effect that Queen Elizabeth, being at the theatre one evening when Shakespeare was playing a king, bowed to him as she crossed the stage. He did not return the salutation, but went on with his part. To ascertain whether the omission was an intentional preservation of assumed character, or an oversight, the Queen again passed him, and dropped her glove. Shakespeare immediately picked it up, and following the royal virgin, handed it to her, adding on the instant these lines to a speech which he was just delivering, and so aptly and easily that they seemed to belong to it.

"And though now bent on this high embassy,
Yet stoop we to take up our cousin's glove."

The Queen, it is said, was highly pleased, and complimented him upon his adroitness and his courtesy. In judging the credibility of this story, it should be remembered that in Shakespeare's time the most distinguished part of the audience went upon the stage, during the performance, in what must have been a very confusing manner ; but the anecdote is plainly one made to meet the craving for personal details of Shakespeare's life. In addition to its inherent improbability, Shakespeare well knew what the author of the verses seems not to have known—that kings cannot go on embassies. Empty compliment and his share of payment to the company for services rendered seem to have been all the benefit that Shakespeare obtained from royal favor. There is not the least reason for believing that either the strong-minded woman or the weak-minded man in whose reigns he flourished recognized his superiority by special distinction or substantial reward.*

* Mr. Peter Cunningham's Extracts from the Accounts of the Revels at Court include the following entries of the performance of Shakespeare's plays before King James, between 1604 and 1611.

The Plaiers.		*The Poets which mayd the plaies.*
By the Kings Ma^tis^ plaiers.	Hallamas day being the first of Novembar, A play in the Banketinge House att Whithall called the Moor of Venis. [Nov. 1st, 1604.]	
By his Ma^tis^ plaiers.	The Sunday ffollowinge, A Play of the Merry Wives of Winsor. [Nov. 4th, 1604.]	
By his Ma^tis^ plaiers.	On St. Stivens night in the Hall a Play called Mesur for Mesur. [Dec. 26th, 1604.]	Shaxberd.
By his Ma^tis^ plaiers.	On Inosents Night The Plaie of Errors. [Dec. 28th, 1604.]	Shaxberd.
By his Ma^tis^ plaiers.	Betwin Newers day and Twelfe day a Play of Loves Labours Lost. [1605.]	
By his Ma^tis^ plaiers.	On the 7 of January was played the play of Henry the fift. [1605.]	
By his Ma^tis^ plaiers.	On Shrovsunday A play of the Marchant of Venis. [Mar. 24th, 1605.]	Shaxberd.
By his Ma^tis^ plaiers.	On Shrovtusday A Play cauled the Marchant of Venis againe commaunded by the Kings Matie. [Mar. 26, 1605.]	Shaxberd.
	[Accounts from Oct. 31st, 1611, to Nov. 1st, 1612.]	
By the Kings players.	Hallomas nyght was presented att Whithall before ye Kinges Matie a play called the Tempest. [Nov. 1st, 1611.]	
The Kings players.	The 5th of November: A play called ye winters nightes Tayle. [1511.]	

On the 5th of June, 1607, Susanna Shakespeare, who was her father's favorite daughter, and who seems to have been a superior woman, was married to Dr. John Hall, a physician of good repute in his county. On the 31st of December of the same year, Edmund Shakespeare was buried in the parish of St. Saviour's, Southwark. He was a player of no distinction, who probably had followed his brother to London and obtained a place in the Black-friars company by his influence.

The inducements presented to Shakespeare by his Puritan townsman Sturley, as early as the year 1597, to the purchase of tithes in his native place, were insufficient at the time, or he had not the needful money at hand; for he then acquired no interest in them. But he seems to have entertained the project favorably, and to have formed the design of making an investment of this kind; for in 1605 he bought the moiety of a lease, granted in 1544, of all the tithes of Stratford, Old Stratford, Bishopton, and Welcombe; for which he paid down in cash £440. This is the most important purchase he is known to have made. The consideration was equal to between eleven and twelve thousand dollars of our money.

The natural desire of transmitting an honorable name and a fair estate to descendants seems to have been strong in Shakespeare, and his hopes, sadly disappointed by the early death of his only son, must have been a little dashed again by the event which made him first a grandfather — the birth, in February, 160$\frac{7}{8}$, of a daughter to his daughter Susanna, the wife of Dr. Hall. She brought her husband no other children. In September following Mary Arden died, having survived her husband seven years. Shakespeare's mother must have been about seventy years old at her death, probably in the old home in Henley Street, to which she had gone fifty years before as John Shakespeare's wife, and where the son was born to whom she doubtless owed her undisturbed residence in that house of hope and of sad and tender memories. We do not know that he was present at her funeral; and he seems to have set up no stone to tell us where she or his father lay. But the same is true with regard to his son Hamnet: and it is reasonable to suppose that his own death prevented the completion of designs for a tomb for the family. The next month, October of this same year, 1608, affords us, though in the most formal and unsatisfactory manner, our nearest approximation to a record of a social gathering at which he was present. On the 16th he was sponsor at the baptism of the son of Henry Walker, an alderman of Stratford. The boy was called after his godfather, who remembered him in his will by a legacy of xx. *s.* in gold. So that, after all, as Shakespeare's mother's funeral took place on the 6th of the previous month, we may be pretty sure that he performed for her the last offices, and that he was remaining at Stratford in temporary and much coveted seclusion when he was asked to be William Walker's godfather.

He had produced his great tragedy *King Lear*, the most wondrous work of human genius, in 1605, when he was forty years old. Of this drama the bookseller obtained a copy in 1608, and in that year published three editions of it, the high reputation of its author, as well as the public admiration of this particular work, having been shown not only by the unusual demand which the bookseller was called upon to supply, but by the means which the latter took to make it clear that this was "Mr. William Shakespeare *his* Tragedy of King Lear."*

* See the Introduction to this play, Vol. XI.

For anxious souls who are concerned upon the subject of Shakespeare's taxes, there is a comfortable memorandum preserved at Dulwich College, which professes to give the names of all those who in April, 1609, were rated and assessed for a weekly payment toward the relief of the poor of the Clink Liberty in Southwark. Among fifty-seven names are those of Philip Henslow, Edward Alleyn, and Mr. Shakespeare, who are each assessed weekly at vj. *d.* But, alas! this invaluable evidence also is impeached as spurious; and judging from the fac-simile of it which has been published, it is certainly but a clumsy, and sometimes careless, imitation of 17th century writing. But for this loss there is recompense in the authenticity of a court record, by which we know that in August, 1608, Shakespeare sued John Addenbroke of Stratford, got a judgment for £6, and £1 4 *s.* costs, and that, Addenbroke being returned *non est inventus*, Shakespeare sued his bail Thomas Hornby, the proceedings lasting until June, 1609. Four years before, Shakespeare had sued one Philip Rogers in the Stratford Court of Record for £1 15 *s.* 10 *d.* He had sold Rogers malt to the value of £1 19 *s.* 10 *d.*, and had lent him 2 *s.*, of which the debtor had paid but 6 *s.* And so Shakespeare brought suit for what is called in trade the balance of the account, which represented about $40 of our money. These stories grate upon our feelings with a discord as much harsher than that which disturbs us when we hear of Addison suing poor Steele for £100, as Shakespeare lives in our hearts the lovelier as well as the greater man than Addison. But Addison's case was aggravated by the fact that the debtor was his long-time friend and fellow-laborer. Debts are to be paid, and rogues who can pay and will not pay must be made to pay; but the pursuit of an impoverished man. for the sake of imprisoning him and depriving him both of the power of paying his debt and supporting himself and his family, is an incident in Shakespeare's life which it requires the utmost allowance and consideration for the practice of the time and country to enable us to contemplate with equanimity — satisfaction is impossible.

The biographer of Shakespeare must record these facts, because the literary antiquaries have unearthed, produced, and pitilessly printed them as new particulars of the life of Shakespeare. We hunger, and we receive these husks; we open our mouths for food, and we break our teeth against these stones. What have these law-papers, in the involved verbiage of which dead quarrels lie embalmed, in hideous and grotesque semblance of their living shapes, their life-blood dried that lent them all their little dignity, their action, and their glow, exhaling only a faint and sickly odor of the venom that has kept them from decay, — what have these to do with the life of him whom his friends delighted to call sweet and gentle? Could not these, at least, have been allowed to rest? The parties to them have been two centuries in their graves. Why awake from slumber the empty echoes of their living strife?

It is almost as remote from the purpose of true biography, though it is somewhat more satisfactory, to ascertain the amount of the income which Shakespeare so laboriously acquired and so jealously guarded. That the basis of a calculation might not be lacking, the indefatigable (and ever successful) Mr. Collier produced from the manuscripts at Bridgewater House a memorandum which professes to state the value of Shakespeare's property in the Black-friars. The reader will remember the fruitless opposition of the Lord Mayor and Aldermen of London to the establishment of this theatre. Neither their animosity nor their efforts ceased with their first failure. They neglected no opportunity, no means, to attain their end. Finally, in 1608, Sir Henry Montagu, the then Attorney-General, gave an opinion that the jurisdiction of the corporation of London extended over the Liberty of the Black-friars, and there was another attempt to dislodge Richard Burbadge, William Shakespeare, and their fellows. Either through lack of title or of influence, it was in vain. The players could not be ousted. Then, if we could accept the evidence of Mr. Collier's document, the Mayor and Aldermen thought of buying out the men whom they could not turn out, and had an estimate made of the value of the Black-friars theatrical property, which proved to be in the bulk worth £7000, of which sum Shakespeare's shares and wardrobe property absorbed £1433 6*s.* 8*d.* According to this memorandum Shakespeare's income from his four shares was £133 6*s.* 8*d.*; the rent of a wardrobe and properties set down as worth £500 could not have been less than £50; which makes the Black-friars income £183 6*s.* 8*d.* Reckoning a like return from the Globe, we have £366 13*s.* 4*d.*; and remembering that Shakespeare had other property, and also a productive pen, Mr. Collier, whose calculation this is, certainly rather underrates than overrates his income at £400 — equal at least to $10,000 now — yearly. But, alas! this paper, like so many others brought to light by the same hand, and like the professed Southampton letter which refers to the same circumstances, has been pronounced spurious by high, though perhaps not infallible, authority.* Yet the conclusions based upon it are sustained

* The following is a copy of the memorandum in question. It has been pronounced spurious by Sir Frederic Madden, Mr. T. Duffus Hardy, Mr. N. E. S. A. Hamilton, Professor Brewer (as to whose official positions see the note on p.lxiv), Mr. Richard Giardner, M. W. B. D. D. Turnbull, and Mr. Halliwell.

by a letter of unquestioned authenticity in the State Paper Office at London. Mr. John Chamberlain, writ-

"For avoiding of the playhouse in the Blacke Friers.

Impr	Richard Burbidge owith the Fee and is alsoe a sharer therein. His interest he rateth at the grosse summe of 1000li for the Fee and for his foure Shares the summe of 933li 6s 8d	1933 li 6s 8d
Item	Laz Fletcher owith three shares wch he rateth at 700li that is at 7 years purchase for eche share or 33li 6s 8d one year with an other.	700 li
Item	W. Shakspeare asketh for the wardrobe and properties of the same playhouse 500li, and for his 4 shares, the same as his fellowes Burbidge and Fletcher 933li 6s 8d	1433 li 6s 8d
Item	Heminges and Condell eche 2 shares	933 li 6s 8d
Item	Joseph Taylor one share and an halfe	350 li
Item	Lowing one share and an halfe	350 li
Item	foure more playeres with one halfe share unto eche of them	466 li 13s 4d
	Suma totalis	6166. 13. 4.

Moreover, the hired men of the Companie demaund some recompence for their greate losse and the Widowes and Orphanes of players who are paide by the Sharers at diuers rates & proporcōns soe as in the whole it will coste the Lo. Mayor and Citizens at the least	7000 li"

Here may conveniently be added another document from the same source, which rests under even graver imputations against its genuineness. It professes to be a draught or abridged transcript of a warrant, appointing Robert Daiborne, William Shakespeare and others instructors of the Children of the Queen's Revels. But aside from the palæographic condemnation of the paper, its contents have been shown by Mr. Halliwell (in his *Curiosities of Shakespearian Criticism*, p. 22) to be entirely incongruous with the circumstances under which it professes to have been written.

"Right trusty and welbeloved, &c., James, &c. To all Mayors, Sheriffs, Justices of the Peace, &c. Whereas the Queene, our dearest wife, hath for her pleasure and recreation appointed her servaunts Robert Daiborne, &c. to provide and bring upp a convenient nomber of children, who shall be called the Children of her Majesties Revells, knowe ye that we have appointed and authorized, and by these presents doe appoint and authorize the said Robert Daiborne, William Shakespeare, Nathaniel Field, and Edward Kirkham, from time to time to provide and bring upp a convenient nomber of children, and them to instruct and exercise in the quality of playing Tragedies, Comedies, &c., by the name of the Children of the Revells to the Queene, within the Blackfryers, in our Citie of London, or els where within our realme of England. Wherefore we will and command you, and everie of you, to permitt her said servaunts to

ing to Sir Dudley Carleton at the Hague in 1619, mentions that the death of the Queen hinders the players from the exercise of their calling, and adds, "One speciale man among them, Burbadge, is lately dead, and hath left, they say, better than £300 land." Now, if Burbadge, who was but an actor, could acquire landed property to the value of £300 yearly, surely Shakespeare might well receive £100 more from all his sources of income. A chancery suit upon which Shakespeare was obliged to enter, apparently in 1612, for the protection of his interests in the tithes of Stratford and

keepe a convenient nomber of children, by the name of the Children of the Revells to the Queene, and them to exercise in the qualitie of playing according to her royal pleasure. Provided alwaies, that no playes, &c. shall be by them presented, but such playes, &c. as have received the approbation and allowance of our Maister of the Revells for the tyme being. And these our lres. shall be your sufficient warrant in this behalfe. In witnesse whereof, &c., 4° die Janij. 1609.

Bl Fr and globe Wh Fr and parish garden Curten and fortune Hope and Swanne	All in & neere London

"Proud povertie.	Engl tragedie.
Widow's mite.	False Friendes.
Antonio kinsmen.	Hate and love.
Triumph of Truth.	Taming of S.
Touchstone.	K. Edw 2.
Grissell.	

Stayed."

I here remark upon a hitherto unnoticed but very significant and suspicious fact in connection with this paper, and one of a very unpleasant nature for Mr. Collier. It will be observed that the list of plays which follows the essential part of the paper, and which is followed by the memorandum "Stayed," ends with "K. Edw 2." According to the fac-simile made by a fac-similist of high repute in London, this list is in a single line, and between the title of the last play and the word "Stayed" there is a blank space about two inches wide. Now, in the copy of this paper given in Mr. Collier's Life of Shakespeare (p. ccxxix.) "K. Edw 2" is followed by the name of another play, "Mirror of Life." Whence did Mr. Collier derive the name of that play, which does not exist upon the document itself as it appears in the Bridgewater MSS.? From a draught from which the Bridgewater MS. was written out? How else? For it must be noted that this is not an instance of error in reading or copying, but an absolute interpolation, like that in the letter of Mrs. Alleyn given on p. cclxxxviii of this volume. See the Southampton letter above referred to on p. 37 of Vol. II.

neighboring parishes, shows us that his receipts from that quarter were £60 (now full $1500) yearly.* To finish all that need be said about mere business transactions, in March, 161$\frac{2}{3}$, Shakespeare, in connection with "William Johnson citizein and vintner of London and John Jackson and John Hemynge gentlemen" purchased from "Henry Walker citizein and minstrell" a house and the land attached, not far from the Black-friars theatre; paying for it £140, of which £60 were left on bond and mortgage. Mr. Collier has reasonably conjectured that Shakespeare joined in this purchase to serve his fellow-actor, Heminge; and that Heminge and the two other purchasers not being able to discharge the amount which he had paid and assume the mortgage, the property fell to him. The deed of conveyance has a peculiar interest as bearing one of the four certainly authentic signatures of Shakespeare. It is now preserved in the library of the city of London, at Guildhall.

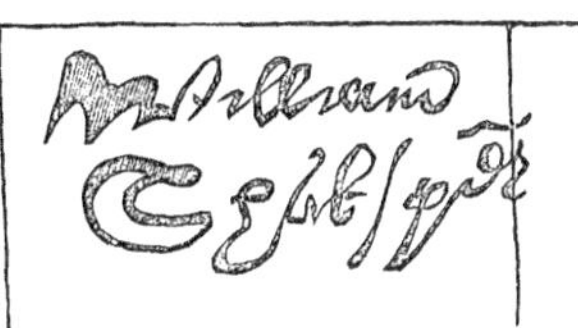

Shakespeare had been about eighteen years in London, and with the approach of his fortieth year was

* The Bill, which may be found at full length in Mr. Halliwell's *Life of Shakespeare*, furnishes the following single paragraph of interest: —

"—— and your oratour William Schackspeare hath an estate and interest of and in the moyty or one half of all tythes of corne and grayne aryseing within the townes, villages and ffields, and of and in the moity or half of all tythes of wool and lambs, and of all small and privy tythes, oblacions and alterages arisinge or increasing in Old Stratford, Bishopton, and Welcome, being in the said parishe of Stratford, or within the wholl parishe of Stratford uppon Avon aforesaid, for and during all the residue of the said terme, beinge of the yearly value of threescore pounds."

attaining the height of his reputation, when a club was established there, which owes a wide celebrity and perpetual fame chiefly to him, although there is no evidence that he was one of its members. It was founded by Sir Walter Raleigh, and met at the Mermaid — a favorite tavern in Bread Street. Here Raleigh himself, Jonson, Beaumont, Fletcher, Selden, Colton, Carew, Donne, and others their chosen companions met for social and convivial enjoyment; and that they did not admit Will Shakespeare of their crew, who can believe? Yet our confidence that he sat with them round that board which Beaumont celebrates in his well-known lines,* can only rest upon the moral impossibility that he should have been absent. There all students of the literature and manners of those days have reasonably agreed in placing the scene of the wit combats between Shakespeare and Jonson, the fame of which had reached Fuller's time, and caused him to imagine the encounter of the two like that between a Spanish great galleon and an English man-of-war; Jonson, like the former, built far higher in learning, and solid, but slow in his performances; Shakespeare, like the latter, less in bulk, but lighter in movement, turning and tacking nimbly, and taking every advantage by the

* "What things have we seen
Done at the Mermaid! heard words that have been
So nimble, and so full of subtle flame,
As if that every one from whom they came
Had meant to put his whole wit in a jest,
And had resolv'd to live a fool the rest
Of his dull life; then when there hath been thrown
Wit able enough to justify the town
For three days past, wit that might warrant be
For the whole city to talk foolishly
Till that were cancell'd, and, when that was gone,
We left an air behind us which alone
Was able to make the two next companies
Right witty, though but downright fools, more wise."
Letter to Ben Jonson.

quickness of his wit and invention. This, however, is only Fuller's imagination. We have no testimony as to the quality or the style of wit exhibited by either of these redoubted combatants; and all the pretended specimens of their colloquial jests and repartees that have reached us are so pitiably tame and forced that they are plainly foolish fabrications.

Of Shakespeare's social life during his long residence in London we have not even a tradition. We can form an idea of it only upon surmise. But at twenty-eight years of age he had won the respect of men very far above him in social position; and we may reasonably believe that his intercourse with people of the higher classes was not confined to casual meetings at the theatre and at taverns. Men of his personal qualities, rating him only at contemporary estimation, are too rare not to be welcomed in any society, unless there are special reasons for their exclusion. The very observable change in his representations of female character after the production of his earliest plays is such as would have been the natural result of association with women of a higher social culture than that of the female acquaintances of his youth; and I am inclined to the opinion that this elevated appreciation of woman is due to such intercourse, and that in some of his sonnets we have traces of an attachment between him and some lady whose regard for him was stronger than the restraints of morality and the barriers of society.

Tradition tells us that he went yearly to Stratford, where he left his wife and children. This may well have been. The interests which he looked after so carefully would be likely to take him into the society of his wife as often as once in a twelvemonth. Tradition also tells us that on his way back and forth on these dutiful journeys he used to stop in Oxford, at the Crown Tavern, which was kept by John Davenant, a grave and melancholy citizen who had to wife a beautiful and charming woman. Sir William Davenant, who was born in February, $160\frac{5}{6}$, was her son; and Shakespeare, it is said, was his godfather. And the story goes that one day an old townsman, seeing Will running homeward in great haste "to see his godfather Shakespeare," told him to be careful lest he took God's name in vain. This may all be true; but a story essentially the same is not uncommon in very old jest books. Indeed the humorous quibble is so apparent and so inviting, that if the tale is not as old as the custom of having fathers, it is only because it cannot be older than that of having godfathers. Now Sir William Davenant gave countenance to this report of his origin; but what credit shall be given to the testimony of a man who would welcome an aspersion upon his mother's reputation for the sake of being believed to write, by inheritance, "with the very spirit of Shakespeare," as he said he thought he did. Davenant was morally a poor creature, and in this he only did his kind.

Another story is also told of Shakespeare's fortunes with the sex. Having been long current as a tradition, it was afterwards found recorded in Manningham's diary among the Ashmolean MSS., under the date March 13th, 1601. It is, that a woman, "a citizen," seeing Richard Burbadge, the great actor of the day, play Richard III., was so carried away by her admiration that she asked him to visit her after the play — an invitation to supper from ladies to favorite actors being then not uncommon. Shakespeare overheard the appointment, (the custom of admitting spectators upon the stage during the performance must again be remembered,) and, resolving to supplant his friend, went to the rendezvous before him, announced himself as the crook-backed tyrant, and was as successful as his own hero in winning female favor under adverse circumstances. Burbadge arrived soon after, and sending word that Richard III. was at the door, received for answer, from a source as to which he could have had no doubt, that "William the Conqueror was before Richard III." But it was not by adventures of this kind that a soul like Shakespeare's could be satisfied; nor could it have been under the influence of women of this sort that with the advance of years the striking change above mentioned took place in the traits of his female characters.

V.

We are as ignorant, upon direct evidence, of the exact date at which Shakespeare at last withdrew from London to live at ease in Stratford, as we are of that at which he fled from Stratford to enter upon a life of irksome toil in London. But all circumstances which bear upon this question point to some time between 1610 and 1612. He retired from active life a wealthier man than he could reasonably have hoped to become when he entered it. He had achieved a fame and attained a social standing which must have been very far beyond his expectations; and he had won the favor and enjoyed the society of men of high rank and great public distinction. But yet even to William Shakespeare, with his surpassing genius, his worldly wisdom, his prudence and his thrift, all culminating in a success which made him the mark of envy at the end, as he had been at the beginning of his career,* life was unsatisfying. He returned to Stratford a disappointed man.

* The following passage in a tract called *Ratsei's Ghost, or the Second Part of his Mad Prankes and Robberies*, of which only one copy is known to exist,

The circumstances which limited his family to the children born at two births before he was of age were aggravated by the loss of the only boy his wife had brought him. He had no son to bear his name, to inherit his property, to glory in his fame, and to be the third gentleman of his family. His daughters, rustic born and rustic bred, were not fitted for circles in which they might otherwise have been sought as wives by men of the position to which their father had raised himself. He saw them married rather late in life to simple village folk, and he resigned himself to simple village society, — wisely, perhaps, but yet, we may be sure, not without a pang and that sense of wrong which afflicts so many of us at the unequal and incongruous distribution of means and opportunities. It must have been with bitterness of soul that he saw the disappearance of his hopes of being the head of a family ranking among the gentry of England.

Rowe says that the latter part of his life was spent,

plainly refers, first to Burbadge and next to Shakespeare. The book is without date, but is believed to have been printed before 1606. Gamaliel Ratsey, who speaks, is a highwayman who has paid some strollers 40 *s.* for playing before him, and afterward robbed them of their fee. The author was probably some inferior player or playwright to whom Shakespeare had been chary of his money and his companionship.

"And for you, sirrah, (says he to the chiefest of them,) thou hast a good presence upon a stage, methinks thou darkenst thy merit by playing in the country: get thee to London, for if one man were dead, they will have much need of such as thou art. There would be none, in my opinion, fitter than thyself to play his parts: my conceit is such of thee, that I durst all the money in my purse on thy head to play Hamlet with him for a wager. There thou shalt learne to be frugal (for players were never so thrifty as they are now about London), and to feed upon all men; to let none feed upon thee; to make thy hand a stranger to thy pocket, thy heart slow to perform thy tongue's promise; and when thou feelest thy purse well lined, buy thee some place of lordship in the country; that, growing weary of playing, thy money may there bring thee to dignity and reputation: then thou needest care for no man; no, not for them that before made thee proud with speaking their [thy] words on the stage. Sir, I thank you (quoth the player) for this good council: I promise you I will make use of it, for I have heard, indeed, of some that have gone to London very meanly, and have come in time to be exceeding wealthy."

as all men of good sense will wish theirs may be, in ease, retirement, and the conversation (i. e. the society, the intercourse) of his friends. He adds that "his pleasurable wit and good nature engaged him in the acquaintance and entitled him to the friendship of the gentlemen of the neighborhood." And Mr. Fullom tells us that the Lucys have lately discovered that his quarrel with their family was made up, and that he lived on pleasant terms with Sir Thomas, the son of his ancient enemy. But this story, though not very improbable, rests on vague and untrustworthy evidence. The very profession which had brought Shakespeare his wealth and his eminence, although it might have given him a certain success in London, would have operated against him as a retired gentleman in a rural community so tinged with Puritanism as that in and about Stratford. Again I remark that it is to this prejudice and to Shakespeare's desire to stand with the world as a gentleman of substance and character, and not as an actor and playwright, that we must attribute his neglect of his dramas after they had discharged their double function of filling his pockets and giving his brain employment and his soul expression. Indifference to the literary fate of their works was common among the playwrights of that day; but to this custom was added, in Shakespeare's case, a motive. The Reverend John Ward, who was made Vicar of Stratford in 1662, records a tradition that Shakespeare in his retirement supplied the stage with two plays every year, and lived at the rate of £1000. This is quite surely but a gross exaggeration of the facts, both as to the rate of his expenditure and the amount of his dramatic labor. We have seen that his income was about £400, though it was rather over than under that then handsome sum; and only three of his plays, *The Tempest*, *The Winter's*

Tale, and *Henry the Eighth*, were produced after his retirement to Stratford. The last of these was brought out at the Globe Theatre, as a spectacle piece, on the 29th of June, 1613; and during its performance the theatre took fire from the discharge of the chambers during one of the pageants, and was burned to the ground.* It is an interesting coincidence that the first performance of the last play that came from Shakespeare's pen was the occasion of the destruction of that "wooden O" in which he had won so many of his imperishable laurels.

Shakespeare is said to have put his poetical powers to use during his later Stratford years in writing epitaphs for friends and neighbors. Such an employment of his pen would be natural. The following verses upon the tomb of Sir Thomas Stanley in Tonge Church are attributed to him by Dugdale in his *History of Warwickshire*. It is possible that he wrote epitaphs no better.

"*Written upon the east end of the Tomb.*

"Ask who lies here, but do not weep;
He is not dead, he doth but sleep.
This stony register is for his bones;
His fame is more perpetual than these stones:
And his own goodness, with himself being gone,
Shall live when earthly monument is none.

"*Written on the west end thereof.*

"Not monumental stone preserves our fame,
Nor sky-aspiring pyramids our name.
The memory of him for whom this stands
Shall out-live marble and defacers' hands.
When all to time's consumption shall be given,
Stanley, for whom this stands, shall stand in heaven."

* See the Introduction to *King Henry the Eighth*, Vol. VIII. p. 319.

Rowe tells us of a tradition that John a Combe, of whose residence and habits something has been said in the earlier part of these Memoirs, told Shakespeare laughingly at a sociable gathering that he fancied he meant to write his epitaph if he happened to outlive him, and begged the poet to perform his task immediately. Upon which Shakespeare gave him these now well-known verses: —

" Ten in the hundred lies here in-grav'd;
'Tis a hundred to ten his soul is not sav'd:
If any man ask, Who lies in this tomb?
Oh ho, quoth the Devil, 'tis my John a Combe."

Much the same story had reached Aubrey's ears, and was of course duly recorded. But according to Aubrey the epitaph was written at a tavern on occasion of the funeral of its subject, and was in these words: —

" Ten in the hundred the Devil allows,
But Combe will have twelve, he swears and he vows.
If any one ask, Who lies in this tomb?
Ho! quoth the Devil, 'tis my John a Combe."

Rowe says that the sharpness of the satire so stung the man that he never forgave it. This, at least, is untrue. Shakespeare and his wealthier neighbor of Stratford College were good friends to the end of the latter's life. John a Combe's will is extant, and in it Shakespeare is remembered by a bequest of five pounds, and Shakespeare himself left his sword to Thomas, John a Combe's nephew. It must be remembered that in those times all interest was called usury, i. e. money paid for the *use* of money, and John a Combe's will is that of a man of true benevolence and mindful friendship. He forgives debts, makes wide and generous provision for the poor, and remembers with much particularity a large circle of friends among the knights, esquires, and gentlemen of his neighborhood.* This jest, turning upon ten in the hundred, (the usual interest at that time,) and a hundred to ten in favor of the Devil, was an old and a common one among our forefathers ; and consequently it has been generally supposed that this epitaph is a fabrication which was foisted upon Shakespeare. But I am inclined to think that he did crack this innocent joke upon his friend, using, as he would be likely to use, an old, well-known jest, and giving it a new turn upon the money-lender's name. For Shakespeare was not always writing *Hamlet*. "'Tis my John a Combe" involves of course the sharp punning jest, 'tis my John ha' come.†

A project for the enclosing of some common lands near Stratford brings Shakespeare forward in 1614 as a man of weight and consideration in his neighborhood.

* Mr. Halliwell discovered among the Ashmolean MSS. one "written," as he says, "not many years after the death of Shakespeare," in which this version of the above anecdote appears : —

"*On John Combe, a coveteous rich man, Mr. Wm. Shak-spear wright this att his request while hee was yett liveing for his epitaphe.*

"Who lies in this tombe ?
Hough, quoth the devil, tis my sone John a Combe
Finis.

"*But being dead and making the poor his heires, hee after wrightes this for his epitaph.*

"Howere he lived judge not,
John Combe shall never be forgott
While poore hath memmorye, for he did gather
To make the poore his issue : he their father,
As record of his tilth and seedes,
Did crowne him in his later needes.
Finis. W. Shak."

† Mr. Hunter says that the verses are "allusive to the double sense of the word *Combe*, as the name of the person there interred, and also the name of a certain measure of corn ; " and this explanation has been hitherto accepted. What point is there in likening John a Combe to a measure of corn ?

It touched his interests in his own acres and in his tithes so closely, that he said to one of the numerous Greenes of Stratford that "he was not able to bear the enclosing of Welcombe." His kinsman Greene, the attorney, who was clerk of Stratford, records in his note book this almost the only speech of Shakespeare which has been authoritatively handed down to us. Shakespeare took all possible measures to secure his threatened interests; and there exists an agreement between him and William Replingham, who appears to have been one of the movers in the affair, by which the latter agrees to make good any damage which the former may receive by the proposed enclosure.* The corporation of Stratford were also opposed to this measure,

* "*Coppy of the articles with Mr. Shakspeare.*

"Vicesimo octavo die Octobris, anno Domini 1614. Articles of agreement made [and] indented between William Shackespeare of Stretforde in the County of Warwick gent. on the one partye, and William Replingham of Great Harborow in the County of Warwick gent. on the other partie, the daye and yeare above said.

"*Item*, the said William Replingham for him, his heires, executors and assignes, doth covenaunte and agree to and with the saide William Shackspeare his heires and assignes, That he, the said William Replingham, his heires or assignes, shall uppon reasonable request, satisfie, content, and make recompense unto him the said William Shackespeare or his assignes, for all such losse, detriment, and hinderance as he the said William Shackespeare, his heirs and assignes, and one Thomas Greene gent. shall or maye be thought in the viewe and judgement of foure indifferent persons, to be indifferentlie elected by the said William and William and their heires, and in default of the said William Replingham, by the said William Shackespeare or his heires onely, to survey and judge the same to sustayne or incurre for or in respecte of the increasinge of the yearlie value of the tythes they the said William Shackespeare and Thomas doe joyntlie or severallie hold and enjoy in the said fieldes or anie of them, by reason of anie inclosure or decaye of tyllage there ment and intended by the said William Replingham; and that the said William Replingham and his heirs shall procure such sufficient securitie unto the said William Shackespeare and his heires for the performance of theis covenauntes, as shall bee devised by learned counsell. In witnes whereof the parties abovsaid to theis presentes interchangeablie their handes and seales have put, the daye and yeare first above wrytten.

"Sealed and delivered in the presence of us,

Tho. Lucas,
Jo. Rogers,
Anthonie Nasshe,
Mich. Olney."

alleging that it would press heavily upon the poorer classes, already distressed by a destructive fire which took place in that town in 1613, but which seems to have left Shakespeare's property untouched. In the autumn of 1614, Thomas Greene was in London about this business; and by one of his memorandums we know that Shakespeare arrived there on the 16th of November of that year, probably upon the same errand. Greene's memorandums show that he was in constant communication with his "cosen Shakespeare" upon this subject, and that the corporation counted much upon their distinguished townsman's influence in the matter.* He remained in London until after the 23d of December in that year: we hear of him from the same authority in the negotiations of 1615, with regard to the same affair, which was not settled until 1618; and this is the last known contemporary record of the life of the great poet of all time.

His younger daughter, Judith, was married on the 11th of February, 161$\frac{5}{6}$, to Thomas Quiney, a vintner of Stratford, and son of the Thomas Quiney who in 1598 had asked Shakespeare to lend him £30. On the 25th of the following March he executed his will, which an erased date shows that he had intended executing on the 25th of the preceding January; and on the 23d of April, 1616, William Shakespeare, of Stratford on Avon, in the county of Warwick, Gentleman, died.

* "1614. Jovis, 17 No. My cosen Shakspear comyng yesterdy to Town, I went to see him how he did. He told me that they assured him they ment to inclose no further than to Gospell Bush, and so upp straight (leavying out part of the Dyngles to the ffield) to the gate in Clopton hedg, and take in Salisburyes peece; and that they mean in Aprill to survey the land, and then to gyve satisfaccion, and not before; and he and Mr. Hall say they think ther will be nothyng done at all."

"23. Dec. A hall. Lettres wrytten, one to Mr Manyring, another to Mr Shakspear, with almost all the company's hands to eyther. I also wrytte myself to my cosen Shakspear the coppyes of all our acts, and then also a not of the inconvenyences wold happen by the inclosure."

Of the cause of his death we only know what Vicar Ward aforesaid heard and noted down half a century after the event. His account is: "Shakespeare, Drayton, and Ben Jonson had a merrie meeting, and it seems drank too hard, for Shakespeare died of a feavour ther contracted." We shrink from the thought of such a close of Shakespeare's life. But looking back upon the manners of the time, and especially its convivial habits, and the inordinate quantities of wine and strong ale then drunk by all who could procure them, we must admit that to die of fever after festivity might have been the fate of any man. Men now living can remember when no person entered a house, at any time, the family of which were not very poor, without being offered and expected to drink some spirituous liquor; cake and wine having been brought forward even to our mothers at morning calls. And Spence tells us in his *Anecdotes*, on the authority of Pope, that Cowley the poet died as Ward says Shakespeare died, but from potations in more reverend, though perhaps not more worshipful company. He and Dean Sprat, afterward Bishop of Rochester, "had been together," Spence says, "to see a neighbor of Cowley's, who (according to the fashion of those times) made them too welcome. They did not set out for their walk home until it was too late, and had drunk so deep that they lay out in the fields all night. This gave Cowley the fever that carried him off. The parish still talk of the drunken Dean." And in the Chamberlain's accounts of Stratford, among the frequent charges for sack and sugar, claret and beer, for such worshipful folk as Sir Fulke Greville and Sir Thomas Lucy, and even Lady Lucy, is one in 1614 for "on quart of sack and on quart of clarett wine geven to a preacher at the New Place," Shakespeare's own house. These considerations make the alleged excess at such a merry meeting of poets as that Ward tells of, a venial sin, and the sad consequences, though uncertain, not improbable.

Shakespeare's remains were interred the second day after his death, the 25th of April, in Stratford church, just before the chancel rail. Above his grave, on the north wall of the church, a monument was erected, at what exact date we do not know; but it was before 1623, as it is mentioned by Leonard Digges in his verses prefixed to the first folio edition of Shakespeare's plays.* The monument shows a bust of the poet in the act of writing. Upon a tablet below the bust is the following inscription:

IVDICIO PYLIVM, GENIO SOCRATEM, ARTE MARONEM,
TERRA TEGIT, POPVLVS MÆRET, OLYMPVS HABET.

STAY PASSENGER, WHY GOEST THOV BY SO FAST?
READ IF THOV CANST, WHOM ENVIOVS DEATH HATH PLAST,
WITH IN THIS MONVMENT SHAKSPEARE WITH WHOME
QVICK NATVRE DIDE: WHOSE NAME DOTH DECK YS TOMBE
FAR MORE THEN COST: SIEH ALL, YT HE HATH WRITT,
LEAVES LIVING ART, BVT PAGE, TO SERVE HIS WITT.

OBIIT ANO DOI 1616
ÆTATIS 53 DIE 23 AP.

The last line of this inscription, and a tradition unheard of until Oldys wrote his notes in Langbaine, have raised the question whether Shakespeare died on the same day of the month on which he is supposed to have been born. But what matter whether he lived a day more or less than fifty-two full years? He had lived long

* See Preliminary Matter in Vol. II.

enough. His work was done, and he had tasted, nay, had drained, life's cup of bitter-sweet. Dugdale tells us that his monument was the work of Gerard Johnson, an eminent sculptor of the period; others have attributed it to Thomas Stanton; and experts have supposed that the face was modelled from a cast taken after death.

Be this as it may, the bust must be accepted as the most authentic likeness that we have of Shakespeare. It was originally colored after life. The eyes were light hazel, the hair and beard auburn, the complexion fair; the doublet was scarlet; the tabard, or loose gown without sleeves thrown over the doublet, black; the neck and wristbands white; the upper side of the cushion green, the under, crimson; its cord and tassels, gilt. The colors were renewed in 1749; but in 1793 Malone, tastelessly and ignorantly classic, had the whole figure painted white by a house-painter. A flat stone covers the grave. Upon it is the following strange inscription:

GOOD FREND FOR IESVS SAKE FORBEARE,
TO DIGG THE DVST ENCLOASED HEARE:
BLESE BE Y^{E} MAN Y^{T} SPARES THES STONES,
AND CVRST BE HE Y^{T} MOVES MY BONES.

A Mr. Dowdall, in an existing letter to Mr. Edward Southwell, dated April 10th, 1692, says that these lines were written by the poet himself a little before his death. Dowdall plainly records a tradition which possibly may have been well founded. It is more probable, however, that to prevent the removal of Shakespeare's remains to the charnel-house of the church, when time made other demands upon the space they occupied, in compliance with a custom of the day and place, some member of his family, or some friend, had this rude, hearty curse cut upon his tomb-stone. Tradition, not traceable higher than 1693, says his wife and daughters earnestly desired to be laid in the same grave with him, but that "not one for fear of the curse above said dare touch his grave-stone." It has had one good effect, at least. It has kept at Stratford those relics which but for it would probably have been removed to Westminster Abbey.

Shakespeare's wife and his two daughters — Susannah, married to Dr. Hall, and Judith, married to Thomas Quiney — survived him. His granddaughter, Elizabeth Hall, who also was living at the time of his death, was twice married; first, to Thomas Nash, an esquire of Stratford, and afterward to Mr. John Barnard of Abington in Northamptonshire, who was knighted by Charles II. in 1661; but she had no children. Judith had three sons, who died unmarried; and with Lady Barnard, who died in 1669-70, Shakespeare's family became extinct. His property was strictly entailed upon the male issue of his daughter Susannah, which failed to appear. The entail was broken by legal contrivance; and soon after the death of Lady Barnard, the estate which he had gathered with so much labor and solicitude was dispersed. New Place, which was the home of his later years, was distinguished, in Lady Barnard's time, by the brief residence there of Queen Henrietta Maria, during the troubles of the Great Revolution. Mr. and Mrs. Nash entertained the Queen there for three weeks, in June, 1643, when, escorted by Prince Rupert and his troops, she was on her progress to join King Charles at Oxford — an incident which would have been well pleasing to Mistress Nash's grandfather. Afterward, as we have already seen, New Place fell into the hands of Sir Hugh Clopton, a descendant of its builder, who renovated and altered it; and it was finally bought by the Reverend Francis Gastrell as his residence. He lived there several years, much annoyed by curious pilgrims to his house and to his garden, in which there was a mulberry tree, which, according to the tradition of the town, Shakespeare planted with his own hands. This Reverend gentleman was wealthy enough to indulge in that very expensive luxury, a high temper. So at last he gave his vexation vent by cutting down the mulberry tree,* and afterward, in 1759, having quarrelled with the magistrates about assessments, he razed his house to the ground, and left the place, a petty ecclesiastic Erostratus, hooted and execrated by the Stratford people. Thus, within less than one hundred and fifty years of his death, all trace of Shakespeare had disappeared from Stratford, except his birthplace and his tomb.

This is all that we know by authentic record, by tradition, and by inference of him who stands alone in the highest niche of literary fame. But this is much. It seems little only because of his greatness. Of many men not to be thought of in comparison with him, we know indeed much more, and in these days, when every man seems, like Pepys, to be his own Boswell, we are likely to know all; but of many who occupy a place only second to his, we know much less. The causes of our ignorance of Shakespeare's life are partly the Puritanism which developed itself in the mother country during his life, and the consequent political convulsions which came so soon after his death, and lasted so long; partly the frivolous and grovelling taste of the literary and dramatic school which came in with the Restoration, and prevailed for more than half a century, and which

* The wood of this tree was bought by a watchmaker of Stratford, who made it into boxes and similar articles. It must have attained an enormous size; for there is enough of it extant to make a line-of-battle ship. But my piece and yours, reader, are genuine.

cared little about the works and less about the life of William Shakespeare; partly, too, we may be sure, a desire on his part, characteristic of all cultivated people of English race, to keep personal affairs from publicity. But the effect of these causes is small in comparison with the results of the indifference which prevailed among people of all ages and countries, until within the last hundred or hundred and fifty years, to the personal character and private lives of poets, painters, scientific men, and generally of all public persons not concerned in government. We know more of Shakespeare than the Greeks knew of Æschylus, the father of their tragedy, or of Aristophanes, the father of their comedy, two centuries after they died. Public functions partially preserved the personal history of Sophocles from similar obscurity. Of Molière, the greatest and most original of French dramatic writers, there is almost equal ignorance; and it is remarkable that not a page of his manuscripts is known to be in existence. The personal history of Shakespeare's great contemporary Bacon is well known; but had he not become the king's Attorney General, Sir Francis Bacon, Lord Verulam, Viscount St. Albans, and Lord High Chancellor of England, Master Bacon might have written his Essays and worked out his Novum Organon in happy unobserved obscurity, and the world might have begun to inquire into his every-day life only after it had discovered that he was the greatest philosopher of modern times. Of Shakespeare's fellow-craftsmen we are yet more ignorant than we are of him. Of Beaumont and Fletcher, both born in the rank of gentry, one the son of a Judge, the other of a Bishop, we know little more than that they wrote their plays and lived in the society of the most intelligent men of their day. Chapman's associations and what he did are discovered only by indirect collateral evidence; but eminent as he was, and highly esteemed as he appears to have been, nothing is recorded of his personal history. We are obliged to infer the year of his birth from the record of his age upon his portrait; and time has left us no guide-post to his birthplace. The minor stars of the Elizabethan galaxy, the Greenes, Peeles, Marlowes, Websters, Fords, and such like, left hardly a trace behind them which their own pens had not written. Ben Jonson, who lived to see all the poets of the Elizabethan period in their graves, and to be an object of literary and almost antiquarian interest to a new generation and a new school, left more materials for his memoirs than any contemporary poet. But it is only with his later years that we are thus acquainted. Of his youth and early manhood we are not less ignorant than we are of Shakespeare's.

Unlike Dante, unlike Milton, unlike Goethe, unlike the great poets and tragedians of Greece and Rome, Shakespeare left no trace upon the political, or even the social life of his era. Of his eminent countrymen Raleigh, Sidney, Spenser, Bacon, Cecil, Walsingham, Coke, Camden, Hooker, Drake, Hobbes, Inigo Jones, Herbert of Cherbury, Laud, Pym, Hampden, Selden, Walton, Wotton, and Donne may be properly reckoned as his contemporaries; and yet there is no evidence whatever that he was personally known to either of these men, or to any others of less note among the statesmen, scholars, soldiers, and artists of his day, except the few of his fellow-craftsmen whose acquaintance with him has been heretofore mentioned in these Memoirs.

Shakespeare's character, entirely free from those irregularities which are usually, but unreasonably, regarded as almost the necessary concomitants of genius, seems to have been of singular completeness and of perfect balance. Of his transcendent mental gifts, the results of the daily labor by which he first earned his bread and then made his fortune remain as evidence; and what else we know of him shows him to us, in the common business and intercourse of life, upright, prudent, self-respecting; a man to be respected and relied upon. An actor at a time when actors were held in the lowest possible esteem, he won the kind regard and consideration of those who held high rank and station: a poet, he was not only thrifty but provident. Though careful of his own, he was not only just, but generous, to others. His integrity was early noticed; and Jonson says "he was indeed honest, and of an open and free nature." Surpassing all his rivals, after the recoil of the first surprise he was loved by all except the meanest souls among them; and such men only love themselves. 'Sweet' and 'gentle' are the endearing epithets which they delighted to apply to him. In his position, to have produced this effect upon high and low, he must have united a native dignity to a singular kindness of heart, evenness of temper, and graciousness of manner. His ready wit and his cheerfulness in social intercourse are particularly mentioned in tradition. To these qualities it is plain that he added a sympathy that was universal — a gift which more than any other wins the love of all mankind. And, indeed, it is to the effect of this moral quality that we owe the complete and multitudinous manifestation of his intellectual greatness. The Reverend Mr. Davies, writing after 1688, says that "he died a papist." If he became a member of the Church of Rome, it must have been after he wrote *Romeo and Juliet*, in which he speaks of "evening mass;" for the humblest member of that church knows that there is no mass at vespers. The expression used by Davies implies, indeed, that Shakespeare died in a faith in which he had not been educated. But his report is improbable. In the over-much righteousness of the puritanical period in which Shakespeare's last years were passed, a moderate degree of cheerfulness and Christian charity, to say nothing of conformity to the Church of England, might easily have brought the reproach of papistry upon men less open to suspicion than a retired player. Shakespeare, although he seems to have been a man of sincere piety, seems also to have been without religious convictions. His works are imbued with a high and heartfelt appreciation of the vital truths of Christianity; but nowhere does he show a leaning towards any form of religious observance, or of church government, or toward any theological tenet or dogma. No church can claim him; no simple Christian soul but can claim his fellowship. Such, as this imperfect record shows, was William Shakespeare; a man who adorned an inferior and dignified an equivocal station in life, and who raised himself from poverty and obscurity to competence and honorable position by labors which, having their motive not in desire of fame, but in duty and in manly independence, have placed him upon an enduring eminence to which in after ages sane ambition does not aspire.

Globe Theatre.

Chancel of Stratford Church, with Shakespeare's Monument.

SHAKESPEARE'S WILL.*

Vicesimo quinto die *Martii*,† Anno Regni Domini nostri Jacobi nunc Regis Angliæ, &c. decimo quarto, et Scotiæ xlix°. Annoque Domini 1616.

T. W^mj Shackspeare

In the name of god, Amen! I William Shackspeare of Stratford upon Avon, in the countie of warr. gent, in perfect health and memorie, god be praysed! doe make and Ordayne this my last will and testament in manner and forme followeing; That ys to saye, First I Comend my Soule into the handes of god my Creator, hoping, and assuredlie beleeving, through thonelie merites of Jesus Christe my Saviour, to be made partaker of lyfe everlastinge, And my bodye to the Earth whereof yt ys made. Item, I Gyve and bequeath unto my Daughter ‡ Judyth, One hundred and Fyftie poundes of lawfull English money, to be paied unto her in manner and forme followeing, That ys to saye, One hundred poundes *in discharge of her marriage porcion* within one yeare after my deceas, with consideracion after the Rate of twoe Shillinges in the pound for soe long tyme as the same shalbe unpaied unto her after my deceas, and the Fyftie poundes Residewe thereof, upon her Surrendring *of* or gyving of such sufficient Securitie as the overseers of this my Will shall like of, to Surrender or graunte All her estate and Right that shall discend or come unto her after my desceas, or *that shee* nowe hath, of in or to one Copiehold tenemente with thappurtenaunces, lyeing and being in Stratford upon Avon aforesaied, in the saied county

* The will is on three sheets of paper, fastened together at the top. The poet's name is signed at the bottom of the first and of the second sheet, and his final signature is near the middle of the third sheet. Malone was of opinion that he signed the last sheet first, and that his hand grew gradually weaker in signing the second and first pages. The words printed in Italics are those which in the original are interlined.

† Originally written, "*Januarii.*"

‡ Originally, "*sonne and* daughter."

of warr. being parcell or holden of the mannour of Rowington, unto my Daughter Susanna Hall, and her heires for ever. Item, I Gyve and bequeath unto my saied Daughter Judith One hundred and Fyftie Poundes more, if shee, or Anie issue of her bodie, be Lyvinge att thend of three yeares next ensueing the Daie of the Date of this my Will, during which tyme my executours to paie her consideracion from my deceas according to the Rate aforesaied; And if she dye within the saied tearme without issue of her bodye, then my will ys, and I Doe gyve and bequeath One Hundred Poundes thereof to my Neece Elizabeth Hall, and the Fiftie Poundes to be sett fourth by my executours during the lief of my Sister Johane Harte, and the use and proffitt thereof Cominge, shalbe payed to my saied Sister Jone, and after her deceas the said l[li]. shall Remaine Amongst the children of my saied Sister Equallie to be Devided Amongst them; But if my saied Daughter Judith be lyving att thend of the saied three Yeares, or anie yssue of her bodye, then my will ys, and soe I Devise and bequeath the saied Hundred and Fyftie Poundes to be sett out *by my executors and overseers* for the best benefitt of her and her issue, and *the stock* not *to be* paied unto her soe long as she shalbe marryed and Covert Baron; but my will ys, that she shall have the consideracion yearelie paied unto her during her lief, and after her deceas, the saied stock and consideracion to bee paied to her children, if she have Anie, and if not, to her executours or assignes, she lyving the saied terme after my deceas: Provided that yf such husbond as she shall att thend of the saied three yeares be marryed unto, or at anie [time] after, doe sufficientlie Assure unto her, and thissue of her bodie landes Answereable to the porcion by this my will gyven unto her, and to be adjudged soe by my executours and overseers, then my will ys, that the said Cl[li]. shalbe paied to such husbond as shall make such assurance, to his owne use. Item, I gyve and bequeath unto my saied sister Jone xx[li], and all my wearing Apparrell, to be paied and delivered within one yeare after my Deceas; And I doe will and devise unto her *the house* with thappurtenaunces in Stratford, wherein she dwelleth, for her natural lief, under the yearlie rent of xij[d]. Item, I gyve and bequeath unto her three sonnes, William Harte, [Thomas *] Hart, and Michaell Harte, Fyve Poundes Apeece, to be paied within one Yeare after my decease.† Item, I gyve and bequeath unto *the saied Elizabeth Hall* ‡ All my plate, *except my brod silver and gilt bole*, that I now have att the Date of this my will. Item, I gyve and bequeath unto the Poore of Stratford aforesaied tenn poundes; to Mr. Thomas Combe my Sword; to Thomas Russell, Esquier, Fyve pounds; and to Frauncis Collins of the Borough of warr. in the countie of warr. gentleman, thirteene poundes Sixe shillinges and Eight pence, to be paied within one Yeare after my Deceas. Item, I gyve and bequeath to *Hamlett Sadler* § xxvi^{s} viij^{d}, to buy him A Ringe; to *William Raynoldes*, gent. xxvi^{s} viij^{d}, *to buy him A Ringe;* to my godson William Walker xx^{s} in gold; to Anthonye Nashe, gent. xxvi^{s} viij^{d}; and to Mr. John Nashe, xxvi^{s} viij^{d}; ‖ *and to my Fellowes, John Hemynges, Richard Burbage, and Henry Cundell*, xxvi^{s} viij^{d} *Apeece, to buy them ringes.* Item, I Gyve, will, bequeath, and devise, unto my daughter Susanna Hall, *for better enabling of her to performe this my will, and towardes the performans thereof*, All that Capital messuage or tenemente, with thappurtenances, *in Stratford aforesaid*, Called the new place, wherein I nowe Dwell, and two Messuages or tenementes, with thappurtenaunces, scituat, lyeing, and being in Henley-streete, within the borough of Stratford aforesaied; And all my barnes, stables, Orchardes, gardens, landes, tenementes, and hereditamentes whatsoever, scituat, lyeing, and being, or to be had, Receyved, perceyved, or taken, within the townes, Hamletes, Villages, Fieldes, and groundes of Stratford upon Avon, Oldstratford, Bushopton, and Welcombe, or in anie of them, in the said countie of warr. And alsoe All that messuage or tenemente, with thappurtenaunces, wherein One John Robinson dwelleth, scituat, lyeng, and being, in the blackfriers in London nere the Wardrobe; and all other my landes, tenementes, and hereditamentes whatsoever: To have and to hold All and singular the saied premisses, with their appurtenaunces, unto the saied Susanna Hall, for and during the terme of her naturall lief; and after her deceas to the first sonne of her bodie law-

* This Christian name is omitted in the original will, but, like "time" above, appears in the copy of the probate.

† The following words were here at first inserted, but afterwards cancelled: "to be sett out for her within one yeare after my decease by my executours with thadvice and direccions of my overseers, for her best profitt, until her marriage, and then the same with the increase thereof to be paied unto her."

‡ Originally, "*her*."

§ Originally, "*Mr. Richard Tyler thelder*."

‖ Originally, "xxvi^{s} *in gold*."

fulle yssueinge, and to the heires Males of the bodie of the saied first Sonne lawfully yssueinge; and for defalt of such issue, to the second Sonne of her bodie lawfullie issueinge, and to the heires males of the bodie of the said Second Sonne lawfully yssueing; and for defalt of such heires, to the third Sonne of the bodie of the saied Susanna Lawfullie yssueinge, and to the heires males of the bodie of the saied third sonne lawfullie yssueing; And for defalt of such issue, the same soe to be and Remaine to the Fourth,* Fyfth, sixte, and Seaventh sonnes of her body, lawfullie issueinge one after Another, and to the heires Males of the bodies of the said Fourth, fifth, Sixte, and Seaventh sonnes lawfullie yssueing, in such manner as yt is before Lymitted to be and Remaine to the first, second, and third Sonns of her bodie, and to their heires Males; And for defalt of such issue, the saied premisses to be and Remaine to my sayed Neece Hall, and the heires Males of her bodie lawfullie yssueing; And for defalt of such issue, to my Daughter Judith and the heires Males of her bodie lawfullie issueinge, And for defalt of such issue, to the Right heires of me the saied William Shackspeare for ever. *Item, I gyve unto my wief my second best bed, with the furniture.* Item, I gyve and bequeath to my saied Daughter Judith my broad silver gilt bole. All the rest of my goodes, Chattel, Leases, plate, Jewels, and houshold stuffe whatsoever, after my Dettes and Legacies paied, and my funerall expences discharged, I gyve, devise, and bequeath to my Sonne-in-Lawe, John Hall, gent. and my Daughter Susanna his wief, whom I ordaine and make executours of this my Last will and testament. And I doe intreat and Appoint *the saied* Thomas Russell, Esquier, and FraunCis Collins, gent. to be overseers hereof, And doe Revoke All former wills,

* Originally, "Fourtn *sonne.*"

and publishe this to be my last will and testament. In Witness whereof I have hereunto put my *hand*,* the Daie and Yeare first above written.

By me William Shakspeare

Witnes to the publyshing hereof,

FRA: COLLYNS
JULYUS SHAWE
JOHN ROBINSON
HAMNET SADLER
ROBERT WHATTCOTT

Probatum coram Magistro Willielmo Byrde, Legum Doctore Comiss. &c. xxjj.[do] die mensis Junii, Anno Domini 1616; juramento Johannis Hall, unius executorum &c. cui &c. de bene &c. jurat. reservat. potestate &c. Susannæ Hall, alteri executorum &c. cum venerit petitur, (Inv[t]. ex[t].)

* Originally, "*Seale*."

CHRONOLOGICAL TABLE

OF SHAKESPEARE'S WORKS.

[The appearance of the title of a play between brackets indicates the first form of a play afterward rewritten.]

	Probable Date of Writing.	Date of First Mention or Publication.
Venus and Adonis,	1584–5,	1593, first quarto.
The Passionate Pilgrim,	1584–6,	1599, first quarto.
[*Part I. of the Contention, &c.*], [*The True Tragedy, &c.*], Titus Andronicus, [*Taming of a Shrew*],	1587–9,	1592, Greene's Groats-worth of Wit. (1594, first quarto?) 1598, Meres's Palladis Tamia.
Love's Labour's Lost,	1588–9,	1598, Meres's Pall. Tamia.
Comedy of Errors,	1589,	1598, Meres's " "
[*Love's Labour's Won*],	1589,	1598, Meres's " "
The Two Gentlemen of Verona,	1589–90,	1598, Meres's " "
King Henry the Sixth, Part I., " " Part II., " " Part III.,	1590–91,	1623, first folio. 1623, first folio. 1623, first folio.
Sonnets,	1590?–1605?,	1609, first quarto.
[*Romeo and Juliet* (?)],	1591–2.	
Lucrece,	1593,	1594, first quarto.
Richard the Third,	1593,	1597, first quarto.
[*All's Well that Ends Well*],	1593-4.	
A Midsummer-Night's Dream,	1594,	1598, Meres's Pall. Tamia.
The Merchant of Venice,	1594,	1598, Meres's " "
Richard the Second,	1594–5,	1598, Meres's " "
Romeo and Juliet,	1596,	1597, first quarto.
King John,	1596,	1598, Meres's Pall. Tamia.
King Henry the Fourth, Part I.,	1596,	1598, first quarto.
" " " Part II.,	1597,	1598, Stationers' Register.
[*Troilus and Cressida?*],	1597–8,	1602, " "
[*The Merry Wives of Windsor*],	1598,	1602, first quarto.
Much Ado about Nothing,	1598–9,	1600, first quarto.
Twelfth Night,	1599,	1601, Manningham's D'ry.
Henry the Fifth,	1599,	1600, first quarto.
As You Like It,	1599,	1600, Stationers' Register.
Hamlet,	1600,	1603, first quarto.
The Taming of the Shrew,	1601,	1623, first folio.

Pericles,	1602,	1609, first quarto.
The Merry Wives of Windsor,	1603,	1623, first folio.
Measure for Measure,	1603–4,	1604, Acc't of Rev'ls at C't.
All's Well that Ends Well,	1604,	1623, first folio.
A Lover's Complaint,	1605 (?),	1609, first quarto.
King Lear,	1605,	1607, Stationers' Register.
Timon of Athens,	1605–7,	1623, first folio.
Macbeth,	1605,	1610, Forman's Diary.
Julius Cæsar,		1623, first folio.
Antony and Cleopatra,	1606–8,	1608, Stationers' Register.
Troilus and Cressida,		1609, first quarto.
Cymbeline,		1623, first folio.
Coriolanus,	1609–11,	1623, first folio.
Othello,		1621 (?), Stationers' Reg.
The Winter's Tale,	1611,	1611, Forman's Diary.
The Tempest,	1611,	1611, Acc't of Rev'ls at C't.
Henry the Eighth,	1613,	1623, first folio.

NOTE ON THE PORTRAITS AND AUTOGRAPH SIGNATURES OF SHAKESPEARE.

NO painting is known which can be accepted as an authentic portrait of William Shakespeare. The number of pigmentary representations of countenances, more or less human, for which pretensions to such honor, more or less unworthy of consideration, have been set up, may be reckoned at somewhere between three and three hundred; but only two of these have sufficient claims upon attention to make them worthy of particular notice. These are the widely known, and for a long time generally accepted, Chandos portrait, and the Felton portrait, which, once in high favor, has for many years been lost sight of, except by Shakespearian enthusiasts and collectors. The former may be traced from its present place in the Bridgewater collection, up through the Chandos collection, and the hands of a Mr. Nicol, a Mr. Robert Keck, and Mrs. Barry the actress, to the possession of Betterton the actor. While it was his property, an engraving was made from it by Vandergucht for Rowe's edition of the poet's works, which was published in 1709. So far its descent from the antiquity of more than a century and a half as an accepted portrait of Shakespeare is well established. But its pedigree, (so to speak,) like many others, fails at the most interesting and important stage. It was said in the last century that Davenant was the possessor of this picture next before Betterton, and that he had it as a legacy from a John Taylor, who painted it from life. But there is not a particle even of presumptive evidence in favor of either one of these assertions. And were the portrait clearly traceable to Davenant, some better testimony than his bare word, or even his actual belief, is necessary to establish the authenticity of such a picture. Indeed, upon any subject connected with the godfather whose son he was so weakly willing to be reputed, the evidence of Charles the Second's Poet Laureate must be regarded as of little value. Looking to the picture itself, we find a notable absence of internal evidence of its authenticity. For we are able to compare it with two portraits of Shakespeare as to which there is evidence that they were regarded by his friends as faithful representations of their great original. These are the print from Droeshout's engraving, which appears on the title page of the first folio, and the bust in the church at Stratford. To the correctness of the former of these Ben Jonson bears testimony in language which may mean that the engraver made his drawing from the life; * and the latter was set up between the date of Shakespeare's death, 1616, and that of the publication of the folio, 1623, and without a doubt by the surviving members of the poet's immediate family. These are the only authentic portraits of Shakespeare. The print is a hard, wooden, staring thing, which yet holds its own on comparison with similar publications of its time; and the bust is likewise not the loveliest creation of the chisel. Yet the resemblance between the two is such that each supports the pretensions of the other. The print represents its subject as about thirty or thirty-five years of age: the bust has the appearance of a man about fifty years old, and is supposed to have been modelled from a cast taken after death. Unlike as these portraits are in their material, and in the means upon which they depend for effect, the one being in the round and the other flat, they evidently represent the same man. The individual features, and the countenance as a whole, correspond as nearly as portraits by different artists are apt to do, especially when we consider the different periods of life at which they were manifestly taken. To neither of these heads does the Chandos portrait present other than the most superficial resemblance; no more, in fact, than might well exist between it and the "effigies" of hundreds of bald-fronted and oval-cheeked men of the period. Did the print and the bust not exist, we might accept this stolid countenance as Shakespeare's; for the faces of men of genius not unfrequently misrepresent their minds. But the preservation of those authentic and agreeing portraits makes it impossible for us to accept this ear-ringed, full-bearded, heavy-eyed, simple-mouthed thing, unsupported as it is by a particle of evidence that reaches to within three quarters

* See Vol. II. of this edition, p. 2 of Preliminary Matter, &c.

of a century of the time at which it must have been painted, if it really were authentic. In my judgment the Chandos head has no claim whatever to be regarded as a contemporary portrait of Shakespeare.

Of the history of the Felton head nothing whatever is known before the year 1792. In that year it was exhibited at the European Museum, King Street, St. James's Square, London, as "a curious portrait of Shakespeare, painted in 1597." It was bought for five guineas by a Mr. Felton. He, making inquiries concerning the history of the picture, was informed by the keeper of the Museum that it "was purchased out of an old house known by the sign of the Boar, in Eastcheap, London, where Shakespeare and his friends used to resort; and, report says, was painted by a player of that time." This story was plainly a shallow fabrication made to fit the traditions that Shakespeare used to frequent the Boar's Head Tavern in Eastcheap, which was burned down in 1666, and that Burbage had painted his portrait. Two years after, the same Museum man ager — a Mr. J. Wilson — assured Steevens, who, with many other men of note, critics and painters of repute, was much impressed by this picture, that it had been found, four or five years before, "at a broker's shop in the Minories, by a man of fashion whose name must be concealed," and that it was sold as a part of that gentleman's collection to the Museum. This story, which itself could give neither authenticity nor value to the picture, was probably as sheer a fabrication as the other. The very period at which this head first came into public notice casts suspicion upon it; for Shakespearian forgery and fabrication then were rife. On the back of the panel upon which this head is painted is an inscription in black and white paint, the style of the characters being that of the Elizabethan period. This inscription was, by those who first brought the picture into notice, and by the publisher of the first engraving from it, supposed to be "*Guil Shakspeare* 1597 *R N*."; and it was not until some years after that Mr. Abraham Wivell, a painter, having rubbed some linseed oil upon the back of the picture to nourish the decayed wood, brought out the writing more clearly, and discovered that it was "*Gul. Shakspear.* 1597. *R B*." Now, as R B are the initials of Richard Burbage, and R N those of no one known as having had any connection with Shakespeare, or as having been a painter in his day, it is at least worthy of note that if this inscription were spurious, the fabricators strangely failed to take any advantage of their invention. This, however, is the only circumstance connected with the known history of the picture which affords any support (if, indeed, it does afford any) to its claims to be accepted as an original portrait of Shakespeare.

The picture itself presents this appearance: The head almost fills the ground upon which it appears, because a piece of the panel, on which was part of the ruff, had been split off on one side before it attracted attention as a portrait of Shakespeare, and what remained was cut down in proportion, that it might be suitably framed.* The surface is, or was, "covered all over with dark spots," which are supposed to have been the result of its "being a long time in a damp place without varnish." † The head presents remarkable likeness in form and feature both to the Stratford bust and the Droeshout print, corresponding in cut of beard and fashion of costume to the latter. The height of the forehead is very much exaggerated; the distance from the eyebrow to the top of the head being nearly as great as that from the same line down to the chin.‡ This fault and that of a long upper lip are common in portraits taken at the time in question. A high forehead, or more properly a bald brow, was then regarded as a beauty, as Shakespeare's own works bear witness; and the artists sought to flatter their subjects. But neither this fault nor the very careless drawing of the costume can detract from the intrinsic interest of this picture. The correspondence of the face both in general form and particular feature to the two authenticated portraits is so remarkable that it may be accepted in those respects at least as truthful; while the expression is so peculiar and so suited to the character of the man it professes to represent, and yet so unlike that which a mere mercenary fabricator would have been likely to give his work, that it seems as if one of two conclusions must be accepted: — Either we have here a genuine portrait of Shakespeare painted from the life, or the work of a man of genius and insight who prostituted his powers to the fabrication of a portrait and the forgery of a signature, and then let

* Richardson's *Proposals*, &c.

† Wivell's *Inquiry*, &c.

‡ See the beautiful stipple print from this picture in Wivell's *Inquiry*, &c.

his work go from him, careless even of attaining the success within the reach of a clever impostor. This sweet, grave, sensitive face, with its serene, all-observant eye, and its mouth almost sad, but to all perception capable of smiles as bright as sunlight, if it were not painted from Shakespeare's self, yet does express that self in a fashion which, mere feature accuracy being secured, leaves nothing to be desired. For these reasons this portrait has been engraved to accompany the present edition. The forehead and the costume have been corrected by the Stratford bust and the Droeshout print; but in all other respects the engraver has most faithfully and sympathetically reproduced the traits and the expression of the original. The portrait is not presented as having considerable claims to authenticity. Not improbably a fabrication based upon the Droeshout print, it may yet possibly be the original from which Droeshout engraved. But in either case it gives us, with the same features which the two authentic portraits give, such a fitting expression of the mind and soul of Shakespeare, that, in fault of a better which is well authenticated, it matters little whether it is *vero* or only *ben trovato.*

The signature, a fac-simile of which accompanies this portrait in the present edition, is in like manner utterly without evidence of its authenticity. The only authenticated signatures of Shakespeare known to exist are the three upon his will and the one on a conveyance, of which fac-similes are given in the foregoing pages. But a fifth, above mentioned, has been accepted by eminent experts in paleography as genuine. This signature appears upon the title page of a copy of the first edition of Florio's translation of Montaigne's Essays, published in 1603. This volume was for sixty years in the possession of the Reverend Edward Patteson of Smethwick, near Birmingham, England. In 1838 it was bought by the British Museum for £100; that sum having been paid for it only because of the signature in question. The purchase was made on the recommendation of Sir Frederic Madden, Keeper of the Manuscripts in the British Museum, who believes in the authenticity of the signature, and who has published a pamphlet in its support. Nothing is known of the whereabout of the volume previous to the year 1778, a time when the interest in Shakespeare was so great and the investigations of his personal history so recent and so imperfect that it was both tempting and propitious to the fabricator. It is true that the well known passage in the *Tempest* in which *Gonzalo* appropriates the words of Montaigne,* and the fact that Florio and Shakespeare were under the protection of the same patron, make it very probable that the latter did at one time possess a copy of the former's version of Montaigne. But for these very reasons that book would have been selected by a fabricator of any sagacity for the introduction of a spurious signature, and they therefore tell quite as much against as for the genuineness of this one. In fact its claims to authenticity have no support but mere opinion based upon its style and general appearance, and its resemblance to originals of unquestionable genuineness — a position which it occupies in common with the Felton portrait. Like that portrait, however, it is probably, whether genuine or a fabrication, the best accessible representation of that which it professes to be; and, like the portrait, it is given here, as it has been received into the British Museum, not as supported by evidence of authenticity, or even of high antiquity, but solely on account of its intrinsic interest.

* See Vol. II. p. 88, of this edition.

THE ENGLISH DRAMA.

AN ACCOUNT OF THE RISE AND PROGRESS OF

THE ENGLISH DRAMA

TO THE TIME OF SHAKESPEARE.

THE English drama, like the Greek, has a purely religious origin. The same is true of the drama of every civilized people of modern times. It is worthy of particular remark that the theatre, denounced by churchmen and by laymen of eminently evangelical profession, as base, corrupting, and sinful, not in its abuse and its degradation, but in its very essence, should have been planted and nourished by churchmen, having priests for its first authors and actors, and having been for centuries the chief school of religion and of morals to an unlettered people. Theatrical representations have probably continued without interruption from the time of Æschylus. Even in the dark ages, which we look back upon too exclusively as a period of gloom, tumult, and bloodshedding, people bought and sold, and were married and given in marriage, and feasted and amused themselves as we do now; and we may be sure that among their amusements dramatic representations of some sort were not lacking. The earliest dramatic performances in the modern languages of Europe of which we have any record or tradition were representations of the most striking events recorded in the Hebrew Scriptures and in the Christian Gospels, of some of the stories told in the Pseudo Evangelium, or Spurious Gospel, or of legends of the saints. On the continent these were called Mysteries; in England both Mysteries and Miracle-plays. The ancient Hebrews had at least one play. It was founded upon the exodus of their people from Egypt. Fragments of this play in Greek iambics have been preserved to modern times in the works of various authors. The principal characters are Moses, Zipporah, and God in the Bush. The author, one Ezekiel, is called by Scaliger the tragic poet of the Jews. His work is referred by one critic to a date before the Christian era; others suppose that he was one of the Seventy Translators; but Warton, my authority in this instance, supposes that he wrote his play after the destruction of Jerusalem, hoping by its means to warm the patriotism and revive the hopes of his dejected countrymen.

The Eastern Empire long clung to all the glories to which its name, its language, and its position gave it a presumptive title; and the tragedies of Sophocles and Euripides were performed after some fashion at Constantinople until the fourth century. At this period Gregory Nazianzen, archbishop, patriarch, and one of the fathers of the church, banished the pagan drama from the Greek stage, and substituted plays founded on subjects taken from the Hebrew or the Christian Scriptures. St. Gregory wrote many plays of this kind himself; and Warton says that one of them, called *Χριστος Πασχων*, or Christ's Passion, is still extant.* In this play, which, according to the Prologue, was written in imitation of Euripides, the Virgin Mary was introduced upon the stage, making then, as far as we know, her first appearance. St. Gregory died about A. D. 390. His dramatic productions more than rivalled his other theological writings in the favor of the people; for, as Warton also men-

* *History of English Poetry*. sec. xxxiv. vol. ii. p. 517. ed. 1840.

tions, St. Chrysostom, who soon succeeded Gregory in the see of Constantinople, complained that in his day people heard a comedian with much more pleasure than a minister of the gospel. St. Chrysostom held the see of Constantinople from A. D. 398 to A. D. 404. In this quarter also another kind of dramatic representation — that of mummery or masking — developed itself in a Christian or a modern form. It is known that many of the Christian festivals which have come down to us from the dark ages were the fruits of a grafting of Christian legends upon pagan ceremonies — a contrivance by which the priests supposed that they had circumvented the heathen, who would more easily give up their religion than their feasts and their holidays. And the introduction of religious mumming and masking by Theophylact, patriarch of Constantinople, about the year 990, has been reasonably attributed to a design of giving the people a Christian performance which they could and would substitute in place of the Bacchanalian revels. He is said by an historian of the succeeding generation to have "introduced the practice which prevails even at this present day of scandalizing God and the memory of his saints, on the most splendid and popular festivals, by indecent and ridiculous songs, and enormous shoutings, . . . diabolical dances, exclamations of ribaldry, and ballads borrowed from the streets and brothels." The Feast of Fools and the Feast of Asses — the latter of which was instituted in honor of Balaam's beast — had this origin. Such mingling of revelry and religion as these Feasts, and of amusement and instruction in the faith as the Mysteries, suited both the priestly and the popular need of the time; and they soon found their way westward, and particularly into France. There, not long after, the Feast of Asses was performed in this manner: The clergy walked on Christmas day in procession, habited to represent Moses, David, the prophets, other Hebrews, and Assyrians. Balaam, with an immense pair of spurs, rode on a wooden ass, which enclosed a speaker. Virgil was one of the procession, which moved on, chanting versicles and dialoguing in character on the birth of Christ, through the body of the church, until it reached the choir.* The fairs of those days, which were the great occasions of profit and amusement, offered opportunities for the performance of these "holy farces," or of the soberer mysteries or miracle-plays, of which the priests did not fail to avail themselves; and thus this rude form of religious drama spread gradually, but not slowly, throughout Europe.

Warton and his editor Price found that religious plays were performed in Italy at a period very much earlier than either Riccoboni or Crescembini, the principal Italian authorities on this subject, supposed; in fact, that they were common as early as 1250. In the natural order of things this species of performance would pass from Italy to France and from France to England; and the supposition that it was brought into the latter country across the channel is supported by the fact that there is evidence that the first religious plays performed in England were translations from the French. Some yet extant have passages in that language scattered through them — a fact which can be most reasonably accounted for by the supposition that these isolated passages are parts of the original, left untranslated in the manuscripts which have come down to us. It has even been supposed that the first miracle-plays produced in England were performed in French. Possibly this supposition is well founded; but we may be sure that these plays soon received an English dress. For the mir-

* Warton's *History of English Poetry*, sec. vi. vol. ii. p. 2, ed. 1840.

acle-plays were used by the priesthood for the religious instruction, not only of those who could not read,—among whom were the Norman nobles who could understand French,—but also, and chiefly, of the middle and lower classes, to whom French was almost as incomprehensible as the Latin in which their prayers were vicariously mumbled. Miracle-plays seem to have been, in some measure at least, the fruit of the same laudable desire on the part of the Roman Catholic priesthood for the instruction of their people in religious truth, to which we owe the rhymed homilies or gospel paraphrases of the thirteenth century, in which the lesson of the day, read of course in Latin, was translated, amplified, and illustrated in octosyllabic rhymes, which were read to the people by the priest. Six ancient manuscript collections of these homilies are known to exist; and in the prologue to the oldest one of them, which is of the fourteenth century, and which has recently been printed, the writer expressly says that he has undertaken his task of thus preaching in English that all may understand what he says, because both clerks and ignorant men understand English, but all men cannot understand Latin and French.

The earliest performance of a miracle-play in England of which any record has been discovered took place within about ten years previous to 1119. The play, founded upon the legend of St. Catherine, was written by Geoffrey, afterward Abbot of St. Albans, before he became abbot, and was performed in Dunstable. So says Matthew Paris in his Lives of the Abbots, which was written before 1240. Geoffrey, a Norman monk and a member of the University of Paris, became Abbot of St. Albans in 1119. But his miracle-play was no novelty; for Budæus, the historian of the University of Paris, tells us that it was at that time common for teachers and scholars to get up these performances.* Fitz-Stephen, Thomas à Becket's contemporary and biographer, also records that in London, during the life or soon after the death of that stiff-necked priest, who was put to death in 1170, there were performed in London religious plays representing the miracles wrought by saints, or the sufferings and constancy of martyrs.† These miracle-plays or mysteries derived their name from the fact that, whether founded upon the Old or the New Testament, the spurious Gospel attributed to Nicodemus, or church tradition, they almost without exception represented a display of supernatural power. Made the means of teaching not only religious history, but religious dogmas, these miracle-plays often represented a display of supernatural power in the support of those dogmas; and naturally that one most in need of such extra-rational aid, transubstantiation, received most of this bolstering. One of the oldest manuscript miracle-plays extant, the manuscript being, in the judgment of experts, as old as 1460–70, is upon this subject. It is called "The Play of the Blessed Sacrament," and dramatizes a miracle said to have been worked in the forest of Aragon in the year 1461; but doubtless the tradition is older. Among the characters are Christ, five Jews, a bishop, a curate, a Christian merchant, and a physician. The merchant steals the Host and sells it to the Jews, on condition that they shall become Christians if they find that it has miraculous powers. To test its character, they stab it; it bleeds, and one of them goes mad at the sight: one attempts to nail it to a post; he has his hand torn off: the phy-

* I have seen neither Matthew Paris's *Historia Major*, &c., nor Budæus's *Historia Universitatis Parisiensis*. Both are cited by Markland and Warton, who are my authorities.

† Fitz-Stephens's *Description of London*, ed. Pegge, 1773, p. 73.

sician is called in, but after a comic scene is turned out as a quack. They then boil the Host, and the water turns to blood. Finally, they try to consume it in a blazing furnace, when the oven bursts asunder, and an image of Christ arises, before which the Jews prostrate themselves, and become Christians on the spot. The bishop now forms a procession, enters the Jew's house, and addresses the image, which changes to bread again. He then "improves the occasion" offered by this comic-pantomime-like performance, in an epilogue, which is a rhymed homily on transubstantiation.

There were neither theatres nor professional actors in England, indeed in Europe, at the period when miracle-plays first came in vogue. Their first performers were clergymen; the first stages or scaffolds on which they were presented were set up in churches. Evidence that this was the case has been discovered in such profusion that it is needless to specify it more particularly in this place, than to remark that councils and prelates finally found it necessary to forbid such performances, either in churches or by the clergy. After the exclusion of the clergy from the religious stage, lay brothers, parish clerks, and the hangers-on of the priesthood naturally took the place of their spiritual fathers, under whose superintendence, or, to speak precisely, management, the miracle-plays were brought out. Excluded from the church itself, like the strange *Danse Macabre*, or Dance of Death, like that dance the miracle-play found fitting refuge in the churchyard. But it was finally forbidden within all hallowed precincts, and was then presented upon a movable scaffold or pageant, which was dragged through the town, and stopped for the performance at certain places designated by an announcement made a day or two before. At last the presentation of these plays fell entirely into the hands of laymen, and the handicraftsmen became their actors; the members of the various guilds undertaking respectively certain plays which they made for the time their speciality. Thus the Shearmen, or Tailors, would represent one, the Cappers another, and so with the Smiths, the Skinners, the Fishmongers, and others. In the Chester series Noah's Flood was very appropriately assigned to the Water Dealers and Drawers of the Dee. It is almost needless to remark that the female characters were always played by striplings and young men. Women did not appear upon the English stage until the middle of the 17th century. It would seem that the priests appeared only as amateurs, and that their performances were gratuitous. But when the laymen, or at least when the handicraftsmen, undertook the business, they were paid, as we know by the memorandums of account still existing.*

The oldest manuscript of an English miracle-play known to exist is that of *The Harrowing of Hell*, which is among the Harleian MSS. in the British Museum. This manuscript is believed to have been written about 1350; but that date of course does not help us to determine the period when the play was composed, or give it priority in this respect to others which have been preserved only in more modern writing. *The Harrowing of Hell* is supposed with probability to have

* The following items of account are taken from one of many memorandums discovered by Mr. Sharp in the archives of Coventry, and published in his Essay on the Coventry Mysteries:—

Md. payd to the players for corpus christi daye
Imprimis, to God ij[s]
Itm to Cayphas iij[s] iiij[d]
Itm to Heroude iij[s] iiij[d]
Itm to Pilatt is wyff ij[s]
Itm to the Bedull iiij[s]
Itm to one of the knights ij[s]
Itm to the devyll and Judas xviij[d]

been one of a series; and its subject, the descent of Christ into hell for the purpose of bringing away thence the saints and prophets, has its place in collections or series which have from their completeness greater interest and importance.

The three most important sets of miracle-plays in our language are known as the Townley, the Coventry, and the Chester collections. The Townley collection is supposed to have belonged to Widkirk Abbey, and is hence sometimes called the Widkirk collection. The manuscript, in the opinion of Mr. Collier, is of the time of Henry VI.* The Coventry collection is so called because there is reason to believe that it was the property of the Gray Friars of Coventry, who were famous for the performance of miracle-plays at the feast of Corpus Christi. The principal part of the manuscript copy extant was written in the year 1468, as appears by that date upon one page of the volume.†

* The following are the titles of the thirty plays in the Townley series: I. The Creation and the Rebellion of Lucifer. II. Mactatio Abel. III. Progressus Noæ cum Filiis. IV. Abraham. V. Jacob and Esau. VI. Processus Prophetarum. VII. Pharao. VIII. Cæsar Augustus. IX. Annunciatio. X. Salutatio Elizabethæ. XI. Pastorum. XII. Alia eorundem. XIII. Oblatio Magorum. XIV. Fugatio Josephi et Mariæ in Egiptum. XV. Magnus Herodus. XVI. Purificatio Mariæ. XVII. Johannes Baptista. XVIII. Conspiratio Christi. XIX. Colaphizatio. XX. Flagellatio. XXI. Processus Crucis. XXII. Processus Talentorum. XXIII. Extractio Animarum. XXIV. Resurrectio Domini. XXV. Peregrini. XXVI. Thomas Judiæ. XXVII. Ascensio Domini. XXVIII. Judicium. XXIX. Lazarus. XXX. Suspensio Judæ.

† The Coventry series contains forty-two plays, upon the following subjects: I. The Creation. II. The Fall of Man. III. The Death of Abel. IV. Noah's Flood. V. Abraham's Sacrifice. VI. Moses and the Ten Tables. VII. The Genealogy of Christ. VIII. Anna's Pregnancy. IX. Mary in the Temple. X. Mary's Betrothment. XI. The Salutation and the Conception. XII. Joseph's Return. XIII. The Visit to Elizabeth. XIV. The Trial of Joseph and Mary. XV. The Birth of Christ. XVI. The Adoration of the Shepherds. XVII. The Adoration of the Magi. XVIII. The Purification. XIX. The Slaughter of the Innocents. XX. Christ disputing in the Temple. XXI. The Baptism of Christ. XXII. The Temptation. XXIII. The Woman taken in Adultery. XXIV. Lazarus. XXV. The Council of the Jews. XXVI. The Entry into Jerusalem. XXVII. The Last Supper. XXVIII. The Betraying

The Chester series, of which there are three existing manuscript copies, the oldest only of the year 1600, belonged to the city of Chester. Its author was one Randle, a monk of Chester Abbey. They were played upon Whitsunday by the tradesmen of that city, and Mr. Markam, one of the earliest, and, in the phrase of his day, most ingenious writers upon this subject, has pretty clearly established that they were first produced in 1268, four years after the establishment of the feast of Corpus Christi, under the auspices of Sir John Arneway, mayor of Chester.* A brief analysis of some of the plays of the Coventry series will give a correct notion of the character of these queer compositions.

A prologue, in stanzas, spoken alternately by three vexillators, tells in detail the subjects of the forty-two plays. The first, *The Creation*, is opened by God, who, after declaring in Latin that he is alpha and omega, the beginning and the end, goes on in English to assert his might and his triune existence, and then announces his creative intentions. A chorus of angels then sing in Latin the *Tibi omnes angeli*, &c., of the *Te Deum*.

of Christ. XXIX King Herod. XXX. The Trial of Christ. XXXI. Pilate's Wife's Dream. XXXII. The Crucifixion. XXXIII. The Descent into Hell. XXXIV. The Burial of Christ. XXXV. The Resurrection. XXXVI. The three Marys. XXXVII. Christ appearing to Mary Magdalen. XXXVIII. The Pilgrims of Emmaus. XXXIX. The Ascension. XL. Descent of the Holy Ghost. XLI. The Assumption. XLII. Doomsday.

* The Chester series contains but twenty-four plays, upon the following subjects: I. The Fall of Lucifer. II. De Creatore Mundi. III. De Deluvio Noæ. IV. De Abrahamo, Melchisedech, et Loth. V. De Mose et Rege Balak, et Balaam Propheta. VI. De Salutatione et Nativitate Salvatoris. VII. De Pastoribus Greges pascentibus. VIII. De Tribus Regibus Orientalibus. IX. De Oblatione Tertium Regum. X. De Occisione Innocentium. XI. De Purificatione Virginis. XII. De Tentatione Salvatoris. XIII. De Chelidonio et Resurrectio Lazari. XIV. De Jesu intrante Domum Simeonis Leprosi. XV. De Cœna Domini. XVI. De Passione Christi. XVII. De Descensu Christi ad Inferos. XVIII. De Resurrectione Jesu Christi. XIX. De Christo ad Castellum Emmaus. XX. De Ascensione Domini. XXI. De Electione Matthæ. XXII. Ezekiel. XXIII. De Adventu Antichristi. XXIV. De Judicio Extremo.

Lucifer next appears, and asks the angels whether they sing thus in God's honor or in his, asserting that he is the most worthy. The good angels declare for God; the bad for Lucifer. God then dooms him to fall from heaven to hell. Lucifer submits to his sentence without murmuring, and expresses his emotion only in a manner most likely to deprive the scene of any dignity it might otherwise have exhibited. The second play, *The Fall of Man*, opens with a speech by Adam and a reply by Eve, in which they set forth their happy condition and the command concerning the tree of knowledge of good and evil. The serpent then appears, and tempts Eve to violate this command. The action, if action it must be called, follows in the most servile manner, and with no expansion, the narrative in Genesis; and Adam and Eve are expelled from paradise.* It is clear that the representatives of the types of our race appeared upon the stage innocently free from "the troublesome disguises that we wear;" and that they afterward faithfully followed the Hebrew lawgiver's narrative in the use of fig leaves.† In the third play, *Cain and Abel*,

* Here is Eve's lamentation.

"*Eva.* Alas! alas! and wele away,
That evyr towchyd I the tre;
I wende as wrecche in welsome way,
In blake busshys my boure xal be.
In paradys is plente of playe,
ffayr frutys ryth gret plente,
The ȝatys be schet with Godys keye,
My husbond is lost because of me.
Leve spowse now thou fonde,
Now stomble we on stalk and ston.
My wyt awey is fro me gon,
Wrythe on to my necke bon
With hardnesse of thin honde."

† In the Chester miracle-play the stage direction is, "*Here shall Adam and Eve stand nackede and shall be not ashamed.*" In the Coventry play Adam speaks thus immediately after he has eaten the apple.

"*Adam dicet sic.*
Alas! alas! ffor this fals dede,
My fleshy frend my fo I fynde,

the only noteworthy points are, first, that Cain speaks very disrespectfully of Adam and his counsels, saying that he cares not a hair if he never sees him; and next that, when Abel's offering is accepted and consumed by fire, Cain breaks out into abuse of him, calling him a "stinking losel." * This, by the way, is one of the few representations of contemporary manners furnished by these miracle-plays. If we accept them as truthful in this regard, we must credit our forefathers with a ready resort to foul language when they were angered. Afterward, in the play on *Noah's Flood*, Lamech calls a young man "a stinking lurdane," and in that on the Woman taken in Adultery, the Scribes and Pharisees call her forth to be taken to judgment in language more pharisaic than decent. The Towneley mystery, which represents the first fratricide, is even more grotesque and

Schameful synne doth us unhede,
  I se us nakyd before and behynde.
Our lordes wurd wold we not drede,
  Therfore we be now caytyvys unkynde,
Oure pore prevytes ffor to hede,
  Somme ffygge-levys fayn wolde I fynde
      ffor to hyde oure schame.
Womman, ley this leff on thi pryvyte,
And with this leff I xal hyde me,
Gret schame it is us nakyd to se,
      Oure lord God thus to grame."

* Cain's speech, which here follows, will give a notion of the language and the action of the play at the point of highest interest.

"*Caym.* What? thou stynkyng losel, and is it so?
  Doth God the love and hatyht me?
Thou xalt be ded I xal the slo,
  Thi Lord thi God thou xalt nevyr se!
Tything more xalt thou nevyr do,
  With this chavyl bon I xal sle the,
Thi deth is dyht, thi days be go,
  Out of myn handys xalt thou not fle,
      With this strok I the kylle.—
Now this boy is slayn and dede,
O hym I xal nevyr more han drede,
He xal hereafter nevyr ete brede,
      With this gresse I xal him hylle."

indecent than that in the collection which we are examining. Cain comes upon the stage with a plough and team, and quarrels with his ploughboy for refusing to drive the oxen. Abel enters, bids speed the plough to Cain, and in reply is told to do something quite unmentionable. After Abel is killed, the boy counsels flight for fear of the bailiffs. Cain then makes a mock proclamation, which his boy blunderingly repeats; and after this clownish foolery, Cain bids the audience farewell before he goes to hell. The personages in the fourth play, *Noah's Flood*, are God, Noah and his wife, his three sons and their wives, an angel, Cain, Lamech, and a young man. Noah and his family talk pharisaic morality for about the first third of the play. God then declares his displeasure, and that he "wol be vengyd;" to which end he will destroy all the world, except Noah and his family. The angel announces the coming flood to Noah, and bids him build a ship to save his household, and "of every kynds bestes a cowpyl." Noah and his family go out to build the ship, and Lamech enters blind and conducted by a young man. In spite of his infirmity, at the suggestion of his guide, he shoots at a supposed beast in a bush; but, like another hapless person known to rhyme who "bent his bow," he hits what he did not shoot at, and kills Cain, who mysteriously happens to be in the bush. Aroused to wrath, and moved by fear of the fate predicted of him who should slay Cain, Lamech kills the young man who had misled him into shooting at the beast. He goes out, and Noah comes in with his ship — "*et statim intrat Noe cum navi cantantes* [sic]." This ship, as we learn from the direction in the corresponding play of the Chester Mysteries, was customarily painted over with figures of the beasts supposed to be within, as if they had struck through, and come out like an eruption. In that play, too, and also in the corresponding Towneley play, Noah's wife refuses to enter the ark. Indeed, in those plays she is represented as an arrant scold. In the first scene she berates Noah, who gives her as good as she sends, and both swear roundly by the Virgin Mary ; and as to going into the ark, the patriarch, "the secunde fathyr," as he styles himself, edified the female part of the audience by fairly flogging his wife on board with a cart whip. The flood comes on, (we have returned to the Coventry plays ;) Noah and his wife speak thirty lines of dialogue, and then he says, —

"xl[ti] days and nightes hath lasted thys rayn,
And xl[ti] days this grett flood begynnyth to slake ;
This crowe xal I sende out to seke sum playn,
Good tydynges to brynge this message I make."

The crow does not return, and the dove is sent, "*qua redeunte cum ramo viride olivæ*," as the stage direction says, Noah and his family leave the ark, singing, "*Mare videt et fugit*," &c.

The fourteenth play, which represents the *Trial of Joseph and Mary* on accusations based upon the latter's mysterious pregnancy, is opened by a crier, who summons the jurors and people who have causes to come into court. Although the trial is supposed, of course, to take place in Palestine before the Christian era, it is presided over by "my lorde the buschop," and the people summoned are English folk of the lower class, whose surnames have plainly been given to them on account of their occupation or their personal traits.* The crier lets us into a judge's secret, by warning those who have causes to be tried to put money in their purses, or their cause may speed the worse. In the next play, which

* John Jurdon, Geffrey Gile, Malkin Milkdoke, Stephen Sturdy, Sawdor Saddler, Tom Tinker, Peter Potter, Lucy Liar, Miles Miller, &c.

represents the *Birth of Christ*, Mary, as she and Joseph are on their way to Bethlehem, longs for cherries from a tree which they pass. Joseph is old, lazy, and huffish, and tells her that the tree is too high, and that he may get her cherries who got her with child. Whereupon Mary prays for the cherries, and the boughs bend down to her; at which Joseph repents. Plainly there were properties, and even machinery, upon the stage at this rude and early period; and, indeed, the lists of properties (for they seem always to have been so called) which have been preserved show that no small pains were taken to portray the glories and the horrors of the various scenes presented, and especially in the imitations of such miraculous events as that of the bowing down of the branches of the cherry tree. The seventeenth play, *The Adoration of the Magi*, introduces the most famous character in these dramas — Herod. He is always represented in them not only as wicked and cruel, but as a tremendous braggart. He raves and swaggers and swears without stint; his favorite oath being by Mahound, i. e., Mohammed; for in all respects these miracle-plays set chronology at defiance. The speeches put into his mouth, more than any others, are written in the old Anglo-Saxon alliterative style, of which *Piers Ploughman's Vision* is a well-known example.* Herod, in spite of his heathenism, his cruelty,

* Perhaps the most characteristic speech of his in every respect is the following from *The Slaughter of the Innocents:* —

"*Herodes Rex.* I ryde on my rowel ryche in my regne,
Rybbys ffnl rede with rape xal I sende;
Popetys et paphawkes I xal putten in peyne,
With my spere provyn, pychen, and to-pende.
The gowys with gold crownys gete thei nevyr ageyn,
To seke tho sottys sondys xal I sende;
Do howlott howtyn hoberd heyn,
Whan here barnys blede undyr credyl bende;
Sharply I xal hem shende!

his profanity, and his braggadocio, — perhaps by reason of them, — used to be a favorite character with young men of spirit and parts who were stage-struck. Chaucer, it will be remembered, says, in the Miller's Tale, of his "Absolon, that joly was and gay," —

"Sometime to shew his lightness and maistrie
He plaieth Herode on a skaffolde hie."

The knave childeryn that be
In alle Israel countré,
Thie xul have blody ble,
ffor on I calde unkende.
It is tolde in Grw,
His name xulde be Jhesu
I fownde.
To have hym ȝe gon,
Hewe the flesche with the bon.
And gyff hym wownde!
Now kene knyghtes kythe your craflys.
And kyllyth knave childeryn and castyth hem in clay;
Shewyth on ȝour shulderes scheldys and schaftys,
Schapyht amonge schel chowthys ashyrlyng shray;
Doth rowncys rennen with rakynge raftys,
Tyl rybbys be to rent with a reed ray.
Lete no barne beleve on bete baftys,
Tyl a beggere blede be bestys baye,
Mahound that best may;
I warne ȝow my knyghtes,
A barn is born I plyghtes,
Wold clymbyn kynge and kyknytes,
And lett my lordly lay.
Knyghtes wyse
Chosyn ful chyse
Aryse! aryse!
And take ȝour tolle!
And every page
Of ij. ȝere age
Or eveyr ȝe swage,
Sleythe ilke a fool.
On of hem alle
Was born in stalle
ffolys hym calle
Kynge in crown
With byttyr gallo,
He xalle down falle. —
My myght in halle
Xal nevyr go down."

But more than by the indecency, the coarseness, the bombast, and the vapidity of these miracle-plays, we are astonished and repulsed by the degrading familiarity with which they treat the most awful and most moving incidents of the Gospel history. The Last Supper was actually played; the Crucifixion was actually played; and even the Resurrection was not too sacred or mysterious a subject to be represented. Conforming both to the religious spirit and the taste of the time, the clerical dramatist spared his audience the sight of no indignity, of no torture, suffered by Christ, but took delight in representing all the physical circumstances attending his death with gross and bald particularity.* And as we

* The following passage, it will be seen, shows that the crucifixion was represented even to the minutest of its attendant circumstances: —

"*Than xul thei pulle Jhesu out of his clothis, and leyn them togedyr; and then thei xul pullyn hym down and leyn along on the cros, and after that naylyn hym thereon.*

Primus Judæus. Come on now here, we xal asay
Yf the cros for the be mete;
Cast hym down here in the devyl way,
How long xal he standyn on his fete?

Secundus Judæus. Pul hym down, evyl mote he the
And gyf me his arm in hast;
And anon we xal se
Here good days thei xul be past!

Tertius Judæus. Gef hese other arm to me, —
Another take hed to hese feet;
And anon we xal se
Yf the borys be for hym mete.

Quartus Judæus. This is mete, take good hede;
Pulle out that arm to the sore.

Primus Judæus. This is short, the devyl hym sped,
Be a large fote and more.

Secundus Judæus. ffest on a rop and pulle hym long,
And I xal drawe the ageyn;
Spare we not these ropys strong,
Thow we brest both flesch and veyn!

Tertius Judæus. Dryve in the nayle anon, lete se,
And loke and the flesch and sennes welle last.

Quartus Judæus. That I graunt, so mote I the;
Lo! this nayl is dreve ryth wel and fast.

Primus Judæus. ffest a rope than to his feet,
And draw hym down long anow.

close our examination of the miracle-plays, a reflection of their mingled childishness and temerity must be uppermost in the mind of every reader. Had it not been done, it would seem almost impossible that such subjects could be so unworthily treated by men of sense and education, which the better class of Roman Catholic priests were even in the days when these plays were written. Here were the grandest themes handled by authors to whom they were matters of religious faith and supreme concern; and all that was done was to degrade, to belittle, and to make ridiculous. The rudeness of the people for whose instruction and pleasure the miracle-plays were produced, and the gross and material character of religion in that day, account in a great measure for this shocking contrast between subject and treatment. But yet it would seem that, though rude and simple, these compositions might have preserved some little of the spirit of the Hebrew writers from whom their subjects were taken, and who themselves wrote for people only a little advanced beyond the pale of semi-barbarism. And one subject, by remarkable coincidence, was treated with a certain degree of simplicity and pathos by the writers of all of the three great collections of English miracle-plays. This was the story of Abraham and Isaac. And it is worthy of special remark that it was a subject of which the interest is purely human, or at least that part of the subject in question which exhibited paternal love on the one side and filial love and devotion on the other, which raised all these writers out of their slough of coarseness and buffoonery into the region of healthy sentiment. The Coventry series, which we have been examining, offers the best

Secundus Judæus. Here is a nayl for both good and greet,
I xal dryue it thorwe, I make a vow!
Here xule thei leve of and dawncyn abowte the cros shortly."

treatment of this incident; which in itself, and in the barest relation of it, is, if one can repress an outbreak of rebellious indignation and disbelief, the most pathetic and heart-breaking told in all the Hebrew Scriptures. With an extract from this composition, which I shall put in modern language, I shall close this notice of English miracle-plays: —

"*Isaac.* All ready, father, even at your will
And at your bidding I am you by,
With you to walk over dale and hill;
At your calling I am ready.
To the father ever most comely
It behoveth the child ever obedient to be;
I will obey, full heartily,
To every thing that ye bid me.

Abraham. Now, son, in thy neck this fagot thou take,
And this fire bear in thy hand;
For we must now sacrifice go make,
Even after the will of God's command.
Take this burning brand
My sweet child, and let us go;
There may no man that liveth upon land
Have more sorrow than I have woe.

Isa. Father, father, you go right still;
I pray now, father, speak unto me.
Abra. My good child, what is thy will?
Tell me thy heart, I pray to thee.
Isa. Father, fire and wood here is plenty;
But I can see no sacrifice;
What ye will offer fain would I see,
That it were done at best advice.

Abra. God shall that ordain that is in heaven,
My sweet son, for this offering;

A dearer sacrifice may no man name
  Than this shall be, my dear darling.
Isa. Let be, dear father, your sad weeping;
  Your heavy looks agrieve me sore.
Tell me, father, your great mourning,
  And I shall seek some help therefor.

Abra. Alas, dear son, for needs must me
  Even here thee kill, as God hath sent;
Thine own father thy death must be,—
  Alas, that ever this bow was bent!
With this fire bright thou must be brent;
  An angel said to me right so;
Alas, my child, thou shalt be shent!
  Thy careful father must be thy foe."

Isaac yields to what Abraham tells him is the divine command, which yet he says makes his heart "cling and cleave as clay."

"*Isa.* Yet work God's will, father, I you pray,
  And slay me here anon forthright;
And turn from me your face away
  My head when that you shall off smite.

Abra. Alas! dear son, I may not choose,
  I must needs here my sweet son kill;
My dear darling now must me lose,
  Mine own heart's blood now shall I spill.
Yet this deed ere I fulfil,
  My sweet son, thy mouth I kiss.
Isa. All ready, father, even at your will
  I do your bidding, as reason is.

Abra. Alas! dear son, here is no grace,
  But need is dead now must thou be.
With this kerchief I hide thy face;

In the time that I slay thee,
Thy lovely visage would I not see,
Not for all this world's good."

It is true that the incident here represented is in itself the most touching that can be conceived; but the author of the play has amplified the very brief account in Genesis, and worked it out in a dialogue, which, rude although it be, is full of nature and simple pathos. The conditions of the action are monstrous and incredible, if we leave out the supernatural element; and the situation, unrelieved by the ever-present consciousness that the sacrifice is not to be made, would be too heart-rending for contemplation. But an unquestioning belief in the supernatural, even to the literal acceptance of the figurative style and extravagant phraseology of the Orient, was assumed by the writers of miracle-plays. The son's love, submission, and self-devotion, and the father's anguish, are expressed with tenderness and truth. Abraham's silent woe, as they walk together, is exhibited with really dramatic power in Isaac's exclamation, "Father, father, you go right still;" and Abraham's reply, "Tell me thy heart," and his after exclamation, "Alas, that ever this bow was bent!" are full of pathos. And when at last the child tells the father to work God's will, yet begs him to turn away his face when he strikes, and Abraham kisses his son, and hides from his own eyes the boy's lovely visage, the interest is wrought up to such a pitch that supernatural intervention is demanded by the holiest instincts of that very nature which supernatural intervention has so pitilessly outraged.

II.

Rude, gross, and childish as were the miracle-plays, they yet contained the germ of our drama; and from them its development, for a long time slow, but never checked, can be traced up to the sudden splendid maturity of the Elizabethan era. The Coventry series, which we have just been examining, differs from the Towneley and the Chester series by the introduction of allegorical personages into some of the plays. In the earlier miracle-plays the personages all belonged to the religious history which the plays were written to teach; and the author confined his work to the putting of the scriptural story or saintly legend into the form of dialogue and soliloquy. But as time wore on, virtues, vices, and even modes of mental action, were impersonated, and mingled upon the pageant or the scaffold with patriarchs, apostles, and saints. Thus the eighth of the Coventry series, *The Barrenness of Anna*, is opened with a kind of prologue or introductory chorus by Contemplation, a character which reappears in the series; and in *The Salutation and Conception* the Virtues, collectively embodied, with Truth, Pity, and Justice, perform functions like those of the Greek chorus. At last, in *The Slaughter of the Innocents*, Death (Mors) takes part in the action; and in some of the other plays impersonal Detractors, Accusers, and Consolers also appear. In the three Digby Miracle-plays * there is one formed upon the life of Mary Magdalen, which is interesting in this respect. And in the first of the set which represents the Conversion of St. Paul, it is noteworthy that of two devils which are among the characters, one is

* So called because they are preserved among the Digby MSS. in the Bodleian Library. See Collier's *Annals of the Stage*, &c., Vol. II. p. 230.

named Belial and the other Mercury! The first is instructed to enter thus: "Here to enter a Dyvel with thunder and fyre, and to avaunce hym selfe saying as folowyth; and his spech spoken to syt downe in a chayre." While he is thus making himself comfortably at home in a devilish way, and complaining of the lack of news, his attendant or messenger comes in, according to this direction: "Here shall entyre a nother devyll, calld Mercury, with a fyering, coming in hast, cryeing and roryng." After a consultation as to the bad way their friend Saul appears to be in, to wit, peril of salvation, body and soul, they both "vanyshe away with a fyrye flame and a tempest." * The play on the *Life of Mary Magdalen*, rather a late miracle-play, was intended to be a spectacle of unusual attraction. It required four pageants or scaffolds. Tiberius, Herod, Pilate, and the Devil — personages of apparently equal dramatic dignity — had each his own station before the audience; and the entrance of the latter is thus directed: "Here shal entyr the prynce of devylls in a stage, and hell onder neth that stage." Indeed, the representation of hell, or of hell-mouth, into which demons and their victims were sent, was a standing, and, it would seem, a much prized effect in the performance of the miracle-plays. In the account books of the expenses of the Coventry plays, there are many charges for "the repayring of Helmought." † To return to the play of *Mary Magdalen*: — a ship appears between the scaffolds; the mariners spy the castle of Mary, which the Devil and the Seven Deadly Sins besiege and capture. Lechery addresses the heroine in a speech, the following extract from which will give a notion of the style of the composition: —

* Collier, as above.

† Sharpe's *Dissertation on the Coventry Mysteries.*

"Heyl, lady, most lawdabyll of alyauns!
Heyl, orient as the sonne in his reflexite!
Much pepul be comfortyd be your benignaunt affyauns;
Brighter than the bornyd is your bemys of bewte:
Most debonarious with your aungelly velycyte."

The appearance of the Seven Deadly Sins and of the Kings of the World, the Flesh, and the Devil in this play as ten distinct characters, is not only very curious, but is a noteworthy step toward the next stage of our drama, which now took the allegorical form of the moral-play. Of character and action, in a true dramatic sense, the miracle-plays, with one or two exceptions to be noticed hereafter, had really none. The personages came upon the stage and described themselves, giving a dry catalogue of their qualities, conditions, and relations, and then went formally through the speech and action prescribed for them in Scripture or legend. But when allegorical personages began to multiply, as they did in the miracle-plays, they began also to interfere with and modify this slavish adherence to Scripture story and church tradition; until finally these personages, who, it will be seen upon a moment's reflection, represent an extraneous human element, and are, in fact, clumsy embodiments alternately of the mental conditions of the other characters and of the audience, obtained possession of the stage, and completely expelled the angels, saints, and patriarchs, in aid of whose waning power to interest the people they had been created.

In a moral-play, pure and simple, the personages are all embodiments of abstract ideas, and the motive of the play is the enforcement of moral truth as a guide to human conduct. The abstract ideas may be virtues, as

Justice, Mercy, Compassion; or vices, as Avarice, Malice, Falsehood; or a state, condition, or mode of life, as Youth, Old Age, Poverty, Abominable Living; or an embodiment of the human race, as in the character Every Man in the moral-play of that name; or of a part of it, in the play of Lusty Juventus; or of the end of all men, for in these compositions Death itself is not unfrequently embodied. But there were two prominent, and, so to speak, stock characters, which were as essential to a moral-play as Harlequin and Columbine to an old pantomime. These were the Devil and the Vice; the former being an inheritance from the miracle-plays, but the latter a new creation. Exactly why and how this personage came into being with the moral-play, we do not know; but may it not have been with the purpose of having ever present an embodied antithesis to the motive of the play — morality? That the name was derived from the nature of the character would seem manifest without a word, were it not that other and fantastic derivations have been suggested.* The Devil was represented as the hideous monster evolved by the morbid religious imagination of the dark ages, having horns, at least one hoof, a tail, a shaggy body, and a visage both frightful and ridiculous. The Vice wore generally, if not always, the costume of the domestic fool, or jester, of the period, which is now worn by clowns of the circus. He was at first called the Vice; but as the Vice became a distinct line of character, as much as walking gentleman on our stage, or *père noble* on the French, his name and his functions were afterward those of Infidelity, Hypocrisy, Desire, and so forth. Sometimes the part of a gallant or bully was written for the Vice, and was named accordingly; and sometimes he was called Iniquity.

* The reader who cares to see them may find them stated and confuted in Douce's *Illustration of Shakespeare*, Vol. I. p. 468.

When he bore this name he would seem to have been not a mere buffoon or clown, making merriment with gibes and antics, but a sententious person, with all his fun; for Shakespeare makes the following descriptive mention of this kind of Vice: —

> "Thus, like the formal vice, Iniquity,
> I moralize two meanings in one word."
> *Richard the Third*, Act III. Sc. 1.

But the Vice generally performed the mingled functions of scamp, braggart, and practical joker. There was a conventional make-up for his face. Barnaby Rich, in *Adventures of Brusanus*, published 1592, says that a certain personage had "his beard cut peecke a devant, turnde uppe a little, like the Vice of a playe." He was armed with a dagger or sword of lath, with which he beat the Devil; that personage having his revenge almost invariably, at the end of the play, by taking his tormentor upon his back and running off with him into "hellmought."

Moral-plays were first performed upon the pageants or scaffolds from which they were driving the miracle-plays. But at last it was thought that people might better go to the play than have the play go to them; and it was found that barns and great halls were more convenient for actors and audience than movable scaffolds. Yet later, people discovered that best of all available places were inn yards, where windows, and galleries, and verandas commanded a view of a court round which the house was built. Sometimes moral-plays were written to be played in the interval between a feast or dinner and a banquet; the banquet having corresponded to what we call the dessert, and having been usually served in another room. Hence the name of *interlude*, which was frequently given to these plays. Yet the name interlude came to be almost confined to a kind of play shorter than a moral-play, and without allegorical characters or significance, and so better suited to the occasion for which it was intended. John Heywood was the master of this kind of play-writing, if indeed he were not its inventor; but his proper place is at a later period of our little history.

The oldest English moral-play yet discovered exists in manuscript, and is entitled *The Castle of Perseverance.** It was written about 1450. The principal character is Humanum Genus, an embodiment of mankind, whose moral enemies, the World, the Flesh, and the Devil, (Mundus, Caro, and Belial,) open the play by a conference in which they boast of their powers. Mankind (Humanum Genus) then appears, and announces that he has just come into the world naked; and immediately a good and a bad angel present themselves, and assert their claims to his confidence. He gives himself up to the latter, who, through the agency of the World, places him in the hands of Voluptuousness and Folly, (Voluptas and Stultitia. — But let it suffice to say that the characters have Latin names.) Backbiter then makes him acquainted with Avarice and the other deadly sins, of whom Luxury — in these plays always a woman — becomes his leman. The good angel sends Confession to him, who is told that he is come too soon, he having then more agreeable matters in hand than the confessing of sin. But at last, by the help of Penitence, Mankind is reclaimed, and got off into the strong Castle of Perseverance in company with the seven Cardinal Virtues. Belial and the Deadly Sins lay siege to the castle, the leader having first berated and beaten his forces for

* Once in possession of Dr. Cox Macro; it passed into the collection of Mr. Hudson Gurney, who submitted it to Mr. Collier. See that gentleman's *Annals of the Stage*, Vol. II. p. 278.

having allowed his prey to escape him.* Belial and the Sins are defeated, chiefly by the aid of Charity and Patience, who pelt them with roses from the battlements. But Mankind begins to grow old, and Avarice undermines the castle, and persuades him to leave it. Garcio (a boy) claims all the goods which Mankind has gathered with the aid of Avarice, when Death and the Soul appear, and the latter calls on Pity for help. But the bad angel takes the hero on his back, and sets off with him hell-ward. The scene changes to heaven, where Pity, Peace, Justice, and Truth plead for him with God, and we are left to infer that Mankind is saved. God speaks the moralizing epilogue. A rude drawing on the last leaf of the manuscript shows the castle with a bed beneath it for Mankind, and five scaffolds for God, Belial, the World, the Flesh, and Avarice. Mr. Collier is of opinion that so carefully constructed and varied an allegory "must have predecessors in the same kind;" but this supposition seems to me by no means necessary. An allegorical purpose once formed, the miracle-plays furnished all the necessary precedents for the development of the idea. In another play in the same collection, called *Mind Will and Understanding*, Anima, the Soul, also appears, and, having been debauched by the three personages who give the play its name, she

* Belial thus incites his followers to the assault:—

"I here trumpys trebelen all of tene:
The wery world walkyth to werre . .
Sprede my penon upon a prene
And stryke we for the now undyr sterre.
Schapyth now your sheldys shene
Yone skallyd skrouts for to skerre
Buske ye now, boys, belyve,
For ever I stond in mekyl stryve
Whyl Mankind is in clene lyve."

Mr. Collier, from whom I copy them, justly remarks upon a certain degree of life and spirit in these rude lines.

"apperythe in most horribul wyse, fowler than a fend," and gives birth to six of the deadly sins according to this direction: "Here rennyt out from undyr the horrybull mantyle of the Soul six small boys in the lyknes of devyllys, and so retorne ageyn." Conscious of her degradation, she goes out with her three seducers, and it is directed that "in the going the Soule syngyth in the most lamentabull wyse, with drawte notes, as yt ys songyn in the passyon wyke." In the end, Mind, Will, and Understanding are converted from their evil ways, to the great joy of Anima.

John Skelton, poet-laureate to Henry VII. and his son, wrote two moral-plays, *The Necromancer*, and *Magnificence.* A copy of the latter still exists; and one of the former was seen and described by Collins, although it has since been lost. The characters are a Necromancer, the Devil, a Notary, Simony, and Avarice; and the action is merely the trial of the last two before the Devil. The Necromancer calls upon the Devil, and opens the court. The prisoners are found guilty, and are sent straightway to hell. The Devil abuses the conjurer, and disappears in flame and smoke. This play, which was played before King Henry VII., at Woodstock, on Palm Sunday, was printed in 1504. When *Magnificence* was produced we do not know, as its title page is without date; but Skelton mentions it in a poem printed in 1523. Its purpose is to show the vanity of magnificence. The hero, Magnificence, — eaten out of house and home by a raft of friends called Fancy, alias Largess, Counterfeit-countenance, Crafty-conveyance, Cloked-collusion, Courtly-abusion, and Folly, — falls into the hands of Adversity and Poverty, and finally is taken possession of by Despair and Mischief, who persuade him to commit suicide, which he is about to do, when Good-hope stays his hand, and Redress, Circumspection, and Perseverance sober him down to a humble frame of mind. The piece is intolerably long, and much of it is written in that wearisome verse called "Skeltonic."* To relieve it, some fun is introduced, which is of the coarsest kind, but which was probably more to the taste of all the poet's audience, high and low, than his heavy moralizing.† Of pure moral-plays the reader has probably had quite enough; but two others may well be noticed, on account of traits peculiar to them. In one, called *The longer thou livest the more Foole thou art*, the chief character is Moros, a mischievous fool, who enters upon this direction: "Here entreth Moros, counterfaiting a vaine gesture and a foolish countenaunce, synging the foote of many songes as fools were wont."

* Of which the following passage is an example: —

"For counterfet countenaunce knowen am I.
This worlde is full of my foly.
I set not by hym a fly
That cannot counterfet a lye,
Swere and stare and byde therebye,
And countenaunce it clenly,
And defende it manerly.
A knave will counterfet now a knyght,
A lurdayne lyke a lorde to fyght,
A mynstrell lyke a man of myght,
A tappyster lyke a lady bryght.
Thus make I them wyth thryff to fyght;
Thus at the last I brynge hym ryght
To Tyburne, where they hange on hyght."

† As for instance, the following passage, quoted by Mr. Collier, in which Folly wins a wager that he will laugh Crafty-conveyance out of his coat: —

"[*Here foly maketh semblaunt to take a lowse from crafty conveyaunce shoulder*]
Fancy What hast thou found there?
Foly By god, a lowse
Crafty-convey By cockes harte I trow thou lyste.
Foly By the masse, a spanyshe moght with a gray lyste
Fancy Ha, ha, ha, ha, ha, ha!
Crafty-convey. Cockes armes, it is not so, I trowe
[*Here crafty-conveyaunce putteth of his gowne*
Foly Put on thy gowne agayne for now thou hast lost.
Fancy Lo, John a bonam, where is thy brayne?"

This brings to mind Shakespeare's fools and clowns, who are always singing the foot of many songs; and we see the making them do so was no device of his, but a mere faithful copying of the living models before him; though the lyric sweetness and the art and the wisdom which he puts into their mouths were in most instances, we may be sure, his own. The other moral-play in question, *The Marriage of Wit and Science*,* is remarkable not only for its very elaborate and ingenious, though equally dull and wearisome, allegory, but for the fact that it is regularly divided into acts and scenes, which is not the case with even many of the early comedies and tragedies by which the miracle-plays were succeeded. One of the very latest of the moral-plays was *The Three Lords and Three Ladies of London*, which was written after 1588, and printed in 1590. But, as its title would indicate, this is in reality a kind of comedy; and it is also remarkable as being written for the most part in blank verse.

III.

As allegory had crept into the miracle-plays, and, by introducing the impersonation of abstract qualities, had worked a change in their structure and their purpose, which finally produced the moral-play, so personages intended as satire upon classes and individuals, and as representations of the manners and customs of the day, took, year after year, more and more the place of the cold and stiff abstractions which filled the stage in the pure moral-play, until, at last, comedy, or the ideal representation of human life, appeared in English drama. Thus in *Tom Tyler and his Wife*, which, according to

* Reprinted by the Shakespeare Society.

Ritson, was published in 1578, and which contains internal evidence that it was written about eight years before that date, the personages are Tom Tyler, his good woman, who is a gray mare of the most formidable kind, Tom Tailor, his friend, Desire, Strife, Sturdy, Tipple, Patience, and the Vice. In *The Conflict of Conscience*, written at about the same date, among Conscience, Hypocrisy, Tyranny, Avarice, Sensual-suggestion, and the like, appear four historical personages — Francis Spiera, an Italian lawyer, who is called Philologus, his two sons, and Cardinal Eusebius. Mr. Collier also mentions a political moral-play written about 1565, called *Albion Knight*, in which the hero, a knight named Albion, is a personification of England, and the motive of which is satire upon the oppression of the commons by the nobles. But before this date, and probably in the reign of Edward VI., Bishop Bale had written his *Kynge Johan*, a play the purpose of which was to further the Reformation, and which partook of the characters of a moral-play, and a dramatic chronicle-history. Indeed, neither the reformers nor their opponents were slow to take advantage of the stage as a means of indoctrinating the people with their peculiar views; and as the government passed alternately into the hands of Papists and Protestants, plays were suppressed, or dramatic performances interdicted altogether, as the good of the ecclesiastical party in power seemed to require. In the very first year of Queen Mary's reign, 1558, a politico-religious moral-play, called *Respublica*, was produced, the purpose of which was to check the Reformation. The kingdom of England is impersonated as Respublica, and, by the author's own admission, Queen Mary herself figures as Nemesis, the goddess of redress and correction.*

* Described in Collier's edition of Shakespeare's Works. 1843. Vol. I. p. xviii.

John Heywood, whose interludes have been already mentioned, produced his first play before the year 1521. Yet, in turning our eyes back two generations to glance at his compositions, we may obtain, perhaps, a more correct view of the gradual development of the English drama than if we had examined them in the order of time. Heywood was attached to the court of Henry VIII. as a singer and player upon the virginals. His interludes were short pieces, about the length of one act of a modern comedy. Humorous in their motive, and dependent for all their interest upon their extravagant burlesque of every-day life, upon the broadest jokes and the coarsest satire, they were, indeed, but a kind of farce. That which is regarded as Heywood's earliest extant production is entitled *A mery play between the Pardoner and the Frere, the Curate and neybour Pratte.* The Pardoner and the Friar have got leave of the Curate to use his church, the former to show his relics, the latter to preach; both having the same end in view — money. They quarrel as to who shall have precedence, and at last fight. The Curate, brought in by this row between his clerical brethren, attempts to separate and pacify them; but failing to accomplish this single-handed, he calls the neighbors to his aid. In vain, however; for the Pardoner and the Friar, like man and wife interrupted in a quarrel, unite their forces, and beat the interlopers soundly. After which they depart, and the play ends. In *The Four P's*, another of Heywood's interludes, the personages are the Palmer, the Pardoner, the Poticary, and the Pedlar. In this play there is little action; and the four worthies, after gibing at each other's professions for a while, set out to see which can tell the biggest lie. After much elaborate and ingenious falsehood the Palmer beats by the simple assertion that he never saw a woman out of patience in his life; at which his opponents "come down" without another word. The satire in these plays is found in the inconsistency between the characters of the personages and their professions, and particularly in the absurd and ridiculous pretensions of the clergymen as to their priestly functions, and the nature of their relics. In *The Pardoner and the Friar*, the Pardoner produces "the great too of the holy trynyte," and

> "of our Ladye a relyke full good,
> Her bongrace, which she ware with her French hode,
> Whan she wente oute al wayes for sonne bornynge;"

also, "of all halowes the blessed jaw bone;" and in *The Four P's* there is a "buttocke-bone of Pentecoste." And yet Heywood was a stanch Romanist.

There are certain passages in Heywood's plays, which, considering the period at which he wrote, are remarkable for genuine humor and descriptive power, as well as for spirited and lively versification.* And coarse and

* See the following description of an alleged visit to hell by the Pardoner in *The Four P's*:—

> "Thys devyll and I walket arme in arme
> So farre, tyll he had brought me thyther,
> Where all the dyvells of hell togyther
> Stode in a ray, in suche apparell
> As for that day there metely fell.
> Theyr hornes well gylt, theyr clowes full clene,
> Theyr taylles wel kempt, and as I wene,
> With sothery butter theyr bodyes anoynted;
> I never sawe devylls so well appoynted.
> The master devyll sat on his jacket,
> And all the soules were playinge at racket.
> None other rackettes they hadde in hande
> Save every soule a good fyre brand;
> Wherewith they played so pretely,
> That Lucyfer laughed merely:
> And all the resedew of the feends
> Did laugh thereat ful wel like freends.
> But of my frende I sawe no whyt,
> Nor durst not axe for her as yet.

indecent as his productions must be pronounced, they exhibit more real dramatic power than appears in those of any other playwright of the first half of the sixteenth century.

Heywood founded no school, seems to have had no imitators; there is no line of succession between him and the man who must be regarded as the first writer of genuine English comedy. We have seen that plays in which characters drawn from real life, mingled with the allegorical personages proper to moral-plays, were written as late as 1570. Such were *Tom Tyler and his Wife* and *The Conflict of Conscience*, mentioned above. But as early as the year 1551, Nicholas Udall, who became Master of Eton, and afterward of Westminster, had written a play divided into acts and scenes, with a gradually developed action tending to a climax, and the characters of which were all ideal representations of actual life; a play which was, in short, a comedy. The

Anone all this rout was brought in selens,
And I by an usher brought in presens,
Of Lucyfer: then lowe, as wel I could,
I knelyd whiche he so well alowde,
That thus he beckte, and by saynt Antony
He smyled on me well favouredly,
Bendynge his browss as brode as barne durres,
Shakynge his eares as ruged as burres;
Rolyng his eyes as rounde as two bushels;
Flashynge the fyre out of his nose thryls;
Gnashinge his teeth so vaynglorously,
That me thought tyme to fall to flatery,
Wherwith I tolde as I shall tell.
O plesant pycture! O prince of hell!
Feutred in fashyon abominable
And syns that is inestimable
For me to prayse the worthyly,
I leve of prayse as unworthy
To geve the prays besechynge the
To heare my sewte, and then to be
So good to graunt the thynge I crave."

play is named after its hero, *Ralph Roister Doister*. The scene is laid in London, and Ralph, who is a conceited, rattle-pated young fellow about town, and amorous withal, fancies himself in love with Dame Custance, a gay young widow with "a tocher," as he thinks, of a thousand pounds and more. But upon this point Matthew Merry-greek,* his poor kinsman and attendant, a shrewd, mischievous, time-serving fellow, remarks to him, that

> "An hundred pounde of marriage money doubtless,
> Is ever thirtie pounde sterlyng or somewhat less;
> So that her thousande pounde yf she be thriftie
> Is much neere about two hundred and fiftie.
> Howbeit wowers and widows are never poore."

Which shows that our ways, in this respect at least, have not changed much in three hundred years from those of our forefathers. When the play opens, Custance is betrothed to Garvin Goodluck, a merchant who is then at sea. But Merry-greek crams his master with eagerly swallowed flattery, and puts him in heart by telling him that a man of his person and spirit can win any woman. Ralph encounters three of Custance's handmaids, old and young, and by flattering words and caresses tries to bring them over to his side. He leaves a letter with one of them for Custance, which is delivered, but not immediately opened. The next day Dobinet Doughty, the merchant's servant, brings a ring and token from Master Goodluck to Dame Custance; but Madge, having got a scolding for her pains in delivering Ralph's letter, refuses to carry the ring and token. Other servants entering, Dobinet introduces himself as a mes-

* Merry-greek was slang three hundred years ago for what we now call a "jolly fellow." "Then she's a merry Greek indeed."
Troilus and Cressida, Act I. Sc. 2.

senger from the dame's betrothed husband; and they, especially one Tibbet Talk-a-pace, being delighted at the idea of a wedding, and mistaking the man who is thus to bless the household, fall out as to who is to deliver Ralph's presents. But Tib triumphs by snatching the souvenirs and running out with them to her mistress. A reproof to Tib in her turn ends the second act. The third opens with a visit by Merry-greek to Dame Custance, that he may find out if the ring and token have worked well for his master's interest. But he only learns from Dame Custance that she is fast betrothed to Goodluck, that she has not even opened Ralph's letter, but knows that it must be from him, —

"For no mon there is but a very dolte and lout
That to wowe a widowe would so go about."

She adds that Ralph shall never have her for his wife while he lives. On receiving this news, Ralph declares that he shall then and there incontinently die; when Merry-greek takes him at his word, pretends to think that he is really dying, and calls in a priest and four assistants to sing a mock requiem. Ralph, however, like most disappointed lovers, concludes to live; and Merry-greek advises him to serenade Custance, and boldly ask her hand. So done; but Custance snubs him, and produces his yet unread letter, which Merry-greek reads to the assembled company with such defiance of the punctuation that the sense is perverted, and all are moved to mirth except Ralph, who in wrath disowns the composition. Dame Custance retires, and Merry-greek, again flattering his master, advises him to refrain himself awhile from his lady-love, and that then she will seek him, for, as to women,

"When ye will they will not; will not ye, then will they."

Ralph threatens vengeance upon the scrivener who copied his letter; but when the penman reads it with the proper pauses, he finds out who is the real culprit; and thus the third act ends. The fourth opens with the entrance of another messenger from Goodluck to Dame Custance. While he is talking to the lady Ralph enters, ostentatiously giving orders about making ready his armor, takes great airs, calls Custance his spouse, and tells Goodluck's messenger to tell his master that "his betters be in place now." The angered Dame Custance summons maid and man, and turns Ralph and Merry-greek out of doors; but the latter soon slips back, and tells her that his only purpose is to make sport of Ralph, who is about returning armed, "to pitch a field" with his female foes. Roister Doister soon enters armed with pot, pan, and popgun, and accompanied by three or four assistants. But the comely dame, who seems to be a tall woman of her hands, stands her ground, and, aided by her maids, "pitches into" the enemy, and with mop and besom puts him to ignominious flight; in which squabble the knave Merry-greek, pretending to fight for his rich kinsman, manages to belabor him soundly. At the beginning of the fifth act Garvin Goodluck makes his appearance, and Sim Suresby tells him of what he saw and heard at his visit to Dame Custance. Goodluck is convinced of the lady's fickleness. She arrives, and would welcome him tenderly; but of course there is trouble. Finally, however, on the evidence of Tristram Trusty, she is freed from suspicion; and Ralph, petitioning for pardon, is invited to the wedding supper, and the play is at an end. It is rather a rude performance;*

* The following extract from the opening of the third scene of the fourth act of this comedy is a fair example of its style: —

"*Custance.* What meane these lewde felowes thus to trouble me stil?
Sym Suresby here, perchaunce, shal thereof deme som yll,

but it contains all the elements of a regular comedy of the romantic school; and it must be confessed that many a duller one has been presented to a modern audience.

Yet ruder and coarser than *Ralph Roister Doister*, and

And shall suspect me in some point of naughtinesse,
And they come hitherward.
Sym Suresby. What is their businesse?
Cust. I have nought to them, nor they to me, in sadnesse.
Sure. Let us hearken them; somewhat there is, I feare it.
Ralph Roister. I wil speake out aloude best, that she may heare it.
Merry-greek. Nay, alas! ye may so feare hir out of hir wit.
Roister. By the crosse of my sworde, I will hurt hir no whit.
Merry. Will ye doe no harme in deede? Shall I trust your worde?
Roister. By Roister Doister's fayth, I will speak, but in borde.
Sure. Let us hearken them; somewhat there is, I feare it.
Roister. I will speake out aloude, I care not who heare it. —
Sirs, see that my harnesse, my tergat, and my shield,
Be made as bright now as when I was last in field,
As white as I shoulde to warre againe tomorrowe —
For sicke shall I be but I worke some folke sorrowe.
Therefore see that all shine as bright as sainct George,
Or as doth a key newly come from the smith's forge.
I woulde have my sworde and harnesse to shine so bright
That I might therewith dimme mine enimies sight;
I woulde have it cast beames as fast, I tell you playne,
As doth the glittering grass after a showre of raine.
And see that, in case I shoulde have to come to arminge,
All things may be ready at a moment's warning.
For such a chaunce may chaunce in an houre, do ye heare?
Merry. As perchaunce shall not chaunce againe in seven yeare.
Roister. Now draw we neare to hir, and heare what shal be sayde.
Merry. But I woulde not have you make hir too muche afrayde.
Roister. Well founde, sweete wife (I trust) for al this your soure looke
Cust. Wife! Why cal ye me wife?
Sure. Wife! this geare goeth acrook.
Merry. Nay Mistresse Custance, I warrant you our letter
Is not as we redde e'en nowe, but much better;
And where ye half stomaked this gentleman afore,
For this same letter ye wyll love him nowe therefore;
Nor it is not this letter though ye were a queene
That shoulde breake marriage betweene you twaine, I weene.
Cust. I did not refuse hym for the letter's sake.
Roister. Then ye are content me for your husbande to take.
Cust. You for my husbande to take! Nothing lesse truely.
Roister. Yea, say so sweete spouse, afore strangers hardly.
Merry. And though I have here his letter of love with me,
Yet his rings and his tokens he sent keepe safe with ye.
Cust. A mischief take his tokens, and him, and thee too."

less amusing, is *Gammer Gurton's Needle*, which, until 1818, was supposed to be the earliest extant English comedy, but which was not written until about thirty years later than Udall's play, it having been first performed, as Malone reasonably concludes, at Christ College, Cambridge, in 1566. Its author was John Still, afterward Bishop of Bath and Wells, who was born in 1543. The personages in this play are all, with two or three exceptions, rustics, and their language is a broad, provincial dialect. The plot turns upon the simple incident of Gammer Gurton's loss of her needle while she is mending her servant Hodge's breeches. Sharp is the hunt through five acts after this needful instrument — Hodge even pretending to have an interview with the Devil upon the subject. But the needle is not found until Hodge, having on the mended garment, is hit "a good blow on the buttocks" by the bailiff, whose services have been called in; when the clown discovers that Gammer Gurton's needle, like Old Rapid's in the *Road to Ruin*, does not always stick in the right place. The second act of this farrago of practical jokes and coarse humor opens with that jolly old drinking song beginning, —

> "I cannot eat but little meat,
> My stomach is not good,"

which may be found in many collections of lyric verse.

IV.

Whether it was that moral-plays satisfied for a long time our forefathers' desire for serious entertainment, and furnished them sufficient occasion for that reflection upon the graver interests and incidents of human life which it is tragedy's chief function to suggest, or whether the public, wearied by the sententious gravity of the moral-plays, (which, however, their authors had often sought to retrieve by humorous character and incident,) demanded, on the introduction of real life into the drama, that only its light and merry side should be presented, it is certain that comedy entered upon the English stage much in advance of her elder sister. It is barely possible that a play upon the story of *Romeo and Juliet* was performed in London before the year 1562;* but the earliest tragedy extant in our language is *Ferrex and Porrex*, or *Gorboduc*, all of which was probably written by Thomas Sackville, Earl of Dorset, but to the first three acts of which Thomas Norton has a disputed claim. This play is founded on events in the fabulous chronicles of Britain. The principal personages are Gorboduc, King of Britain, about B. C. 600, Videna, his wife, and Ferrex and Porrex, his sons. But nobles, councillors, parasites, a lady, and messengers make the personages number thirteen. The first act is occupied with the division of the kingdom by Gorboduc to his sons, and the talk thereupon. The second, with the fomenting of a quarrel between the brothers for complete sovereignty. The third, with the events of a civil war, in which Porrex kills Ferrex. In the fourth, the queen, who most loved Ferrex, kills Porrex while he is asleep at night in his chamber; the people rise in wrath and avenge this murder by the death of both Videna and Gorboduc. The fifth act is occupied by a bloody suppression of this rebellion by the nobles, who, in their turn, fall into dissension; and the land, without a rightful king, and rent by civil strife, becomes desolate. This tragedy was written for one of the Christmas festivals of the Inner Tem-

* See the Introduction to *Romeo and Juliet*, Vol. X. p. 7.

ple, to be played by the gentlemen of that society; and by desire of Queen Elizabeth it was performed by them at White-hall on the 18th of January, 1561. It is plain that the author of this play meant to be very elegant, decorous, and classical; and he succeeded. Of all the stirring events upon which the tragedy is built, not one is represented; all are told. Even Ferrex and Porrex are not brought together on the stage, and Videna does not meet either of them before the audience after the first act. Each act is introduced by a dumb show, intended to be symbolical of what will follow — a common device on our early stage which was ridiculed by Shakespeare in the third act of *Hamlet;* * and each act, except the last, is followed by a moralizing and explanatory chorus recited by "four ancient and sage men of Britain."

Ferrex and Porrex is remarkable as being the first English play extant in blank verse, and probably it was the first so written. It is to be wondered that even in this respect it was ever taken as a model. For although Sir Philip Sidney in his *Defence of Poesy*, finding fault with *Ferrex and Porrex* for its violation of the unities of time and place, admits that it is so "full of stately speeches and well sounding phrases, climbing to the hight of Senaca his stile, and full of notable morality,

* "*The Order and Signification of the Domme Shew before the fourth Act.*

"First the musick of howeboies began to playe, during which came from under the stage, as though out of hell, three furies, Alecto, Megera, and Ctisiphone clad in blacke garmentes sprinkled with bloud and flames, their bodies girt with snakes, their heds spred with serpentes in stead of heire, the one bearing in hand a snake, the other a whip, and the third a burning firebrand; ech driving before them a king and a queene, which moved by the furies unnaturally had slaine their owne children. The names of the kings and queenes were these, Tantalus, Medea, Athamas, Ino, Cambises, Althea; after that the furies and these had passed about the stage thrise, they departed, and than the musick ceased: hereby was signified the unnatural murders to follow, that is to say, Porrex, slaine by his owne mother; and of king Gorboduc and queene Videna, killed by their owne subjects."

which it doth most delightfully teach," yet it may be safely said that another play so lifeless in movement, so commonplace in thought, so utterly undramatic in motive, so oppressively didactic in language, so absolutely without distinction of character among its personages, cannot be found in our dramatic literature. From *Ferrex and Porrex* we turn even to the miracle-plays and moral-plays with relief, if not with pleasure. Some notion of its tediousness may be gathered from the fact that it closes with a speech one hundred lines in length, and that the first act is chiefly occupied with three speeches by three councillors, which together make two hundred and sixty verses.* This play demands notice because

* The following passage, in which the death of Porrex is announced, is a favorable example of the style of this play: —

"*Marcella.* Oh where is ruth or where is pitie now?
Whether is gentle hart and mercy fled?
Are they exiled out of our stony brestes,
Never to make returne? is all the world
Drowned in blood and sonke in crueltie?
If not in woman mercy may be found
If not (alas) within the mother's brest
To her owne childe to her owne flesh and blood;
If ruthe be banished thence, if pitie there
May have no place, if there no gentle hart
Do live and dwell, where should we seek it then?
Gorboduc. Madame (alas) what means your wofull tale?
Marcella. O silly woman I! why to this houre
Have kinde and fortune thus deferred my breath,
That I should live to see this dolefull day?
Will ever wight beleve that such hard hart
Could rest within the cruell mother's brest,
With her owne hande to slaye her only sonne?
But out (alas) these eyes behelde the same,
They saw the driery sight, and are become
Most ruthfull recordes of the bloody fact.
Porrex (alas) is by his mother slaine,
And with her hand and wofull thing to tell;
While slumbring on his carefull bed he restes,
His hart stabde in with knife is reft of life.
Gorboduc. O Eubulus, oh draw this sword of ours,
And pearce this hart with speed! O hateful light,
O loathsome life, O sweete and welcome death,
Deare Eubulus, worke this we thee besech!

it is our first tragedy, our first play written in blank verse, but for no other reason. It had no perceptible effect upon the English drama, and marks no stage in its progress. In that regard it might as well have been written in Greece and in Greek, or in ancient British by Gorboduc himself; for in either case its motive and plan could not then have been more foreign to the genius of English dramatic literature. And it is now proper to say that translated plays adapted from Greek and Latin authors, of which there were many performed in the earlier part of Elizabeth's reign, are here passed by without notice, not merely because they were translations and adaptations, but because, not being an outgrowth of the English character, they were entirely without influence upon the development of the English drama, in an account of which they have no proper place. *The Supposes* translated from Ariosto by George Gascoigne, and acted at Gray's Inn in 1566, must be mentioned as the earliest extant play in English prose. The fact is significant indeed, that none of the many plays written especially for the court and for the learned societies and the elegant people of that day have left any traces even of a temporary influence upon our stage. The English drama, unlike that of France, had its germ in the instincts, and its growth with the growth, of the whole English people.

Up to, and even past, the Elizabethan era, the English drama was rude in style and in construction, gross in sentiment and in language. Its personages had little char-

Eubulus. Pacient your grace, perhappes he liveth yet,
With wound receaved, but not of certain death.
Gorboduc. O let us then repayre unto the place,
And see if Porrex live, or thus be slaine.
Marcella. Alas he liveth not, it is to true,
That with these eyes of him a perelesse prince,
Sonne to a king and in the flower of youth,
Even with a twinkle a senselesse stock I saw."

acter or keeping, its incidents little probability or connection. A true dramatic style, by which character is evolved and emotion revealed, was yet unformed. The cultivated people of that time saw these defects, except the last, but devised for them the wrong remedy. With their heads full of the ancient classics, they judged their own theatre by a foreign standard, to which they would have forced it to conform.* In this English drama,

* George Whetstone, in the dedication of his Promos and Cassandra, the incidents of which Shakespeare used in his *Measure for Measure*, and which was published in 1578, gives us the following criticism upon the English drama of that day: —

"The Englishman in this qualitie is most vaine, indiscreete, and out of order: he first groundes his worke on impossibilities: then, in three howers, ronnes he throwe the worlde: marryes, gets children, makes children men, men to conquer kingdomes, murder monsters, and bringeth Gods from Heaven, and fetcheth divils from Hel. And (that which is worst) their ground is not so imperfect as their workinge indiscreete; not waying, so the people laugh, though they laugh them (for their follies) to scorn. Manye tymes, to make myrthe, they make a clowne companion with a Kinge: in theyr grave Councils they allow the advice of fools; yea, they use one order of speach for all persons, a grose *Indecorum*," &c.

Sir Philip Sidney, in a passage of his *Defence of Poesy* (written about 1583) which has been often quoted, but which is too important to be omitted here, says, —

"Our Tragedies and Comedies are not without cause cried out against, observing rules neither of honest civilitie nor skilfull Poetrie. Excepting Gorboduck (againe I say of those that I have seene) which notwithstanding, as it is full of statelie speeches, and well sounding phrases, climing to the height of Seneca his stile, and as full of notable moralitie, which it doth most delightfully teach, and so obtaine the verie end of Poesie, yet in truth it is very defectious in the circumstances, which grieves me, because it might not remaine as an exact modell of all Tragedies. For it is faulty in place and time, the two necessarie companions of all corporall actions. For where the Stage should alway represent but one place, and the uttermost time presupposed in it, should be both by Aristotle's precept and common reason, but one day, there is both many dayes and manie places artificially imagined. But if it bee so in *Gorboduck*, how much more in all the rest, where you shall have *Asia* of the one side, and *Africk* of the other, and so many other under kingdoms, that the Player, when he comes in, must ever begin with telling where he is, or else the tale will not be conceived. Now you shall have three ladies walke to gather flowers, and then we must believe the stage to be a garden. By and by we hear newes of a shipwrack in the same place; then we are to blame if we accept it not for a rocke. Upon the backe of that comes out a hideous monster with fire and smoke, and then the miserable beholders are bound to take it for a cave; while, in the meantime, two armies flie in, represented with four swords and bucklers, and then what hard hart will not receive it for a pitched

rude, coarse and confused, there was yet an inherent vitality. It was native to the English mind, and it sought to present even in tragedy an idealized picture of real life which had never yet been attempted.

Our drama, advancing through centuries, had slowly reached this stage of growth, where if its development had been stayed, its history would have been almost without interest, except to the literary antiquary, when suddenly its homely, uncouth bud burst into flower so sweet, of beauty so glorious, so perennial, as ever after to gladden, to perfume, and to adorn the ages. The rapidity of this transition is astonishing. It is almost like magical transformation. In less than twenty years from the time when the best plays yet produced by English authors were intrinsically unworthy of a place in literature, the English stage had become illustrious.

This change was brought about by the great and increasing taste of the day for dramatic performances, which called into the service of the theatre every needy hand that held a ready pen. A crowd of young men left the learned professions in London, or abandoning rustic homes, flocked thither to make money by writing plays. Among these men seven attained distinction; and yet not only so inferior, but of so little intrinsic enduring interest, was the work of six of them, that, with one and hardly one exception, their names would

field? Now, of time they are much more liberal; for ordinarie it is that two young Princes fall in love: after many traverses she is got with child, delivered of a fair boy; he is lost, groweth a man, falleth in love, and is ready to get another child, and all this in two houres' space; which how absurd it is in sense, even sense may imagine and art hath taught, and all ancient examples justified, and at this daye the ordinarie players in *Italie* wil not erre in . . . But besides these grosse absurdities how all their Playes be neither right Tragedies nor right Comedies, mingling Kings and Clownes not because the matter so carieth it, but thrust in the Clowne by head and shoulders, to play a part in Majestical matters with neither decencie nor discretion; so as neither the admiration and commiseration, nor right sportfulness is by their mongrel Tragi-comedy obtained."

not have been known outside of purely literary circles, but for the seventh. They were Thomas Kyd, John Lilly, George Peele, George Chapman, Robert Greene, Christopher Marlowe, and William Shakespeare. Of the six, the oldest whose age is known to us was only ten years the senior of the seventh, and the most eminent, Marlowe, was born but two years before him.* Shakespeare got to work in London very early in life. He was using his pen as a dramatic writer there before he was twenty-four years old.† These men were therefore in both the strictest and in the broadest sense his contemporaries — his contemporaries as men and as authors. The mere fact that he found four of them, Kyd, Peele, Greene, and Marlowe, in the front rank of dramatic writers on his arrival in London, does not properly entitle them to consideration as his predecessors in English drama. Being so absolutely contemporaneous with him in age, they could be justly regarded as his predecessors only as having been the founders of a school of which he was an eminent disciple, or to which he had established a rival or a successor. But he stood to them in neither of these relations. He and they were all, with a single exception, of one school, of which neither one of them was the founder. With this one exception these men were all striving to do the same thing, at the same time, in the same way. The time had come when it was to be done, and the time brought the men who were to do it, each according to his ability. And not only were their aims identical, but there is the best reason, short of competent contemporary testimony,

* Lilly was born about 1553, Peele about the same year, Chapman in 1559, Greene about 1560, Marlowe about 1562, Shakespeare in 1564. The date of Kyd's birth can only be conjectured.

† See Section XII. of the Essay on the Authorship of *King Henry the Sixth*. Vol. VII.

for believing that four of them, including Shakespeare, were colaborers upon still existing works.*

The exception to this unity of purpose was John Lilly, the author of *Euphues*. Lilly is known in dramatic literature as the author of eight comedies written to be performed at the court of Elizabeth.† They are in all respects opposed to the genius of the English drama. They do not even pretend to be representations of human life and human character, but are pure fantasy pieces, in which the personages are a heterogeneous medley of Grecian gods and goddesses, and impossible, colorless creatures with sublunary names, all thinking with one brain, and speaking with one tongue — the conceitful, crotchety brain and the dainty, well-trained tongue of clever, witty John Lilly. They are all in prose, but contain some pretty, fanciful verses called songs, which are as unlyrical in spirit as the plays in which they appear are undramatic. From these plays Shakespeare borrowed a few thoughts; but they exercised no modifying influence upon his genius, nor did they at all conform to that of the English drama, upon which they are a mere grotesque excrescence. Chapman, one of the elder and the stronger of the six above named, is not known as the author, even in part, of any play older than Shakespeare's earliest performances. He probably entered upon dramatic composition at a somewhat later period in life than either of the others; and as a dramatist he is properly to be passed over in this place,

* See the introduction to *The Taming of the Shrew* and the Essay upon *King Henry the Sixth*.

† Lilly's Plays are *Endimion*, *Campaspe*, *Sapho and Phaon*, *Gallathea*, *Mydas*, *Mother Bombie*, *The Woman in the Moone*, and *Love's Metamorphosis*. *The Maid's Metamorphosis*, which was published anonymously in 1600, has been attributed to him, as also has *A Warning for Fair Women*, which was published anonymously in 1599; but neither of them bears traces of his style.

as not even having been Shakespeare's predecessor, in the mere order of time, by even that very brief period which may be admitted in the cases of Peele, Greene, and Marlowe. The styles of these three dramatists are commented upon, and extracts from their plays are given, in the Essay upon the Authorship of King Henry the Sixth, in another volume of this work, where they are particularly considered in their relation to Shakespeare. I will, however, notice here the opinion generally received, that Marlowe's talents were very far superior to those of either Greene or Peele — a judgment to which I cannot entirely assent, as far as Peele is concerned. Peele's plays, it is true, lack some of Marlowe's fire and fury; but they are also without much of his fustian. Peele's characters are less strongly marked than Marlowe's; but they are also less absurd and extravagant, and, in my opinion, they are equally well discriminated, though that is little praise. Peele's *David and Bathsheba* is a play which for the genuineness of its feeling, if not for the harmony of its verse, Marlowe might have been glad to own; and *The Battle of Alcanzar* is in the same furious, bloody vein with his *Tamburlaine*, and equal, if not superior, to it in sense and keeping. It is also noteworthy that the Prologue to Peele's *Arraignment of Paris*, which was published in 1584, when Marlowe was but twenty years old, and before he had taken his Bachelor's degree at Cambridge, is, for its union of completeness of measure with variety of pause, unsurpassed by any dramatic blank verse, that of one play excepted, which was written before the time of Shakespeare. The critical reader who is familiar with Marlowe's works must constantly remember that there is every reason for believing that *Edward the Second* — his best play in versification no less than in style, sentiment, and character — was written after 1590, and after the production of *The First Part of the Contention* and *The True Tragedy*.*

With regard to these dramatists there only remains to be noticed the claim which has been set up for one of them, Marlowe,† that he was the first who used blank verse upon our public stage, and "the first who harmonized it with variety of pause." As to which I will only say, briefly, that although it is probably true that he in his *Tamburlaine* made one of the earliest efforts to bring blank verse into vogue in plays written for the general public, and to substitute the roll and flow of measured rhythm for the feebler and more monotonous music of rhyme in dramatic poetry intended for uncultured as well as cultured ears, I cannot find in this endeavor reason for giving him the credit due to an innovator, much less that which belongs to an inventor. Blank verse, as we have seen, was used in plays produced for special occasions and audiences many years before Marlowe wrote; and he, writing only for the general theatre-going public, seems merely to have used, and somewhat improved, an instrument which he found made to his hand. Among the dramatists who preceded Marlowe in the use of blank verse on the public stage is one who, in my judgment, wrote it with a spirit and a freedom which Marlowe himself hardly excelled. This dramatist is the author of *Jeronimo*. A continuation of this play, called *The Spanish Tragedy, or Hieronimo is mad again*, which we know, upon Thomas Heywood's testimony, was written by Thomas Kyd, was one of the most popular plays of the Elizabethan era. Hitherto it has been assumed that Kyd was also the author of *Jeronimo*. But a comparison of the two plays shows them to be so unlike

* See pp. 438, 439 of the Essay upon the Authorship of King Henry the Sixth. Vol. VII.

† By Mr. Collier in his History of English Dramatic Poetry, &c., and by Mr. Dyce in his Life of Shakespeare.

in all respects — in versification, in language, in dramatic characterization, and in all distinctive poetic traits — that it seems very clear that the fact that Kyd did write *The Spanish Tragedy* is conclusive evidence against his authorship of the elder play. It would be difficult for two contemporary dramatic poets, in their treatment of the same or a very similar subject, to produce two works more unlike in all particulars. *The Spanish Tragedy* had been written, as we know upon Ben Jonson's testimony, long enough before 1587 to be then an old story. We may be equally sure that the play of which it is a continuation had preceded it some years. In structure *Jeronimo* bears strong traces of the pre-Elizabethan era. It opens with a dumb show explanatory of the situation of the characters before the action commences; the action does not "grow to a point," and the play consequently reads less like a tragedy than an episode of history dramatized with little art; quite one half of the play is in rhyme; and among its *dramatis personæ* one is allegorical — Revenge. This personage and the Ghost of Andrea, the slain lover who appears with him in the last scene of *Jeronimo*, are also used by Kyd in *The Spanish Tragedy;* but in that they merely form a chorus, and neither mingle in nor influence the action. The traits of *Jeronimo* just mentioned, and particularly the first and last, are indicative of a period earlier than that known as the Elizabethan era; while the versification and characterization belong to that era, and indeed would disgrace none of its dramatists except Shakespeare himself, and are hardly unworthy of his prentice hand. Dumb shows went out as Elizabethan dramatists began to occupy the stage; and allegory is the distinctive trait of the period of the moral-plays, although, as we have seen, it yielded place gradually to real life. The use of dumb show, and especially the introduction of an allegorical character among the *dramatis personæ* of a tragedy of real life written in blank verse, of which no other example is known to me, distinctly mark the transitional type of *Jeronimo*, which may be regarded as a fine and characteristic example of English tragedy in the stage of its development immediately preceding that which produced Shakespeare. And indeed this play and its continuation, in spite of the crudeness of both and the childishness of the latter, seem to have left stronger traces of influence upon Shakespeare's works than any other, or than all others, written by his predecessors or his contemporaries.

The English drama, and not the stage and the theatres, before the time of Shakespeare, is the subject of this account; but it may be fitly closed with a very brief description of the play-houses and the theatrical management of his early years. The general use of inn-yards as places of dramatic amusement has been already mentioned in the course of remarks upon the moral-play; and when Shakespeare arrived in London, at least three inns there — the Bull, the Cross Keys, and the Bell Savage — were thus regularly occupied. But, by a striking coincidence, with the Elizabethan era of our drama came theatres proper, buildings specially adapted to the needs of actors and audiences. Shakespeare found three such in the metropolis, — four, if to The Theatre, The Curtain, and Black-friars, we are to add Paris Garden, where bear-baiting shared the boards with comedy. All the theatres of Shakespeare's time were probably built of wood and plaster. Of the three above mentioned, the Blackfriars belonged to the class called private theatres — we know not why, unless because the private theatres were entirely roofed in, while in the others the pit was uncovered, and of course the stage and the gallery exposed to the external air. A flag was kept flying from a staff on the roof during the performance. Inside there were the stage, the pit, the boxes and galleries, much as we have them nowadays. In the public theatres, the pit, separated from the stage by paling, was called the yard, and was without seats. The price of admission to the pit or yard varied, according to the pretensions of the theatre, from twopence, and even a penny, to sixpence; that to the boxes or rooms from a shilling to two shillings, and even, on extraordinary occasions, half a crown.

The performances usually commenced at three o'clock in the afternoon; but the theatre appears to have been always artificially lighted, in the body of the house by cressets, and upon the stage by large rude chandeliers. The small band of musicians sat, not in an orchestra in front of the stage, but, it would seem, in a balcony projecting from the proscenium. People went early to the theatre for the purpose of securing good places, and while waiting for the play to begin, they read, gamed, smoked, drank, and cracked nuts and jokes together. Those who set up for wits, gallants, or critics, liked to appear upon the stage itself, which they were allowed to do all through the performance, lying upon the rushes with which the stage was strewn, or sitting upon stools, for which they paid an extra price.

Pickpockets, when detected at the theatre, seem to have been put in an extempore pillory on the stage, among the wits and gallants, at whose tongues, if not whose hands, they doubtless suffered. Kempe, the actor, in his *Nine Daies' Wonder*, A. D. 1600, compares a man to "such a one as we tye to a poast on our stage for all the people to wonder at when they are taken pilfering."

Certain very peculiar dramatic companies should not

be passed by entirely without notice. They were composed altogether of children. The boys of St. Paul's choir, those of Westminster school, and a special company called the Children of the Revels, were the most important. The first two acted under the direction of the Master of St. Paul's choir and of the school, the last under that of the Master of the Revels. Their performances were much admired, and the companies of adult actors at the theatres were piqued, and perhaps touched in pocket, by the public favor of these younkers. Shakespeare shows this by a speech which he puts into Rosencranz's mouth. (*Hamlet*, Act. II. Sc. 2.) Their audiences were generally composed of the higher classes, and they acted plays of established reputation only. This appears from the following passage in *Jack Drum's Entertainment*, published in 1601, which was itself played by the children of Paul's, as appears by its title page: —

" *Sir Edward.* I sawe the Children of *Pawles* last night,
And troth they pleas'd me prettie, prettie well.
The Apes in time will do it handsomely.
Planet. I' faith I like the Audience that frequenteth there,
With much applause. A man shall not be choakte
With the stench of Garlicke, nor be pasted
To the barny Iackett of a Beer-brewer.
Brabant, Jn. 'Tis a good gentle audience, and I hope the Boyes
Will come one day into the Courte of Requests.
Brabant, Sig. I, and they had good playes, but they produce
Such mustie fopperies of antiquitie
As do not sute the humorous ages backs
With cloathes in fashion."

Sig. H, 3 *b.*

The performance was announced by three flourishes of trumpets. At the third sounding, the curtain, which was divided in the middle from top to bottom, and ran upon rods, was drawn, and after the prologue the actors entered. The prologue was spoken by a person who wore a long black cloak and a wreath of bays upon his head. The reason of which costume was, that prologues were first spoken by the authors of plays themselves, who wore the poetical costume of the middle ages, such as we see it in the old portraits of Ariosto, Tasso, and others. When the authors themselves no longer appeared as prologue, the actors who were their proxies assumed their professional habit. Poor Robert Greene, the debauched playwright and poet, begged upon his miserable death-bed that his coffin might be strewed with bays; and the cobbler's wife, at whose house he died, respected this clinging of the wretched author to his right to Parnassian honors, and fulfilled his last request. In the earlier part of the Elizabethan era it was common for all the actors who were to take parts in the play to appear in character and pass over the stage before the performance began. This was a relic of the days of the miracle-plays and moral-plays. In the course of the play he who played the clown would favor the audience with outbreaks of extemporaneous wit and practical joking, in virtue of a time-honored privilege claimed by the clowns to "speak more than was set down for them." Indeed, extempore dialogue seems to have been permitted to, if not expected from, the representatives of comic characters. Such stage directions as the following from Greene's *Tu quoque* (A. D. 1614) are not uncommon: "*Here they two talke and rayle what they list; then Rash speakes to Staynes.*"

"*All speake.* Ud's foot dost thou stand by and do

nothing? come talke and drown her clamors. *Here they all talke and Joyce gives over weeping and Exit.*"

Between the acts there was dancing and singing; and after the play, a jig, which was a kind of comic solo sung, said, acted, and danced by the clown to the accompaniment of his own pipe and tabor. Each day's exhibition was closed by a prayer for the Queen, offered by all the actors kneeling.

The stage exhibited no movable scenery. It was hung with painted cloths and arras; when tragedy was played, the hangings were sometimes, at least, sable; over the stage was a blue canopy, called "the heavens." Although there was no proper scenery, there was ample provision of rude properties, such as towers, tombs, dragons, painted pasteboard banquets, and the like. Furniture was used, of course, and was, in many cases, the only means of indicating a change of scene, which, indeed, in most cases was left to the imagination of the audience, helped, it might be, as Sir Philip Sidney says, if the supposed scene were Thebes, by "seeing *Thebes* written in great letters on an old door." * Machinery and trap-doors were freely used, and gods and goddesses

* Such stage directions as the following show how very rude were the devices for indicating a change of scene in the latter part of the 16th and the early part of the 17th centuries: —

"*Enter Sybilla lying in child bed with her child lying by her.*"
Heywood's *Golden Age*, 1611.

"*Enter a shoemaker sitting on the stage at work. Jenkins to him.*"
Greene's *George-a-Greene*, 1599.

In the following passage the audience were evidently expected to "make believe" that a few steps across the stage was a going to the town's end.

"*Shoemaker.* Come, sir, will you go to the town's end now, sir?
Jenkins. Ay sir, come. — Now we are at the town's end; what say you now?"
Idem, ut supra.

In the plays of that period, after a murder or killing in combat, the direction is generally to the survivor, "Exit with the body." There was no device by which the dead body could be shut out from the audience, that the next scene might go on without its presence.

were let down from and hoisted up to the heavens in chairs moved by pulleys and tackle that creaked and groaned in the most sublunary and mechanical manner. At the back of the stage was a balcony, which, like the furniture in the Duke Aranza's cottage, served "a hundred uses." It was inner room, upper room, window, balcony, battlements, hill side, Mount Olympus, any place, in fact, which was supposed to be separated from and above the scene of the main action. It was in this balcony, for instance, that Sly and his attendants sat while they witnessed the performance of *The Taming of the Shrew*. The wardrobes of the principal theatres were rich, varied, and costly. It was customary to buy for stage use slightly worn court dresses and the gorgeous robes used at coronations. Near the end of the last century, Steevens tells us, there was "yet in the wardrobe of Covent Garden Theatre a rich suit of clothes that once belonged to James I." Steevens saw it worn by the performer of Justice Greedy in Massinger's *New Way to pay Old Debts*. The Allen papers and Henslowe's Diary* inform us fully upon this point. In the latter there is a memorandum of the payment of £4 14s., equal to $120, for a single pair of hose; and by the former we see that £16. equal to $400, was the price of one embroidered velvet cloak, and £20 10s., equal to $512, that of another. Costume of conventional significance was also worn; for Henslowe records the purchase at the large price of £3 10s, of "a robe for to goo invisibell."

A comparison of the prices paid for dresses, with those paid for the plays in which they were worn, shows us that the absence of scenery and of stage decoration, to which it has been supposed we owe much of the rich imagery

* Both published by the Shakespeare Society.

in the Elizabethan drama, was due only to poverty of resource, and not to the higher value set by the public, and consequently by the theatrical proprietors, upon the intellectual part of their entertainment. The highest sum which Henslowe records as having been paid by him before 1600, as the full price of a play, is £8 — not half what was given for a cloak that might have been worn in it; the lowest sum is £4 — not as much as the hero's hose might have cost. By 1613, theatrical competition had raised the price of a play by a dramatist of repute to £20, which, being equal to $500 of the present day, was perhaps quite as much as the proprietors could afford, and was not an inadequate payment for such plays as went to make up the bulk of the dramatic productions of the day. Happily, nearly all of these have perished; and of those which have survived, the best claim the attention of posterity only because Shakespeare lived when they were written.

ESSAY ON SHAKESPEARE'S GENIUS.

AN ESSAY TOWARD THE EXPRESSION OF

SHAKESPEARE'S GENIUS.

THE student of language, or the mere intelligent observer of the speech of his own day, cannot but notice how surely men supply themselves with a word when one is needed. The new vocal sign is sometimes made, but is generally found. A lack is felt, and the common instinct, vaguely stretching out its hands, lays hold of some common, or, mayhap, some half-forgotten or rarely-used word, and, putting a new stamp upon it, converts it into current coin of another denomination, a recognized representative of new intellectual value. Purists may fret at the perversion, and philologers may protest against the genuineness of the new mintage; but in vain. It answers the needs of those who use it, and that is all that they require. The word 'talent,' in the sense of mental faculty, affords an example both of the appropriation and the perversion in question. Its appropriation took place about three centuries ago; but its perversion has been gradually going on within the memory of men yet living, and is perhaps hardly yet completed. And there is this singularity in its history, that it was taken at about the same time into the vocabulary not of one language, but into those of several; into all those, in fact, which felt the influence of the Christian Scriptures at the time of the revival of learning. Christ's parable of the servants who received a different number of talents in trust during their master's absence, in which the word is used with its original meaning of a sum of money, but figuratively to signify those personal gifts and advantages for the use of which each man is responsible, is the origin of the word in the sense in which it is used in modern languages, it having been taken into them in its purely metaphorical signification. But at first it was used to mean the natural bent of the mind; and in fact, until the present generation, it was synonymous with 'genius,' a word which, in its application to the mind or soul, is, in our tongue at least, of later introduction. The earlier as well as the later lexicographers of the English, French, and Italian languages give definitions of these words which are really identical. And Crabbe himself, although his function is that of nice discrimination, can divide them no farther than by saying that "genius is the particular bent of the intellect which is born with a man," and that "talent is a particular mode of intellect which qualifies its possessor to do some things better than others;" thus furnishing as perfect an example as could be given of distinction without difference. But since the author of the Synonymes issued the last edition of his work, 1837, the usage of intelligent people has been drawing a sharper line of demarcation between these two words. One, 'genius,' has been raised, and the other has been degraded, from their former common level. The next lexicographer who does his work with nicety and thoroughness must define 'genius' as original, creative mental power, and 'talent' as that inferior and more common, though sometimes more expanded and more beneficent, faculty which puts to new use facts already known, principles already discovered, methods of thought or expression already established, or which, in literature and the arts of design, produces by labor and taste, rather than by new conception. Genius may be of high or of low order; talent may be great or small. Genius may be pestilent; talent beneficent. But the former in its lower grades is not approached in kind by the latter in its larger development, any more than a poor diamond is rivalled by a fine quartz crystal, or a living spring, from which flows but a thread of water, by a reservoir which supplies the daily needs of millions. The apothegm, *Poeta nascitur, non fit*, is true only if by 'poet' we mean only the poet of genius. But so we do not mean; and we have crowned, and worthily crowned, a made-poet with bays, and left a poet-born to live by gauging the liquor that quickened his inspiration and soothed his grief. Perhaps Gray affords the most signal example of poetic talent developed and cultivated to its utmost capability and perfection, and his *Elegy in a Country Churchyard* the most admired instance of an exquisite work of poetic art produced by taste and fine susceptibility and labor — in a word, by talent. But certainly the highest manifestation of genius in poetry is Shakespeare; who, indeed, united in himself genius in its supremest nature and talent in its largest development, adding to the peculiar and original powers of his mind a certain dexterity and sagacity in the use of them which are frequently the handmaids of talent, but which are rarely found in company with genius.

There are two great divisions of genius. One supplies the needs and expresses the spirit of its age; the other finds its inspiration in elemental truth, and deals only with that which is eternal. Of the three great poets of the world, (if we pass by the author of the Book of Job,) Homer, working in the simplest elements of human nature, limited less than any one of his successors by artificial modes of thought and forms of life, himself a mere voice chanting an unconscious epic in the dim twilight beyond the farther verge of history, and telling the story of man's youth before his anxious eyes had been turned inward, belongs preëminently to the universal type of genius, and therefore appeals directly to both instructed and uninstructed minds; while of those who found their inspiration in their own experience, Dante, the chief, as much politician as poet, making a hell for his foes and a heaven for his friends, cannot be fully understood without some knowledge of the period and the country in which he lived. Hence it is that even among his countrymen Dante is, and always must remain, the poet of the instructed few; while unlearned men of all bloods and all ages find in the barrier of a foreign tongue their only hindrance to perusing, with a common delight, the ever fresh and living page of Homer. But Shakespeare presented as simply and directly as Homer to the universal mind of man the perennial truth of unchanging nature. This seems to have been perceived by his very contemporaries. Ben Jonson, in the only line of his eulogy of Shakespeare which is generally known, and which, continually cited, is almost as often destructively misquoted, expresses this appreciation of his beloved friend and fellow. It will be recognized by nearly every reader in these words: —

> "He was not for an age, but for all time."

But this was not what Jonson wrote. He said of Shakespeare, —

> "He was not of an age, but for all time;"

and the almost universal substitution of the one preposition for the other shows a failure to appreciate Jonson's meaning, and degrades a most remarkable expression of the high quality of Shakespeare's genius into a clever antithetical utterance of the commonplace eulogy that his fame would endure forever. Jonson said (and the context, as well as the line itself, shows his meaning) that Shakespeare was not a man of his age, but that what he wrote was for, adapted to, all time. The voice of more than two centuries has confirmed this far-reaching and discriminating judgment. Yet it but partly told the truth; for Shakespeare alone, of all great poets, attained the highest and rarest combination of power, and united in himself the two kinds of genius. He was both of his age and for all time. Only his race could have produced him, — for a Celtic, a Scandinavian, or even a German Shakespeare is inconceivable, — and that race only at the time when he appeared. The English, or so-called Anglo-Saxon, race is distinguished by a sober earnestness and downrightness of character which manifests itself even in its narrative, dramatic, and poetical literature; and our greatest poet, universal although he was, marked himself peculiarly ours by raising his dizzy pile of fancy and imagination upon the broad and solid foundation of English common sense. But Shakespeare not only thought as an Englishman, and spoke as an Englishman, and so was always truly national, although outside of history he chose only one English subject for dramatization,— he thought and spoke only as an Englishman could speak in the Elizabethan era. His plays could have been produced neither before the middle of the sixteenth century nor after the reign of Charles the First. Yet bearing thus plainly the mark of the time, as well as of the race, which produced them, these writings have as their chief distinction, that whatever they possess of beauty is beautiful, and whatever they tell of truth is true, to all mankind forever. The attempt to explain such an intellectual phenomenon seems indeed presumptuous. We may rightly admire what we cannot fully understand; we may apprehend what we cannot comprehend, and comprehend that which we cannot worthily express; and I own that I shrink back as I essay to measure with my little line and fathom with my puny plummet the vast profound of Shakespeare's genius.

Individual organization determines preference; but organization and circumstances together determine choice, which is preference moved by will, or preference in action. Happily both these joined to make a dramatist of Shakespeare. Circumstances took him to London to earn his bread; circumstances made the theatre the aptest field for his labor; and his organization fitted him supremely for the dramatic function. Yet, had he been born in the present day, it may at least be questioned whether he would have chosen the drama as his profession. He would probably have sought a more remunerative or a less preoccupied field of labor than that of the English drama in the present day. But living in the reign of Elizabeth, he went to London to become an actor and write plays for a London audience.

Never, perhaps, did imaginative works, written to please the public of a great city, have less of a town air, of that urban quality which, for instance, is so striking in Pope's poems, in Addison's essays, and in the plays of their period and of Dryden's, than is to be found in Shakespeare's dramas. Yet it was only in London that those plays could have been written. London had but just before Shakespeare's day made its metropolitan supremacy felt, as well as acknowledged, throughout England. As long as two hundred years after that time the county of each member of Parliament was betrayed by his tongue ; but then the speech of the cultivated people of Middlesex and its vicinity had become, for all England, the undisputed standard. Northumberland, or Cornwall, or Lancashire might have produced Shakespeare's mind; but had he lived in any one of those counties, or in another, like them, remote in speech as in locality from London, and written for his rural neighbors instead of the audiences of the Blackfriars and the Globe, the music of his poetry would have been lost in sounds uncouth and barbarous to the general ear, the edge of his fine utterance would have been turned upon the stony roughness of his rustic phraseology. His language would have been a dialect, which must needs have been translated to be understood by modern English ears, with the loss of that heavy discount which is always paid at the desk of the broker in literary exchange. For us of after ages, and so for the perpetuity and diffusion of Shakespeare's fame, he appeared at a most propitious period of the history of our race, not only as to its language, but as to its political and social condition. As to language, there was then a freedom from critical and scholastic restraint which has never since existed, united to a copiousness of vocabulary, which, except in the direction of philosophy and science, has not been materially enlarged. The English language, even the English of London, although Chaucer and Spenser had used it, was regarded then, in England itself, as unfit for the use of scholars; English literature held no admitted place in the realm of letters; and the English people were of small consideration in Europe. We are accustomed to think of London as the capital of a great kindred empire, which is in letters, as well as in arms and commerce, one of the five or six great powers of civilized Christendom. We measure its importance by the fact of its being the time-honored literary metropolis of the great kingdom and the great republic whose tongue it speaks. But at the time of Shakespeare's arrival there, although that time was the glorious reign of Queen Elizabeth, London was only the chief city of the southern part of a little island which then contained the whole English race — a race which had not yet taken its appointed place among the nations. Indeed, as a people, it was not until the beginning of Elizabeth's reign that we attained to the full maturity of our English-hood. The great civil wars, which involved three generations, though lasting but thirty years, and which ended by placing the Tudors on the throne, were not only the expiring throes of feudalism, they were the pangs of a new birth; and that birth was the English nation. To the land made more nearly homogeneous by the upturning and intermingling of its elements in this long civil convulsion, the Reformation came, and completed the enfranchisement which the destruction of feudalism had but partly accomplished. The English character did not completely attain its ideal type until after it had freed itself from the fetters of feudality, and cast off the yoke of Rome. During the century which succeeded the latter event it seems to have been more purely and absolutely, and at the same time unconsciously and generously, English than the influences of party politics, the entangling interests of an extended empire, and the artificial sustaining of a dead form of society have permitted it to be since that period. Then, from this people, thus interfused, thus tried and purified, thus invigorated by repose, in the first flush and strength of its perfected and awakened nature, there sprang an array of men glorious in arts and arms, in learning and in literature, in commerce and in statesmanship. It was this period, celebrated under the name of the princess whose reign filled the greater part of it, and which extended from about 1575 to 1625, which produced the men who changed the position of the English people before the world; and chief among them, though not then reckoned of them, was William Shakespeare.

Not until the beginning of the nineteenth century did Shakespeare's own race acknowledge, with one consent, that the rustic-bred playwright was the greatest of poets and one of the wisest, if not the wisest, of men. It took us two hundred years to bring ourselves with unanimity to the simple acceptance of that miracle. We literally brought ourselves to it; for the professed scholars and critics rather hindered than helped our progress to that large appreciation in which they were ever behind the people. In fact, Shakespeare's supreme popularity dates from his own day; and in this respect it was not exceptional, but conformed to a rule which is almost universal. The judgment of posterity may reverse, or it may confirm, enhance, and diffuse, the approval of contemporaries; but in literature the man who fails to please those to whom he addresses himself has failed forever. We have contemporary testimony to the fact that Shakespeare's plays were regarded by the public of his own day as incomparably superior to those of all his rivals; and it may be doubted whether a remarkable appreciation of them which was printed in the bookseller's Address to the Reader of *Troilus and Cressida* in 1609 — that "they serve for the most common commentaries of all the actions of our lives" — has been more than decorated and illustrated, amplified and weakened, by all subsequent criticism. It was the demand of succeeding generations for these dramas, the delight in them which was constantly felt and expressed, broadening, deepening, strengthening steadily year by year, and the moral and intellectual influence which they exerted, which compelled the critics to undertake to account for this extraordinary phenomenon in literature. The literary history of the seventeenth century, during the first sixteen years of which Shakespeare was alive, shows a demand for his plays by the reading public unapproached in the case of any other author. The fondness grew. It included all classes of readers, from the most thoughtful to those who merely sought in books a momentary pastime. In the first half of the eighteenth century the demand of the public for Shakespeare's plays was at least fourfold greater than that for any other book, notwithstanding the great number already issued from the press, and in spite of the fact that the most admired and elegant writer of the early part of that period had devoted his best powers to the diffusion of a taste for the works of our great epic poet, while he hardly mentions those of the greater dramatist. Yet the literary men of his own day who praise Shakespeare, almost without exception, leave his plays unnoticed, and limit their eulogy to his *Venus and Adonis* and his *Lucrece;* and the critics of the eighteenth century, yielding, personally, as we can see, to the spell of his genius, were yet reluctant, doubtful, and troubled with many scruples when they came to account for all the admiration of which they themselves and their labors were living witnesses. True, one of them, himself a poet, Pope, passed in happy phrase one of the most penetrative judgments that has been uttered upon him when he said, "The poetry of Shakespeare is inspiration indeed. He is not so much an imitator, as an instrument, of Nature; and it is not so just to say that he speaks for her as that she speaks through him." But he, like all his contemporaries and immediate successors, thought it necessary to praise and blame with alternate breath, and to point out deformities, manifold and monstrous, in this bewitching, but untutored and half savage child of nature. Yet, at this very time, the intelligent love of Shakespeare was so deeply rooted in the English breast that his words and thoughts pierced, like multitudinous fibres, the intellectual life of the people; and while these men, and their little rhymes, and their bulbous sentences might have lived or perished and no harm been done, and little notice taken, he could not have been displaced without a disturbance of the whole English nature, and a destruction of no small part of the phraseology of common life. This being true as to the relative position of our own critics to our own spontaneous appreciation of Shakespeare, still more is it true with regard to the relations of foreign critics to that appreciation. Some people, who ought to have known better, have more than half admitted that the German critics taught us to understand our own poet. I am unwilling to believe this of the English race in Europe; I know that it is not true of that part of it in America. Here, at least, there is, and always has been, a class of people so large and so diffused through society that it cannot be rightly called a class, who do not know that there are German critics, who have little acquaintance with any criticism, to whom Schlegel is unrevealed, and Coleridge is but a name, and who yet read, and understand, and love, and delight in Shakespeare, and who would quietly smile at the notion that "at last" we understand Shakespeare because some learned people have said very profound sayings about his revelations of the "inner life." We must be careful not to confound perception with expression, or comprehension with power of analysis. Newton saw no better, rejoiced no more in the beauty of color, than other people because he analyzed the sunbeam. The ignorant monk, who would have burned him as a sorcerer, illuminated missals with an intuitive mastery of the harmonies of the prism, which he could not have attained by all his experiments, or explained by all his theories. Shakespeare himself, who seems to have seen and understood all mental relations and conditions, saw this, and, as if with an eye of favor upon the millions who would read him with simple pleasure, made *Birone* say of the astronomers, —

"These earthly godfathers of heaven's lights,
That give a name to every fixed star,
Have no more profit of their shining nights
Than those that walk and wot not what they are."

That which first distinguished Shakespeare from the little throng of dramatists among whom, and with some of whom, he first labored, was the character of his thought, and the language in which he clothed it — in a word, his style. It is that which first strikes the attention of the reader of the present day when he takes up Shakespeare's works. It is that by which we are enabled to distinguish his writing from that of other dramatists in the same play, as in the First and Second Parts of *King Henry the Sixth*, *The Taming of the Shrew*, and *Pericles*. The distinction can be made with a very great degree of certainty by any one qualified by natural gifts and practice for such investigations, even with regard to Shakespeare's earliest writing. It is not that Shakespeare is all fine gold, and others are all dross; but when we know that of several mines one produces gold, another silver, and another lead, and when we find gold and dross, or silver and dross, or lead and dross, or gold and silver and lead together, we need not be in much doubt as to the distribution of the ownership.

Purely English as Shakespeare was in what we may call the externals of his dramatic art, he was in no respect more so than in his style. In the earlier half of the sixteenth century Italian literature had begun to exercise a modifying influence upon that of England, and especially upon English poetry. Surrey, Spenser, Sidney, Daniel, Jonson, Beaumont, Fletcher, Drayton, Milton, all show the effect of this influence. In Shakespeare's writings it does not appear, except, perhaps, in his erotic pastoral poem *Venus and Adonis.* His very sonnets are free from any traces of Italian spirit or versification. He went to Italian literature, — at his time the great mint and treasure-house of fiction, — but it was only for the mere incidents of a tragedy like *Othello*, or a comedy like *The Merchant of Venice.* He doubtless read Italian well enough to master the works of the early Italian novelists; but although the literature of that language could not but have insensibly enlivened his genius, and enriched his stores of thought, it had no perceptible effect upon his mental tone, his turn of expression, or his choice of imagery. He is as free from the influence of this as he is from that of classic literature, the imitation of which was in vogue with the regularly educated writers of his day. His vocabulary, at once his means of thought and medium of expression, is merely that of his time, that which was used by his dramatic contemporaries and by the translators of our Bible. Writing for the general public, he used such language as would convey his meaning to his auditors — the common phraseology of that period. But what a language was that! In its capacity for the varied and exact expression of all moods of mind, all forms of thought, all kinds of emotion, all the reasoning of philosophy and the subtleties of metaphysics, a tongue unequalled by any other known to literature; a language of exhaustless variety, strong without ruggedness, and flexible without effeminacy; a manly tongue, yet bending itself gracefully and lovingly to the tenderest and the daintiest needs of woman, and capable of giving utterance to the most awful and impressive thoughts in homely words that come from the lips and go to the heart of childhood! It would seem as if that language had been preparing itself for centuries to be the fit medium of utterance for the world's greatest poet. Hardly more than a generation had passed since the English tongue had reached its perfect maturity, — just time enough to have it well worked into the unconscious usage of the people, — when Shakespeare appeared, to lay upon it a burden of thought which would test its extremest capability. He could not exhaust, but he fully exhibited, all the capacities of the English tongue. His distinction was not in the words which he used, but in the use to which he put them. No unimportant condition of his supreme mastery over expression was his entire freedom from restraint, it may almost be said of consciousness, in the choice of language. He was no precisian, no etymologist, no purist. He was not purposely writing literature. The only criticism that he feared was that of his audience, which represented the English people of all grades above the peasantry. These he wished should not find his writing incomprehensible or dull; no more.

If we except the translators of our Bible, Shakespeare wrote the best English that has yet been written; but they who speak of it as remarkably pure, that is, as having a notably small admixture of Romance words, utter mere vague, unwarranted encomium. In the sixteenth century there were probably more Romance words adopted into our language than there had been before, or have been since, if we exclude words of technical or quasi-technical character. These words Shakespeare and the translators of the Bible used at need with unconscious freedom. The vocabularies both of the Bible and of Shakespeare's plays show forty per cent. of Romance or Latin words, which, with the exception just named, is probably a larger proportion than is now used by our best writers, certainly larger than is heard from those who speak their mother tongue with spontaneous idiomatic correctness.* So many Latin words having been adopted into the English language in the Elizabethan era, and English having been, up to that period, almost excluded from literature, the Latin element then retained much of its native character; to which fact is due, in some measure, Shakespeare's use of words of Latin origin in their radical signification. But although he does this much more than any of his contemporaries, we may be sure that it was the result of no yielding to the constraints of scholarship. In brief, words were his slaves, not he theirs; and if one could serve his purpose better than another, he did not stop to ask the birthplace or to trace the lineage of his servant. He will compose verse after verse almost wholly of Anglo-Saxon monosyllables; and this equally in passages descriptive, dramatic, and lyric in character, and of the utmost dissimilarity of sentiment. On the other hand, he will make two Latin words fill an entire verse, except, perhaps, one or two syllables. Again, Shakespeare mingles words of native and of foreign origin which are synonymes so closely as to subject him to the charge of pleonasm — a charge which can for like reason be brought against the noble liturgy of the Church of England. It is thus manifest that Shakespeare was secure and thoughtless in his use of words, except as to their power to serve his present purpose. So that there can be no more futile objection to a reading in his plays than that the doubtful word occurs in no other passage of his writing. For if he had occasion to use a word but once, or, for

* See *Lectures on the English Language*, by the Hon. George P. Marsh, LL. D., pp. 124, 125.

that matter, to make it for his single need, he would have used or made it without hesitation. Yet his intuitive knowledge of the peculiar value of words of various derivation is continuously manifest. That he was keenly sensible of the ludicrous effect of long Latin words in certain situations is manifest, not only from such instances as *Costard's* conclusion that 'remuneration' is "the Latin word for three farthings," and *Bardolph's* definition of 'accommodated,' "That is, when a man is, as they say, accommodated; or when a man is — being — whereby — he may be thought to be accommodated, which is an excellent thing," but from such usage as that in *Sir Toby Belch's* rejoinder to *Maria's* remonstrance against his roistering behavior, "Tilly vally, am I not consanguineous?" where the use of the Latin word and the abstract idea has a humor which would have been lost had he said, "Am I not her kinsman?"

Shakespeare's freedom in the use of words was but a part of that conscious irresponsibility to critical rule which had such an important influence upon the development of his whole dramatic style. To the working of his genius under this entire unconsciousness of restraint we owe the grandest and the most delicate beauties of his poetry, his most poignant expressions of emotion, and his richest and subtlest passages of humor. For the superiority of his work is just in proportion to his irresponsibility to literary criticism. His poems, the least excellent of his writings, were written for the literary world; and it is upon them that his contemporaries, in passing literary judgment, found his reputation. His sonnets, which occupy a middle place, were written for himself or for his private friends, and were obtained for publication in some indirect way. His plays were mere entertainments for the general public, written not to be read, but spoken; written as business, just as

Rogers wrote money circulars, or as Bryant writes leading articles. This freedom was suited to the unparalleled richness and spontaneousness of his thought, of which it was, in fact, partly the result, and itself partly the condition. Ben Jonson had these traits of his friend's genius in his mind when he wrote that passage in which he tells us that he "had an excellent phantasy, brave notions, and gentle expressions; wherein he flowed with that facility that it was sometimes necessary he should be stopped. *Sufflaminandus erat*, as Augustus said of Haterius. His wit was in his own power; would the rule of it had been so too." We, with our dictionaries, and our books of synonymes, our thesauruses of words and phrases, to facilitate literary composition, our Blairs and our Kameses, may think, some of us, that we have smoothed the road to literary distinction, when we have but cumbered our movement and distracted our attention. After all, the secret of the art of writing is to have somewhat to say, and to say just that and no other. We think in words, and when we lack fit words we lack fit thoughts. When we strive to write finely for the sake of doing so, we become bombastic or inane. Oldisworth, quoted by Dr. Johnson in his *Lives of the Poets*, says of Edmund Neale, (known under the assumed name of Smith,) who had a great reputation in his own day, "Writing with ease what could easily be written moved his indignation. When he was writing upon a subject he would seriously consider what Demosthenes, Homer, Virgil, or Horace, if alive, would say upon that occasion, which whetted him to exceed himself as well as others." Which, I take it, is one principal reason why, although the world yet hears something of Demosthenes, of Homer, of Virgil, and of Horace, it has long ceased to hear any thing of Neale. It must not be supposed, however, that Shakespeare, in the composition of his plays, was guided by no written law because in his day, in England, no literary law had yet been written. In *The Garden of Eloquence*, by Henry Peacham, published in 1577, there are forms and figures of speech described, and classified, and named to the number of two hundred and more, with apt rules to use them withal. But not seeking to square his work by these rules, Shakespeare wrote in his marvellous fashion, because, if he wrote at all, it was just as easy for him to write in that way as in any other. When Lear says, —

> "Down, thou climbing sorrow;
> Thy element's below," —

the critics of the last century, walking through the clipped verdure and formal alleys of the Garden of Eloquence, point out, with dignified complacency, that "here is a most remarkable prosopopœia." So there is, if they must have it so. But it comes from Shakespeare's pen as a matter of course; as if no other thought, no other words, could have occurred to him on that occasion. And what cared he what Homer or what Virgil would have said? But it is always thus with him. Unlike other great writers, he does not seem to scatter his riches with a lavish hand; they drop from him like fatness from the clouds of heaven; as if with the intellectual riches of a god he had a godlike serenity in their possession and their bestowal.

Notwithstanding Shakespeare's copiousness of thought and affluence of imagery, no remark upon his style could be more erroneous than that so often made by his critics, that he does not repeat himself. It has even been attempted to regulate his text upon this assumption. But Shakespeare did not hesitate to repeat either his own thoughts or words, or, for that matter, those of other writers, when to do so served his present purpose. Examples are scattered all through his plays.

In no respect was Shakespeare's art classical. He was essentially a Goth, and his style corresponded entirely to the character of his mind. English is a Gothic language; yet there can be classical English, as we have been shown by Addison and Goldsmith. In the former of these eminent writers we find the perfection of ease, clearness, harmony, and dignity. So we do in Shakespeare, except that some passages, from compression of many thoughts, from neglect of elaboration, and sometimes from corruption, lack clearness. But it is not thus that Shakespeare's style is to be defined. It is not to be defined at all: it is a mystery. Addison's sound sense, the eminently graceful character of his mind, and his lambent humor, were individual qualities which marked his thought; but as to his style, it can be easily analyzed; its elements can be detected, and their proportions declared. But you cannot take certain qualities of style and combine them in certain proportions, and by certain rules, and make your Shakespeare's mixture. A nameless something — not grace, not harmony, not strength — which yet mingles with them all in Shakespeare, would be lacking. Addison's perfect style has been perfectly imitated. There have been men, there might be many men, who could produce not what would properly be called an imitation of it, but the thing itself. But the man has never yet written, except Shakespeare, who could produce ten lines having that quality, which, for lack of other name, we call Shakespearian.

It is, however, not only in this nameless charm and happy audacity that Shakespeare differs from those writers of our language whose style may be regarded as models of correctness. He is often undeniably incorrect, in consequence, partly, of the syntactical usage of his day, which, upon minor points, had not yet attained a complete logical conformity to the very principles then recognized, and partly of his own neglect to revise carefully that which he wrote so fluently. His occasional errors which are not of the former kind appear only in his plays; they are not found in the poems, which he wrote for perusal.

There is, however, a vagueness in some passages of Shakespeare's poetry which is intentional, and which is a result of the highest art — a vagueness which magnifies an image, generally of terror, which would be belittled by being drawn with sharper outline. This is a trait of Gothic art, and is not peculiar to Shakespeare, or indeed to poetry, for it finds its place in Gothic architecture. Schiller has been much praised, and somewhat over-praised, for his use of the indefinite neuter pronoun 'it,' in his ballad *The Diver*, to indicate the fabled polypus, which, however, he immediately describes.* But Shakespeare, who seems to have been beforehand with most modern poets in all their happiest devices, had in this effect anticipated and surpassed Schiller, and had availed himself of our indefinite dread of unknown horrors in the recesses of the sea, not only, like Schiller, to leave upon the mind a vague image of the unknown creature itself, but to heighten our dread of, and aversion to, unnatural crime. How indefinite the comparison when *Lear* exclaims, —

"Ingratitude, thou marble-hearted fiend,
More hideous when thou show'st thee in a child
Than the sea-monster!"

What is *the* sea-monster? Yet how much more of

* "It saw — a hundred-armed creature — its prey."
Sir E. Bulwer Lytton's Translation.

horror is suggested by that definite indefinity than if the comparison had been in terms to a crocodile or a kraken! And in other modes, and for other reasons than the strengthening of an image, Shakespeare is sometimes vague, and, in expressing abstract thought or simple emotion, seems purposely indefinite. He is aided in his effect of this kind by a singular felicity in framing phrases which convey ideas by mere suggestion, and which at once fill mind and ear with a satisfaction the reason for which escapes close analysis.

Akin to this power in Shakespeare is that of pushing hyperbole to the verge of absurdity; of mingling heterogeneous metaphors and similes, which, coldly examined, seem discordant; in short, of apparently setting at nought all rules of rhetoric, without paying the penalty by the critics in such case made and provided. There is in a play, which, though not the greatest production of Shakespeare's genius, displays more completely than any other all the qualities of his style, — *The Second Part of Henry the Fourth*, — a passage, which, in its resistless sweep and majestic imagery, is not surpassed by any other of his writing, and which is an extreme example at once of the vagueness, the mingling of metaphor, and the extravagance with which he could dare to write, and splendidly succeed. *Northumberland*, — after several speeches, during which he, with rapidly rising emotion, is led to the certain knowledge of his son *Hotspur's* death, — enraged with grief, thus closes his outbreak of wrath and sorrow: —

"Now bind my brows with iron, and approach
The ragged'st hour that time and spite dare bring
To frown upon the enrag'd Northumberland.
Let heaven kiss earth: now let not nature's hand
Keep the wild flood confin'd; let order die:

And let this world no longer be a stage,
To feed contention in a lingering act;
But let one spirit of the first-born Cain
Reign in all bosoms, that, each heart being set
On bloody courses, the rude scene may end,
And darkness be the burier of the dead!"

How big this is with strong emotion! how turbulent with grand and multitudinous impersonation! The very abstract subjects are all endowed with life and passion. Yet no clear images are left upon the mind; the attributed actions are, in themselves, preposterous, impossible; and the imprecation of the end of all things, upon occasion of the death of one man in battle, shows, by attaining it, that there can be a limit even to extravagance. But what reader, except a rhetorician of the last century, ever attempted to form an image of a personified heaven kissing a personified earth! How great a loss would be the knowledge of what the wild flood is which nature keeps confined! Who ever supposed that Shakespeare meant that a stage could strictly be said to feed any thing, much more feed contention! The truth is, that in such passages as that in question, when they are the work of a hand strong enough to carry the reader with the writer, the mind does not take the personifying words in their strict sense. That sense, as in the phrases "let heaven kiss earth," "let order die," "to feed contention," is only suggested, and gives a certain color and intensity to expression. And, in *Northumberland's* speech, the quick opposing changes of impersonation perturb the passage with a stir of words and clash of thought which corresponds to, and portrays the strong, deep agitation of, the speaker's soul.

Shakespeare mixes not only metaphors, but metaphors and plain language. He unites even the material and the spiritual; and yet his image loses neither strength nor beauty because its head is of gold and its feet of clay. When *Hamlet* says,

> "and bless'd are those
> Whose blood and judgment are so well commingled
> That they are not a pipe for Fortune's finger
> To play what stop she please,"

what a union of weight and edge is given to the passage by the welding of the physical idea of blood with the moral idea of judgment! Yet the rhetoricians have forbidden the banns of such unions. But the period as a whole, no less than the first member of it, is obnoxious to their denunciation, for the last half is as apparently incongruous with the first as the elements of the first are with each other. How can the commingling of blood and judgment make a pipe? But Shakespeare did not write for men who read after this mole-eyed fashion. Nor did he here mean that blood and judgment made a pipe. The blood and judgment make the man, and the man is then compared to a pipe in the hands of Fortune. This is not discovered by an analysis, however rapid, but apprehended at once by the understanding of every reader who can and does admit the entrance of more than one idea into his mind at the same time. It is the faculty of combining the expression of an impressive truth, or of a genuine human feeling, with fancies which by themselves would seem extravagant, that gives Shakespeare's style its peculiar and never-failing charm; a faculty which, in its action, transcends all law except that of its own being. He has, in the height of his hyperbole, and even in the occasional inflation of his imagery, a keeping which makes his expressions seem those of simple, though elevated, nature. He possesses also, in its highest manifestation, the correlative power of giving, by the reflected light of his intellect, beauty to that which is in itself repulsive. Not only passion, guilt, and woe, but even inhumanity and baseness, are presented to us so tempered and elevated through the medium of his genius that we are not wounded or repelled by the picture, while we mourn over, or condemn, or even loathe that which it represents. We may say of his genius as *Laertes* says of the crazed *Ophelia*, —

> "Thought and affliction, passion, hell itself,
> She turns to favour and to prettiness."

Thus Shakespeare furnishes us with the very language in which we can pass critical judgment upon himself; so that it is possible that the best and completest expression of his genius could be culled from the works which that genius has produced.

Shakespeare, from the height to which he soars, can overlook and disregard that which affronts lowlier eyes; or, by the universal solvent of his genius, he can compel the union of elements whose natural repugnance resists less potent alchemy. Yet, with no material detriment to his fame, it may be admitted that precisians and purists, and all who admire — as *Samson* fought — only when the law is on their side, can find a true bill of extravagance against him. For what was justly said of Plato, that "if he had not erred he would have done less," is quite as applicable to the great dramatic poet as to the great philosopher; and the allowance may be more reasonably made in the case of Shakespeare. If we will have high-sounding poetry we must risk an occasional flight beyond the bounds of reason. Genius has produced some bombast which is really grand, and some tinsel that will shine forever.

Much more objectionable than such extravagance as

that into which Shakespeare sometimes, though rarely, fell, are the opposite faults of style, an elaboration of nice conceit, and a proneness to verbal quibbling, into which he was led by a conformity to the taste of his period. These trivial blemishes, easily discernible, were just of the kind to bring down the censure of the last century's critics, who were never tired of pecking at Shakespeare for the readiness with which he sprang at an opportunity for a pun; and there can be no doubt that some fine passages of his poetry are less purely beautiful than they would have been were they not spotted with this labored use of words in a double sense. Of the kindred fault, which did not take the form of an absolute pun, but which is hardly less offensive, the *Lucrece* furnishes the following perfect specimen: —

"Even here she sheathed in her harmless breast
A harmful knife, which thence her soul unsheath'd."

Conceits like this, which abound in all departments of the literature of the Elizabethan age, are mere labored, verbal antitheses corresponding to parallel antitheses of thought. The humorous side of this conceit in style is a pun, in which there is correspondence of words, but incongruity of thought. The development of taste has taught us that in serious writing these antitheses are impertinent; but the pleasing surprise of a certain lack of pertinence, which yet seems pertinent, forms no small ingredient in our enjoyment of wit. Of this kind of wit, no less than of that subtler comic quality which we call humor, Shakespeare has shown himself in *Falstaff* the matchless master. And thus we find his most objectionable and most noticeable fault nearly related to one of his most exquisite and charming graces. It is interesting to know that while he conformed to the fashion of his day in this matter of conceits and quibbles, he saw how petty and injurious it was, and visited it with open condemnation. In *Twelfth Night*, after making the *Clown* quibble for three speeches, to *Viola's* bewilderment, upon two words, he makes the same character exclaim, "To see this age! A sentence is but a cheveril glove to a good wit. How quickly the wrong side may be turned outward!" To which *Viola* replies, "Nay, that's certain: they that dally nicely with words may quickly make them wanton." This is one of the very few passages in his plays which may safely be accepted as a mere expression of his own opinions.

But the fashion of his day, at Shakespeare's conformity to which we must chiefly rejoice, was that of using blank verse instead of rhyme in dramatic composition. His choice, doubtless, went with his conformity; but that he yielded in this respect to fashion is plain from the facts that his earlier plays abound in rhymed passages, — a great part of one of them, *The Comedy of Errors*, being in couplets or alternate rhymes, and that he used blank verse only in his plays. Blank verse had been slowly growing in favor with our English poets ever since Surrey used it for his translation of the fourth book of the Æneid, forty years before Shakespeare entered upon his career. At the latter period it was coming into vogue upon the stage, and Shakespeare, who in all that he wrote to set forth as poetry chose rhyme, soon became, in his dramas, the greatest master of English heroic measure. Not much can be said, and if there could, not much need be said, in an attempt to appreciate Shakespeare's genius, of the beauty of his versification. Criticism can do no more than record its various and surpassing beauty. The mere structure of verse is mechanical. It can be, it has been, made perfect by rule. Much good sense has been written in lines composed of five feet of two syllables, with accent duly disposed and tastefully and correctly varied, which are unexceptionable verses, quite as perfect as any that Shakespeare ever wrote. But they are, most of them, a weariness to the flesh, while his delight our ears forever. The reason of this difference it is impossible to set forth. We can no more say why it is than we can say why, when one composer writes a succession of notes which follow each other in perfect conformity to the rules of music, the canons of taste, as well as the laws of composition, we say with *Sly*, "A very excellent piece of work: would 'twere done," and when Mozart writes, conforming to no other laws, he ravishes our souls with melody. The power over sound, whether of words or musical notes, is a personal gift, which, unlike other personal gifts, such as wisdom, logical power, imagination, the mastery of form, as in sculpture and architecture, or of color, as in painting and decoration, is exercised (within certain general limits) purely according to the personal fancy, the spontaneous and intuitive preference of the possessor. The poet, in the sensuous expression of his verse, is guided only by his own sense of what is fit and beautiful. We can see that he attains his purpose by the variation of his pauses, the balance of his sentences, and his choice and arrangement of words in regard to sound. But why and how he does this we cannot tell; nor could he tell himself. We can test one of Shakespeare's characters by the laws of our moral nature; but we have no laws, except those before mentioned, which refer to the rudiments and mechanism of the art, by which we can test the sensuous beauties of his poetry. Except in his songs, he wrote almost entirely in one kind of verse; and he wrote that as he willed; his variations of style, in this respect, resulting only from the greater or less freedom which he allowed himself, guided only by his innate exquisite sense of the beautiful. He had no literary criticism to fear, (it cannot be too constantly kept in mind;) and the success of his plays was not with a public who read, but with an audience who listened. Therefore he admitted hemistichs, defective and redundant lines, the alternation of verse with prose, and of rhymes with blank verse; conscious that so long as the dialogue ran easily and naturally on, the audience would concern themselves with the story, the situations, and the thoughts and feelings of the personages, indifferent to the niceties of versification, which indeed only a reader could detect. In respect to the strict laws of versification, the dramatic poet of the days of Elizabeth was a chartered libertine. Shakespeare availed himself of this freedom to the full; and we can see that as he grew older he allowed himself greater license, the effect of which relaxation was counterbalanced and modified by his greater mastery of the material in which he worked, and his more refined perceptions of beauty. The plays which we know were his latest productions, such as *The Winter's Tale*, *Coriolanus*, and *Henry the Eighth*, are notably freer, free almost to carelessness, when compared with *The Two Gentlemen of Verona* and *King Richard the Second*, for instance, which we know were of his early writing. In some of the Roman plays, and in *King Henry the Eighth*, he reaches the point of almost failing to mark his verse by any cæsural or final pause whatever; very often allowing the place of the last accent to be filled by a syllable, frequently a monosyllabic word, which cannot be accented. It is true that the rhythm of all modern poetry depends merely upon accent, and that the English language has among its happy distinctions that of containing no word which is unfit for poetry. But the facility given by these traits is shared in the first instance by all modern poets, in the second by all English poets.

Yet of all English, as well as of all modern poets, Shakespeare, in respect to his versification as in all other respects, is the supreme master. The rhythm of his verse and the cadence of his periods are determined by an exquisite sense of the beauty of verbal form, working with an intuitive, though not unconscious, power of adaptation of form to spirit.

Like in the irresponsibility and absoluteness of its operation to the faculty of melodious versification is that faculty which we call fancy, touching Shakespeare's exercise of which somewhat has necessarily been said already. Fancy is defined by Johnson as "the power by which the mind forms to itself images of things, persons, or scenes of being," and he gives imagination as its synonyme and first definition; by Webster, as "the faculty by which the mind forms images or representations of things at pleasure;" by Worcester, as "the faculty of combining ideas;" and some metaphysicians, attempting to draw a distinction between fancy and imagination, have attributed to the former faculty the power of forming images or representations of things in the mind, to the latter that of combining and modifying them. If these definitions were correct and sufficient, fancy could not be considered with propriety as a trait of style; which is in poet, painter, or musician, the mode of expression. It would belong to the substance of an author's work, — that which style expresses. But the definitions in question, to which all others known to me conform without essential variation, must be set aside as expressing neither the idea of fancy which is presented by our best writers of any age, nor that which has determined the general use of the word among intelligent people.

This is not the place in which to go into extended dissertation upon the characteristic traits and differences of fancy and imagination; but it may be briefly said that if 'fancy' were ever correctly used as a synonyme of 'imagination,' which is more than doubtful, or as the name of a creative, image-forming faculty, that usage has long since passed away, and that the needs of intelligent people have effected a distinction between the two words, similar in kind to that which has been made between 'talent' and 'genius.' Carlyle, for instance, is celebrated as a writer of vivid and powerful imagination; but no person of ordinary discrimination would speak of fancy as one of his characteristic mental traits. So the style of *A Midsummer-Night's Dream* is peculiarly rich and brilliant in fancy; but except in the personages of Puck and the clowns, it is not distinguished among Shakespeare's plays for imagination, which, as exhibited in his works, finds its highest manifestation in *King Lear*, *Macbeth*, and *The Tempest*. In brief, imagination is that creative faculty of the mind by which images of men and things, and their relations, are conceived and brought forth with seeming reality. It is the correlative of faith, which is the substance of things hoped for, and the evidence of things not seen. Fancy is the faculty which illustrates, enriches, and adorns a person, a thing, or a statement of fact or truth by association, comparison, and by attributed function or action.

Never did intellectual wealth equal in degree the boundless riches of Shakespeare's fancy. He compelled all nature and all art, all that God had revealed and all that man had discovered, to contribute materials to enrich his style — to enforce his thought; so that the entire range of human knowledge must be laid under contribution to illustrate his writings. This inexhaustible mine of fancy — furnishing metaphor, comparison, illustration, impersonation, in ceaseless alternation, often intermingled, so that the one cannot be severed from the other, although the combination is clearly seen, and leaves a vivid impression upon the mind — is the great distinctive intellectual trait of Shakespeare's style. In his use of simile, imagery, and impersonation, he exhibits a power to which that of any other poet in this respect cannot be compared even in the way of derogation; for it is not only superior to, but unlike, that which we find in any other. He very rarely institutes a formal comparison, rarely uses the word 'like,' which is so common with other poets. Nor does the condensation of simile called metaphor, or the attribution of will called impersonation, furnish a medium quite sufficient for his fancy. He does not set off his thought and his image against each other, or formally illustrate one by the other. He fuses a thought, or a feeling, and an image together. They are not even twins, but a single birth; thought giving soul to image, and image embodying thought. When Milton, in a passage of justly celebrated beauty, would exhibit the bashfulness of a modest new-made wife, he makes Adam say,

> "To the nuptial bower
> I led her, blushing like the morn."

But Shakespeare makes Posthumus say, that in like circumstances Imogen showed

> "A pudency so rosy, the sweet view on't
> Might well have warm'd old Saturn."

In the epic poet there are two ideas, not only distinct, but severed: the dramatist presents one, which suggests two. Again, Milton, in a passage yet more beautiful than the last quoted from him, describing the dawn, says,

> "Now Morn, her rosy steps i' th' eastern clime,
> Advancing, sow'd the earth with orient pearl."

This is nearer, especially in the rosy steps; but still

there is a severance between morn and the eastern clime, between morn and the pearl. Shakespeare, describing the same event, says, in his compact way, —

"Morn, in russet mantle clad,
Walks o'er the dew of yon high eastern hill."

This is the production of no acquired art, but of an inborn faculty. Shakespeare displayed the fulness of its strength in his earliest plays. Who has not already thought of Romeo's announcement of the dawn? —

Night's candles are burn'd out, and jocund day
Stands tiptoe on the misty mountain top."

But this is mere description of natural phenomena; Shakespeare's peculiar power in this respect is the vividness with which his fancy illustrates thought, action, and emotion. This highest exercise of that faculty appears in the following passage, which has never been surpassed in the grandeur of its imagery, or the felicity of its illustration. *Queen Margaret*, taunting *York*, after the battle of Sandal Castle, with his disappointed ambition, says, —

"Come, make him stand upon this mole-hill here,
That raught at mountains with outstretched arms,
Yet parted but the shadow with his hand."

Yet this passage is from a speech in *The True Tragedy of Richard Duke of York*, which was written when Shakespeare was but about twenty-five years of age, and an unknown dramatist, working in company with others. He transferred the speech bodily to his Third Part of *King Henry the Sixth*. It is of his writing. Its mere excellence does not alone stamp it as his; but no other poet has made such a use of imagery.

It has been already remarked that the richness of Shakespeare's style is due in great measure to the variety of his allusions, and the extended knowledge from which he draws his illustrations. His knowledge of man and of nature was chiefly intuitive, although it was developed and perfected by observation and reflection. But so intimate is the acquaintance which he exhibits with certain arts and occupations, and certain departments of learning, that hence hypotheses have been framed and supported by argument, that he passed some of his early years in the professional acquirement of the knowledge which he afterward put so dexterously to use — a dangerous foundation for such a supposition in regard to any author of quick observation and a lively fancy; most dangerous with regard to Shakespeare. Johnson's dictum, that Nature gives no man knowledge, is, to say the least, too general in its terms to be true in all its bearings. It is hardly less safe to limit the power of genius in expressing emotions by the bounds of individual experience, than to assume that it cannot describe actual occurrences which it has not witnessed, or places which it has not seen. And although it is clear that genius cannot furnish its possessor with knowledge of facts, or with technical knowledge, men whose faculties do not rise to the plane of genius may, by powers of keen observation, quick perception, retentive memory, and ready combination, acquire, in the ordinary intercourse of life, without special study, a technical knowledge which up to a certain point shall be real, and, dexterously deployed, seem thorough. It is not derogatory to Shakespeare's genius, but rather the reverse, to believe that in his works much of what appears to be the fruit of a special knowledge was acquired in this manner. Of all men known to the history of literature, he seems to have had the most subtle and sensitive intellectual apprehension. What he casually heard, and what he saw by side glances, he seems to have understood by intuition, and to have made thenceforth a part of his intellectual resources. As to book knowledge, it is certain that, although he was not what scholars call a scholar, he had as much learning as he had occasion to use, or even more. His plays and poems teem with evidence that he devoured books, and that he assimilated what he read with marvellous celerity and completeness. Even when we can trace in his poetry the very passages of the authors to whom he was indebted, they reappear from the mysterious recesses of his brain, transmuted and glorified. When we see what it was that he absorbed, and how he produced it, we are reminded of *Ariel's* song,—

"Full fathom five thy father lies;
Of his bones are coral made;
Those are pearls that were his eyes;
Nothing of him, that doth fade,
But doth suffer a sea change
Into something rich and strange."

His early plays are full of allusions to ancient classic literature, showing no great learning indeed, but a mind fresh from academic studies, such as they were. But he soon discontinued this school-boyish habit: the fulness of his brain with his own thoughts left no room for second-hand lumber. He imbibed the spirit of Greek and Roman history, through whatever channel he received it, although he sometimes violated chronology and costume, to the annoyance of some critics hardly worthy to have been his readers. Where, even in Plutarch's pages, are the aristocratic republican tone and the tough muscularity of mind which characterized the Romans so embodied as in Shakespeare's Roman plays? Where, even in Homer's song, the subtle wisdom of the crafty Ulysses, the sullen selfishness and conscious martial might of broad Achilles, the blundering courage of thick-headed Ajax, or the mingled gallantry and foppery of Paris, so vividly portrayed as in *Troilus and Cressida?* What matter is it that he committed such an error in costume as to make Aufidius say to Coriolanus, that he joyed more at welcoming him a friend and ally of Corioli, than when he first saw his wedded mistress bestride his threshold — the fact having been that the newly-married wife of Latin race was carefully lifted over the threshold on her first entrance to her husband's house? What that he made Hector cite Aristotle, who lived eight hundred years after the siege of Troy? He did not care; nor did his hearers; and why should we be troubled? Must our little learning so cripple our imagination? Shakespeare's genius could not have taught him the relation which Greek literature bore to that of Rome; but he having acquired that knowledge, his intuitive perception of higher relations taught him what function the Greek language would perform for an accomplished Roman orator, statesman, and philosopher, and his dramatic imagination of the scene, when Cæsar fell into a fit after having refused the crown, showed him Cicero speaking Greek, so that "those that understood him smiled at one another, and shook their heads." But when, in *Henry the Fifth*, the Bishop of Exeter makes his comparison of government to the subordination and harmony of parts in music, —

> "For government, though high, and low, and lower,
> Put into parts, doth keep in one concert,
> Congreeing in a full and natural close
> Like music," —

it is more than superfluous to seek, as some have sought, in Cicero *De Republica* the origin of this simile; for that book was lost to literature, and unknown, except by name, until Angelo Mai discovered it upon a palimpsest in the Vatican, and gave it to the world in 1822. Cicero very probably borrowed the fancy from Plato; but it was not Shakespeare's way to go so far for that which lay near at hand. Music, and particularly vocal part-music, was much cultivated by our forefathers in Shakespeare's time; and he seems to have been a proficient in the art. The comparison is one that might well occur to any thoughtful man who is also a musician; but it is not every such man who would use it with so much aptness, and make it with so much beauty.

No less noticeable than this display of knowledge more or less recondite, yet no less easy to understand, is Shakespeare's use in illustration of natural phenomena which must have been beyond his personal observation. Of all negative facts in regard to his life, none perhaps is surer than that he never was at sea; yet in *Henry the Eighth*, describing the outburst of admiration and loyalty of the multitude at sight of Anne Bullen, he says, as if he had spent his life on shipboard, —

"Such a noise arose
As the shrouds make at sea in a stiff tempest;
As loud and to as many tunes."

We may be very sure that he made no special study of geology; certainly he could have had no instructor in a science which dates its birth almost within the present century. Yet in the following lines from his 64th sonnet, an important geological fact serves him for illustration: —

"When I have seen the hungry ocean gain
Advantage on the kingdom of the shore,
And the firm soil win of the watery main,
Increasing store with loss and loss with store," &c.

Where, and how, and why, had Shakespeare observed a great operation of nature like this, which takes many years to effect changes that are perceptible? Yet we may be sure that Shakespeare had this knowledge in no miraculous way, though his possession of it might be mysterious to the many who did not possess it themselves. For we find that his knowledge of that which he could not learn of his own soul, which could teach him every thing with regard to man, but nothing with regard to material nature, was limited to what he had observed, and to the knowledge of his time, even in the simplest matters. He knew that Cicero would be likely to veil a sententious comment upon an important political event in Greek; he knew that the shrouds of a ship howled dismally in a tempest; he even knew that a compensating loss and gain is going on between the great waters and the continents; but he did not know what every lad fit to enter college now knows, and what it would seem that any intelligent man, who considered the subject, must have discovered for himself, that the sparks produced by flint and steel are minute pieces of steel struck off and heated to redness by friction. Like all his contemporaries, he supposed that the fire was in the flint. Thersites says that Ajax's wit "lies as coldly in him as fire in a flint, which will not shew without knocking." But the limits of Shakespeare's knowledge did not mark the scope of his genius, and his ignorance or his learning is of small account in estimating the quality of his poetry or the truth and interest of his dramatic conceptions. Would either of two passages from which lines have just been quoted have been more impressive if Aufidius had spoken of his new-married wife being lifted over his threshold, or if Shakespeare had known that steel was burned by collision with flint? It matters little what naturalists and scholars think of the material which Shakespeare used for the illustration of his thought, and less whence those materials were derived. Of no more importance is it that he has transferred thoughts from forgotten wastes to his own blooming pages. What matter that he has taken some from Lilly? It is he alone who makes those thoughts admired. Those which he did not take the world has quite forgotten. The glory is not in the cloud, but in the eternal light that falls upon the fleeting exhalation. Even in regard to the special knowledge which is most strikingly exhibited in Shakespeare's writings, — that of the law, — of how little real importance is it to establish the bare fact that Shakespeare was an attorney's clerk before he was an actor! Suppose it proved, — what have we learned? Nothing peculiar to Shakespeare, but merely what was true of a great number of other young men, his contemporaries. It has a naked material relation to the other fact, that he uses legal phrases oftener than any other dramatist or poet; but with his plastic power over those grotesque and rugged forms of language, it has nought to do whatever. That was his inborn mastery. Legal phrases did nothing for him; but he did much for them. Chance cast their uncouth forms around him, and the golden overflow from the furnace of his glowing thought fell upon them, enshielding and glorifying them forever. The same fortune might have befallen the lumber of any other craft; it did befall that of some others — the difference being one of quantity, and not of kind. The certainty that Shakespeare had been bred to the law, would it even help us to the knowledge of his life — of what he did for himself, thought for himself, how he joyed, how he suffered, what he was? No more would it help us to understand his genius.

Whatever Shakespeare may have learned, he did not

learn his dramatic art, in which he had not only no instructor, but no model. By dramatic art is not here meant the principles which guided him in the construction of his plays. In that he had teachers, who were also his examples. The form and the action of all his dramas, whether comedies, histories, or tragedies, were determined by laws over which he had, or at least exercised, no control. At the time of his arrival in London the English drama had attained a recognized, if not an established, form, which was not an imitation of an elder type, or the invention of an individual, but an outgrowth of the national character. Not only was the form of plays thus determined, but the manner of writing them. It was the settled practice of the dramatic writers of that day, most of whom were connected with one theatre or another, either as actors or retained play-wrights, to take plots wherever they could find them — from popular novels, old plays, or well-known passages of history, and to work these up as quickly as possible into an effective play, which, by its story and its characters, would interest the public. Preference was given to the plots of old plays, or the stories of novels which already had a hold upon popular favor. To all these usages Shakespeare conformed. It is worth while to bring to mind these well-established facts in regard to Shakespeare's dramatic writing, because it is the fashion of some critics to regard him as writing, like Sophocles or Euripides, to a listening nation, conscious that its fame was partly involved in his productions, the judgment of which was worthy of the grave consideration of gravest men, and because much superfine subtlety and ingenuity have been exhibited in tracing his purposes, and in providing him with psychological theories, according to which he gave certain traits to certain characters, and led them through such and such experience, when in fact he was but following the old play or the old story to which he had gone for the framework or the material of his drama. Even his historical pieces, which all the evidence shows were written at hap-hazard as far as regards their order, or at least only with the public taste in view, have been solemnly resolved into tetralogies and cycles, with a central thought and a ruling purpose, as if Shakespeare meant in writing them to give the world a philosophy of history; which indeed can be extracted from them by the thoughtful reader for himself, but only because they are an idealized picture, in little, of real life. And what wonderful psychological knowledge has one of Shakespeare's later critics found in the bringing *Romeo* upon the scene enamoured of *Rosaline*, to have this passion supplanted by the purer and tenderer one for *Juliet!* which, on the contrary, critics of the last century regarded as a great fault in the amorous Veronese's character. But the truth, which these critics did not know, is, that in this transfer of affection Shakespeare merely followed the novel and the poem to which he went for his plot. There he found the incident of *Romeo's* earlier love; there he found the old Nurse, and even her praise of *Paris* to *Juliet*, and her underrating of *Romeo* after his banishment, with her counsel to the second marriage; all of which have been lauded as exquisite and subtly-drawn traits of nature; which again indeed they are, and Shakespeare could doubtless have invented them; but the truth is, that he found them. So in the tale which he dramatized and called *Othello*, he found *Iago*, with his craft and his spontaneous and almost superfluous fiendishness, the reason and the right of which have been the occasion of so much profound psychological discussion. There is reason for believing that the sudden changes in the feelings of lovers and tyrants in some of Shakespeare's plays, and such unaccountable acts, for instance, as *Valentine's* willingness to resign his mistress to *Proteus*, would be accounted for, although perhaps not explained, by the discovery of some lost play or novel. In plays written as daily labor, by a man whose sole object in writing was to please a promiscuous audience, by a play-wright who worked merely as one of a company or partnership, his part of the business being to furnish words for others to speak, who composed sometimes in joint authorship, and who worked over the old material which lay nearest to his hand, and was best suited to his money-making purpose, always saving time and trouble as much as possible, — in such plays, so produced, what folly to seek, as some have sought, a central thought, a great psychological motive! From all that we know of Shakespeare and his circumstances, and all that can be extracted from his plays without torture, we may be sure that the great central thoughts and inner motives which have been sought out for his various dramas, by critics of the German school, could he but come back and hear them, would excite only his smiling wonder. In the mere construction of his dramas, although Shakespeare sometimes displays great skill, not only in the working of the plot, but in the manner in which he conformed his genius to the taste and the dramatic fashions of his day, he exhibits nowhere a conformity to principles of art unknown before his era.

Every worthy reader of Shakespeare must see that his peculiar power as a dramatist lies in his treatment of character. The interest which distinguishes his plays, as plays, from all others, is that which centres in the personages, in their expressions of thought and emotion, and in their motives and modes of action. *This* was his dramatic art, and this it was in which he had neither teacher nor model. For at the time when he wrote, character, properly so called, was almost, if not quite, unknown to English literature, and but little more to that of the Latin races. In English dramatic literature, Marlowe alone had attempted character, but in a style extremely coarse and rudimentary. The Italian and French novelists who preceded Shakespeare, including even Boccaccio himself, interest by mere story, by incident and sentiment. Their personages have no character. They are indeed of different kinds, good and bad, lovers, tyrants, intriguers, clowns, and gentlemen, of whom some are grave and others merry. But they are mere human formulas, not either types or individuals. It has been much disputed whether Shakespeare's personages are types or individuals. They are both. Those which are of his own creation are type individuals. So real are they in their individuality, so sharply outlined and compactly construed, that the men and women that we meet seem but shadows compared with them ; and yet each one of them is so purged of the accidental and non-essential, as to become typical, ideal. He made them so by uniting and harmonizing in them a variety of traits, all subordinated to, yet overwhelmed by, one central and dominating trait, and by so modifying and coloring the manifestation of this trait, that of itself it has individuality. Shakespeare's personages are thoroughly human, and therefore not embodiments of single traits or simple impulses, but complicated machines ; and the higher their type the more complex their organization. He combines in one individual, and harmonizes, qualities apparently incongruous, his genius revealing to him their affinities. It is the consequent complication of motive which causes the characters of Shakespeare's personages to be read differently by different people. This variety of opinion upon them, within certain wide and well-determined limits, is evidence of the truthfulness of the characters. Not only does their complex organization give opportunity for a different appreciation of their working, but, as in real life, the character, nay, the very age of those who pass judgment upon them, is an element of their reputation. Not only will two men of equal natural capacity, and equally thoughtful, form different opinions of them, but the judgment of the same man will be modified by his experience. Unlike the personages of the world around us, some of whom pass from our sight, while others come forward, and all change with the lapse of time, those of Shakespeare's microcosm, by the conditions of their existence, remain the same. But our view of them is enlarged and modified by advancing years. As we grow older we look upon them from a higher point, and the horizon of our sympathy with them broadens. We lose little, and we gain much. For manhood's eye, ranging over its wider scope, finds that the eminences which were the boy's bounds of admiration, do not pass out of sight, but become parts of a grander and more varied prospect, while distance, in diminishing their importance, casts upon them the tender light of that happy memory which ever lingers upon pure and early pleasures. But as in real life again, Shakespeare's characters, during their mimic existence, depend upon and develop each the other. We see how they are mutually worked upon and moulded. And in this interdependence and reciprocal influence, more than in mere structure of plot, consists the unity of Shakespeare's plays as organic wholes. His personages are not statuesque, with sharp, unchanging outlines. His genius was not severe and statuesque, as, for instance, Dante's was. His men and women are singularly flexile; and not only so, but they seem to have that quality of flesh and blood which unites changeableness with identity; as a man's substance changes, and his soul grows older year by year, and yet he is the same person. It is not only the story in Shakespeare's dramas which makes progress, but the characters of the personages. *Lear*, *Romeo*, *Macbeth*, *Othello*, are, as the phrase is, not the same men at the end of the play as at the beginning. Their experience has modified their characters; yet each is the same, though *quanto mutatus!* This it is which exhibits Shakespeare's supreme peculiar power. What he did, for instance, for *Iago*, was not to make him a villain, but to provide the ready-made villain with a soul. He worked out in poetry a great psychological problem: — Given such and such hellish deeds, what kind of man is he who does them? and how does he think, and feel, and act? Shakespeare *made* souls to his characters; he did not give them his own. It is now the most commonly recognized truth in regard to him, that he is a self-oblivious poet. But this is not true of him without important qualification. In his sonnets, whether they were written in his own person or in another's, he was not oblivious of self. On the contrary, his own thoughts, his own feelings, constantly appear. He pours out his own woes with a freedom in which he equals, but with a manliness in which he far surpasses, Byron. It is as a dramatist that he is self-oblivious; and he is so to a degree too absolute, it would seem, for the ever-conscious people of the world to apprehend. Else we should not hear, as we continually do hear, an opinion or a course of conduct sustained, with an air of triumph, by the citation of Shakespeare's opinion in its favor. For there is hardly a course of conduct, or an opinion, upon a moral question, which cannot be thus supported. Shakespeare disappeared in his personages; and it is they who speak, and not their creator. The value, nay, the very meaning, of what his creatures say, must be measured by their characters, and the circumstances under which it is spoken. Attempts have been made on the one hand to show that Shakespeare was an infidel, and on the other that he was a Roman Catholic. Both might have been equally successful. A bishop has, by ingenious and elaborate collation of passages of the player's works, set forth certain religious principles and sentiments derived from the Bible as Shakespeare's. But by a like process just the opposite might have been shown with equal certainty. In this regard, as in all others, what Shakespeare wrote was the outgrowth of character and circumstance. Religious subjects could not be treated with more solemnity than by some of his personages, as the reader of *Henry the Eighth*, *Richard the Second*, and *Measure for Measure*, will remember; nor, on the other hand, could the most imposing dogmas of divinity be touched with more daring or more disrespectful hands, than are laid upon them in *King Henry the Fourth*, *Cymbeline*, *Macbeth*, and *Much Ado about Nothing*.

It is thus upon every question. Because a usurper, wishing to build up in himself a belief that he rules by the grace of God, says, —

> "There's such divinity doth hedge a king
> That treason can but peep to what it would,
> Acts little of his will," —

it no more follows that Shakespeare believed in the absolute and divine right of kings, than because one of *Jack Cade's* followers lays it down that the command, Labor in thy vocation, "is as much to say as, Let the magistrates be laboring men; and therefore should we be magistrates," it follows that he was a radical democrat. For he made both the usurper and the demagogue.

It would seem as if, in all Shakespeare's thickly-peopled plays, we might find at least one character which he meant should represent his own. But the longer and the closer our study of those plays, the more clearly it appears that of all his creatures, none think his thoughts or express his preferences, except his Fools. And perhaps the Fool in *King Lear* more nearly represents Shakespeare's tone of mind and view of life than any other of his personages. All Shakespeare's Fools are wise; but this one has wisdom enough to teach prudence to men of the world, and to set up a college of philosophers. A tinge of sadness, almost of melancholy, tempers all the sallies of his wit. He is as true as *Kent*, and as tender as *Cordelia*. Comparison to him were compliment to any other man than Shakespeare. His use of the Jester exhibits in a striking manner two marked traits of Shakespeare's method: one, the ease with which he adapted himself to circumstances, and bent his mighty genius to the little needs of his profession; the other, the profusion with which he poured out his thoughts, and the impartiality with which he bestowed his labor. He seems never to have husbanded his resources, or thought any work beneath his dignity. It is a poor workman who complains of his tools; and Shakespeare, finding the Fool in possession of an established place upon the stage, and thus essential to the popularity of his plays with a mixed audience, instead of rebelling against or fretting at this necessity, made him the vehicle of his sentiment, his fancy, his practical wisdom, and even of his pathos.

Shakespeare has minor personages, but no slighted characters. They all have individuality, and he will waste on a messenger a sentiment or a simile that would grace a hero's tongue, or add dignity to a royal proclamation. The *personnage prostatique* of the pseudo-classic French stage has no place in Shakespeare's drama. This completeness of his minor characters is the more remarkable because he has whole scenes which were manifestly written merely to meet the exigencies of stage management. Such, for instance, is the second scene of Act III. of *Othello*. It consists of but six lines, and merely gives a glimpse of *Othello*, as he goes to walk upon the works. But it separates two others, in both of which *Cassio* appears, at the end of the first and the beginning of the second; and it tells us that *Iago* is to meet *Othello* upon the works, from which they afterward enter together, the latter already made a little sensitive upon the subject of his lieutenant's nearness to his wife. And in *The Merry Wives of Windsor*, the first Scene of Act IV., in which *Sir Hugh Evans* plays pedagogue to *William Page*, has nothing whatever to do with the plot, but it serves to separate the scene in which *Falstaff* receives his second invitation from that which exhibits the entertainment to which he is invited. These are mere contrivances to preserve the appearance of probability in action, which, when it has its formal name, is called the unity of time and place. It would have been well, for instance, in this respect, if a scene could have been thrown in between the first and second scenes of Act I. of *All's Well that Ends Well*, which present one of the most striking examples of Shakespeare's disregard of that unity. For although one is at Roussillon and the other at Paris, *Bertram* and *Parolles* appear in both; the latter's entrance before the King in his palace being separated by only seven short speeches from his exit at Roussillon, to accompany *Bertram* on his journey. But of how small importance is such discrepancy! No dramatic interest is broken by it, no essential propriety violated. It would be open to no objection in a story; and in regard to their construction, English plays are only acted stories. But in fact, Shakespeare, as we have just seen, was put to shifts in common with the merest journeyman play-wright that ever wrote to-day to get him bread to-morrow. Yet these straits only ministered occasion to his genius. He went to his work like a faithful servant, but he did it like a King. The very superfluous scene in *The Merry Wives of Windsor* just cited, one of the least important its author wrote, bears unmistakable marks of his hand, and for its character and humor will always be read with pleasure.

Hardly less remarkable than Shakespeare's vigorous and vivid style of dramatic portraiture are the range of his subjects and the variety of his characters. He left no department of his art untried, and sounded the dramatic lyre from its lowest note to the top of its compass. The same hand that struck from it the woes of *Lear* and the troubled harmonies of Hamlet's soul drew forth also its most fantastic strains, and left us in *The Comedy of Errors* a farce equally extravagant and jocular. No other writer has so run through the scale of humanity. In this respect it is safe to say, that Shakespeare will never be surpassed, because he left no important type of character untouched. From *Hamlet* to *Abhorson*, from *Imogen* to *Mistress Quickly*, what a descent! Yet between these extremes the full gradation is maintained. Nay, the lower extreme is passed. *Caliban* bridges the gap between the human creature and the brute; and *Crab* stands upon the other side with cur-like thanklessness for a character as sharply drawn as his master's.

Whence did Shakespeare draw the characters of such a multitude of various and well-defined personages? From models? Did he, as some would have it, keep watch upon the world around him, and seizing upon the individuals that suited his purposes, put them into his dramas? Great painters have thus filled their canvases;

and dramatists of high rank have manifestly drawn their characters from people whom they saw around them. Hence it is that we find the same face doing duty for like characters in the works of painters, from Raphael to Leech, so that we recognize their pictures by traces of some lovely woman, or some strongly-marked man, whose traits have seized upon their imaginations. Hence, that throughout Beaumont and Fletcher's and Jonson's plays, and much more in those of inferior dramatists, the men and women who fulfil certain functions, good or bad, have an unmistakable resemblance. But among Shakespeare's personages there is not this family likeness. There is no likeness whatever, except in the style of their portrayal. These are plainly from the same mint, but do not, like those, seem to have been struck with the same die. Gustave Doré is the only painter who shows a similar fecundity. Had Shakespeare, working, as he did, merely to make money, drawn his characters from models, he surely must have fallen into a habit which would have saved him much labor, and have satisfied his audience. He would have had his stock of models; and these, worked into each new plot as they were needed, speaking his fancy, his wisdom, his wit, and his humor, and dressed in different costume, would have filled the eye and ear of his public. It is true that he must have observed. He was probably the most observant of men, as well as the most reflective; and his works had of necessity the advantage of his observation as well as of his reflection and his imagination. Nor did the greatness of his mind absolve it from the law of development and progress common to humanity. Although wise in his youth, — and his early plays show wisdom, — he must, by the very exercise of his faculties, and the habit of introspection, have grown wiser as he grew older. But, if we may judge by the ruling sentiment of his plays, while he seems early to have understood the world, he seems also to have long retained the hope and trustfulness of youth. When we consider that *The Merry Wives of Windsor*, *King Henry the Fifth*, and *Hamlet* were written within two years, we shall see that it is difficult, if not impossible, to mark his periods by sentiments, choice of subject, or manner of treatment. It is only by his literary or external style that we trace his passage from youth to maturity. Otherwise Shakespeare seems to have had moods, not periods. Age, too, although it brings more acquaintance with mankind, does not necessarily bring better knowledge of human nature. That knowledge is not an aggregation, but a growth; its germ is born with him who has it, and it spreads from within. Individuals are mere opportunities for its development, occasions for its manifestation. That Shakespeare availed himself of all such opportunities and occasions, that he tested his judgments by experiment, and his conceptions by comparison, that he watched in the men and women around him the operation of those laws to which his creations must conform, cannot reasonably be doubted. It is probable, too, that he found here and there a trait, or even a character, which, though not a model, was a suggestion. His women especially show the fruit of this kind of study. That he did not draw his personages from life is manifest from the fact that all the principal of them, those the creation of which made his fame what it is, are such as he could not possibly have seen, except in mental vision, and that the experiences through which they pass, and by which their living prototypes must have manifested their intellectual and moral traits to him, are such as he could not have had the opportunity of observing. Did Shakespeare ever meet a mad king, a king whose conscious kingliness is supreme even in his madness, but whose dawning madness tinges the first manifestations of his kingly power? As well suppose that he had met a Caliban. Shakespeare's mind contained, but it had not received, his characters. In that play so marvellously full of thought, *Troilus and Cressida*, perhaps the most thoughtful of his works, *Ulysses* rises to the full height of our idea of the wandering Ithacan. Whence came this Ulysses? Not from Homer's brain; for although Homer *tells* us that the King of Ithaca was "divine" and "spear-renowned," and "well skilled in various enterprise and counsel," the deeds and words of the hero, as represented by the Greek poet, hardly justify these epithets. Here we see that Shakespeare was even wiser than the Homeric ideal of human wisdom. For this Shakespeare made our *Ulysses*. It was but his name and his reputation that had come down from antiquity. It was the character that corresponded to and justified these that Shakespeare supplied in this instance, as in many others. He did not restore a limb, or even supply a head; but as if catching and filling the outline of a shadow vanished for centuries, he surmounted with the speaking substance of that shadow an inscribed and empty pedestal.

Shakespeare thus used the skeletons of former life that had drifted down to him upon the stream of time, and were cast at his feet, a heap of mere dead matter. But he clothed them with flesh and blood, and breathed life into their nostrils; and they lived and moved with a life that was individual and self-existent after he had once thrown it off from his own exuberant intellectual vitality. He made his plays no galleries of portraits of his contemporaries, carefully seeking models through the social scale from king to beggar. His teeming brain bred lowlier beggars and kinglier kings than all Europe could have furnished as subjects for his portraiture. He found in his own consciousness ideals the like of which, for beauty or deformity, neither he nor any other man had ever looked upon. In his heart were the motives and the passions of all humanity; in his mind the capability, if not the actuality, of all human thought. Nature, in forming him, alone of all the poets, had laid that touch upon his soul, which made it kin with the whole world, and which enabled him at will to live throughout all time, among all peoples. Capable thus, in his complete and symmetrical nature, of feeling with and thinking for all mankind, he found in an isolated and momentary phase of his own existence the law which governed the life of those to whom that single phase was their whole sphere. From the germ within himself he produced the perfected individual as it had been or would have been developed. The eternal laws of human life were his servants by his Heaven-bestowed prerogative, and he was yet their instrument. Conformed to them because instinct with them, obedient to, yet swaying them, he used their subtle and unerring power to work out from seemingly trivial and independent truths the vast problems of humanity; and standing ever within the limits of his own experience, he read and reproduced the inner life of those on the loftiest heights or in the lowest depths of being, with the certainty of the physiologist, who from the study of his own organization recreates the monsters of the ante-human world, or of the astronomer who, not moving from his narrow study, announced the place, form, movement, and condition of a planet then hidden from earthly eyes in the abyss of space.

It is a vain notion, put forth by some who should know better, that much study, reflection, and earnest endeavor are required to understand Shakespeare rightly. Culture, and discipline, and natural powers of analysis are doubtless demanded for the explanation of the motives and characteristic traits of Shakespeare's personages, and for the unravelling of some of his involved passages, (which are very few,) or the following of some of his highest flights of fancy. But almost all of us must have something of Shakespeare latent in our souls, voiceless and unexpressed; else we should be incapable of that sympathetic comprehension of his thoughts and his characters, the existence of which among ever increasing multitudes for many generations is the only possible condition of his peculiar and enduring fame. Some men, it is true, will never understand him in some passages; and some — happily for the world, very few — will not be able to understand him at all by any study or reflection of which they are capable. This from no proneness of the poet to paradox, or to eccentric or sentimental views of life, or to over-subtlety of thought. For although of all poets he is most profoundly psychological, as well as most fanciful and most imaginative, yet with him philosophy, fancy, and imagination are penetrated with the spirit of that unwritten law of reason which we speak of as if it were a faculty — common sense. His philosophy is practical, and his practical views are fused with philosophy and poetry. He is withal the sage and the oracle of this world. Subjects which are essentially, and in other hands would seem, prosaic and almost sordid, are raised by him into the realms of poetry, and yet in language so clearly expressive of their essential character as to be adopted as shrewd maxims by the worldly wise.

In this constant presence and rule of reason in his most exalted flights, we recognize again a trait of the English origin and character of his genius — a trait which is at the foundation of its eminence even in the realm of imagination, but at which other peoples often jeer. Even in our passions we will ask, Why, and say, Because. "*Voilà*," cries the French maid in one of the few passages of insight in Vanbrugh's *Provoked Wife*, "*Voilà un vrai Anglais! Il est amoureux, et cependant il veut raisonner.*"

Many people have given themselves serious concern as to the moral influence of Shakespeare's plays; and critics of great weight, fulfilling their function, have gone down far, and staid down long, in the attempt to fathom the profound moral purpose which they were sure must be hidden in the depths of these grand compositions. But the direct moral influence of Shakespeare is nothing, and we may be sure that he wrote with no moral purpose. He sought only to present life; and the world which he shows us, like that in which we live, teaches us moral lessons according to our will and our capacity. Johnson, meaning censure of "his first defect," wrote Shakespeare's highest praise in this respect, in saying of him that "he carries his persons indifferently through right or wrong, and at the close dismisses them without further care, and leaves their example to operate by chance." That word "indifferently" is Shakespeare's eulogy. He gives the means of study, and leads insensibly to reflection. Men resent, or turn away from, conviction at the lips of others, which they will receive and lay to heart if they hear it from the lips of the inward monitor. And even children see through and despise the shallow device which makes goodness always lead to happiness, and flout the stories which conduct them through artificial paths to bring them out upon a moral. Man, however gifted, can never teach more than life and nature; and among gifted men there has been only

Shakespeare who could teach as much. The moral unity which distinguishes his plays is not, as some would have it, especially among the Germans, the result of a moral purpose deliberately planned and well worked out, but of the fact that those dramatic poems were the spontaneous manifestation of one great symmetrical mind in complete and intimate accordance with nature. Shakespeare is able to teach as much as nature — nay, even more than unmitigated nature — for two reasons. One is, that he presents us something which is not nature, but is a perfect reflex of nature. It is strange, but true as strange, that imitation always interests us more than reality. The very reflection of a beautiful landscape in a mirror wins our attention more, nay, seems more beautiful, than the landscape itself. Seen in a Claude glass it becomes a picture, a *quasi* work of art, which we study, over which we muse, and to which we again and again recur; while the scene itself, if we see it often, may become to us an unnoticed part of our daily life, like the rising of the sun, that daily miracle. And so the mirror which, following his own maxim, Shakespeare holds up to nature, is more studied by us than Nature herself, and by means of it nature is better understood. The phenomena are brought by him within the range of our mental vision. Reduced in their dimensions, but kept perfect in proportion and true in color, they are transferred to and fixed upon his pages; and we can take down from our shelves these specimens of thought and passion, and muse and ponder over them at leisure. This is measurably true of all imaginative writing; but it is preëminently true of Shakespeare's.

But the chief reason of Shakespeare's ability to teach us as much as nature, is a breadth of moral sympathy, a wide intellectual charity, which makes him as impartial as nature. His mirror tinges with no color of its own the scene which it reflects. The life-giving rain of his genius falls equally upon the just and the unjust; and as the sunshine and the shower develop both tares and wheat according to their kind, so he never seeks to modify the nature, or the seeming, of that which he quickens into life; and he is never more impartial than when he is most creative.

It was this quality of universal sympathy in Shakespeare's mental constitution which enabled him to unite to his knowledge of man and of truth that knowledge of men and of things which is called knowledge of the world. He seems to have had this latter knowledge in as great a degree as that more abstract knowledge which made him a great dramatic and philosophical poet, and to have been the most perfect man of the world whose name appears upon the roll of literature. All that we know of his life shows him in full possession of this great qualification of the perfect social man, so rarely found in poets; and his works are pervaded with its exhibition. Consider well such characters as *Angelo*, *Parolles*, *Faulconbridge*, *Polonius*, *Jaques*, *Falstaff*, such gentlemen as *Bassanio*, *Mercutio*, *Prince Henry*, *Cassio*, *Antony* (in *Julius Cæsar*), and see what knowledge, not only of the human heart, but of society, of manners, of actual life, in short, — to return to the accepted phrase, — of knowledge of the world, these characters display. It is this knowledge, this tact, which enables him to walk so firmly and so delicately upon the perilous edge of essential decency, and not fall into the foul slough below, where the elegant dramatists of the last century lie wallowing. This he does notably, for instance, in *Faulconbridge* and *Falstaff* — *Falstaff*, a gentleman by birth and breeding, yet coarse, gross, mean, and selfish, a degraded castaway, yet with consummmate tact and exquisite art, never allowed to be vulgar or repulsive, and whose matchless humor makes his company delightful.

It has been objected to the assertion of the amplitude of Shakespeare's mind and to the generosity of his character, that he always represents the laborer and the artisan in a degraded position, and often makes his ignorance and his uncouthness the butt of ridicule. The charge is brought by reformers and philanthropists of such narrow views that they cannot see that art is not the pioneer, but the landscape-gardener, of society. Shakespeare, although he thought as a philosopher, wrought as an artist; and art has to do with the facts of the world before it, idealizing them, but not changing their nature. Three hundred years ago, the husbandman and the mechanic were degraded in the world's eyes; and Shakespeare, the healthiness of whose understanding is as remarkable as any trait of his genius, knew that the world's appreciation is generally right of men in mass, and that these hard-handed men had all the consideration that was their due, though not all the rights or the advantages. It is always so. Individual men may fail to receive a just appreciation; but, as surely as water finds its level, classes of men always command the standing that they can maintain. It is because the working man, whether his labor be rude or skilled, has raised himself, has, in fact, become another man, that the world now awards him a consideration which he did not receive in the days of Queen Elizabeth. Shakespeare, although he represented thê world as he saw it, was no panegyrist of things as they were, no mere *laudator temporis acti.* He was no sycophant to power. Whatever might have been the faults of others in this regard (and they seem to have been fewer and less in the mother country in those days than in the present), Shakespeare did not hesitate to tell kings and nobles all the truth, and even to put it into their own mouths.

The personal opinions and inclinations of Shakespeare are so little traceable in his works, that we can only judge of his feeling toward the wretched and oppressed by the intimate sympathy which he shows with their privations, their sufferings, and their lowly pleasures. In *King Lear*, *Edgar's* disguising himself as an Abraham-man, gave Shakespeare an opportunity, which so thrifty a householder as he was might well have seized, to hold up those tramping pests of our forefathers to condemnation, or, at least, to ridicule. But his picture presents the sufferer's side of the case, and tells us how he "eats the swimming frog, the toad, the tadpole, the wall newt, and the water, swallows the old rat and the ditch dog, drinks the green mantle of the standing pool, who is whipped from tything to tything, and stocked, punished, and imprisoned." Shakespeare must have well known the ways of the begging impostor; but he chose to show us, in this most touching manner, the dreadful extremities and sufferings of the vagrant pauper.

The little that remains to be said is of a general nature.

Shakespeare's art was not simple, its manifestation was not serene. Simplicity and serenity are the highest ideal in the arts of design. The Greeks attained it in their sculptures and their temples, Raphael in his Madonnas; and even in landscape art, the highest style is that which, rising above the representation of phenomenal effects, presents the ideal of Nature in her wonted phases. But this limitation does not hold in literature, especially in dramatic literature, in which action, complication, intensity, and variety approaching incongruity, are compatible with, if not essential to, the attainment of the highest excellence. Grecian architecture is simple and serene, but not, therefore, the highest type of architecture; and Shakespeare's genius may be well compared — and, I believe, the comparison is not new — to a Gothic cathedral, vast, grand, and solemn in its general aspect, and single in its general impression, yet on closer view seen to bear the stamp of various periods, and to be filled with airy, light, upspringing columns, and minutely decorated with delicate tracery, and with grotesque, humorous, and even indecorous details, correspondent to each other, yet all unlike, though seeming like, and, to an eye capable of the great whole, blending into rich harmony.

But may not the time arrive when the world will say, We have had enough of Shakespeare? May not men become pardonably weary of hearing of this one matchless man, and so ostracize him for his very excellence? It might possibly be so if men lived forever; but generation succeeds to generation, and to each one he is new, and so will be new as long as the tongue in which he wrote is spoken. To each new reader Shakespeare brings more than one life can exhaust, and those who have studied him longest are they who are best assured that no man ever laid his head so close upon the great heart of Nature, and heard so clearly the throb of her deep pulses.

All that I have so inadequately said is true; and yet it is no less true that Shakespeare revealed to the world no new truth in ethics, in politics, or in philosophy. He was not an intellectual discoverer. If the plague had not spared him in his cradle, the great movements of the world would have been deprived of no direct impulse coming from his mind. They would have gone on without, much as they have gone on under the influence of his writings. No social or political development of his race or of mankind would have been checked, except in so far as a diffusion of intellectual and moral culture and refinement might have been retarded. For man's knowledge of himself would have been very much more limited, because of the lack of those works which afford at once the most alluring temptations to the study of human nature and the best field and school for its pursuit. The English, or, if we choose to call it so, the Anglo-Saxon race, both in Europe and in America, would have lacked a certain degree of that general elevation of mental and moral tone and that practical wisdom which distinguish it among the peoples. A source of pleasure more exquisite and more refining than is elsewhere to be found, of instruction more nearly priceless than any except that which fell from the lips of Jesus of Nazareth, would not have been opened. Thus, although Shakespeare exercised no direct influence upon the world's progress, that which he has exercised indirectly is large, and is constantly increasing; and it will increase with the diffusion of our race, its language, and a knowledge of its literature.

It has been before remarked that the dramatists of Shakespeare's time, writing only to please the people, had only to consult the general taste, and were free from any restraint, except that imposed by their own judgment. Some of them did attempt to work, measurably at least, according to classical formulas; and these failed entirely to attain the ends which they had in view — popularity and profit. Of the rest, all, with one or two exceptions, being without a trusty monitor, external or internal, fell into monstrous extravagance, coarseness, conceit, and triviality. But Shakespeare, save for his conformity to mere outside fashion, was entirely unlike his contemporaries. He is among them, but not of them. Their minds run in the same channel, but do not mingle. The clear and powerful current of his thought flows swiftly and clearly side by side with their sluggish and turbid outpourings, leaving them behind, and taking no tint or taint from its surroundings. To him there was gain, instead of loss, in the disregard of formulas. Creative genius is mostly great, not by means of formulas, but in their despite. Almost inevitably it provokes censure by breaking through established rules — a truth which has at last obtained such recognition that defiance of rule is sometimes ignorantly set up as evidence of genius, of which only individuality, and inherent vitality and strength, are witnesses. The so-called extravagances of genius establish its claims by themselves becoming formulas for minds of lower rank; and thus schools are formed, of which no one is really great except the founder. Yet poets of the highest order of the seraphs of the art, do not have followers, because they soar too far in the empyrean for the manner of their flight to be observed and imitated. It is the second-rate men, great yet second, who form schools. For their way of working is discernible, comprehensible, imitable. But the supremely divine is ever a mystery. This is especially true of Shakespeare. As he worked in the manner of no school, so he founded none. He adopted the old forms indeed, and he labored with the same artistic motive, as well as the same material objects as his contemporaries and immediate predecessors and successors. But this produced no living likeness between their offspring. The mistakes which have been made upon this subject, by writers of mark, are so great as to cast a doubt upon the soundness of all critical judgment. His plays and those of Marlowe, Jonson, Massinger, Marston, Middleton, Ford, and Field, have neither in their dramatic nor poetical traits the least family likeness; none, in fact, except a certain affluence and strength of diction, and certain colloquial tricks of expression, characteristic of the period.

May the world expect another Shakespeare? Not unless circumstances corresponding to those which produced this Shakespeare should occur again. Shakespeare marked a stage in the world's progress, or at least in the history of a race which since his time has more than any other influenced that progress. He appeared at the period when the English character, slowly forming through centuries, had attained its typical development; when the English language had assumed a form from which it has not varied sensibly for three centuries; and when our race, having freed itself from the restraints of feudalism, had attained the most symmetrical and harmonious social development possible to it under an established gradation of classes. A new Shakespeare may be born to us, but only as the fruit of a new condition. He can only appear when essential civilization, not mere outward refinement, has advanced so far as to have established radically new relations among men, and when our language has so far changed as to be the fitting vehicle for the expression of a new philosophy, a new worldly wisdom, a new range of sympathy, new sentiment both high and homely, and a new cast of thought. For in him of whom we speak, the old has had its full expression. It may be doubted whether these conditions will, even in the new England, ever be fulfilled. But should they be, then Nature, at once chary and inexhaustible, never working in vain, but ever prompt and able to supply the needs which she creates, will produce another Shakespeare, because then, and not till then, another will be required.

HISTORICAL SKETCH OF

THE TEXT OF SHAKESPEARE.

HISTORICAL SKETCH OF

THE TEXT OF SHAKESPEARE.

SHAKESPEARE'S care for the preservation of his works was in notably inverse proportion to their merit. He gave his *Venus and Adonis* and his *Lucrece* to the press himself; and we may be quite sure that they were printed under his own immediate supervision. His sonnets appear to have been placed in the publisher's hands with his consent, and by some one who had access to the original manuscripts for the correction of the text, even if the author himself did not read the proofs. But there is little room for doubt that his plays were published in all cases without his agency; in most, there is good reason for believing, without his consent; and in many, without his knowledge. Eighteen of them — *The Merry Wives of Windsor*, *Much Ado about Nothing*, *A Midsummer Night's Dream*, *Love's Labour's Lost*, *The Merchant of Venice*, *King Richard II.*, *The First Part of King Henry IV.*, *The Second Part of King Henry IV.*, *King Henry V.*, *The Second Part of King Henry VI.*, *The Third Part of King Henry VI.*, *King Richard III.*, *Troilus and Cressida*, *Titus Andronicus*, *Pericles*, *King Lear*, *Romeo and Juliet*, and *Hamlet* — were printed separately during his lifetime.* The copies

* *The First Part of the Contention between the two Famous Houses of York and Lancaster*, and *The True Tragedy of Richard, Duke of York*, are here

of most of these plays used by their first printers were, almost without doubt, surreptitiously obtained, and they are of comparatively inferior authority in determining the text; their office being mainly auxiliary. But some of them, having been made into prompter's books for the theatre to which Shakespeare was attached, and afterwards placed in the printer's hand as copy for the first authentic edition of the plays, are of higher authority than others.

In 1623, seven years after Shakespeare's death, the first collected edition of his plays was published in folio, under the title, "Mr. William Shakespeare's Comedies, Histories and Tragedies. Published according to the True Originall Copies." This is known in Shakespearian literature as the first folio; and it is the only authentic form in which the text of his dramatic works has reached us. It contains all his plays except one; nineteen which had been surreptitiously or carelessly printed before its publication (one — *Othello* — having been published in quarto after his death), and seventeen which appeared in it for the first time. The play not included is *Pericles, Prince of Tyre;* and it has been conjectured that the refusal of the holder of the copyright of that play to part with it, or to come into the enterprise of publishing the first folio, caused its omission. It is more than possible, however, that in this case there was an unsettled question as to Shakespeare's authorship. This first folio was published under the direction of John Heminge and Henry Condell, who were Shakespeare's friends, fellow-actors, and joint theatrical proprietors. Their

regarded as early forms of the Second and the Third Parts of *King Henry VI.*, and they are as much entitled to be classed with Shakespeare's plays as *Pericles, Timon of Athens,* and *Titus Andronicus.* See Vol. VII. pp. 402, 468.

Address "to the great variety of Readers,"* which is a sort of preface, shows that they sent the volume to the press with a full consciousness of their responsibility, and with the intention of giving to the world an authentic text of the works of their "worthy friend and fellow." They were fully aware of the existence of many incorrect and spurious copies of his plays; and they did not fail to appreciate, or hesitate to avow, the advantages which they possessed for the protection of their author's fame. Indeed, such is the authority given to this volume by the auspices under which it appeared, that had it been thoroughly prepared for the press, and printed with care, there would have been no appeal from its text; and editorial labor upon Shakespeare's plays, except that of an historical or exegetical nature, would have been not only without justification, but without opportunity.

Heminge and Condell, however, seem to have done little else for Shakespeare than furnish the publishers with the copies of his plays which had been in use on the stage of the Globe Theatre; and though this insured the highest authenticity attainable in the absence of copies prepared for the press by the author's own hand, in the case of many plays it did not even secure an immaculate text for the printer. For, as I have already remarked, copies of some of the surreptitiously published single plays had been used as prompter's books for the theatre. They necessarily received some correction to make them serviceable in their new function; and, in part of them, the text was subjected to modification, curtailment, and even addition, — which we have no reason to doubt was the

* See this Address and the remarks upon it, Vol. II. p. xi. and p. xxxi. of this work.

work of the author himself. But many errors, which, though of little or no importance in a stage copy, are serious blemishes to even an uncritical reader's eye, were allowed to remain; and of these errors, not a few were literally repeated in the printing of the first folio. And that precious volume itself, like the quarto editions of the single plays which preceded it, and like almost the entire body of the printed dramas of its period, is filled with traces of neglect. Beside minor errors, the correction of which is obvious, words are in some cases so transformed as to be past recognition, even with the aid of the context; lines are transposed; sentences are sometimes broken by a full point followed by a capital letter, and at other times have their members displaced and mingled in incomprehensible confusion; verse is printed as prose, and prose as verse; speeches belonging to one character are given to another; and, in brief, all possible varieties of typographical derangement may be found in this volume, in the careful printing of which the after world had so deep an interest.

The defects and blemishes of the first folio must be attributed merely to the lack of proper editorial supervision; for its general appearance shows that it was designed to be a first-rate book for its day. Its price was one pound sterling — equal to twenty-five dollars at the present measure of value. Although published at so high a price, at a time when quarto copies of the single plays must have been numerous, when the class which furnished book buyers, or even readers, was comparatively very small, and during the rapid increase of the Puritanic school, which taught abhorrence of stage-plays in any form as a cardinal point of doctrine, this edition was so entirely exhausted within nine years, and so much in demand, that a second folio was published in 1632. This second folio is, in fact, little more than a reprint, page for page, of its predecessor. Comparatively few of the typographical errors of the first are corrected in the second; and not only are the remainder exactly reproduced, but to them are added others hardly less grave and confusing. On the very points, therefore, in which the text of the first folio is faulty, that of the second is much inferior. It also shows numerous traces of modernization and sophistication.*

It is not surprising that Shakespeare's plays were not reprinted during the Commonwealth; but in 1664 a third folio was issued, containing, in addition to those which had appeared in its two predecessors, *Pericles* and six spurious plays which had been published as "by William Shakespeare," or "by W. S." during his life.† A fourth folio appeared in 1685. Its contents are the same as those of the third.

* Such, for instance, as the readings, "deserts *wild*," for "deserts *idle*," *Othello*, Act I. Sc. 3, and "that cries *out* murther" for "that cries *on* murther." *Idem*, Act V. Sc. 1.

† These six plays are *The London Prodigal*, *Thomas Lord Cromwell*, *Sir John Oldcastle*, *The Puritan*, *A Yorkshire Tragedy*, and *Locrine*. Of these, the first, third, and fifth had been published as Shakespeare's, and the second, fourth, and sixth as by W. S. But so great was the value of Shakespeare's name, and so entire appears to have been his indifference to literary fame as a dramatist, that the presence of his name upon the title pages of the three of these plays which bear it, is of no weight as evidence of authorship; and as to the initials, W. S., they may have stood for one or more of a hundred other names. These plays have been rejected by all of Shakespeare's editors (including the players who stood godfathers to the first folio) except Rowe, who merely reprinted what he found in the last folio edition. Eighteen years after Shakespeare's death the *Two Noble Kinsmen* was published as by him and Fletcher. There is no other authority for assigning it in part to him; and conclusion must be based entirely upon internal evidence. Some lost dramas also have been attributed to Shakespeare.

John Warburton, Somerset Herald, and an antiquarian, who was born in 1682, and died in 1759, had made a collection of old manuscript plays, which most lamentably were destroyed. A list of them in his own handwriting is preserved among the Lansdowne Manuscripts. It enumerates fifty-three manuscripts, including two or three poems; and the names of Greene, Massinger, Marlowe, Ford, and Middleton appear as the authors of plays which they are

Neither of the last three folios is of the slightest authority in determining the text of Shakespeare ; and the second is only of service in those instances in which it corrects the typographical errors of the first.

II.

Up to this time Shakespeare had gained or suffered through no other editing than the very limited care of his brother players. In the seventeenth century there was no collation or verbal criticism of his text; but his style and matter and the construction of his plays were made the subjects of incidental comment and discussion by Mr. Thomas Rymer, the Reverend Jeremiah Collier,* Mr. John Dennis, and an anonymous opponent of Mr. Collier.†

known to have written, but which were never printed, and which have been lost. In this list are the following items : —

"Henry ye 1st, by Will. Shakespear and Rob. Davenport.
Duke Humphrey, Will. Shakespear.
A Play by Will. Shakespear."

At the end of the list is the following memorandum : —

"After I had been many years collecting these manuscript playes, through my own carelesness and the ignorace of my Sir. in whose hand I had lodgd them, they was unluckely burnd, or put under pyes, excepting ye three^{b} wch followes. J. W."

Of the three plays above mentioned by John Warburton, the first was entered on the books of the London Stationers' Company in 1653, and the second in 1660. In the latter year *Iphis and Ianthe, or a Marriage without a Man*, and *The History of King Stephen* were also entered on that register, and attributed to Shakespeare. (See *Biographia Dramatica*, Lond. 1812.) Nothing else is known of these five plays. Other dramatic writings have been graced by Shakespeare's name, but not in such a manner as to make the question of his connection with them worth considering; except, indeed, by some of those German critics who have undertaken to teach the English race how to appreciate its own great poet, and whose penetration. able to discover any thing in any thing. finds wonderful manifestations of Shakespeare's power in the dullest and silliest of these false pretenders.

* "A Short View of the Immorality and Profaneness of the English Stage: Together with the sense of Antiquity upon this subject. By Jeremy Collier, M. A. 8vo. London, 1698."

† "The Antient and Modern Stages survey'd — Or Mr. Collier's view of the Immorality and Profaneness of the English Stage set in a True Light, &c. London 1699."

In the year 1709, Shakespeare's Plays, "Revised and Corrected, with an account of his Life and Writings, by N. [icholas] Rowe," were published, in seven volumes octavo. This edition, beside all of the authentic plays, contains the six which are accounted apocryphal. Shakespeare had now for the first time an editor, in the proper sense of the word. Rowe was a poet of merit, a man of excellent sense, a scholar, and, withal, a modest and somewhat pains-taking editor. The fruit of his labors was a great improvement in the text of Shakespeare, chiefly by the rectification of a large proportion of the grosser typographical errors which deform the previous impressions. Rowe first divided all the plays into Acts and Scenes, added many stage directions, and supplied lists of the dramatis personæ.*

Rowe was succeeded as an editor of Shakespeare by Pope, who, in 1725, published a luxurious edition in six volumes 4to. But the master of Twickenham, though a subtle thinker, a keen epigrammatist, and an exquisite versifier, made a very poor editor of the works of that poet, who, beside all other superiority, was a thinker so much subtler, an epigrammatist so much keener, and a versifier so much more exquisite than he. Pope used the quartos somewhat to the advantage, but more to the detriment of his author, foisting into the text what Shakespeare never wrote, or, having written, had rejected. He made a few good, and several very pretty and plausible emendations of typographical errors; but he added to these a far

* A very considerable number of the stage directions which appear in the modern editions of Shakespeare's plays were inserted by Rowe or Theobald. To these I have added a very few, which seemed to be needed. Some plays in the old editions are almost bare of stage directions, and are not divided into Scenes. Ignorance of these facts on the part of quarterly reviewers and other critics, who speak downward and with authority, has been the cause of some strange blunders.

greater number which were only exponents of his personal conceit, and of that unkindred estimation of Shakespeare's genius which was characteristic of his age. Presuming, too, to strike out of the text passages which did not suit his taste, and bearing off as many as a dozen speeches at a swoop, he left his edition both mutilated and corrupt, so that, as a whole, it is the poorest that was ever published.

Theobald, — "poor piddling Theobald," — the first hero of the Dunciad, who succeeded his satirist, is one of the best of Shakespeare's editors. He was the first who did any remarkable service by conjectural emendation, — Rowe's corrections of this kind having been rather of the obvious sort, — and he also first laid the quartos under important and judicious contribution. But he had not sufficiently studied, or, in consequence, justly appreciated the text of the first folio. He issued first a book devoted almost entirely to the examination of the text of *Hamlet*, which was well entitled "Shakespeare Restored; or a Specimen of the Many Errors, as well committed as unamended, in Pope's edition of this Poet," 4to., 1726, — a publication the unanswerable strictures of which Pope never forgave. In 1733 his own edition of Shakespeare's works was published in seven octavo volumes. It contained by far the best text of its author that had yet appeared. A great number of its conjectural emendations of corrupted passages remain undisturbed to this day, and have passed, by the successive consent of generation after generation, into the accepted text. Of Theobald's readings, the greater number which have been rejected were introduced by him at the suggestion of his "ingenious friend Mr. Warburton."

After Theobald came Sir Thomas Hanmer, a baronet, who published an edition, magnificent for its day, in six volumes 4to., at Oxford, in 1744. Hanmer was a man of taste, and an accomplished gentleman. He did somewhat to better, and somewhat more to harm the text which Theobald had produced. His labors were received with favor; but he was indebted for his reputation rather to fashion than to any remarkable merit, and his edition, full of faults and innovations, and marred by mutilation, is rarely consulted; the few received, or favorably regarded, emendations which he proposed being perpetuated in the text, or in the notes of other editors.*

Hanmer's edition was followed, in 1747, by Bishop Warburton's. This prelate, not then mitred, was very learned, very able; but he was equally assuming and arrogant in his personal demeanor, and he treated Shakespeare's works as he probably would have treated the player himself, had he been his contemporary. He set himself not so much to correcting the text, as to improving the thoughts and amending the style of Shakespeare. His tone is that of haughty flippancy. Does he find a passage in which the thought or the expression of William Shakespeare is at variance with the judgment of William Warburton, — he immediately alters it to suit the taste of that distinguished scholar and divine, saying, "Without a doubt, Shakespeare wrote, or meant, thus." As, for instance, of the fine line in *Hamlet*, —

"Or to take arms against a sea of troubles," —

* Collins, who wrote "To fair Fidele's grassy tomb," as a dirge for *Imogen* (*Cymbeline*, Act IV. Sc. 2), addressed an epistle in verse to Sir Thomas Hanmer on his edition of Shakespeare, in which there are these lines: —

"Those Sibyl leaves, the sport of every wind,
(For poets ever were a careless kind)
By thee dispos'd *no further toil demand*,
But just to Nature, *own thy forming hand*."

If editor or eulogist had but known what he had been about!

he says, "Without question Shakespeare wrote,

'— against *assail* of troubles,'

i. e., assault."

The reckless editing, of which this is a characteristic specimen, soon brought forward defenders of the integrity of Shakespeare's text. But it would be strange indeed, if in such a flight of random shots Shakespeare-ward, all had missed the mark; and so, like all his predecessors, and many of his successors, Bishop Warburton left amid his heaps of editorial chaff some grains of sense, which have been carefully winnowed out for the Shakespearian garner.

In 1745 appeared a duodecimo volume entitled "Miscellaneous Observations on the Tragedy of Macbeth, with Remarks on Sir T. H.'s [Sir Thomas Hanmer's] edition of Shakespear; to which is affixed, proposals for a new edition of Shakespear, with a specimen." It was written, as its author might have said, with combined perspicuity of thought and ponderosity of language. It was by Samuel Johnson, then rapidly rising to the highest position in the world of letters; and, in 1765, an edition of Shakespeare, "with the corrections and illustrations of various commentators: to which are added notes, by Samuel Johnson," was published in eight octavo volumes. It is giving the Doctor but little praise to say that he was a better editor than his reverend predecessor. The majority of his emendations of the text were, nevertheless, singularly unhappy; and his notes, though often learned, and sometimes sensible, were generally wanting in just that kind of learning and of sense most needful for his task.* The chief

* In *King Lear*, Act I. Sc. 2, *Edmund*, the bastard, according to the old text, says in reference to his schemes for supplanting his brother, —

defect in Dr. Johnson's mind, when we consider it as one of a high order, appears to have been an incapacity of the sympathetic apprehension of imaginative truth and beauty. In this he represented the period in which he lived; for, unlike the man whose works he undertook to edit, and presumed to patronize, he was of an age, and was not for all time. But when he opened Shakespeare's pages, even his common sense, which has been justly styled "colossal," seems to have forsaken him, and his candor, in some degree, to have followed it; for he assumes the settlement of disputes about various readings of folios and quartos, and yet leaves unmistakable evidence that he has neglected the examination and comparison of those texts — that first and most laborious part of editorial duty.*

Edward Capell, who next claims attention, was one of the most learned and assiduous of the editors. He published in 1759 a quarto volume entitled "Notes and various Readings of Shakespeare;" in 1768 he issued an edition of Shakespeare in ten volumes octavo; and in 1779 his "Notes and Various Readings," with many additions, and the "School of

"Edmund the base
Shall to' th' legitimate."

This, Edwards corrected, by reading, "Shall *top* the legitimate;" and yet seventeen years afterward Dr. Johnson could read, "shall *toe* the legitimate," with the note, "To toe him is, perhaps, to kick him out." Not many of Johnson's notes are quite so ridiculous as this; but many approach it in absurdity; and it shows what a tremendous step nonsense-ward he could take when he was given up to his own imaginations.

* For this opinion of Johnson as an editor of Shakespeare, which was published in *Shakespeare's Scholar*, (New York: 1854,) I was gravely rebuked both at home and abroad; and perhaps it was presuming in so young a man as I then was to write thus, even if I thought thus, upon such a subject. But further consideration has confirmed me in my judgment; and I am not the less willing to stand by this verdict that so eminent a critic as Lord Macaulay has since written thus concerning Johnson's Shakespeare: "It would be difficult to name a more slovenly and worthless edition of any great classic. The reader may turn over play after play without finding one happy conjectural emendation, or one ingenious and satisfactory explanation of a passage which had baffled preceding commentators." *Biographies:* Edinburgh, 1860. p. 112.

Shakespeare," were published in three quarto volumes. The editor of Shakespeare must have these books, and, alas! must read them. Capell's words are not without knowledge; but they often do as much to darken counsel as those uttered by the most ignorant of his co-laborers. Much patience and close thinking are sometimes needed to divine his meaning. The obscurest passage in the author whom he strives to elucidate is luminous as the sun, compared with the convoluted murkiness of his page; and when sometimes he quotes the passage upon which he comments, as its clear meaning flashes on the mind, we involuntarily think of the people who sat in darkness and saw a great light. And yet Capell did somewhat for the text, although the mass of his labors is thrust aside, for rare consultation, upon the shelves of the critical or the curious. He preserved the rhythm of Shakespeare's prose, and a characteristic trait of the speech of his time, by retaining carefully the contractions of the original. His collocation of the various readings of the old editions is invaluable for reference.

At about this period Shakespearian criticism became rampant. The publication of Warburton's edition in 1747 had provoked controversy, and given new stimulus to investigation. From that day commentary trod upon the heels of commentary, and panting pamphleteers toiled after each other in the never-ending struggle to reach the true text of Shakespeare, with as little hope of attaining it as old Time has of overtaking Shakespeare himself in Johnson's monstrous personification.* The commentators were nearly all

* "Existence saw him spurn its bounded reign,
And panting Time toil'd after him in vain."
Prologue at the Opening of Drury Lane Theatre, 1747.

of them scholars, and many were men of much critical acuteness. But their labors were almost altogether fruitless. When they displayed most learning, and exercised most ingenuity, they used to be most at fault; when they were successful it was often by chance, and generally upon some point which they regarded as of little consequence. To estimate their services to the text, compared with the harm they did it, as "two grains of wheat hid in two bushels of chaff," is to pass a lenient judgment upon their labors. There were reasons for all this. Critical Dogberrys that they were, they went not the way to examine. Their pedantry and the artificial taste of the day, joined to their own conceit and the want of a just appreciation of the genius of Shakespeare, led most of them far astray. They did not recognize him as their master, at whose feet they were to sit and learn. They did not go to their task in a humble, docile spirit. Milton had written, —

> "— sweetest Shakespeare, Fancy's child,
> Warbles his native wood-notes wild;" —

a driblet of belittling, patronizing praise, for which he should never have been forgiven, had he not atoned for it by that grand line in the epitaph, in which he calls Shakespeare

> "Dear son of memory, great heir of fame."

But the first encomium chimed with the tinkling criticism of the middle of the last century; and Shakespeare was regarded as an untutored genius, sadly in need of pruning and training; a charming, but unsophisticated songster, whose "native wood-notes wild," if their exuberance could be tamed down to the barrel-organ standard of the poet-fanciers of the day, would be meet entertainment for persons of quality — if they were not too exacting as to the unities.* In editing his works for perusal, the

* This criticism, which was first made in *Putnam's Magazine*, May, 1853, and afterwards embodied in *Shakespeare's Scholar*, has provoked much censorious remark, pitched in the admonitory key, but all of it entirely from the purpose. Those who have taken the writer so severely to task have done so upon grounds which show, I think, that they fail to appreciate the passage in *L'Allegro*. The object of that passage is not the characterization of Shakespeare "by one trait of his genius," in the words of one objector who leads the chorus, but the contrast of the so-called "Fancy's child," as a pretty little wild-bird-like creature, with Jonson, as the high and mighty master of the stage.

> "Then to the well-trod stage anon
> If Jonson's learned sock be on,
> Or sweetest Shakespeare, Fancy's child,
> Warble his native wood-notes wild."

That such was the universal apprehension of the passage is shown by the fact that this appreciation and comparison infested English literature until the beginning of the present century. So Phillips, Milton's nephew and pupil, in his *Theatrum Poetarum*, gives it as characteristic of Shakespeare that "he pleaseth with a certain *wild and native elegance*." Dryden, in his Epilogue to the *Conquest of Granada*, Part 2d, writing of the dramatists of the preceding age, says, —

> "But were they now to write, when critics weigh
> Each line and every word throughout a play,
> Not one of them, not *Jonson in his height*
> Could pass!"

thus plainly indicating who was regarded as the great and all-accomplished man at the period of the Restoration, even in the judgment of a Dryden. So Thomson says, —

> "Is not *wild* Shakespeare thine and Nature's boast?"

And Warburton, describing *The Winter's Tale* as "a homely and simple, though agreeable, country tale," brings his characterization to a focus by saying that in telling this country tale "Our 'Sweetest Shakespeare, Fancy's child,warbles,'" &c., &c. In a Sonnet "To the Right Hon. Mr. ———," written by Mr. T. E., [Thomas Evans?] Dodsley's Collection, Vol. II. p. 398, Ed. 1765, are these lines: —

> "Amid this feast of Mind, when *Fancy's child*,
> *Sweet* Shakespeare raps the soul to virtuous deed."

Dr. Sewall in the Preface to his edition of Shakespeare's Poems (4to. 1725) — and he was a champion of his author — says, "Milton seems to have *hit his character best* when he says,

> — 'Shakespear, Fancy's sweetest child,
> Warbles his native wood-notes wild.'"

Lord Shaftesbury is also kind enough to say of Shakespeare that, "Notwithstanding his *natural Rudeness, his unpolish'd Style*, his antiquated Phrase and

constant effort was, not to imbibe his spirit and touch his work with reverential hand, but to make him conform as much as possible to the standard which the critics had adopted. No one of them seemed to suspect that Shakespeare could have been a law unto himself. In putting his plays upon the stage, a yet more outrageous desecration of his genius was the fashion for nearly a hundred years. The soul of Procrustes seemed to have migrated into every

Wit, his *want of Method and Coherence* and his Deficiency in almost all the Graces and Ornaments of this kind of Writing; yet by the Justness of his Moral, the Aptness of many of his Descriptions and the plain and natural turn of several of his characters, he pleases his Audience, and often gains their Ear without a single Bribe from Luxury or Vice," — including, let us trust, that of my Lord of Shaftesbury.

Now, if the modern echoes or apologists of these people, emulating their example, like to go to Shakespeare when some literary Captain Cuttle tells them to "overhaul their little warbler," they may do so, and welcome; but there are those to whom the Swan of Avon sings another note.

The delay in the sending of this volume to press, consequent upon the distracted state of our country, enables me to add to this note the following passage from the last Imaginary Conversation written by Walter Savage Landor, which was published in the London *Athenæum* for May 18th, 1861. Andrew Marvel and John Milton speak.

"*Marvel.* . . . . I am about to find fault with you on the score of poetry. 'Surgit amari aliquid quod in ipsis floribus angit.'

"*Milton.* After the sweet I am prepared for the bitter, which often happens in life, and it is only children who take the bitter first.

"*Marvel.* Now for it. You were not a very young man when you wrote how

> 'Sweetest Shakespeare, Fancy's child,
> Warbled his native wood-notes wild.'

After acknowledging the *prettiness* of the verses, *I deny the propriety of the application. No poet was ever less a warbler of 'wood-notes wild.'* In his earlier poems he was elaborate, and not exempt from stiff conceits — the fault of the age as exemplified by Spenser.

"*Milton.* In his later he takes wing over the world, beyond human sight, but heard above the clouds."

Essentially identical as this criticism is with that which I had ventured eight years before the Conversation between Marvel and Milton was published, it is more than probable that Mr. Landor has no knowledge of either the magazine or the book in which the former had been previously printed; and I, at least, would unwillingly believe that he has not afforded my humble opinion the very important support which it thus receives from the independent concurrence of my judgment with that of so accomplished a scholar, so subtle and so sound a critic, and so eminent an author as himself.

playwright and stage-manager in England, from the day of the Restoration; and Shakespeare's plays, when they were presented at all, were so curtailed, distorted, patched, vamped and garbled, that the original work was lost almost beyond recognition. The shelves of the stage library groan under heaps of these abominations; and to this day we have not escaped their baleful influence.

The appearance of George Steevens and Edmund Malone in the field of Shakespearian literature produced greater and more permanent changes in the text than had been achieved by any of their predecessors, save Theobald. They were not co-workers, but at least, in the latter part of their critical careers, opponents. Steevens reprinted the quartos, and wrote notes and comments upon the text, which, in 1773, were embodied in an edition in ten octavo volumes. He is one of the most acute and accomplished of Shakespeare's commentators; but rarely have abilities and acquirements been more abused. To show his ability to suggest "ingenious" readings, he wantonly rejected the obvious significance of the text, and perverted the author's meaning, or destroyed the integrity of his work. He was witty, and not only launched his shafts at his fellow-commentators, but turned them against his author. He had an accurate — mechanically accurate — ear, and ruthlessly mutilated, or patched up, Shakespeare's lines to a uniform standard of ten syllables.* Beside all this, a mocking, jeering style, and an apparent

* Of the way in which Steevens worked here is a characteristic example. In a passage in *The Winter's Tale*, Act II. Sc. 1, he reads, "And why so, my *good* lord," with this note: "The epithet *good*, which is wanting in the old copies, is transplanted (for the sake of metre) from a redundant speech in the following page." It is sometimes hard to believe that Steevens was in earnest.

lack of earnestness of purpose, combine to confirm the impression that he is an editor not to be relied upon.

But in Malone he found an adversary who, in spite of a defective ear and a somewhat sluggish apprehension, was entirely too powerful for him. Malone published in 1780 two volumes, containing notes and comments upon the text as it was left by Johnson and Steevens, and other miscellaneous Shakespearian matter; and in 1790 appeared his edition of Shakespeare, "collated verbatim with the most authentic copies, and revised; with the corrections and illustrations of various commentators; to which are added, an essay on the chronological order of his plays; an essay relative to Shakespeare and Jonson; a dissertation on the three parts of *King Henry VI.*; an historical account of the English stage; and notes."* This title gives a just idea of the wide field of Shakespearian inquiry, covered by the labors of Malone. Though not highly accomplished, he was a fair scholar, a man of good judgment, and, for his day, of good poetical taste.† He was patient, indefatigably laborious, and honestly devoted to his task; he sought the glory of his author, not his own — except in so far as the latter was involved in the former. We of to-day can see that he committed many and great blunders; but he saved the text of Shakespeare from

* This edition was eight years in passing through the press. See its fourth volume, p. 112.

† But Malone, as above mentioned, had a poor ear, and an Irish one. He having remarked on a passage in *Titus Andronicus*, Act IV. Sc. 2, "Arm, my lords," &c., that "*arm* is here used as a dissyllable," Steevens replied that he had seen correct and harmonious verses of Malone's, and therefore wondered if he (Malone) had written a tale of persecuted love he would have ended it with a couplet like this, —

"Escaping thus Aunt Tabby's larums,
They triumphed in each other's arums."

wide and ruthless outrage, and by painful and well-directed investigation into the literature and manners contemporary with his author, cast new light upon his pages. To Edmund Malone the readers of Shakespeare, during the last decade of the last century and the first quarter of this, were indebted for the presentation of his works in a condition more nearly approaching their integrity than any other in which they had yet been exhibited.

The next important edition to Malone's was published in twenty-one octavo volumes, in 1803, and afterward in 1813. It was based chiefly upon that of Johnson and Steevens, with the corrections and illustrations of various commentators, all revised and augmented by Isaac Reed, an editor qualified for his task by patience, accuracy, and much reading of our early dramatic literature. This edition effected little for the text of Shakespeare, and was rather remarkable for the copiousness and variety of its prolegomena, notes, and illustrative essays. It is one of the two most important of the Variorum editions.

Malone had planned and nearly completed a second edition of his work when he died in 1812. The materials which he left were prepared and superintended through the press by James Boswell Jr., — the son of Johnson's biographer, — who, taking the Variorum of 1813 as his model, produced an edition, also in twenty-one octavo volumes, which was published in 1821, and which is a monument to the industry, research, and good judgment of its principal editor, whose labors appear to best advantage when placed beside those of his immediate predecessors and his contemporaries. This edition is usually spoken of as eminently *the* Variorum. It is a rich storehouse of Shakespearian literature, and, in addition to Malone's latest notes and comments, contains most of those which appeared in its immediate predecessor. But it is purged of heaps of smutty matter which befoul the pages of the elder book, labelled with the names Amner and Collins — pseudonymes of Steevens and Ritson. Boswell also played dustman to a mass of not indecent nonsense scraped up by Reed, although he left so much untouched.

To the editions which have now been mentioned must be added those of Alexander Chalmers, published in 1805, and several times reprinted, of the Reverend William Harness, in 1825, and of Samuel Weller Singer, at Chiswick, in 1826; though the text of neither of these was formed upon a collation of the early editions, but upon an eclectic use of the labors of preceding editors. The text of Chalmers's edition, a great favorite, does not differ materially from that of Reed's Variorum of 1803; and Singer went for his text to the editions of Steevens and Malone, with an occasional reference to an old folio or quarto. Singer's edition was highly prized, and, until within a few years past, was the favorite for general reading among cultivated people. The causes of this favor were its convenient size, the excellence of its typography, and its frugal selection from the notes of all the commentators. It was, in fact, an abridged variorum. Its editor belonged essentially to the old eighteenth century school, and though laborious, and a great reader of old books, showed neither real scholarship, critical acumen, nor power of generalization. His text was formed with more care than judgment; but it presented a few plausible emendations. As nearly twenty years elapsed after the publication of Mr. Singer's work without an attempt to rival or surpass it, we have now followed the fortunes of Shakespeare's text down to the editions which are properly of the present day.

Among the commentators on Shakespeare who did not become his editors, the most noteworthy for the purposes of this sketch are — John Upton, who in 1746 published his "Critical Observations on Shakespeare;" Thomas Edwards, whose "Canons of Criticism" first appeared in 1748; Benjamin Heath, who published in 1765 "A Revisal of Shakespear's Text, wherein the alterations introduced into it by the more modern editors and critics are particularly considered;" Thomas Tyrwhitt, the learned editor of Chaucer, whose "Observations and Conjectures upon some passages of Shakespeare" were put forth in 1766; Joseph Ritson, the eccentric and censorious literary antiquary, whose "Remarks Critical and Illustrative on the Text and Notes of the last [Steevens's] Edition of Shakespeare" appeared in 1783; John Monck Mason, who published Comments on the same edition in 1785; Walter Whiter, who in 1794 gave to this department of letters "A Specimen of a Commentary on Shakespeare;" E. H. Seymour, whose two volumes of "Remarks, critical, conjectural, and explanatory, [including also the notes of Lord Chedworth,] upon the plays of Shakspeare," appeared in 1805; Henry James Pye, who came forward in 1807 with his "Commentaries on the Commentators of Shakespeare;" Francis Douce, who issued his "Illustrations of Shakespeare and of Ancient Manners, &c." in 1809; Andrew Becket, who published in 1815 two volumes entitled "Shakspeare's himself again, or the Language of the Poet asserted;" and Zachary Jackson, whose "Shakespeare's Genius Justified, being Restorations and Illustrations of Seven Hundred Passages in Shakspeare," was given to the world in 1819.

Upton's scholarly and systematic labors have interest and value as critical discussions and illustrations of Shakespeare's text. They are instructive, and even suggestive, but over subtle and often pedantic. They did little or nothing towards restoration, but something for the prevention of wanton and ignorant alteration of the readings of the old copies. Edwards's book, written in an ironical vein, was directed chiefly against Warburton, whose conceit, arrogance, and ignorance of his author's language it thoroughly and most serviceably exposed. But Edwards did more than demolish Warburton. His critical acumen, his good taste and good sense, and his quick and sure apprehension of Shakespeare's thought, give him a conspicuous place among those who have been of real service in the preservation and elucidation of Shakespeare's text. His Canons remain, *e converso*, undisputed to this day; and the volume in which they are embodied will long retain its interest and its value. Heath, Tyrwhitt, Ritson, and Mason, each produced a minute but appreciable and beneficial effect upon the text — an effect which in the aggregate is considerable, and which promises to be permanent, although most of their suggestions have been rejected by the verdict of their successors.

Whiter's labors did little for the text; but his book has a permanent value in critical literature from its promulgation and continued application of a new principle of criticism, based upon Locke's doctrine of the association of ideas. Whiter maintained, what no close observer of his own mental action can deny, that the processes of thought are not always logical.

or by way of consequence, but very often associative, and that therefore the intellectual course of an author can be traced through the vestiges or the probabilities of association with such a degree of certainty as to enable us in this way to illustrate obscurity and restore corruption. The principle is one which can be more effectually applied than it was by the critic by whom it was first promulgated.

Eminent among the commentators for various learning, just discrimination, and a becoming deference to the author whose works he came to illustrate, is Mr. Douce. He is among them what Malone is among the editors; save that his volumes exhibit a wider range of knowledge, and a more delicate and sympathetic apprehension of the peculiar beauties of Shakespeare than Malone possessed. Yet much of his illustrative annotation is worthless superfluity, and his few textual comments and suggestions are of little value.

Pye's book was the first deliberate and systematic protest against the pedantic superfluity and the precise and prosaic criticism which marked the eighteenth century school of Shakespearian literature. Its value was rather negative than positive; more in the evil that it exposed than in the good that it accomplished. But it had a restraining influence by its indication of the spirit in which intelligent people were beginning to read these dramas, and of the light in which some of them already regarded the ingenious trifling with which his text had been overlaid, and the unappreciative inflexibility with which its sense had been perverted.

Seymour, Becket, and Jackson are worthy of our attention only as types of certain schools, or rather classes, of commentators who have one endowment in common — utter incapacity for their office. Seymour represents those educated commentators who are pedagogues, not critics. The knowledge that a verb should agree with its nominative case, and that ten syllables make an heroic line, form the staple of the qualifications which he brought to his task. He would have removed the 'from' in all cases in which it is used with 'whence,' or 'thence,' because it is tautological; thus endeavoring to conform the language of Shakespeare's day to that of his own; and he sought, by mutilation, addition, and transposition, to make an unbroken series of perfect lines of ten syllables, from the beginning to the end of every play.

Becket is *facile princeps* of the commentators who have a mission, and nothing else, and who feel that they are sent upon earth to reform the text, with plenary power and special revelation. Of him it is difficult to speak with patience or decorum. His work is stupidity run mad. The time-honored simile of a bull in a china shop was never more applicable than to his delighted plungings among the tender and exquisite beauties fashioned by the hand of Shakespeare. And when he has shivered, and crushed, and scattered to his heart's content, he stands with ineffable complacency amid his fragmentary labors, and, looking round upon them, bellows out, "Shakespeare's himself again." A notion of Becket's book could only be conveyed by extracts; and it would not be worth the space which they would occupy.

Zachary Jackson was a printer; and as the most of the corruptions of Shakespeare's text are due to the carelessness or incompetence of compositors and the lack of proof-reading, he justly thought that a practical knowledge of his art would be of service in their conjectural emendation. He had corrected much proof, and thus, it would seem, should have been able to surmise, with occasional good fortune, what accident had produced the error in the book before him. But even in this he failed almost entirely; and when, forgetting the "*ne sutor*," he ventured into the field of general comment and criticism, he made such absurd and atrocious changes in the text, that it is difficult to believe them the work of a mind above that of an idiot; and yet he utters them with an owlish sapience that makes him the very *Bunsby* of commentators.

But though the text of Shakespeare suffered no permanent injury from such commentators as these, and though the Variorum and the Chiswick editions presented the works of the great dramatist more nearly as he produced them than they had ever before appeared in print, the increasing admiration of the world for those matchless writings, the influence of a humbler, more docile school of criticism upon them, and the well-known fact that there were still many departures in those editions from the authentic text, which, at least, might be needless, created a desire for a text conforming yet more strictly to the primitive standard; and about 1840, two editors stepped forward to supply this want.* These were Mr.

* It would be unjust to pass entirely by the services which Bishop Percy, Chief Justice Blackstone, and Holt White rendered to the text, incidental though they were. Their names often occur in the Variorum, and always in connection with comments or conjectures which are at least intelligent or suggestive. The above notice of the commentators may seem meagre to those who are acquainted with their number and the extent of their labors; but my purpose related only to those who wrote upon the text, and of those only to such as produced an effect upon it, or who were representative men in this department of literature. It is worthy of observation, although it is not surprising, that the German critics have accomplished nothing for Shakespeare in this respect.

Knight and Mr. Collier.* They each did much to effect that nearer approximation of the text to the "True Originall" which was so much needed. Both were sparing of conjectural emendation; but Mr. Collier admitted the "stolen and surreptitious" quartos to a higher authority than that awarded to them by Mr. Knight, who deferred only to the original and authentic but badly printed folio. Mr. Collier had the advantage of a long devotion to the study of old English literature, especially to that of Shakespeare's age; but Mr. Knight brought to his task an intelligent veneration for his author, and a sympathetic apprehension of his thoughts, which distinguished him in this respect above all his predecessors. But both editors committed errors, and left others uncorrected. Mr. Collier admitted readings from the quartos, and the commentators, which are indefensible; and Mr. Knight's almost superstitious veneration for the first folio caused him to reproduce from it, with attempts at explanation, many passages which are evidently corrupted. This was shown with no less admirable temper than ability by the Rev. Alexander Dyce, the editor of Beaumont & Fletcher, Marlowe, Green, and Peele, &c., in his "Remarks on Mr. J. P. Collier's and Mr. C. Knight's Editions of Shakespeare," which appeared in 1844.†

* The publication of Mr. Knight's edition began in 1839, that of Mr. Collier's in 1841; the former was completed in 1841, the latter in 1843.

† Two editions of remarkable merit were afterward published in the United States: one by the Hon. Gulian C. Verplanck, and the other by the Rev. Mr. Hudson. These editors, however, formed their text rather upon an eclectic study of the labors of their immediate predecessors than upon a collation of the old readings, or even a thorough investigation of the whole field of Shakespearian textual criticism. Mr. Verplanck's edition is distinguished by the judgment, taste, and scholarship which guided his editorial labors; Mr. Hudson's by the originality of thought and vigor of style in the critical essays which precede each play.

III.

Having traced the history of the great intellectual heritage of our race through the various fortunes of two hundred and fifty years, we arrive at a period of novel and interesting vicissitude. Hitherto the language of Shakespeare had suffered from his own neglect, from the haste, ignorance, and carelessness of transcribers and printers, and from the incapacity, the presumption, and the pedantry of editors and commentators. Its preservation and its restoration, (for it needed to be fenced as well as to be made whole,) were due only to the faithful labors, the insight, the sensibility, and the constructive ingenuity of some of those who had undertaken to repair its injuries, regulate its confusion, and explain its obscurities. Not a single line written by Shakespeare was known to exist, not a printed play of his which there is reason to believe he saw in proof. Manuscript or contemporary authority for the rehabilitation of the text there was none; and the means of restoration were limited to study, deduction, and conjecture. To these there was now to be added manuscript for which was claimed contemporary, or nearly contemporary, authority. In 1852 Mr. John Payne Collier, whose edition of Shakespeare's works had then been before the public for nine years, who had been favorably known as a student of English, and particularly of Elizabethan, literature for more than thirty years, and who was a man of then unquestioned honor, announced that there had accidentally fallen into his hands a copy of the folio edition of 1632, the margins of which were filled with ancient manuscript corrections of the text, which were of great interest and value. In 1853 Mr. Collier published a history of his discovery, and a detailed exposition of its literary character, in a volume entitled *Notes and Emendations to the Text of Shakespeare from Early Manuscript Corrections in a Copy of the Folio of* 1632.* He therein sustained all the readings, with few exceptions, thus brought forward; and, although his edition of Shakespeare had exhibited an almost slavish deference to "the oldest authority," he now startled his readers not only by expressing his conviction that "far the greater body" of these marginal corrections were "the restored language of Shakespeare," and strongly intimating that their source must have been of higher authority than any theretofore discovered, but by publishing an edition of the plays in which they, or rather such of them as he thought it prudent to make public, were embodied. Only a very few of these substituted readings were manifestly sound, but a multitude of them were plausible: the mysterious manner of their discovery, and their supposed antiquity, excited popular interest, and even blinded critical per-

* According to Mr. Collier's account, he bought this folio, in the spring of 1849, of Mr. Thomas Rodd, a very respectable antiquarian bookseller in London, (who unfortunately died before his evidence was needed,) to complete another imperfect copy of the same edition by the addition of two lacking leaves. Upon examination, he found that the two leaves of his new purchase, of which he was in want, were unfitted for his purpose by being not only too short, but damaged and defaced. He then laid it carelessly away; and it was not until the spring of 1850 that he "observed some marks on the margin of this folio." Yet subsequently, looking farther, he discovered, to his surprise, that "there was hardly a page which did not present, in a handwriting of the time, some emendations in the pointing or in the text." Then, submitting the volume to careful scrutiny, he "became convinced of the value of its marginal corrections." It may be explicable, but it has not yet been explained, how Mr. Collier could open a volume of more than nine hundred pages so directly upon two leaves of which he was in search as not to observe the manuscript which "hardly a page" of that volume was without, or, even supposing that this almost impossible discovery might happen, how it came about that the four pages of these two leaves and the four pages which faced them were also free from writing on their margins. The alternative that Mr. Collier did see these manuscript corrections when he first examined the book, or that they were added afterward, seems unavoidable. Yet that the body of them were so added is not credible, as the reader will see hereafter.

ception; the *Notes and Emendations*, and the new edition of the plays, sold rapidly; and for a short time it seemed as if the whole world would receive with joyful submission the new revelation of Shakespeare. No sooner was the body of the new readings well before the public than strong protests were made against them, and a sharp and minute discussion arose upon their individual merits. But it was plain that their hold upon the faith of the general public would not be shaken by mere critical opinion of their separate value; because to mere opinion opinion could be opposed. A close examination of the body of the readings brought forward in Mr. Collier's *Notes and Emendations* convinced me that, whatever might be their importance on the ground of their antiquity, (they could not have been written until 1632, sixteen years after Shakespeare's death,) or on their own evidence of access by their author to sources of information more authentic than the early printed copies of the plays, they had no such claims to consideration as should remove them from the category of conjectural and arbitrary changes, to be judged solely upon their merits.* This conclusion was based upon the following points, which I believe were sufficiently established: —

The marginal readings, in many instances, debased the poetry of Shakespeare, and extinguished his humor. In some cases they were made in palpable disregard of the context. In others they were no less plainly at variance with Shakespeare's manifest dramatic purpose.

* See *Putnam's Magazine* for October, 1853, and *Shakespeare's Scholar*, 1854, for an examination of Mr. Collier's folio, which, in the words of the preface to the latter, is not a "detailed approval or disapproval" of such of the marginal readings of that volume as had been made public, but "purely an argument, which aims to show that those emendations were made in such a way and at such a time that as to their authority they are utterly without a claim upon our deference."

Some of the changes were made merely because the maker failed to apprehend the meaning of a clear and uncorrupted passage. Many instances of the erasure of a reading once entered, and the substitution of another, showed the vacillation of conjecture, not the record of authority. Some of the readings, the peculiar character of which at the first blush seemed most conclusively to show that they could not have been conjectural, had, on the contrary, been brought forward long before the appearance of this folio, as the fruit of mere conjecture or deduction, by some of the most ignorant and wrong-headed of the commentators.* The margins of the volume were filled with palpable and universally admitted errors of all the various kinds which had been committed by editors and commentators of every grade of capacity and incapacity; and they not only contained a large number of the specific mutilations perpetrated by those editors and commentators, but added to them more than had been before attempted by all mutilators of the text combined. The more important of the obscure passages in the plays were left untouched, except a few which were changed in such a way as to transfer the obscurity from one line to another, or diffuse it through many. The corrector, in disregard or in ignorance of the customs and the phraseology of Shakespeare's day, sought to make Shakespeare's language conform to the fashion of a period half a century later. Finally, the readings were not entered upon the margins of this folio until after the Restoration, at least twenty-eight years subsequent to its publication, and forty-four from the death of Shakespeare, when the poet's contemporaries had passed away, the theatres had been closed, and their

* Even Seymour, Jackson, and Becket.

companies and property dispersed and destroyed during the great civil war and the Commonwealth, and emendation of Shakespeare's plays must, from the nature of things, have been unauthoritative.

As time passed (it is ten years since) the faith of the more thoughtful and best read of those who had welcomed the marginal readings of this folio so heartily, and accepted them so implicitly, began to be shaken in their idol; and in 1856 Mr. Collier himself confessed that he was "convinced that the great majority of the corrections were made, not from better manuscripts, still less from unknown printed copies of the plays, but from the recitations of old actors while the play was proceeding;" adding that he "could adduce various instances never yet pointed out" in which the corrector "inserted what he considered emendations, but what we must look upon as innovations — changes which had crept in [upon the stage] from time to time, to make sense out of difficult passages, but which do not represent the authentic text of Shakespeare." * Again time passed, and the Collier folio (called the Perkins folio in Great Britain, from the name of a former possessor, written upon the cover) was passing out of mind, except among the critical and the studious, when, in April, 1859, seven years after it came into public notice, it was placed in the hands of Sir Frederic Madden, Keeper of the Manuscripts in the British Museum, by the Duke of Devonshire, to whose father it had been given by its discoverer. Previous to this. only a very few persons, and they not Shakespearian scholars, had been favored with a glimpse of it. At the Museum it was closely examined by Mr. N.

* *Seven Lectures on Shakespeare and Milton*, &c. London, 1856, pp. lxxiii., lxxxii.

E. S. A. Hamilton, a palæographer and one of the assistants in the Manuscript Department of that institution. His purpose in making the examination was "to attempt an accurate and unbiased description of the volume."* In the prosecution of this design he discovered that, of the corrections originally made on the margins of this folio, the number which had been wholly or partially "obliterated . . . with a penknife or the employment of chemical agency" were "almost as numerous as those suffered to remain;" he also concluded that, of the corrections allowed to stand, many had been "tampered with, touched up, or painted over, a modern character being dexterously altered, by touches of the pen, into a more antique form;" and he found that the margins were "covered with an infinite number of faint pencil-marks, in obedience to which the supposed old corrector made his emendations," and that these pencilled memorandums had "not even the pretence of antiquity in character or spelling," but were "written in a bold hand of the present century."

Upon this discovery the aid of natural science was invoked, and the volume was placed in the hands of Mr. Nevil Story Maskelyne, Keeper of the Mineralogical Department of the Museum, who examined the margins with a very powerful microscope, and tested the ink of the corrections. Mr. Maskelyne's investigations confirmed entirely the evidence of Mr. Hamilton's eyes. He found the pencilled memorandums "plentifully distributed down the margins," and "the particles of plumbago in the hollows of the paper" in every instance that he examined. He thought, also, that what seemed to be ink was not ink, but "a paint, removable, with the exception of a slight

* See his letter in the London *Times* of July 2d, 1859.

stain, by mere water," — which paint, "formed perhaps of sepia," would enable an impostor to simulate ink faded by time; and, most important of all, in several cases in which "the ink word, in a quaint, antique-looking writing, and the pencil word, in a modern-looking hand, occupy the same ground, and are one over the other," the pencil-marks being obscured or obliterated, Mr. Maskelyne found, on washing off the ink, that at first "the pencil-marks became much plainer than before, and even when as much of the ink-stain as possible was removed, the pencil still ran through the ink line in unbroken, even continuity." These points established, Mr. Maskelyne's conclusion, that in the examples which he tested "the pencil underlies the ink, that is to say, was antecedent to it in its date," was unavoidable.*

These announcements excited hardly less attention than that of the original discovery of the readings. So important a literary fraud, and one which awakened such general interest, had been never before discovered. It seemed as if Mr. Collier must have been either an impostor or a dupe, or the victim of a conspiracy. Investigation was aroused, and the inquiry was prosecuted in regard not only to the folio, but to several other manuscripts relating to Shakespeare, his works, and his contemporaries, which had been brought forward by Mr. Collier as his own discoveries. The literary inquest sat for nearly two years, hearing counsel on both sides, and, in the end, these points were clearly established in regard to this famous folio: —

The volume contains more than twice, nearly three times, as many marginal readings, including stage-directions and changes of orthography, as are enu-

* See his letter in the London *Times* of July 16th, 1859.

merated in a list which Mr. Collier, after having, to use his own words, "often gone over the thousands of marks of all kinds" in his folio, and "reëxamined every line and letter," published as "A List of *Every Manuscript Note and Emendation* in Mr. Collier's Copy of Shakespeare's Works, folio, 1632."*

The margins retain numerous traces of pencil-memorandums.

These pencil-memorandums are in some instances written in a modern cursive hand, to which marginal readings in ink, written in an antique hand, correspond.

There are some pencil-memorandums to which no corresponding change in ink has been made; and one of these is in short-hand of a system which did not come into use until 1774.†

These pencil-memorandums in some instances underlie the words in ink which correspond to them.

Similar modern pencil-writing, underlying in like manner antique-seeming words in ink, appears in the Bridgewater folio, (Lord Ellesmere's,) the manuscript readings in which Mr. Collier was the first to bring into notice.

Some of the pencilled memorandums in Mr. Collier's folio of 1632 seem to be unmistakably in his own handwriting.

Several manuscripts, professing to be contemporary with Shakespeare, and containing passages of interest in regard to him, or to the dramatic affairs of his time, and which Mr. Collier brought forward as the fruits of his researches in the Bridgewater and Dul-

* See the appendix to *Seven Lectures on Shakespeare and Milton.* London, 1856.

† In *Coriolanus*, Act V. Sc. 2, (p. 55, col. 2, of the C. folio,) "*struggles or instead noise*," — plainly a memorandum for a stage-direction in regard to the impending fracas between *Menenius* and the Guard.

wich Collections, have been pronounced spurious by the highest palæographic authorities in England, and in one of them (a letter addressed to Henslow, and bearing Marston's signature) there is a pencilled guide for the ink, like those above mentioned.

In the professed reprint of one manuscript by Mr. Collier, not only are words changed, but several lines relating to Shakespeare appear which could not possibly have formed a part of the passage which he professed to reproduce.*

These are interesting points in the history of the volume and the manuscripts which hold so important a place in the history of Shakespearian literature;

* This manuscript is the postscript of a letter from Mistress Alleyn to her husband, Edward Alleyn, the eminent actor of Shakespeare's day. This letter, dated October 20th or 21st, 1603, was first published by Mr. Collier in his "Memoirs of Edward Alleyn" in 1841, where he represents the following broken passage as part of it: —

"Aboute a weeke a goe there came a youthe who said he was
Mr. Frauncis Chaloner who would have borrowed x$^{li.}$ to
have bought things for . . . *and said he was known*
unto you and Mr. Shakespeare of the globe, who came
. . . *said he knewe hym not, onely he herde of hym that he was*
a roge . . . so he was glade we did not lend him
the monney . . . Richard Johnes [went] to seeke

---

and inquire after the fellow," &c.

The paper on which this postscript is written is very much decayed, and has been broken and torn away by the accidents of time; but enough remains to show that the passage in question really stands thus, — the letters in brackets being obliterated: —

"Aboute a weeke agoe ther[e] [cam]e a youthe who said he was
Mr. Frauncis Chalo[ner]s man [& wou]ld have borrow[e]d x$^{s.}$ to
have ‸bought things for [hi]s Mri[s] . . . . [tru]st hym
Cominge without . . . token . . . . d
I would have . . . .
[i]f I bene sue[r] . . . .

---

and inquire after the fellow," &c.

According to the evidence of Mr. Halliwell, Mr. Hamilton, and Dr. Ingleby, the divisions of the lines in the original manuscript correspond to those above; and a moment's examination will convince the reader that the existence of

but they fail to show that the body of the marginal readings in Mr. Collier's folio are spurious, that is, written in a pretended antique character; and, consequently, they fail to fix on him, in that instance, the guilt of absolute imposture. For such of the pencil tracings on those margins (so worn as to be always faint, and often imperfect) as are not manifestly modern may well have been made as memorandums, or first entries, in the seventeenth century. Lead, or, properly, plumbago pencils were then used; and plumbago is an unalterable, inorganic substance, which does not fade like ink, and the traces of which are very difficult of entire removal, especially when old, even by attrition and washing.* Pencil marks which are certainly two hundred years old are known to exist upon the fly leaves and margins of other books. It is a significant fact in this regard that pencil guides or memorandums were discovered in this volume for even the lines by which long passages are erased.

In the course of their laborious efforts to establish the spuriousness of the marginal readings in Mr.

those words of Mr. Collier's version which are printed in Italic letter in the place to which he assigns them is a physical impossibility. And that the mention of Shakespeare, and what he said, was not on a part of the letter which has been broken away, is made certain by the fortunate preservation of enough of the lower margin to show that no such passage could have been written upon it. The line which separates "and inquire, &c.," from the rest of the postscript, marks the bottom of the first page of the letter. Those words are at the top of the second page.

* M. Bonnardot, the highest French authority upon the subject on which he writes, in his *Essai sur l'Art de Restaurer les Estampes et les Livres*, under the head — "*Taches des crayons.* (*Plombagine, sanguine, crayon noir*," &c.,) — says, "Les traces *récentes* que laissent sur le papier ces divers crayons s'effacent au contact du caoutchouc, ou de la mie de pain; mais, *quand elles sont trop anciennes, elles résistent à ces moyens;* on a recours alors à l'application du savon," &c. "S'il restait, après cette opération, des traces opiniâtres sur le papier, *il faudrait désespérer les enlever.*" p. 81. My own observation confirms M. Bonnardot's.

Collier's folio, the London palæographers and critics unwittingly brought evidence to light, the bearing of which they did not perceive. A part of Mr. Hamilton's valuable and interesting book was devoted to a record of all the manuscript readings on the margins of *Hamlet* in the famous folio.* An examination of this list discovers facts which are irreconcilable with the supposition the great mass of these marginal readings, points, and stage-directions, (many thousand in number,) were written by any one in a pretended antique character, for the purpose of giving them authority on account of their apparent age, and which should settle this part of the question forever.

The number of the manuscript marginal readings in *Hamlet* is four hundred and twenty-six.† But for this large number of readings the sharp eyes and the microscopes of the British Museum, and its co-workers, were able to discover only twelve pencilled memorandums. Of these, three are for mere punctuation, three for stage-directions, and two for the mere adding of letters which do not change the word or the sense,‡ leaving but four instances in which memorandums are found for a change of reading.§ And,

* See *An Inquiry into the Genuineness of the Manuscript Corrections*, &c. By N. E. S. A. Hamilton. London, 1860. pp. 34–55.

† According to Dr. Ingleby, in his *Complete View of the Shakespeare Controversy.*

‡ For instance, "He *smot* the sledded Polax" is changed to "He *smote*," &c., and there is a pencil memorandum for the addition of the *e*!

§ The following are the four passages; the corrections being in Italic letter in the margin:—

"O most pernicious ‸ woman!" Act I. Sc. 5.	*and perfidious*
"With all my love ‸ commend me to you." *Idem.*	*I do.*
"A*nd* thus, I know his father and his friends." Act II. Sc. 1.	*s*
"Or like a creature native and *d*educed." Act IV. Sc. 7	*r*

of these four hundred and twenty-six marginal changes, a very large proportion, quite one half, are mere insignificant literal changes or additions, such as an editor in looking over manuscript, or an author in reading proof, passes by, and leaves to the proof-readers of the printing-office, by whom they are called "literals." * To corrections like these the alleged forger must have devoted more than half his time; and if the thirty-one pages that *Hamlet* fills in the folio furnish a fair sample of the whole of the forger's labors, (and Dr. Ingleby says that it is "a just sample of the other plays in that volume,") we have the enormous sum of more than six thousand four hundred of such utterly useless changes upon the nine hundred pages of that volume. If the author of these corrections was an impostor, such another laborious scoundrel, who labored for the labor's sake, the world has surely never seen.

But among these marginal changes in *Hamlet* a large number present a very striking and significant peculiarity. That peculiarity is a modernization of the text absolutely fatal to the "early" pretensions of the readings; and it appears in the regulation of the loose spelling prevalent at the publication of this folio, and for many years after, by the standard of the more regular and approximately analogous fashion of a later period, and also in the establishment of

* Such are the change of "*Whon* yond same starre" to "*When* yond," &c.; "*Looke* it not like the king" to "*Lookes* it," &c.; "He *smot* the sledded Polax" to "He *smote*," &c.; "*Heaven* will direct it" to "*Heavens* will," &c.; "list, *Hamle*, list," to "list, *Hamlet*, list;" "the *Mornings* Ayre" to "the *Morning* Ayre;" "My Liege and *Madrm*" to "My Liege and *Madam*;" "*locke* of Wit" to "*lacke* of Wit;" "both our *judgement* joyne" to "both our *judgements* joyne;" "my *convseration*" to "my *conversation*;" "the *strucken* Deere" to "the *stricken* Deere;" "*Requit* him for your Father" to "*Requite* him," &c.: "I'll *anoiot* my sword" to "I'll *anoint*," &c.; "the *gringding* of the Axe" to "the *grinding*," &c.

grammatical concords, which, entirely disregarded in the former period, were observed by well-educated people in the latter.* Of such corrections I discovered twenty-eight (and there may be more) among the collations of *Hamlet* alone, which is a "just sample" of the volume. Twenty-eight corrections for the thirty-one pages which *Hamlet* occupies in the folio give, for the nine hundred pages of the whole volume, about eight hundred and fifty instances in which the corrector modernized the text, though he obtained thereby only a change of form, and not a single new reading, in any sense of the term.

Kindred evidence is furnished by the stage-directions to other plays. In *Love's Labour's Lost*, Act IV. Sc. 3, when *Birone* conceals himself from the *King*, the stage-direction in the folio of 1632, as well as in that of 1623, is, "*He stands aside.*" But in Mr. Collier's folio of 1632 this is changed to "*He climbs a tree*," and he is afterward directed to speak "*in the tree.*" So again in *Much Ado about Nothing*, Act II. Sc. 3, there is a manuscript stage-direction to the effect that *Benedick*, when he hides "in the arbour," "*Retires behind the trees.*" Now, as this use of scenery did not obtain until after the Restoration, these stage-directions manifestly could not have been written until after that period.†

* Thus we find "He *smot*" changed to "He *smote;*" "Some *sayes*" to "Some *say;*" "*veyled* lids" to "*vayled* lids;" "*Seemes* to me all the uses" to "*Seem* to me all the uses;" "It lifted up *it* head" to "It lifted up *its* head;" "*dreins* his draughts" to "*drains* his draughts;" "fast in *fiers*" to "fast in *fires;*" "a *vild* phrase, beautified is a *vild* phrase" to "a *vile* phrase, beautified is a *vile* phrase;" "How in my words *somever* she be shent" to "How in my words *soever*," &c.; "*currants* of this world" to "*currents*," &c.; "theres *matters*" to "theres *matter;*" "like some *oare*" to "like some *ore;*" "this *vilde* deed" to "this *vile* deed;" "a sword *unbaited*" to "a sword *unbated;*" "a *stoape* liquor" to "a *stoop* liquor;" and "the *stopes* of wine" to "the *stoopes* of wine."

† Upon this point — which was first made in *Putnams Magazine* for

Yet more: these marginal readings, as shown by the collation of *Hamlet*, not only prove themselves that they were not the work of an impostor, — they show, with an approach to exactness, the period when they were entered upon the margins of the folio. Not more surely did the lacking aspirate betray the Ephraimite at the passage of the Jordan than the spelling, the punctuation, and the grammar of this unknown corrector reveal the period at which he performed his labors. For instance, the word 'vile' was almost universally spelled *vild* or *vilde* down to, and even past, the middle of the seventeenth century; of which no man who could make the body of the corrections in this folio could possibly be ignorant. Yet this marginal corrector modernized *vild* into *vile* in three passages of a single play, — *Hamlet*, — though he thereby obtained not a shade of difference in meaning; and he did likewise in some eight hundred and fifty similar instances. That this is the work of an impostor passes all belief. But to return to the evidence of the period of the marginal writing, which may be briefly shown by tracing the history of 'vile,' which occurs five times in *Hamlet*. In the folio of 1623, in all these cases except the first, it is spelled *vild;*

October, 1853 — Mr. Halliwell says (fol. Shak. Vol. IV. p. 340) that the writer of that article "fairly adduces these MS. directions as incontestable evidences of the late period of the writing in that volume, 'practicable' trees certainly not having been introduced on the English stage until after the Restoration." See, tco, in the following passage from the *Noble Stranger*, by Lewis Sharpe, London, 1640, direct evidence as to the stage customs in London, eight years after the publication of Mr. Collier's folio, in situations like those of *Birone* and *Benedick:* —

"I am resolv'd, I over-
Heard them in the presence appoynt to walke
Here in the garden: now in *yon thicket*
I'll stay," &c.
"*Exit behind the Arras.*"

But no man in the world knows the ancient customs of the English stage better than Mr. Collier.

in the folio of 1632, with the same exception, we also find *vild;* even in the folio of 1664 the spelling in all these instances remains unchanged; but in the folio of 1685, *vild* gives place to *vile* in every case. As with 'vild,' so with the other words subjected to like changes. In brief, the spelling throughout the marginal readings of Mr. Collier's folio, judged by the numerous fac-similes and collations that have been published, indicates the close of the last quarter of the seventeenth century as the period about which the volume in which they appear was subjected to correction. The careful removal throughout the volume (though with some oversights) of those irregularities and anomalies of spelling which were common before the Restoration, and the harmonizing of grammatical discords which were disregarded before that period, and, on the other hand, the retention of the superfluous final *e*, (once the *e* of prolongation,) and of the *l* in the contractions of 'would,' in accordance with a pronunciation which prevailed in Old and New England until 1700 and later, all point to this date, which is also indicated by various other internal proofs, to which attention has been heretofore sufficiently directed. The punctuation, too, which, in Mr. Collier's words, is corrected "with nicety and patience," is that of the books printed after the Restoration.*

* The examples of modernization of the text given in the note upon page 388 indicate a period not earlier than the Restoration.

It is perhaps also worthy of notice that the attempt to make the substitution of the word *cheer* for *chair* in *Coriolanus*, Act IV. Sc. 7, —

"Hath not a tomb so evident as a chair," —

evidence that the marginal readings were entered upon the folio after the close of the eighteenth century, because 'cheer' was not used to mean "a shout of admirative applause" until that date, failed, because the Diary of Henry Teong, a British navy chaplain, dated 1675–79, shows that three cheers were given at that date, as they are now; and in Phaer's translation of the *Æneid*, published

The many erasures throughout this volume must also be taken into consideration, when we examine the question of the good faith in which the bulk of its alterations were made. In *Hamlet* there are no less than thirty-six erasures, which are from a few words to fifty lines in extent, and which include some of the most characteristic, if not some of the finest passages in the tragedy. It is impossible to believe that any man in his senses, making corrections for which he meant to set up a claim for higher authority than that of the earliest printed text, would make such and so numerous erasures.

The foregoing considerations apply to the great mass, in fact to almost the entire body of the marginal readings, and to the pencil-memorandums in Mr. Collier's folio. But there are also, on those margins, many memorandums in cursive pencil writing. The publication of between twenty and thirty fac-similes of this pencil writing, although they consist in only five instances of more than a single word, letter, or point, shows that these memorandums are the work of a hand of the present century, and, according to the judgment of all the British critics who have compared them with Mr. Collier's pencil-writing, and who have borne testimony in the matter, there can, on the score of resemblance, be no doubt as to their origin.

Thus the external, or, more exactly, the physical and literal evidence of this folio sustains, and, I may say, establishes the conclusion which, eight years before it was made public, I had drawn from a crit-

in 1558, the verb is used in this sense: "*Excipiunt plausu pavidos*" is rendered "The Trojans them did chere."

ical examination of the internal or literary evidence, — that its manuscript readings were entered upon its margins in the seventeenth century, and after the Restoration. It seems first to have been submitted to erasure for stage purposes; and afterward (for the changes in text and punctuation extend through the passages marked for omission) to have been carefully corrected for the press, with a view to the publication of a new edition.* Of its fate after it fell into the hands of Mr. Collier, I need say nothing here; and I gladly avail myself of the privilege of silence upon a subject, in my polemical treatment of which heretofore I may unwillingly and unwittingly have wronged a gentleman whose labors have made all readers of our early poetry, and especially of Shakespeare, his debtors, and who, before the appearance of his corrected folio, had borne into the vale of years an unsullied reputation. The topic brings unpleasantly, yet somewhat fitly, to a close the history of a literature often turbid with ignorant presumption, deformed by prejudice, and embittered by acrimony; but I dismiss it not without the hope that facts yet undiscovered, or explanations yet unmade, may preserve this page of letters from the dark stain of imposture.

* This view of the evidence brought forward to establish the spuriousness of the marginal readings in the Collier folio was presented in two articles which I wrote upon the subject, for the *Atlantic Monthly*, in which they were published, October, 1859, and September, 1861.

POEMS.

COMMENDATORY VERSES.

In the volume published in 1640, as "*Poems written by Wil. Shake-speare Gent.*" and which is made up of Shakespeare's Sonnets, fancifully arranged, songs taken from the plays, and poetical translations by other writers, are commendatory verses by Leonard Digges, John Warren, John Milton, William Basse, and an anonymous writer. Of these the second and last are of no interest, and are evidently not contemporary with the works which they celebrate. Milton's, and all that is interesting in Digges', are given in Volume II. of this edition. The following are Basse's lines, which are said by Malone to exist in manuscript written about 1621: —

On the death of WILLIAM SHAKESPEARE, *who died in Aprill, Anno Dom.* 1616.

Renowned *Spenſer,* lie a thought more nigh
To learned *Chauſer*; and rare *Beaumount* lie
A little neerer *Spenſer,* to make roome,
For *Shakeſpeare* in your three-fold, four-fold Tomb.
To lodge all foure in one bed make a shift
Vntill Dommes-day, for hardly will a ſift
Betwixt this day and that by Fate be slaine,
For whom your Curtaines may be drawne again
But if precedencie in death doth barre
A fourth place in your sacred Sepulchre!
Under this ſacred Marble of thy owne,
Sleep rare Tragedian *Shakeſpeare,* ſleepe alone;
Thy unmoleſted peace, in an unſhar'd Cave
Poſſess as Lord, not Tennant, of thy Grave.
That unto us, and others it may be,
Honour hereafter to be laid by thee.

W. B.

VENUS AND ADONIS.

Vilia miretur vulgus: mihi flavus Apollo
Pocula Castalia plena ministret aqua.

"Venvs and Adonis.

Vilia miretur vulgus: mihi flauus Apollo
Pocula Castalia plena ministret aqua.

London Imprinted by Richard Field, and are to be sold at the signe of the white Greyhound in Paules Church-yard. 1593." 4to. 27 leaves.

The title page of the edition of 1594, 4to., does not differ in the most minute particular from that of the edition of 1593, excepting that there is a full point after the word "London." It also has 27 leaves.

"Venvs and Adonis.

Vilia miretur vulgus: mihi flauus Apollo
Pocula Castalia plena ministret aqua.

Imprinted at London by R. F. for Iohn Harison. 1596." 8vo. 27 leaves.

Field's device of the Anchor is found upon each of the above impressions. The edition of 1600, 8vo., only varies from that of 1596 in the imprint, which is "London. Printed by I. H. for Iohn Harison. 1600." The imprint of the 8vo. Edinburgh edition runs thus: "Edinburgh, Printed by John Wreittoun and are to be sold in his Shop a little beneath the salt Trone. 1627." [Collier.

VENUS AND ADONIS.

INTRODUCTION.

THE story of the loves of Venus and Adonis, told by Ovid and by earlier writers, was modified in the middle ages — we know not exactly when or in whose hands — by making Adonis insensible to the transcendent charms of the Goddess of Love and Beauty. Shakespeare adopted this version of the myth, and, when he wrote the following poem, may possibly have been unacquainted with any other.

Venus and Adonis was entered upon the Stationers' Register on the 18th of April, 1593, and published in the same year. How long before that date it was written, cannot be determined. In the dedication Shakespeare calls it "the first heir of his invention," which has been regarded as a designation of it as his earliest work. But such expressions must not be received in evidence implicitly. It would seem from the same dedication that this poem, as well as its successors, was the production of the author's "idle hours." He regarded his dramatic writing as professional business: it was only his leisure that he devoted to the Muse. Still, *Venus and Adonis* is plainly a youthful production, and may have been two or three years in hand before it was published.

The text has come down to us in almost absolute purity.

TO THE RIGHT HONOURABLE

HENRY WRIOTHESLY,

EARL OF SOUTHAMPTON, AND BARON OF TICHFIELD.

RIGHT HONOURABLE,

I KNOW not how I shall offend in dedicating my unpolished lines to your lordship, nor how the world will censure me for choosing so strong a prop to support so weak a burden: only, if your honour seem but pleased, I account myself highly praised, and vow to take advantage of all idle hours, till I have honoured you with some graver labour. But if the first heir of my invention prove deformed, I shall be sorry it had so noble a god-father, and never after ear so barren a land, for fear it yield me still so bad a harvest. I leave it to your honourable survey, and your honour to your heart's content; which I wish may always answer your own wish, and the world's hopeful expectation.

Your honour's in all duty,

WILLIAM SHAKESPEARE.

VENUS AND ADONIS.

EVEN as the sun with purple-colour'd face
  Had ta'en his last leave of the weeping morn,
Rose-cheek'd Adonis hied him to the chase;
Hunting he lov'd, but love he laugh'd to scorn:
  Sick-thoughted Venus makes amain unto him,
  And like a bold-fac'd suitor 'gins to woo him.

"Thrice fairer than myself," thus she began,
"The field's chief flower, sweet above compare,
Stain to all nymphs, more lovely than a man,
More white and red than doves or roses are;
  Nature that made thee, with herself at strife,
  Saith, that the world hath ending with thy life.

"Vouchsafe, thou wonder, to alight thy steed,
And rein his proud head to the saddle-bow;
If thou wilt deign this favour, for thy meed
A thousand honey secrets shalt thou know:
  Here come and sit, where never serpent hisses,
  And being set, I'll smother thee with kisses:

"And yet not cloy thy lips with loath'd satiety,
But rather famish them amid their plenty,
Making them red and pale with fresh variety;
Ten kisses short as one, one long as twenty:
  A summer's day will seem an hour but short,
  Being wasted in such time-beguiling sport."

With this she seizeth on his sweating palm,
The precedent of pith and livelihood,
And, trembling in her passion, calls it balm,
Earth's sovereign salve to do a goddess good:
  Being so enrag'd, desire doth lend her force
  Courageously to pluck him from his horse.

Over one arm the lusty courser's rein,
Under her other was the tender boy,
Who blush'd and pouted in a dull disdain,
With leaden appetite, unapt to toy;
  She red and hot as coals of glowing fire,
  He red for shame, but frosty in desire.

The studded bridle on a ragged bough
Nimbly she fastens; (O, how quick is love!)
The steed is stalled up, and even now
To tie the rider she begins to prove:
  Backward she push'd him, as she would be thrust,
  And govern'd him in strength, though not in lust.

So soon was she along as he was down,
Each leaning on their elbows and their hips:
Now doth she stroke his cheek, now doth he frown,
And 'gins to chide, but soon she stops his lips;
  And kissing speaks, with lustful language broken,
  "If thou wilt chide, thy lips shall never open."

He burns with bashful shame, she with her tears
Doth quench the maiden burning of his cheeks;
Then with her windy sighs and golden hairs,
To fan and blow them dry again she seeks:
  He saith she is immodest, blames her 'miss;
  What follows more she murthers with a kiss.

Even as an empty eagle, sharp by fast,
Tires with her beak on feathers, flesh, and bone,
Shaking her wings, devouring all in haste,
Till either gorge be stuff'd, or prey be gone;
  Even so she kiss'd his brow, his cheek, his chin,
  And when she ends she doth anew begin.

Forc'd to content, but never to obey,
Panting he lies, and breatheth in her face;
She feedeth on the steam as on a prey,
And calls it heavenly moisture, air of grace,
  Wishing her cheeks were gardens full of flowers,
  So they were dew'd with such distilling showers.

Look how a bird lies tangled in a net,
So fasten'd in her arms Adonis lies;
Pure shame and aw'd resistance made him fret,
Which bred more beauty in his angry eyes:
  Rain added to a river that is rank,
  Perforce will force it overflow the bank.

Still she entreats, and prettily entreats,
For to a pretty air she tunes her tale;
Still is he sullen, still he lowers and frets,
'Twixt crimson shame and anger ashy-pale;
  Being red, she loves him best; and being white,
  Her best is better'd with a more delight.

Look how he can, she cannot choose but love;
And by her fair immortal hand she swears
From his soft bosom never to remove,
Till he take truce with her contending tears,
  Which long have rain'd, making her cheeks all wet;
  And one sweet kiss shall pay this countless debt.

Upon this promise did he raise his chin,
Like a dive-dapper peering through a wave,
Who being look'd on ducks as quickly in;
So offers he to give what she did crave,
But when her lips were ready for his pay,
He winks, and turns his lips another way.

Never did passenger in summer's heat
More thirst for drink than she for this good turn.
Her help she sees, but help she cannot get;
She bathes in water, yet her fire must burn.
"O, pity," 'gan she cry, "flint-hearted boy!
'Tis but a kiss I beg; why art thou coy?

"I have been woo'd as I entreat thee now,
Even by the stern and direful god of war,
Whose sinewy neck in battle ne'er did bow,
Who conquers where he comes in every jar;
Yet hath he been my captive and my slave,
And begg'd for that which thou unask'd shalt have

"Over my altars hath he hung his lance,
His batter'd shield, his uncontrolled crest,
And for my sake hath learn'd to sport and dance,
To toy, to wanton, dally, smile, and jest;
Scorning his churlish drum, and ensign red,
Making my arms his field, his tent my bed.

"Thus he that over-rul'd, I oversway'd,
Leading him prisoner in a red rose chain:
Strong-temper'd steel his stronger strength obey'd,
Yet was he servile to my coy disdain.
O, be not proud, nor brag not of thy might,
For mastering her that foil'd the god of fight.

"Touch but my lips with those fair lips of thine, —
Though mine be not so fair, yet are they red, —
The kiss shall be thine own as well as mine: —
What seest thou in the ground? hold up thy head:
  Look in mine eye-balls, there thy beauty lies;
  Then, why not lips on lips, since eyes in eyes?

"Art thou asham'd to kiss? then, wink again,
And I will wink; so shall the day seem night;
Love keeps his revels where there are but twain;
Be bold to play, our sport is not in sight:
  These blue-vein'd violets whereon we lean,
  Never can blab, nor know not what we mean.

"The tender spring upon thy tempting lip
Shows thee unripe, yet may'st thou well be tasted.
Make use of time, let not advantage slip;
Beauty within itself should not be wasted:
  Fair flowers that are not gather'd in their prime,
  Rot and consume themselves in little time.

"Were I hard-favour'd, foul, or wrinkled-old,
I'll-nurtur'd, crooked, churlish, harsh in voice,
O'er-worn, despised, rheumatic, and cold,
Thick-sighted, barren, lean, and lacking juice,
  Then might'st thou pause, for then I were not for thee;
  But having no defects, why dost abhor me?

"Thou canst not see one wrinkle in my brow;
Mine eyes are grey and bright, and quick in turning;
My beauty as the spring doth yearly grow,
My flesh is soft and plump, my marrow burning:
  My smooth moist hand, were it with thy hand felt,
  Would in thy palm dissolve, or seem to melt.

"Bid me discourse, I will enchant thine ear,
Or, like a fairy, trip upon the green,
Or, like a nymph, with long dishevelled hair,
Dance on the sands, and yet no footing seen:
  Love is a spirit all compact of fire,
  Not gross to sink, but light, and will aspire.

"Witness this primrose bank whereon I lie;
These forceless flowers like sturdy trees support me;
Two strengthless doves will draw me through the sky,
From morn till night, even where I list to sport me:
  Is love so light, sweet boy, and may it be
  That thou should'st think it heavy unto thee?

"Is thine own heart to thine own face affected?
Can thy right hand seize love upon thy left?
Then woo thyself, be of thyself rejected,
Steal thine own freedom, and complain on theft.
  Narcissus so himself himself forsook,
  And died to kiss his shadow in the brook.

"Torches are made to light, jewels to wear,
Dainties to taste, fresh beauty for the use;
Herbs for their smell, and sappy plants to bear;
Things growing to themselves are growth's abuse:
  Seeds spring from seeds, and beauty breedeth beauty;
  Thou wast begot, to get it is thy duty.

"Upon the earth's increase why should'st thou feed,
Unless the earth with thy increase be fed?
By law of nature thou art bound to breed,
That thine may live when thou thyself art dead;
  And so in spite of death thou dost survive,
  In that thy likeness still is left alive."

By this, the love-sick queen began to sweat,
For where they lay the shadow had forsook them,
And Titan, 'tired in the mid-day heat,
With burning eye did hotly overlook them;
  Wishing Adonis had his team to guide,
  So he were like him, and by Venus' side.

And now Adonis, with a lazy spright,
And with a heavy, dark, disliking eye,
His lowering brows o'er-whelming his fair sight,
Like misty vapours when they blot the sky,
  Souring his cheeks, cries, "Fie! no more of love:
  The sun doth burn my face; I must remove."

"Ah me!" quoth Venus, "young, and so unkind?
With bare excuses mak'st thou to be gone!
I'll sigh celestial breath, whose gentle wind
Shall cool the heat of this descending sun:
  I'll make a shadow for thee of my hairs;
  If they burn too, I'll quench them with my tears.

"The sun that shines from heaven shines but warm,
And lo! I lie between that sun and thee:
The heat I have from thence doth little harm,
Thine eye darts forth the fire that burneth me;
  And were I not immortal, life were done,
  Between this heavenly and earthly sun.

"Art thou obdurate, flinty, hard as steel?
Nay more than flint, for stone at rain relenteth;
Art thou a woman's son, and canst not feel
What 'tis to love? how want of love tormenteth?
  O, had thy mother borne so hard a mind,
  She had not brought forth thee, but died unkind.

"What am I, that thou should'st contemn me this?
Or what great danger dwells upon my suit?
What were thy lips the worse for one poor kiss?
Speak fair; but speak fair words, or else be mute:
  Give me one kiss, I'll give it thee again,
  And one for interest, if thou wilt have twain.

"Fie! lifeless picture, cold and senseless stone,
Well-painted idol, image dull and dead,
Statue, contenting but the eye alone,
Thing like a man, but of no woman bred:
  Thou art no man, though of a man's complexion,
  For men will kiss even by their own direction."

This said, impatience chokes her pleading tongue,
And swelling passion doth provoke a pause;
Red cheeks and fiery eyes blaze forth her wrong:
Being judge in love, she cannot right her cause;
  And now she weeps, and now she fain would speak,
  And now her sobs do her intendments break.

Sometimes she shakes her head, and then his hand,
Now gazeth she on him, now on the ground;
Sometimes her arms infold him like a band:
She would, he will not in her arms be bound;
  And when from thence he struggles to be gone,
  She locks her lily fingers one in one.

"Fondling," she saith, "since I have hemm'd thee here,
Within the circuit of this ivory pale,
I'll be a park, and thou shalt be my deer;
Feed where thou wilt, on mountain or in dale:
  Graze on my lips, and if those hills be dry,
  Stray lower, where the pleasant fountains lie.

"Within this limit is relief enough,
Sweet bottom-grass, and high delightful plain,
Round rising hillocks, brakes obscure and rough,
To shelter thee from tempest, and from rain:
  Then, be my deer, since I am such a park;
  No dog shall rouse thee, though a thousand bark."

At this Adonis smiles, as in disdain,
That in each cheek appears a pretty dimple:
Love made those hollows, if himself were slain,
He might be buried in a tomb so simple;
  Fore-knowing well, if there he came to lie,
  Why, there Love liv'd, and there he could not die.

These lovely caves, these round enchanting pits,
Open'd their mouths to swallow Venus' liking.
Being mad before, how doth she now for wits?
Struck dead at first, what needs a second striking?
  Poor queen of love, in thine own law forlorn,
  To love a cheek that smiles at thee in scorn!

Now which way shall she turn? what shall she say?
Her words are done, her woes the more increasing;
The time is spent, her object will away,
And from her twining arms doth urge releasing.
  "Pity!" she cries, "some favour, some remorse!"
  Away he springs, and hasteth to his horse.

But lo! from forth a copse that neighbours by,
A breeding jennet, lusty, young, and proud,
Adonis' trampling courser doth espy,
And forth she rushes, snorts, and neighs aloud:
  The strong-neck'd steed, being tied unto a tree,
  Breaketh his rein, and to her straight goes he.

Imperiously he leaps, he neighs, he bounds,
And now his woven girths he breaks asunder;
The bearing earth with his hard hoof he wounds,
Whose hollow womb resounds like heaven's thunder:
  The iron bit he crusheth 'tween his teeth,
  Controlling what he was controlled with.

His ears up prick'd, his braided hanging mane
Upon his compass'd crest now stands on end;
His nostrils drink the air, and forth again,
As from a furnace, vapours doth he send:
  His eye, which scornfully glisters like fire,
  Shows his hot courage, and his high desire.

Sometime he trots, as if he told the steps,
With gentle majesty, and modest pride;
Anon he rears upright, curvets and leaps,
As who should say, lo! thus my strength is tried;
  And this I do, to captivate the eye
  Of the fair breeder that is standing by.

What recketh he his rider's angry stir,
His flattering holla, or his "Stand, I say?"
What cares he now for curb, or pricking spur,
For rich caparisons, or trapping gay?
  He sees his love, and nothing else he sees,
  For nothing else with his proud sight agrees.

Look, when a painter would surpass the life,
In limning out a well-proportion'd steed,
His art with nature's workmanship at strife,
As if the dead the living should exceed;
  So did his horse excel a common one,
  In shape, in courage, colour, pace, and bone.

Round-hoof'd, short-jointed, fetlocks shag and long,
Broad breast, full eye, small head, and nostril wide,
High crest, short ears, straight legs, and passing strong,
Thin mane, thick tail, broad buttock, tender hide:
  Look, what a horse should have he did not lack,
  Save a proud rider on so proud a back.

Sometime he scuds far off, and there he stares;
Anon he starts at stirring of a feather:
To bid the wind a base he now prepares,
And whe'r he run, or fly, they know not whether;
  For through his mane and tail the high wind sings,
  Fanning the hairs, who wave like feather'd wings.

He looks upon his love, and neighs unto her;
She answers him, as if she knew his mind:
Being proud, as females are, to see him woo her,
She puts on outward strangeness, seems unkind;
  Spurns at his love, and scorns the heat he feels,
  Beating his kind embracements with her heels.

Then, like a melancholy malcontent,
He vails his tail, that, like a falling plume,
Cool shadow to his melting buttock lent:
He stamps, and bites the poor flies in his fume.
  His love, perceiving how he is enrag'd,
  Grew kinder, and his fury was assuag'd.

His testy master goeth about to take him,
When lo! the unback'd breeder, full of fear,
Jealous of catching, swiftly doth forsake him,
With her the horse, and left Adonis there.
  As they were mad, unto the wood they hie them,
  Out-stripping crows that strive to over-fly them.

All swoln with chafing, down Adonis sits,
Banning his boisterous and unruly beast:
And now the happy season once more fits,
That love-sick love by pleading may be blest;
  For lovers say, the heart hath treble wrong
  When it is barr'd the aidance of the tongue.

An oven that is stopp'd, or river stay'd,
Burneth more hotly, swelleth with more rage:
So of concealed sorrow may be said,
Free vent of words love's fire doth assuage;
  But when the heart's attorney once is mute,
  The client breaks, as desperate in his suit.

He sees her coming, and begins to glow,
Even as a dying coal revives with wind,
And with his bonnet hides his angry brow;
Looks on the dull earth with disturbed mind,
  Taking no notice that she is so nigh,
  For all askaunce he holds her in his eye.

O, what a sight it was, wistly to view
How she came stealing to the wayward boy;
To note the fighting conflict of her hue,
How white and red each other did destroy:
  But now her cheek was pale, and by and by
  It flash'd forth fire, as lightning from the sky.

Now was she just before him as he sat,
And like a lowly lover down she kneels;
With one fair hand she heaveth up his hat,
Her other tender hand his fair cheek feels:
  His tenderer cheek receives her soft hand's print
  As apt as new-fall'n snow takes any dint.

O, what a war of looks was then between them!
Her eyes, petitioners, to his eyes suing;
His eyes saw her eyes as they had not seen them;
Her eyes woo'd still, his eyes disdain'd the wooing:
  And all this dumb play had his acts made plain
  With tears, which, chorus-like, her eyes did rain.

Full gently now she takes him by the hand,
A lily prison'd in a jail of snow,
Or ivory in an alabaster band;
So white a friend engirts so white a foe:
  This beauteous combat, wilful and unwilling,
  Show'd like two silver doves that sit a billing.

Once more the engine of her thoughts began:
"O fairest mover on this mortal round,
Would thou wert as I am, and I a man,
My heart all whole as thine, thy heart my wound;
  For one sweet look thy help I would assure thee,
  Though nothing but my body's bane would cure thee."

"Give me my hand," saith he, "why dost thou feel it?"
"Give me my heart," saith she, "and thou shalt have it;
O, give it me, lest thy hard heart do steel it,
And being steel'd, soft sighs can never grave it:
  Then, love's deep groans I never shall regard,
  Because Adonis' heart hath made mine hard."

"For shame!" he cries, "let go, and let me go;
My day's delight is past, my horse is gone,
And 'tis your fault I am bereft him so:
I pray you hence, and leave me here alone;
  For all my mind, my thought, my busy care,
  Is how to get my palfrey from the mare."

Thus she replies: "Thy palfrey, as he should,
Welcomes the warm approach of sweet desire:
Affection is a coal that must be cool'd;
Else, suffer'd, it will set the heart on fire.
The sea hath bounds, but deep desire hath none;
Therefore, no marvel though thy horse be gone.

"How like a jade he stood, tied to the tree,
Servilely mastered with a leathern rein;
But when he saw his love, his youth's fair fee,
He held such petty bondage in disdain;
Throwing the base thong from his bending crest,
Enfranchising his mouth, his back, his breast.

"Who sees his true-love in her naked bed,
Teaching the sheets a whiter hue than white,
But, when his glutton eye so full hath fed,
His other agents aim at like delight?
Who is so faint, that dare not be so bold
To touch the fire, the weather being cold?

"Let me excuse thy courser, gentle boy,
And learn of him, I heartily beseech thee,
To take advantage on presented joy;
Though I were dumb, yet his proceedings teach thee:
O, learn to love; the lesson is but plain,
And, once made perfect, never lost again."

"I know not love," quoth he, "nor will not know it:
Unless it be a boar, and then I chase it;
'Tis much to borrow, and I will not owe it;
My love to love is love but to disgrace it;
For I have heard it is a life in death,
That laughs, and weeps, and all but with a breath.

"Who wears a garment shapeless and unfinish'd?
Who plucks the bud before one leaf put forth?
If springing things be any jot diminish'd,
They wither in their prime, prove nothing worth:
  The colt that's back'd and burthen'd being young,
  Loseth his pride, and never waxeth strong.

"You hurt my hand with wringing; let us part,
And leave this idle theme, this bootless chat:
Remove your siege from my unyielding heart;
To love's alarms it will not ope the gate:
  Dismiss your vows, your feigned tears, your flattery,
  For where a heart is hard, they make no battery."

"What! canst thou talk?" quoth she, "hast thou a tongue?
O, would thou hadst not, or I had no hearing!
Thy mermaid's voice hath done me double wrong!
I had my load before, now press'd with bearing:
  Melodious discord, heavenly tune harsh-sounding,
  Ear's deep sweet music, and heart's deep sore wounding.

"Had I no eyes, but ears, my ears would love
That inward beauty and invisible;
Or, were I deaf, thy outward parts would move
Each part in me that were but sensible:
  Though neither eyes nor ears, to hear nor see,
  Yet should I be in love by touching thee.

"Say, that the sense of feeling were bereft me,
And that I could not see, nor hear, nor touch,
And nothing but the very smell were left me,
Yet would my love to thee be still as much;
  For from the stillitory of thy face excelling
  Comes breath perfum'd, that breedeth love by smelling.

"But, O, what banquet wert thou to the taste,
Being nurse and feeder of the other four:
Would they not wish the feast might ever last,
And bid suspicion double lock the door,
  Lest jealousy, that sour unwelcome guest,
  Should by his stealing in disturb the feast?"

Once more the ruby-colour'd portal opened,
Which to his speech did honey-passage yield;
Like a red morn, that ever yet betoken'd
Wreck to the sea-man, tempest to the field,
  Sorrow to shepherds, woe unto the birds,
  Gusts and foul flaws to herdmen and to herds.

This ill presage advisedly she marketh:
Even as the wind is hush'd before it raineth;
Or as the wolf doth grin before he barketh,
Or as the berry breaks before it staineth;
  Or like the deadly bullet of a gun,
  His meaning struck her ere his words begun.

And at his look she flatly falleth down,
For looks kill love, and love by looks reviveth:
A smile recures the wounding of a frown;
But blessed bankrupt that by love so thriveth!
  The silly boy, believing she is dead,
  Claps her pale cheek, till clapping makes it red;

And all amaz'd brake off his late intent,
For sharply he did think to reprehend her,
Which cunning love did wittily prevent:
Fair fall the wit that can so well defend her!
  For on the grass she lies, as she were slain,
  Till his breath breatheth life in her again.

He wrings her nose, he strikes her on the cheeks,
He bends her fingers, holds her pulses hard,
He chafes her lips; a thousand ways he seeks
To mend the hurt that his unkindness marr'd:
  He kisses her; and she, by her good will,
  Will never rise, so he will kiss her still.

The night of sorrow now is turn'd to day:
Her two blue windows faintly she up-heaveth,
Like the fair sun, when in his fresh array
He cheers the morn, and all the earth relieveth:
  And as the bright sun glorifies the sky,
  So is her face illumin'd with her eye;

Whose beams upon his hairless face are fix'd,
As if from thence they borrow'd all their shine.
Were never four such lamps together mix'd,
Had not his clouded with his brow's repine;
  But hers, which through the crystal tears gave light,
  Shone like the moon in water seen by night.

"O, where am I?" quoth she, "in Earth or Heaven,
Or in the ocean drench'd, or in the fire?
What hour is this? or morn or weary even?
Do I delight to die, or life desire?
  But now I liv'd, and life was death's annoy;
  But now I died, and death was lively joy.

"O, thou did'st kill me; kill me once again:
Thy eye's shrewd tutor, that hard heart of thine,
Hath taught them scornful tricks, and such disdain,
That they have murther'd this poor heart of mine;
  And these mine eyes, true leaders to their queen,
  But for thy piteous lips no more had seen.

"Long may they kiss each other for this cure!
O, never let their crimson liveries wear,
And as they last, their verdure still endure,
To drive infection from the dangerous year!
That the star-gazers, having writ on death,
May say, the plague is banish'd by thy breath.

"Pure lips, sweet seals in my soft lips imprinted,
What bargains may I make, still to be sealing?
To sell myself I can be well contented,
So thou wilt buy, and pay, and use good dealing;
Which purchase if thou make, for fear of slips
Set thy seal-manual on my wax-red lips.

"A thousand kisses buys my heart from me,
And pay them at thy leisure, one by one.
What is ten hundred touches unto thee?
Are they not quickly told, and quickly gone?
Say, for non-payment that the debt should double,
Is twenty hundred kisses such a trouble?"

"Fair queen," quoth he, "if any love you owe me,
Measure my strangeness with my unripe years:
Before I know myself, seek not to know me;
No fisher but the ungrown fry forbears:
The mellow plum doth fall, the green sticks fast,
Or being early pluck'd is sour to taste.

"Look, the world's comforter, with weary gait,
His day's hot task hath ended in the west:
The owl, night's herald, shrieks, 'tis very late;
The sheep are gone to fold, birds to their nest,
And coal-black clouds that shadow heaven's light,
Do summon us to part, and bid good night.

"Now let me say good night; and so say you;
If you will say so, you shall have a kiss."
"Good night," quoth she; and, ere he says Adieu,
The honey-fee of parting tender'd is:
  Her arms do lend his neck a sweet embrace;
  Incorporate then they seem, face grows to face.

Till breathless he disjoin'd, and backward drew
The heavenly moisture, that sweet coral mouth,
Whose precious taste her thirsty lips well knew,
Whereon they surfeit, yet complain on drought:
  He with her plenty press'd, she faint with dearth,
  Their lips together glued, fall to the earth.

Now quick desire hath caught the yielding prey,
And glutton-like she feeds, yet never filleth;
Her lips are conquerors, his lips obey,
Paying what ransom the insulter willeth;
  Whose vulture thought doth pitch the price so high,
  That she will draw his lips' rich treasure dry.

And having felt the sweetness of the spoil,
With bindfold fury she begins to forage;
Her face doth reek and smoke, her blood doth boil,
And careless lust stirs up a desperate courage;
  Planting oblivion, beating reason back,
  Forgetting shame's pure blush, and honour's wrack.

Hot, faint, and weary, with her hard embracing,
Like a wild bird being tam'd with too much handling,
Or as the fleet-foot roe that's tir'd with chasing,
Or like the froward infant still'd with dandling,
  He now obeys, and now no more resisteth,
  While she takes all she can, not all she listeth.

What wax so frozen but dissolves with tempering,
And yields at last to every light impression?
Things out of hope are compass'd oft with venturing,
Chiefly in love, whose leave exceeds commission:
  Affection faints not like a pale-fac'd coward,
  But then woos best, when most his choice is froward.

When he did frown, O, had she then gave over,
Such nectar from his lips she had not suck'd.
Foul words and frowns must not repel a lover;
What though the rose have prickles, yet 'tis pluck'd:
  Were beauty under twenty locks kept fast,
  Yet love breaks through, and picks them all at last.

For pity now she can no more detain him;
The poor fool prays her that he may depart:
She is resolv'd no longer to restrain him,
Bids him farewell, and look well to her heart,
  The which, by Cupid's bow she doth protest,
  He carries thence incaged in his breast.

"Sweet boy," she says, "this night I'll waste in sorrow,
For my sick heart commands mine eyes to watch.
Tell me, love's master, shall we meet to-morrow?
Say, shall we? shall we? wilt thou make the match?"
  He tells her, no; to-morrow he intends
  To hunt the boar with certain of his friends.

"The boar!" quoth she; whereat a sudden pale,
Like lawn being spread upon the blushing rose,
Usurps her cheek: she trembles at his tale,
And on his neck her yoking arms she throws;
  She sinketh down, still hanging by his neck,
  He on her belly falls, she on her back.

Now is she in the very lists of love,
Her champion mounted for the hot encounter:
All is imaginary she doth prove,
He will not manage her, although he mount her;
  That worse than Tantalus' is her annoy,
  To clip Elysium, and to lack her joy.

Even as poor birds, deceiv'd with painted grapes,
Do surfeit by the eye, and pine the maw,
Even so she languisheth in her mishaps,
As those poor birds that helpless berries saw.
  The warm effects which she in him finds missing,
  She seeks to kindle with continual kissing:

But all in vain; good queen, it will not be:
She hath assay'd as much as may be prov'd;
Her pleading hath deserv'd a greater fee:
She's love, she loves, and yet she is not lov'd.
  "Fie, fie!" he says, "you crush me; let me go:
  You have no reason to withhold me so."

"Thou had'st been gone," quoth she, "sweet boy, ere this,
But that thou told'st me thou would'st hunt the boar.
O, be advis'd; thou know'st not what it is
With javelin's point a churlish swine to gore,
  Whose tushes, never-sheath'd, he whetteth still,
  Like to a mortal butcher, bent to kill.

"On his bow-back he hath a battle set
Of bristly pikes, that ever threat his foes;
His eyes like glow-worms shine when he doth fret;
His snout digs sepulchres where'er he goes;
  Being mov'd, he strikes whate'er is in his way,
  And whom he strikes his cruel tushes slay.

"His brawny sides, with hairy bristles armed,
Are better proof than thy spear's point can enter;
His short thick neck cannot be easily harmed;
Being ireful on the lion he will venture:
  The thorny brambles and embracing bushes,
  As fearful of him, part; through whom he rushes.

"Alas, he naught esteems that face of thine,
To which love's eyes pay tributary gazes;
Nor thy soft hands, sweet lips, and crystal eyne,
Whose full perfection all the world amazes;
  But having thee at vantage, (wondrous dread!)
  Would root these beauties as he roots the mead.

"O, let him keep his loathsome cabin still;
Beauty hath naught to do with such foul fiends:
Come not within his danger by thy will;
They that thrive well take counsel of their friends.
  When thou did'st name the boar, not to dissemble,
  I fear'd thy fortune, and my joints did tremble.

"Did'st thou not mark my face? Was it not white?
Saw'st thou not signs of fear lurk in mine eye?
Grew I not faint? and fell I not downright?
Within my bosom, whereon thou dost lie,
  My boding heart pants, beats, and takes no rest,
  But like an earthquake shakes thee on my breast.

"For where love reigns, disturbing jealousy
Doth call himself affection's sentinel;
Gives false alarms, suggesteth mutiny,
And in a peaceful hour doth cry, 'kill, kill;'
  Distempering gentle love in his desire,
  As air and water do abate the fire.

"This sour informer, this bate-breeding spy,
This canker that eats up love's tender spring,
This carry-tale, dissentious jealousy,
That sometime true news, sometime false doth bring,
  Knocks at my heart, and whispers in mine ear,
  That if I love thee, I thy death should fear:

"And more than so, presenteth to mine eye
The picture of an angry chafing boar,
Under whose sharp fangs on his back doth lie
An image like thyself, all stain'd with gore;
  Whose blood upon the fresh flowers being shed,
  Doth make them droop with grief, and hang the head.

"What should I do, seeing thee so indeed,
Than tremble at the imagination?
The thought of it doth make my faint heart bleed,
And fear doth teach it divination:
  I prophesy thy death, my living sorrow,
  If thou encounter with the boar to-morrow.

"But if thou needs wilt hunt, be rul'd by me;
Uncouple at the timorous flying hare,
Or at the fox, which lives by subtlety,
Or at the roe, which no encounter dare:
  Pursue these fearful creatures o'er the downs,
  And on thy well-breath'd horse keep with thy hounds.

"And when thou hast on foot the purblind hare,
Mark the poor wretch, to overshoot his troubles,
How he out-runs the wind, and with what care
He cranks and crosses with a thousand doubles:
  The many musets through the which he goes,
  Are like a labyrinth to amaze his foes.

"Sometime he runs among a flock of sheep,
To make the cunning hounds mistake their smell;
And sometime where earth-delving conies keep,
To stop the loud pursuers in their yell;
  And sometime sorteth with a herd of deer.
  Danger deviseth shifts; wit waits on fear:

"For there his smell, with others being mingled,
The hot scent-snuffing hounds are driven to doubt,
Ceasing their clamorous cry, till they have singled
With much ado the cold fault cleanly out;
  Then do they spend their mouths: echo replies,
  As if another chase were in the skies.

"By this, poor Wat, far off upon a hill,
Stands on his hinder legs with listening ear,
To hearken if his foes pursue him still:
Anon their loud alarums he doth hear;
  And now his grief may be compared well
  To one sore sick, that hears the passing bell.

"Then shalt thou see the dew-bedabbled wretch
Turn, and return, indenting with the way;
Each envious briar his weary legs doth scratch,
Each shadow makes him stop, each murmur stay:
  For misery is trodden on by many,
  And being low, never reliev'd by any.

"Lie quietly, and hear a little more;
Nay, do not struggle, for thou shalt not rise:
To make thee hate the hunting of the boar,
Unlike myself thou hear'st me moralize,
  Applying this to that, and so to so;
  For love can comment upon every woe.

"Where did I leave?"—"No matter where," quoth he;
"Leave me, and then the story aptly ends:
The night is spent." "Why, what of that?" quoth she;
"I am," quoth he, "expected of my friends;
And now 'tis dark, and going I shall fall."
"In night," quoth she, "desire sees best of all.

"But if thou fall, O, then imagine this,—
The earth, in love with thee, thy footing trips,
And all is but to rob thee of a kiss.
Rich preys made true men thieves; so do thy lips
Make modest Dian cloudy and forlorn,
Lest she should steal a kiss, and die forsworn.

"Now, of this dark night I perceive the reason:
Cynthia for shame obscures her silver shine,
Till forging Nature be condemn'd of treason,
For stealing moulds from Heaven that were divine,
Wherein she fram'd thee, in high Heaven's despite,
To shame the sun by day, and her by night.

"And therefore hath she brib'd the Destinies,
To cross the curious workmanship of nature;
To mingle beauty with infirmities,
And pure perfection with impure defeature;
Making it subject to the tyranny
Of mad mischances and much misery;

"As burning fevers, agues pale and faint,
Life-poisoning pestilence, and frenzies wood;
The marrow-eating sickness, whose attaint
Disorder breeds by heating of the blood:
Surfeits, impostumes, grief, and damn'd despair,
Swear Nature's death for framing thee so fair.

"And not the least of all these maladies
But in one minute's fight brings beauty under:
Both favour, savour, hue, and qualities,
Whereat th' impartial gazer late did wonder,
  Are on the sudden wasted, thaw'd, and done,
  As mountain snow melts with the midday sun.

"Therefore, despite of fruitless chastity,
Love-lacking vestals, and self-loving nuns,
That on the Earth would breed a scarcity,
And barren dearth of daughters and of sons,
  Be prodigal: the lamp that burns by night
  Dries up his oil to lend the world his light.

"What is thy body but a swallowing grave,
Seeming to bury that posterity
Which by the rights of time thou needs must have,
If thou destroy them not in dark obscurity?
  If so, the world will hold thee in disdain,
  Sith in thy pride so fair a hope is slain.

"So in thyself thyself art made away,
A mischief worse than civil home-bred strife,
Or theirs whose desperate hands themselves do slay,
Or butcher sire that reaves his son of life.
  Foul cankering rust the hidden treasure frets,
  But gold that's put to use more gold begets."

"Nay then," quoth Adon, "you will fall again
Into your idle over-handled theme:
The kiss I gave you is bestow'd in vain,
And all in vain you strive against the stream;
  For by this black-fac'd night, desire's foul nurse,
  Your treatise makes me like you worse and worse.

"If love have lent you twenty thousand tongues,
And every tongue more moving than your own,
Bewitching like the wanton mermaid's songs,
Yet from mine ear the tempting tune is blown;
For know, my heart stands armed in mine ear,
And will not let a false sound enter there;

"Lest the deceiving harmony should run
Into the quiet closure of my breast,
And then my little heart were quite undone,
In his bedchamber to be barr'd of rest.
No, lady, no; my heart longs not to groan,
But soundly sleeps, while now it sleeps alone.

"What have you urg'd that I cannot reprove?
The path is smooth that leadeth on to danger;
I hate not love, but your device in love,
That lends embracements unto every stranger.
You do it for increase: O strange excuse!
When reason is the bawd to lust's abuse.

"Call it not love, for Love to Heaven is fled,
Since sweating lust on earth usurp'd his name;
Under whose simple semblance he hath fed
Upon fresh beauty, blotting it with blame;
Which the hot tyrant stains, and soon bereaves,
As caterpillars do the tender leaves.

"Love comforteth like sunshine after rain,
But lust's effect is tempest after sun;
Love's gentle spring doth always fresh remain,
Lust's winter comes ere summer half be done:
Love surfeits not, lust like a glutton dies;
Love is all truth, lust full of forged lies.

"More I could tell, but more I dare not say;
The text is old, the orator too green.
Therefore, in sadness, now I will away;
My face is full of shame, my heart of teen:
  Mine ears, that to your wanton talk attended,
  Do burn themselves for having so offended."

With this he breaketh from the sweet embrace
Of those fair arms which bound him to her breast,
And homeward through the dark lawn runs apace;
Leaves Love upon her back deeply distress'd.
  Look, how a bright star shooteth from the sky,
  So glides he in the night from Venus' eye;

Which after him she darts, as one on shore
Gazing upon a late-embarked friend,
Till the wild waves will have him seen no more,
Whose ridges with the meeting clouds contend:
  So did the merciless and pitchy night
  Fold in the object that did feed her sight.

Whereat amaz'd, as one that unaware
Hath dropp'd a precious jewel in the flood,
Or 'stonish'd as night wanderers often are,
Their light blown out in some mistrustful wood;
  Even so confounded in the dark she lay,
  Having lost the fair discovery of her way.

And now she beats her heart, whereat it groans,
That all the neighbour-caves, as seeming troubled,
Make verbal repetition of her moans:
Passion on passion doubly is redoubled.
  "Ah me!" she cries, and twenty times, "Woe,
    woe!"
  And twenty echoes twenty times cry so.

She, marking them, begins a wailing note,
And sings extemporally a woeful ditty;
How love makes young men thrall, and old men dote;
How love is wise in folly, foolish witty:
  Her heavy anthem still concludes in woe,
  And still the choir of echoes answer so.

Her song was tedious, and outwore the night,
For lovers' hours are long, though seeming short:
If pleas'd themselves, others, they think, delight
In such like circumstance, with such like sport:
  Their copious stories, oftentimes begun,
  End without audience, and are never done.

For who hath she to spend the night withal,
But idle sounds resembling parasites;
Like shrill-tongu'd tapsters answering every call,
Soothing the humour of fantastic wits?
  She says, "'Tis so:" they answer all, "'Tis so;"
  And would say after her, if she said, "No."

Lo, here the gentle lark, weary of rest,
From his moist cabinet mounts up on high,
And wakes the morning, from whose silver breast
The sun ariseth in his majesty;
  Who doth the world so gloriously behold,
  That cedar-tops and hills seem burnish'd gold.

Venus salutes him with this fair good-morrow:
"O thou clear god, and patron of all light,
From whom each lamp and shining star doth borrow
The beauteous influence that makes him bright,
  There lives a son, that suck'd an earthly mother,
  May lend thee light, as thou dost lend to other."

This said, she hasteth to a myrtle grove,
Musing the morning is so much o'er-worn;
And yet she hears no tidings of her love:
She hearkens, for his hounds, and for his horn:
  Anon she hears them chant it lustily,
  And all in haste she coasteth to the cry.

And as she runs, the bushes in the way
Some catch her by the neck, some kiss her face,
Some twine about her thigh to make her stay.
She wildly breaketh from their strict embrace,
  Like a milch doe, whose swelling dugs do ache,
  Hasting to feed her fawn hid in some brake.

By this she hears the hounds are at a bay,
Whereat she starts, like one that spies an adder
Wreath'd up in fatal folds, just in his way,
The fear whereof doth make him shake and shudder:
  Even so the timorous yelping of the hounds
  Appals her senses, and her spirit confounds.

For now she knows it is no gentle chase,
But the blunt boar, rough bear, or lion proud,
Because the cry remaineth in one place,
Where fearfully the dogs exclaim aloud;
  Finding their enemy to be so curst,
  They all strain courtesy who shall cope him first.

This dismal cry rings sadly in her ear,
Through which it enters to surprise her heart;
Who, overcome by doubt and bloodless fear,
With cold-pale weakness numbs each feeling part:
  Like soldiers, when their captain once doth yield,
  They basely fly, and dare not stay the field.

Thus stands she in a trembling ecstasy,
Till cheering up her senses all dismay'd,
She tells them, 'tis a causeless fantasy,
And childish error that they are afraid;
  Bids them leave quaking, bids them fear no more:
  And with that word she spied the hunted boar;

Whose frothy mouth bepainted all with red,
Like milk and blood being mingled both together,
A second fear through all her sinews spread,
Which madly hurries her she knows not whither:
  This way she runs, and now she will no further,
  But back retires to rate the boar for murther.

A thousand spleens bear her a thousand ways;
She treads the path that she untreads again:
Her more than haste is mated with delays,
Like the proceedings of a drunken brain;
  Full of respects, yet naught at all respecting,
  In hand with all things, naught at all affecting.

Here kennel'd in a brake she finds a hound,
And asks the weary caitiff for his master;
And there another licking of his wound,
'Gainst venom'd sores the only sovereign plaster;
  And here she meets another sadly scowling,
  To whom she speaks, and he replies with howling.

When he hath ceas'd his ill-resounding noise,
Another flap-mouth'd mourner, black and grim,
Against the welkin volleys out his voice;
Another and another answer him,
  Clapping their proud tails to the ground below,
  Shaking their scratch'd ears, bleeding as they go.

Look, how the world's poor people are amazed
At apparitions, signs, and prodigies,
Whereon with fearful eyes they long have gazed,
Infusing them with dreadful prophecies;
  So she at these sad signs draws up her breath,
  And, sighing it again, exclaims on Death.

"Hard-favour'd tyrant, ugly, meagre, lean,
Hateful divorce of love," thus chides she Death,
"Grim grinning ghost, earth's worm, what dost thou mean,
To stifle beauty, and to steal his breath,
  Who when he liv'd, his breath and beauty set
  Gloss on the rose, smell to the violet?

"If he be dead, — O no, it cannot be,
Seeing his beauty, thou should'st strike at it: —
O yes, it may; thou hast no eyes to see,
But hatefully at random dost thou hit.
  Thy mark is feeble age; but thy false dart
  Mistakes that aim, and cleaves an infant's heart.

"Had'st thou but bid beware, then he had spoke,
And hearing him thy power had lost his power.
The destinies will curse thee for this stroke;
They bid thee crop a weed, thou pluck'st a flower.
  Love's golden arrow at him should have fled,
  And not death's ebon dart, to strike him dead.

"Dost thou drink tears, that thou provok'st such weeping?
What may a heavy groan advantage thee?
Why hast thou cast into eternal sleeping
Those eyes that taught all other eyes to see?
  Now Nature cares not for thy mortal vigour,
  Since her best work is ruin'd with thy rigour."

Here overcome, as one full of despair,
She vail'd her eye-lids, who, like sluices, stopped
The crystal tide that from her two cheeks fair
In the sweet channel of her bosom dropped;
  But through the flood-gates breaks the silver rain,
  And with his strong course opens them again.

O, how her eyes and tears did lend and borrow!
Her eyes seen in the tears, tears in her eye;
Both crystals, where they view'd each other's sorrow,
Sorrow that friendly sighs sought still to dry;
  But like a stormy day, now wind, now rain,
  Sighs dry her cheeks, tears make them wet again.

Variable passions throng her constant woe,
As striving who should best become her grief;
All entertain'd, each passion labours so,
That every present sorrow seemeth chief,
  But none is best; then, join they all together,
  Like many clouds consulting for foul weather.

By this far off she hears some huntsman hollow;
A nurse's song ne'er pleas'd her babe so well:
The dire imagination she did follow
This sound of hope doth labour to expel;
  For now reviving joy bids her rejoice,
  And flatters her it is Adonis' voice.

Whereat her tears began to turn their tide,
Being prison'd in her eye, like pearls in glass;
Yet sometimes falls an orient drop beside,
Which her cheek melts, as scorning it should pass
  To wash the foul face of the sluttish ground,
  Who is but drunken, when she seemeth drown'd.

O hard-believing love, how strange it seems
Not to believe, and yet too credulous!
Thy weal and woe are both of them extremes;
Despair and hope make thee ridiculous:
The one doth flatter thee in thoughts unlikely,
In likely thoughts the other kills thee quickly.

Now she unweaves the web that she hath wrought;
Adonis lives, and Death is not to blame:
It was not she that call'd him all-to naught;
Now she adds honours to his hateful name;
She clepes him king of graves, and grave for kings,
Imperious supreme of all mortal things.

"No, no," quoth she, "sweet Death, I did but jest;
Yet pardon me, I felt a kind of fear,
When as I met the boar, that bloody beast,
Which knows no pity, but is still severe;
Then, gentle shadow, (truth I must confess,)
I rail'd on thee, fearing my love's decease.

"'Tis not my fault: the boar provok'd my tongue;
Be wreak'd on him, invisible commander;
'Tis he, foul creature, that hath done thee wrong;
I did but act, he's author of thy slander.
Grief hath two tongues, and never woman yet
Could rule them both, without ten women's wit.

Thus hoping that Adonis is alive,
Her rash suspect she doth extenuate;
And that his beauty may the better thrive,
With Death she humbly doth insinuate;
Tells him of trophies, statues, tombs, and stories,
His victories, his triumphs, and his glories.

"O Jove," quoth she, "how much a fool was I,
To be of such a weak and silly mind,
To wail his death, who lives, and must not die,
Till mutual overthrow of mortal kind!
  For he being dead, with him is beauty slain,
  And, beauty dead, black chaos comes again.

"Fie, fie, fond love! thou art so full of fear,
As one with treasure laden, hemm'd with thieves:
Trifles, unwitnessed with eye or ear,
Thy coward heart with false bethinking grieves."
  Even at this word she hears a merry horn,
  Whereat she leaps that was but late forlorn.

As falcons to the lure, away she flies:
The grass stoops not, she treads on it so light;
And in her haste unfortunately spies
The foul boar's conquest on her fair delight:
  Which seen, her eyes, as murther'd with the view,
  Like stars asham'd of day, themselves withdrew.

Or, as the snail, whose tender horns being hit,
Shrinks backward in his shelly cave with pain,
And there all smother'd up in shade doth sit,
Long after fearing to creep forth again;
  So, at his bloody view, her eyes are fled
  Into the deep-dark cabins of her head:

Where they resign their office and their light
To the disposing of her troubled brain;
Who bids them still consort with ugly night,
And never wound the heart with looks again;
  Who, like a king perplexed in his throne,
  By their suggestion gives a deadly groan;

Whereat each tributary subject quakes,
As when the wind, imprison'd in the ground,
Struggling for passage, Earth's foundation shakes,
Which with cold terror doth men's minds confound.
  This mutiny each part doth so surprise,
  That from their dark beds once more leap her eyes;

And, being open'd, threw unwilling light
Upon the wide wound that the boar had trench'd
In his soft flank; whose wonted lily white
With purple tears, that his wound wept, was drench'd:
  No flower was nigh, no grass, herb, leaf, or weed,
  But stole his blood, and seem'd with him to bleed.

This solemn sympathy poor Venus noteth;
Over one shoulder doth she hang her head,
Dumbly she passions, franticly she doteth;
She thinks he could not die, he is not dead:
  Her voice is stopp'd, her joints forget to bow,
  Her eyes are mad that they have wept till now.

Upon his hurt she looks so steadfastly,
That her sight dazzling makes the wound seem three;
And then she reprehends her mangling eye,
That makes more gashes where no breach should be:
  His face seems twain, each several limb is doubled;
  For oft the eye mistakes, the brain being troubled.

"My tongue cannot express my grief for one,
And yet," quoth she, "behold two Adons dead!
My sighs are blown away, my salt tears gone,
Mine eyes are turn'd to fire, my heart to lead:
  Heavy heart's lead, melt at mine eyes' red fire!
  So shall I die by drops of hot desire.

"Alas, poor world, what treasure hast thou lost!
What face remains alive that's worth the viewing?
Whose tongue is music now? what canst thou boast
Of things long since, or any thing ensuing?
The flowers are sweet, their colours fresh and trim;
But true sweet beauty liv'd and di'd with him.

"Bonnet nor veil henceforth no creature wear;
Nor sun nor wind will ever strive to kiss you:
Having no fair to lose, you need not fear;
The sun doth scorn you, and the wind doth hiss you:
But when Adonis liv'd, sun and sharp air
Lurk'd like two thieves, to rob him of his fair:

"And therefore would he put his bonnet on,
Under whose brim the gaudy sun would peep,
The wind would blow it off, and, being gone,
Play with his locks: then, would Adonis weep,
And straight, in pity of his tender years,
They both would strive who first should dry his tears.

"To see his face, the lion walk'd along
Behind some hedge, because he would not fear him;
To recreate himself when he hath sung,
The tiger would be tame, and gently hear him;
If he had spoke, the wolf would leave his prey,
And never fright the silly lamb that day.

"When he beheld his shadow in the brook,
The fishes spread on it their golden gills:
When he was by, the birds such pleasure took,
That some would sing, some other in their bills
Would bring him mulberries, and ripe red cherries;
He fed them with his sight, they him with berries.

"But this foul, grim, and urchin-snouted boar,
Whose downward eye still looketh for a grave,
Ne'er saw the beauteous livery that he wore;
Witness the entertainment that he gave:
If he did see his face, why then, I know,
He thought to kiss him, and hath kill'd him so.

"'Tis true, 'tis true: thus was Adonis slain.
He ran upon the boar with his sharp spear,
Who did not whet his teeth at him again,
But by a kiss thought to persuade him there;
And nuzzling in his flank, the loving swine
Sheath'd, unaware, the tusk in his soft groin.

"Had I been tooth'd like him, I must confess,
With kissing him I should have kill'd him first:
But he is dead, and never did he bless
My youth with his, — the more am I accurst."
With this she falleth in the place she stood,
And stains her face with his congealed blood.

She looks upon his lips, and they are pale;
She takes him by the hand, and that is cold;
She whispers in his ears a heavy tale,
As if they heard the woful words she told:
She lifts the coffer-lids that close his eyes,
Where lo! two lamps, burnt out, in darkness lies:

Two glasses, where herself herself beheld
A thousand times, and now no more reflect;
Their virtue lost, wherein they late excell'd,
And every beauty robb'd of his effect:
"Wonder of time," quoth she, "this is my spite,
That, thou being dead, the day should yet be light.

"Since thou art dead, lo! here I prophesy,
Sorrow on love hereafter shall attend:
It shall be waited on with jealousy,
Find sweet beginning, but unsavoury end;
Ne'er settled equally, but high or low,
That all love's pleasure shall not match his woe.

"It shall be fickle, false, and full of fraud;
Bud and be blasted in a breathing-while;
The bottom poison, and the top o'er-straw'd
With sweets that shall the truest sight beguile:
The strongest body shall it make most weak,
Strike the wise dumb, and teach the fool to speak.

"It shall be sparing, and too full of riot,
Teaching decrepit age to tread the measures;
The staring ruffian shall it keep in quiet,
Pluck down the rich, enrich the poor with treasures:
It shall be raging mad, and silly mild,
Make the young old, the old become a child.

"It shall suspect, where is no cause of fear;
It shall not fear, where it should most mistrust;
It shall be merciful, and too severe,
And most deceiving when it seems most just;
Perverse it shall be, where it shows most toward;
Put fear to valour, courage to the coward.

"It shall be cause of war and dire events,
And set dissension 'twixt the son and sire;
Subject and servile to all discontents,
As dry combustious matter is to fire:
Sith in his prime death doth my love destroy,
They that love best, their loves shall not enjoy."

By this the boy, that by her side lay kill'd,
Was melted like a vapour from her sight,
And in his blood, that on the ground lay spill'd,
A purple flower sprung up, checquer'd with white;
  Resembling well his pale cheeks, and the blood
  Which in round drops upon their whiteness stood.

She bows her head the new-sprung flower to smell,
Comparing it to her Adonis' breath;
And says, within her bosom it shall dwell,
Since he himself is reft from her by death:
  She crops the stalk, and in the breach appears
  Green dropping sap, which she compares to tears.

"Poor flower," quoth she, "this was thy father's guise, —
Sweet issue of a more sweet-smelling sire, —
For every little grief to wet his eyes:
To grow unto himself was his desire,
  And so 'tis thine; but know, it is as good
  To wither in my breast, as in his blood.

"Here was thy father's bed, here in my breast;
Thou art the next of blood, and 'tis thy right:
Lo, in this hollow cradle take thy rest,
My throbbing heart shall rock thee day and night:
  There shall not be one minute in an hour,
  Wherein I will not kiss my sweet love's flower."

Thus weary of the world, away she hies,
And yokes her silver doves; by whose swift aid
Their mistress mounted through the empty skies
In her light chariot quickly is convey'd;
  Holding their course to Paphos, where their queen
  Means to immure herself and not be seen.

NOTES ON VENUS AND ADONIS.

---

p. 8. "—— blames her '*miss*": — i. e. her amiss, her error.

" "—— she *murthers* with a kiss": — Thus the first three 4tos.; the last three, "she *smothers* with a kiss," which, in my judgment, is the better reading; and any one may see how easily either word might be misprinted for the other. But a change in the text is hardly warranted.

p. 9. "For to a pretty *air*," &c.: — The old editions, "a pretty *ear*," which is plainly a mere phonographic error. See twelve stanzas below, where 'ear' rhymes with 'hair.' Possibly a play upon the two words was intended.

p. 11. "—— *rheumatic*, and cold": — In Shakespeare's time 'rheumatic' was accented upon the first syllable. See *Midsummer Night's Dream*, Act II. Sc. 2, "And rheumatic diseases do abound."

p. 16. "—— now *stands* on end": — Some of the old editions, at least, have "*stand* on end," which I cannot but regard as due to a mere accidental omission of the final *s;* although Malone thought that here 'mane' was used in a plural sense, as composed of many hairs.

p. 17. "*To bid the wind a base*": — See the Note on "bid the base," *Two Gentlemen of Verona*, Act I. Sc. 2.

p. 19. "And all this *dumb play*," &c.: — An allusion to the dumb shows which were explained by a chorus, as in *Pericles*.

p. 27. "To *clip* Elysium": — To embrace Elysium. ....

p. 28. "—— he will *venture*": — In Shakespeare's day 'venture' was pronounced *venter*, and so was a perfect rhyme to 'enter.' See 'venturing' rhymed with 'tempering,' a few stanzas above.

" "Come not *within his danger*": — See the Note on "You stand within his danger," *Merchant of Venice*, Act IV. Sc. 1.

p. 29. "—— to over-*shoot* his troubles": — The old copies, "over*shut*," &c. — a mere phonographic error.

" "The many *musets*": — i. e., little apertures in a hedge through which hares passed.

p. 34. "—— my heart of *teen*": — i. e., of care, trouble.

" "*Passion* on passion *doubly* is redoubled": — The old copies, "*deeply* is redoubled;" and the reading has hitherto been retained without question. But I am sure that here "deeply" is a misprint for 'doubly.' "Deeply redoubled" is a notably infelicitous expression; and the last two lines of the stanza show that the poet had in mind only the number of the repetitions. So in *Macbeth*, Act I. Sc. 2, "doubly redoubled strokes," &c., and in *King Richard II.* Act I. Sc. 3, "thy blows doubly redoubled fall." — 'Passion' here means the *utterance* of emotion. A soliloquy expressive of deep feeling was called a passion.

p. 36. "—— she *coasteth* to the cry": — i. e., she hovereth. See the Note on "will coast my crown," *King Henry Sixth*, Part 3, Act I. Sc. 1.

" Some *twine* about her thigh": — The old copies, "Some *twind*," &c., which has been hitherto retained; but the verbs in the two foregoing and the following lines of the stanza leave no doubt that we have a slight typographical error in the early text.

" "—— and her *spirit* confounds": — This word was pronounced, and perhaps should be here printed, *sprite* or *spright*, the *i* having the sound of *e*.

" "—— who shall *cope* him first": — i. e., cope *with* him. The use of cope, arrive, attain, and like verbs, without a preposition, was common in Shakespeare's day.

p. 37. "—— is *mated* with delays": — i. e., is confounded, overcome.

p. 40. "*When as* I met the boar": — One of the rare instances in which Shakespeare uses 'when as' in the sense of 'when.'

p. 41. "—— *as* murther'd with the view": — The first edition only misprints "*are* murtherd," &c.

p. 42. "—— threw unwilling *light*": — So the earlier editions; those of 1600 and 1627, very plausibly at least, "unwilling *sight*."

p. 44. "—— and *urchin*-snouted boar": — A hedge-hog was called an urchin.

p. 45. "—— and the top *o'er-straw'd*": — i. e., o'er-strewed.

LUCRECE.

"Lvcrece. London. Printed by Richard Field, for Iohn Harrison, and are to be sold at the signe of the white Grey-hound in Paules Churh-yard. 1594." 4to. 47 leaves.

"Lvcrece At London, Printed by P. S. for Iohn Harrison. 1598." 8vo. 36 leaves.

"Lvcrece London. Printed by I. H. for Iohn Harrison. 1600." 8vo. 36 leaves.

"Lvcrece. At London, Printed be N. O. for Iohn Harison. 1607." 8vo. 32 leaves. [COLLIER.

NOTE. The full argument, taken from the early Roman annals, which the author prefixed to this poem, its dedication, and the above transcript of the titles of its old editions, leave no occasion for any introductory remarks upon it. It was entered upon the Stationers' Register on the 9th May, 1594, and was doubtless written in 1593.

TO THE RIGHT HONOURABLE

HENRY WRIOTHESLY,

EARL OF SOUTHAMPTON, AND BARON OF TICHFIELD.

THE love I dedicate to your lordship is without end; whereof this pamphlet, without beginning, is but a superfluous moiety. The warrant I have of your honourable disposition, not the worth of my untutored lines, makes it assured of acceptance. What I have done is yours; what I have to do is yours; being part in all I have, devoted yours. Were my worth greater, my duty would show greater; mean time, as it is, it is bound to your lordship, to whom I wish long life, still lengthened with all happiness.

Your Lordship's in all duty,

WILLIAM SHAKESPEARE.

THE ARGUMENT.

Lucius Tarquinius (for his excessive pride surnamed Superbus) after he had caused his own father-in-law, Servius Tullius, to be cruelly murdered, and, contrary to the Roman laws and customs, not requiring or staying for the people's suffrages, had possessed himself of the kingdom, went, accompanied with his sons and other noblemen of Rome, to besiege Ardea: during which siege, the principal men of the army meeting one evening at the tent of Sextus Tarquinius, the king's son, in their discourses after supper every one commended the virtues of his own wife; among whom, Collatinus extolled the incomparable chastity of his wife Lucretia. In that pleasant humour they all posted to Rome; and intending, by their secret and sudden arrival, to make trial of that which every one had before avouched, only Collatinus finds his wife (though it were late in the night) spinning amongst her maids: the other ladies were all found dancing and revelling, or in several disports; whereupon the noblemen yielded Collatinus the victory, and his wife the fame. At that time Sextus Tarquinius, being inflamed with Lucrece's beauty, yet smothering his passions for the present, departed with the rest back to the camp; from whence he shortly after privily withdrew himself, and was (according to his estate) royally entertained and lodged by Lucrece at Collatium. The same night he treacherously stealeth into her chamber, violently ravished her, and early in the morning speedeth away. Lucrece, in this lamentable plight, hastily dispatcheth messengers, one to Rome for her father, another to the camp for Collatine. They came, the one accompanied with Junius Brutus, the other with Publius Valerius; and finding Lucrece attired in mourning habit, demanded the cause of her sorrow. She, first taking an oath of them for her revenge, revealed the actor, and whole manner of his dealing, and withal suddenly stabbed herself: which done, with one consent they all vowed to root out the whole hated family of the Tarquins; and bearing the dead body to Rome, Brutus acquainted the people with the doer, and manner of the vile deed, with a bitter invective against the tyranny of the king; wherewith the people were so moved, that, with one consent and a general acclamation, the Tarquins were all exiled, and the state government changed from kings to consuls.

LUCRECE.

FROM the besieged Ardea all in post,
Borne by the trustless wings of false desire,
Lust-breathed Tarquin leaves the Roman host,
And to Collatium bears the lightless fire
Which, in pale embers hid, lurks to aspire,
And girdle with embracing flames the waist
Of Collatine's fair love, Lucrece the chaste.

Haply that name of 'chaste' unhappily set
This bateless edge on his keen appetite;
When Collatine unwisely did not let
To praise the clear unmatched red and white,
Which triumph'd in that sky of his delight;
Where mortal stars, as bright as heaven's beauties,
With pure aspects did him peculiar duties.

For he the night before, in Tarquin's tent,
Unlock'd the treasure of his happy state;
What priceless wealth the Heavens had him lent
In the possession of his beauteous mate;
Reckoning his fortune at such high proud rate,
That kings might be espoused to more fame,
But king nor peer to such a peerless dame.

O happiness enjoy'd but of a few!
And, if possess'd, as soon decay'd and done
As is the morning's silver-melting dew
Against the golden splendor of the sun;
An expir'd date, cancell'd ere well begun:
  Honour and beauty, in the owner's arms,
  Are weakly fortress'd from a world of harms.

Beauty itself doth of itself persuade
The eyes of men without an orator;
What needeth, then, apologies be made
To set forth that which is so singular?
Or why is Collatine the publisher
  Of that rich jewel he should keep unknown
  From thievish ears, because it is his own?

Perchance his boast of Lucrece's sovereignty
Suggested this proud issue of a king,
For by our ears our hearts oft tainted be:
Perchance that envy of so rich a thing,
Braving compare, disdainfully did sting
  His high-pitch'd thoughts, that meaner men should vaunt
  That golden hap which their superiors want.

But some untimely thought did instigate
His all too timeless speed, if none of those:
His honour, his affairs, his friends, his state,
Neglected all, with swift intent he goes
To quench the coal which in his liver glows.
  O rash, false heat, wrapt in repentant cold,
  Thy hasty spring still blasts, and ne'er grows old!

When at Collatium this false lord arrived,
Well was he welcom'd by the Roman dame,
Within whose face beauty and virtue strived
Which of them both should underprop her fame:
When virtue bragg'd, beauty would blush for shame;
  When beauty boasted blushes, in despite
  Virtue would stain that o'er with silver white.

But beauty, in that white intituled,
From Venus' doves doth challenge that fair field;
Then, virtue claims from beauty beauty's red,
Which virtue gave the golden age to gild
Their silver cheeks, and call'd it then their shield;
  Teaching them thus to use it in the fight,
  When shame assail'd, the red should fence the white.

This heraldry in Lucrece' face was seen,
Argu'd by beauty's red, and virtue's white:
Of either's colour was the other queen,
Proving from world's minority their right,
Yet their ambition makes them still to fight,
  The sovereignty of either being so great,
  That oft they interchange each other's seat.

This silent war of lilies and of roses,
Which Tarquin view'd in her fair face's field,
In their pure ranks his traitor eye encloses;
Where, lest between them both it should be kill'd,
The coward captive vanquished doth yield
  To those two armies that would let him go.
  Rather than triumph in so false a foe.

Now thinks he, that her husband's shallow tongue,
The niggard prodigal that prais'd her so,
In that high task hath done her beauty wrong,
Which far exceeds his barren skill to shew:
Therefore, that praise which Collatine doth owe,
  Enchanted Tarquin answers with surmise,
  In silent wonder of still gazing eyes.

This earthly saint, adored by this devil,
Little suspecteth the false worshipper,
For unstain'd thoughts do seldom dream on evil;
Birds never lim'd no secret bushes fear:
So guiltless she securely gives good cheer,
  And reverend welcome to her princely guest,
  Whose inward ill no outward harm express'd:

For that he colour'd with his high estate,
Hiding base sin in plaits of majesty;
That nothing in him seem'd inordinate,
Save sometime too much wonder of his eye,
Which, having all, all could not satisfy;
  But, poorly rich, so wanteth in his store,
  That cloy'd with much, he pineth still for more.

But she, that never cop'd with stranger eyes,
Could pick no meaning from their parling looks,
Nor read the subtle shining secrecies
Writ in the glassy margents of such books:
She touch'd no unknown baits, nor fear'd no hooks;
  Nor could she moralize his wanton sight,
  More than his eyes were open'd to the light.

He stories to her ears her husband's fame,
Won in the fields of fruitful Italy;
And decks with praises Collatine's high name,
Made glorious by his manly chivalry,
With bruised arms and wreaths of victory:
  Her joy with heav'd-up hand she doth express,
  And wordless so greets Heaven for his success.

Far from the purpose of his coming thither,
He makes excuses for his being there:
No cloudy shew of stormy blustering weather
Doth yet in his fair welkin once appear;
Till sable night, mother of dread and fear,
  Upon the world dim darkness doth display,
  And in her vaulty prison stows the day.

For then is Tarquin brought unto his bed,
Intending weariness with heavy sprite;
For after supper long he questioned
With modest Lucrece, and wore out the night:
Now leaden slumber with life's strength doth fight,
  And every one to rest themselves betake,
  Save thieves, and cares, and troubled minds, that wake.

As one of which doth Tarquin lie revolving
The sundry dangers of his will's obtaining;
Yet ever to obtain his will resolving,
Though weak-built hopes persuade him to abstaining:
Despair to gain doth traffick oft for gaining;
  And when great treasure is the meed proposed,
  Though death be adjunct, there's no death supposed.

Those that much covet are with gain so fond,
That what they have not, that which they possess,
They scatter and unloose it from their bond,
And so, by hoping more, they have but less;
Or, gaining more, the profit of excess
  Is but to surfeit, and such griefs sustain,
  That they prove bankrupt in this poor-rich gain.

The aim of all is but to nurse the life
With honour, wealth, and ease, in waning age,
And in this aim there is such thwarting strife,
That one for all, or all for one we gage;
As life for honour in fell battles' rage;
  Honour for wealth, and oft that wealth doth cost
  The death of all, and all together lost.

So that in venturing ill, we leave to be
The things we are for that which we expect;
And this ambitious foul infirmity,
In having much, torments us with defect
Of that we have: so then we do neglect
  The thing we have; and, all for want of wit,
  Make something nothing by augmenting it.

Such hazard now must doting Tarquin make,
Pawning his honour to obtain his lust,
And for himself himself he must forsake:
Then, where is truth, if there be no self-trust?
When shall he think to find a stranger just,
  When he himself himself confounds, betrays
  To slanderous tongues, and wretched hateful days?

Now stole upon the time the dead of night,
When heavy sleep had clos'd up mortal eyes;
No comfortable star did lend his light,
No noise but owls' and wolves' death-boding cries:
Now serves the season that they may surprise
  The silly lambs. Pure thoughts are dead and still,
  While lust and murder wake, to stain and kill.

And now this lustful lord leap'd from his bed,
Throwing his mantle rudely o'er his arm,
Is madly toss'd between desire and dread;
Th' one sweetly flatters, th' other feareth harm;
But honest fear, bewitch'd with lust's foul charm,
  Doth too-too oft betake him to retire,
  Beaten away by brain-sick rude desire.

His falchion on a flint he softly smiteth,
That from the cold stone sparks of fire do fly,
Whereat a waxen torch forthwith he lighteth,
Which must be lode-star to his lustful eye;
And to the flame thus speaks advisedly:
  "As from this cold flint I enforc'd this fire,
  So Lucrece must I force to my desire."

Here, pale with fear, he doth premeditate
The dangers of his loathsome enterprise,
And in his inward mind he doth debate
What following sorrow may on this arise:
Then, looking scornfully, he doth despise
  His naked armour of still slaughtered lust,
  And justly thus controls his thoughts unjust.

"Fair torch, burn out thy light, and lend it not
To darken her whose light excelleth thine;
And die, unhallow'd thoughts, before you blot
With your uncleanness that which is divine:
Offer pure incense to so pure a shrine:
  Let fair humanity abhor the deed,
  That spots and stains love's modest snow-white weed.

"O, shame to knighthood and to shining arms!
O, foul dishonour to my household's grave!
O, impious act, including all foul harms!
A martial man to be soft fancy's slave!
True valour still a true respect should have;
  Then, my digression is so vile, so base,
  That it will live engraven in my face.

"Yea, though I die, the scandal will survive,
And be an eye-sore in my golden coat;
Some loathsome dash the herald will contrive,
To cipher me how fondly I did dote;
That my posterity, sham'd with the note,
  Shall curse my bones, and hold it for no sin
  To wish that I their father had not been.

"What win I, if I gain the thing I seek?
A dream, a breath, a froth of fleeting joy.
Who buys a minute's mirth to wail a week,
Or sells eternity to get a toy?
For one sweet grape who will the vine destroy?
  Or what fond beggar, but to touch the crown,
  Would with the sceptre straight be stricken down?

"If Collatinus dream of my intent,
Will he not wake, and in a desperate rage
Post hither, this vile purpose to prevent?
This siege that hath engirt his marriage,
This blur to youth, this sorrow to the sage,
  This dying virtue, this surviving shame,
  Whose crime will bear an ever-during blame.

"O, what excuse can my invention make,
When thou shalt charge me with so black a deed?
Will not my tongue be mute, my frail joints shake,
Mine eyes forego their light, my false heart bleed?
The guilt being great, the fear doth still exceed;
  And extreme fear can neither fight nor fly,
  But, coward-like, with trembling terror die.

"Had Collatinus kill'd my son or sire,
Or lain in ambush to betray my life,
Or were he not my dear friend, this desire
Might have excuse to work upon his wife,
As in revenge or quital of such strife;
  But as he is my kinsman, my dear friend,
  The shame and fault finds no excuse nor end.

"Shameful it is; — ay, if the fact be known:
Hateful it is; — there is no hate in loving:
I'll beg her love; — but she is not her own:
The worst is but denial and reproving.
My will is strong, past reason's weak removing:
  Who fears a sentence, or an old man's saw,
  Shall by a painted cloth be kept in awe."

Thus, graceless, holds he disputation
'Tween frozen conscience and hot burning will,
And with good thoughts makes dispensation,
Urging the worser sense for vantage still;
Which in a moment doth confound and kill
  All pure effects, and doth so far proceed,
  That what is vile shows like a virtuous deed.

Quoth he, "She took me kindly by the hand,
And gaz'd for tidings in my eager eyes,
Fearing some hard news from the warlike band
Where her beloved Collatinus lies.
O, how her fear did make her colour rise!
  First red as roses that on lawn we lay,
  Then, white as lawn, the roses took away.

"And how her hand, in my hand being lock'd,
Forc'd it to tremble with her loyal fear!
Which struck her sad, and then it faster rock'd,
Until her husband's welfare she did hear;
Whereat she smiled with so sweet a cheer,
  That had Narcissus seen her as she stood,
  Self-love had never drown'd him in the flood.

"Why hunt I, then, for colour or excuses?
All orators are dumb when beauty pleadeth:
Poor wretches have remorse in poor abuses;
Love thrives not in the heart that shadows dreadetl
Affection is my captain, and he leadeth;
  And when his gaudy banner is display'd,
  The coward fights, and will not be dismay'd.

"Then, childish fear, avaunt! debating, die!
Respect and reason, wait on wrinkled age!
My heart shall never countermand mine eye:
Sad pause and deep regard beseem the sage;
My part is youth, and beats these from the stage.
  Desire my pilot is, beauty my prize;
  Then, who fears sinking where such treasure lies?'

As corn o'er-grown by weeds, so heedful fear
Is almost chok'd by unresisted lust.
Away he steals with open listening ear,
Full of foul hope, and full of fond mistrust;
Both which, as servitors to the unjust,
  So cross him with their opposite persuasion,
  That now he vows a league, and now invasion.

Within his thought her heavenly image sits,
And in the self-same seat sits Collatine:
That eye which looks on her confounds his wits;
That eye which him beholds, as more divine,
Unto a view so false will not incline;
  But with a pure appeal seeks to the heart,
  Which, once corrupted, takes the worser part;

And therein heartens up his servile powers,
Who, flatter'd by their leader's jocund show,
Stuff up his lust, as minutes fill up hours;
And as their captain, so their pride doth grow,
Paying more slavish tribute than they owe.
  By reprobate desire thus madly led,
  The Roman lord marcheth to Lucrece' bed.

The locks between her chamber and his will,
Each one by him enforc'd retires his ward;
But as they open they all rate his ill,
Which drives the creeping thief to some regard:
The threshold grates the door to have him heard;
  Night-wandering weasels shriek, to see him there;
  They fright him, yet he still pursues his fear.

As each unwilling portal yields him way,
Through little vents and crannies of the place
The wind wars with his torch to make him stay,
And blows the smoke of it into his face,
Extinguishing his conduct in this case;
  But his hot heart, which fond desire doth scorch,
  Puffs forth another wind that fires the torch:

And being lighted, by the light he spies
Lucretia's glove, wherein her needle sticks:
He takes it from the rushes where it lies,
And griping it, the needle his finger pricks;
As who should say, this glove to wanton tricks
  Is not inur'd; return again in haste;
  Thou seest our mistress' ornaments are chaste.

But all these poor forbiddings could not stay him;
He in the worst sense construes their denial:
The doors, the wind, the glove, that did delay him,
He takes for accidental things of trial,
Or as those bars which stop the hourly dial;
  Who with a ling'ring stay his course doth let,
  Till every minute pays the hour his debt.

"So, so," quoth he; "these lets attend the time,
Like little frosts that sometime threat the Spring,
To add a more rejoicing to the prime,
And give the sneaped birds more cause to sing.
Pain pays the income of each precious thing;
  Huge rocks, high winds, strong pirates, shelves and
    sands,
  The merchant fears, ere rich at home he lands."

Now is he come unto the chamber-door
That shuts him from the heaven of his thought,
Which with a yielding latch, and with no more,
Hath barr'd him from the blessed thing he sought.
So from himself impiety hath wrought,
  That for his prey to pray he doth begin,
  As if the Heavens should countenance his sin.

But in the midst of his unfruitful prayer,
Having solicited th' eternal power
That his foul thoughts might compass his fair fair,
And they would stand auspicious to the hour,
Even there he starts: — quoth he, "I must deflower:
  The powers to whom I pray abhor this fact,
  How can they, then, assist me in the act?

"Then Love and Fortune be my gods, my guide!
My will is back'd with resolution:
Thoughts are but dreams, till their effects be tri'd;
The blackest sin is clear'd with absolution;
Against love's fire fear's frost hath dissolution.
  The eye of heaven is out, and misty night
  Covers the shame that follows sweet delight."

This said, his guilty hand pluck'd up the latch,
And with his knee the door he opens wide.
The dove sleeps fast that this night-owl will catch:
Thus treason works ere traitors be espi'd.
Who sees the lurking serpent steps aside;
  But she, sound sleeping, fearing no such thing,
  Lies at the mercy of his mortal sting.

Into the chamber wickedly he stalks,
And gazeth on her yet-unstained bed.
The curtains being close, about he walks,
Rolling his greedy eye-balls in his head:
By their high treason is his heart misled;
  Which gives the watch-word to his hand full soon,
  To draw the cloud that hides the silver moon.

Look, as the fair and fiery pointed sun,
Rushing from forth a cloud, bereaves our sight;
Even so, the curtain drawn, his eyes begun
To wink, being blinded with a greater light:
Whether it is that she reflects so bright,
  That dazzleth them, or else some shame supposed,
  But blind they are, and keep themselves enclosed.

O, had they in that darksome prison di'd,
Then had they seen the period of their ill:
Then Collatine again, by Lucrece' side,
In his clear bed might have reposed still;
But they must ope, this blessed league to kill,
  And holy-thoughted Lucrece to their sight
  Must sell her joy, her life, her world's delight.

Her lily hand her rosy cheek lies under,
Cozening the pillow of a lawful kiss,
Who therefore angry, seems to part in sunder,
Swelling on either side to want his bliss,
Between whose hills her head intombed is;
  Where, like a virtuous monument, she lies,
  To be admir'd of lewd unhallowed eyes.

Without the bed her other fair hand was,
On the green coverlet; whose perfect white
Show'd like an April daisy on the grass,
With pearly sweat, resembling dew of night.
Her eyes, like marigolds, had sheath'd their light,
  And canopied in darkness sweetly lay,
  Till they might open to adorn the day.

Her hair, like golden threads, play'd with her breath;
O modest wantons! wanton modesty!
Showing life's triumph in the map of death,
And death's dim look in life's mortality:
Each in her sleep themselves so beautify,
  As if between them twain there were no strife,
  But that life liv'd in death, and death in life.

Her breasts, like ivory globes circled with blue,
A pair of maiden worlds unconquered;
Save of their lord, no bearing yoke they knew,
And him by oath they truly honoured.
These worlds in Tarquin new ambition bred;
  Who, like a foul usurper, went about
  From this fair throne to heave the owner out.

What could he see, but mightily he noted?
What did he note, but strongly he desired?
What he beheld, on that he firmly doted,
And in his will his wilful eye he tired.
With more than admiration he admired
  Her azure veins, her alabaster skin,
  Her coral lips, her snow-white dimpled chin.

As the grim lion fawneth o'er his prey,
Sharp hunger by the conquest satisfi'd,
So o'er this sleeping soul doth Tarquin stay,
His rage of lust by gazing qualifi'd;
Slak'd, not suppress'd; for standing by her side,
  His eye, which late this mutiny restrains,
  Unto a greater uproar tempts his veins:

And they, like straggling slaves for pillage fighting,
Obdurate vassals fell exploits effecting,
In bloody death and ravishment delighting,
Nor children's tears, nor mothers' groans respecting,
Swell in their pride, the onset still expecting:
  Anon his beating heart, alarum striking,
  Gives the hot charge, and bids them do their liking.

His drumming heart cheers up his burning eye,
His eye commends the leading to his hand;
His hand, as proud of such a dignity,
Smoking with pride, march'd on to make his stand
On her bare breast, the heart of all her land,
  Whose ranks of blue veins, as his hand did scale,
  Left their round turrets destitute and pale.

They, mustering to the quiet cabinet
Where their dear governess and lady lies,
Do tell her she is dreadfully beset,
And fright her with confusion of their cries:
She, much amaz'd, breaks ope her lock'd-up eyes,
  Who, peeping forth this tumult to behold,
  Are by his flaming torch dimm'd and controll'd.

Imagine her as one in dead of night
From forth dull sleep by dreadful fancy waking,
That thinks she hath beheld some ghastly sprite,
Whose grim aspect sets every joint a shaking;
What terror 'tis! but she, in worser taking,
  From sleep disturbed, heedfully doth view
  The sight which makes supposed terror true.

Wrapp'd and confounded in a thousand fears,
Like to a new-kill'd bird she trembling lies;
She dares not look; yet, winking, there appears
Quick-shifting antics, ugly in her eyes:
Such shadows are the weak brain's forgeries;
  Who, angry that the eyes fly from their lights,
  In darkness daunts them with more dreadful sights.

His hand, that yet remains upon her breast,
(Rude ram to batter such an ivory wall)
May feel her heart (poor citizen!) distress'd,
Wounding itself to death, rise up and fall,
Beating her bulk, that his hand shakes withal.
  This moves in him more rage, and lesser pity,
  To make the breach, and enter this sweet city.

First, like a trumpet, doth his tongue begin
To sound a parley to his heartless foe;
Who o'er the white sheet peers her whiter chin,
The reason of this rash alarm to know,
Which he by dumb demeanour seeks to shew;
  But she with vehement prayers urgeth still,
  Under what colour he commits this ill.

Thus he replies: "The colour in thy face
That even for anger makes the lily pale,
And the red rose blush at her own disgrace,
Shall plead for me, and tell my loving tale;
Under that colour am I come to scale
  Thy never conquer'd fort: the fault is thine,
  For those thine eyes betray thee unto mine.

"Thus I forestall thee, if thou mean to chide:
Thy beauty hath ensnar'd thee to this night,
Where thou with patience must my will abide,
My will that marks thee for my earth's delight,
Which I to conquer sought with all my might;
  But as reproof and reason beat it dead,
  By thy bright beauty was it newly bred.

"I see what crosses my attempt will bring,
I know what thorns the growing rose defends,
I think the honey guarded with a sting;
All this beforehand counsel comprehends,
But will is deaf, and hears no heedful friends:
  Only he hath an eye to gaze on beauty,
  And dotes on what he looks, 'gainst law or duty

"I have debated, even in my soul,
What wrong, what shame, what sorrow I shall breed;
But nothing can affection's course control,
Or stop the headlong fury of his speed.
I know repentant tears ensue the deed,
  Reproach, disdain, and deadly enmity,
  Yet strive I to embrace mine infamy."

This said, he shakes aloft his Roman blade,
Which, like a falcon towering in the skies,
Coucheth the fowl below with his wings' shade,
Whose crooked beak threats if he mount he dies:
So under his insulting falchion lies
  Harmless Lucretia, marking what he tells,
  With trembling fear, as fowl hear falcon's bells.

"Lucrece," quoth he, "this night I must enjoy thee:
If thou deny, then force must work my way,
For in thy bed I purpose to destroy thee.
That done, some worthless slave of thine I'll slay,
To kill thine honour with thy life's decay;
  And in thy dead arms do I mean to place him,
  Swearing I slew him, seeing thee embrace him.

"So thy surviving husband shall remain
The scornful mark of every open eye;
Thy kinsmen hang their heads at this disdain,
Thy issue blurr'd with nameless bastardy:
And thou, the author of their obloquy,
  Shalt have thy trespass cited up in rhymes,
  And sung by children in succeeding times.

"But if thou yield, I rest thy secret friend:
The fault unknown is as a thought unacted;
A little harm, done to a great good end,
For lawful policy remains enacted.
The poisonous simple sometimes is compacted
  In a pure compound; being so applied,
  His venom in effect is purified.

"Then, for thy husband and thy children's sake,
Tender my suit: bequeath not to their lot
The shame that from them no device can take,
The blemish that will never be forgot;
Worse than a slavish wipe, or birth-hour's blot;
  For marks descried in men's nativity
  Are nature's faults, not their own infamy."

Here, with a cockatrice' dead-killing eye,
He rouseth up himself, and makes a pause;
While she, the picture of pure piety,
Like a white hind under the gripe's sharp claws,
Pleads in a wilderness, where are no laws,
  To the rough beast that knows no gentle right,
  Nor aught obeys but his foul appetite.

But when a black-fac'd cloud the world doth threat,
In his dim mist th' aspiring mountains hiding,
From Earth's dark womb some gentle gust doth get,
Which blows these pitchy vapours from their biding,
Hindering their present fall by this dividing:
  So his unhallowed haste her words delays,
  And moody Pluto winks, while Orpheus plays.

Yet, foul night-waking cat, he doth but dally,
While in his hold-fast foot the weak mouse panteth:
Her sad behaviour feeds his vulture folly,
A swallowing gulf that even in plenty wanteth.
His ear her prayers admits, but his heart granteth
No penetrable entrance to her plaining:
Tears harden lust, though marble wear with raining.

Her pity-pleading eyes are sadly fixed
In the remorseless wrinkles of his face;
Her modest eloquence with sighs is mixed,
Which to her oratory adds more grace.
She puts the period often from his place;
And 'midst the sentence so her accent breaks,
That twice she doth begin, ere once she speaks.

She conjures him by high almighty Jove,
By knighthood, gentry, and sweet friendship's oath,
By her untimely tears, her husband's love,
By holy human law, and common troth,
By Heaven and Earth, and all the power of both,
That to his borrow'd bed he make retire,
And stoop to honour, not to foul desire.

Quoth she, "Reward not hospitality
With such black payment as thou hast pretended;
Mud not the fountain that gave drink to thee;
Mar not the thing that cannot be amended;
Mend thy ill aim before thy shoot be ended
He is no wood-man that doth bend his bow
To strike a poor unseasonable doe.

"My husband is thy friend, for his sake spare me;
Thyself art mighty, for thine own sake leave me;
Myself a weakling, do not then ensnare me;
Thou look'st not like deceit, do not deceive me:
My sighs, like whirlwinds, labour hence to heave thee.
  If ever man were mov'd with woman's moans,
  Be moved with my tears, my sighs, my groans.

"All which together, like a troubled ocean,
Beat at thy rocky and wreck-threatening heart,
To soften it with their continual motion;
For stones dissolv'd to water do convert.
O, if no harder than a stone thou art,
  Melt at my tears and be compassionate!
  Soft pity enters at an iron gate.

"In Tarquin's likeness I did entertain thee;
Hast thou put on his shape to do him shame?
To all the host of heaven I complain me,
Thou wrong'st his honour, wound'st his princely name:
Thou art not what thou seem'st; and if the same,
  Thou seem'st not what thou art, a god, a king;
  For kings like gods should govern every thing.

"How will thy shame be seeded in thine age,
When thus thy vices bud before thy spring?
If in thy hope thou dar'st do such outrage,
What dar'st thou not, when once thou art a king?
O, be remember'd, no outrageous thing
  From vassal actors can be wip'd away;
  Then, kings' misdeeds cannot be hid in clay.

"This deed will make thee only lov'd for fear;
But happy monarchs still are fear'd for love:
With foul offenders thou perforce must bear,
When they in thee the like offences prove:
If but for fear of this, thy will remove;
  For princes are the glass, the school, the book,
  Where subjects' eyes do learn, do read, do look.

"And wilt thou be the school where lust shall learn?
Must he in thee read lectures of such shame?
Wilt thou be glass, wherein it shall discern
Authority for sin, warrant for blame,
To privilege dishonour in thy name?
  Thou back'st reproach against long-living laud,
  And mak'st fair reputation but a bawd.

"Hast thou command? by him that gave it thee,
From a pure heart command thy rebel will:
Draw not thy sword to guard iniquity,
For it was lent thee all that brood to kill.
Thy princely office how canst thou fulfil,
  When, pattern'd by thy fault, foul sin may say,
  He learn'd to sin, and thou didst teach the way?

"Think but how vile a spectacle it were,
To view thy present trespass in another.
Men's faults do seldom to themselves appear;
Their own transgressions partially they smother;
This guilt would seem death-worthy in thy brother.
  O, how are they wrapp'd in with infamies,
  That from their own misdeeds askance their eyes!

"To thee, to thee, my heav'd-up hands appeal,
Not to seducing lust, thy rash relier;
I sue for exil'd majesty's repeal;
Let him return, and flattering thoughts retire:
His true respect will prison false desire,
 And wipe the dim mist from thy doting eyne,
 That thou shalt see thy state, and pity mine."

"Have done," quoth he: "my uncontrolled tide
Turns not, but swells the higher by this let.
Small lights are soon blown out, huge fires abide,
And with the wind in greater fury fret:
The petty streams, that pay a daily debt
 To their salt sovereign with their fresh falls' haste,
 Add to his flow, but alter not his taste."

"Thou art," quoth she, "a sea, a sovereign king;
And lo! there falls into thy boundless flood
Black lust, dishonour, shame, misgoverning,
Who seek to stain the ocean of thy blood.
If all these petty ills shall change thy good,
 Thy sea within a puddle's womb is hears'd,
 And not the puddle in thy sea dispers'd.

"So shall these slaves be king, and thou their slave;
Thou nobly base, they basely dignifi'd;
Thou their fair life, and they thy fouler grave:
Thou loathed in their shame, they in thy pride:
The lesser thing should not the greater hide;
 The cedar stoops not to the base shrub's foot,
 But low shrubs wither at the cedar's root.

"So let thy thoughts, low vassals to thy state"—
"No more," quoth he; "by Heaven, I will not hear
thee:
Yield to my love; if not, enforced hate,
Instead of love's coy touch, shall rudely tear thee;
That done, despitefully I mean to bear thee
Unto the base bed of some rascal groom,
To be thy partner in this shameful doom."

This said, he sets his foot upon the light,
For light and lust are deadly enemies:
Shame, folded up in blind concealing night,
When most unseen, then most doth tyrannize.
The wolf hath seiz'd his prey, the poor lamb cries;
Till with her own white fleece her voice controll'd
Entombs her outcry in her lips' sweet fold:

For with the nightly linen that she wears,
He pens her piteous clamours in her head,
Cooling his hot face in the chastest tears
That ever modest eyes with sorrow shed.
O, that prone lust should stain so pure a bed!
The spots whereof could weeping purify,
Her tears should drop on them perpetually.

But she hath lost a dearer thing than life,
And he hath won what he would lose again;
This forced league doth force a further strife;
This momentary joy breeds months of pain:
This hot desire converts to cold disdain.
Pure chastity is rifled of her store,
And lust, the thief, far poorer than before.

Look, as the full-fed hound, or gorged hawk,
Unapt for tender smell, or speedy flight,
Make slow pursuit, or altogether balk
The prey wherein by nature they delight:
So surfeit-taking Tarquin fares this night:
  His taste delicious, in digestion souring,
  Devours his will, that liv'd by foul devouring.

O, deeper sin than bottomless conceit
Can comprehend in still imagination!
Drunken desire must vomit his receipt,
Ere he can see his own abomination.
While lust is in his pride, no exclamation
  Can curb his heat, or rein his rash desire,
  Till, like a jade, self-will himself doth tire.

And then, with lank and lean discolour'd cheek,
With heavy eye, knit brow, and strengthless pace,
Feeble desire, all recreant, poor, and meek,
Like to a bankrupt beggar wails his case:
The flesh being proud, desire doth fight with grace,
  For there it revels; and when that decays,
  The guilty rebel for remission prays.

So fares it with this faultful lord of Rome,
Who this accomplishment so hotly chased;
For now against himself he sounds this doom,
That through the length of times he stands disgraced:
Besides, his soul's fair temple is defaced;
  To whose weak ruins muster troops of cares,
  To ask the spotted princess how she fares.

She says, her subjects with foul insurrection
Have batter'd down her consecrated wall,
And by their mortal fault brought in subjection
Her immortality, and made her thrall
To living death, and pain perpetual:
  Which in her prescience she controlled still,
  But her foresight could not fore-stall their will.

Even in this thought through the dark night he stealeth,
A captive victor that hath lost in gain;
Bearing away the wound that nothing healeth,
The scar that will despite of cure remain;
Leaving his spoil perplex'd in greater pain.
  She bears the load of lust he left behind,
  And he the burthen of a guilty mind.

He, like a thievish dog, creeps sadly thence,
She like a wearied lamb lies panting there;
He scowls, and hates himself for his offence,
She desperate with her nails her flesh doth tear;
He faintly flies, sweating with guilty fear;
  She stays, exclaiming on the direful night;
  He runs, and chides his vanish'd, loath'd delight.

He thence departs a heavy convertite,
She there remains a hopeless cast-away;
He in his speed looks for the morning light,
She prays she never may behold the day;
"For day," quoth she, "night's scapes doth open lay,
  And my true eyes have never practis'd how
  To cloak offences with a cunning brow.

"They think not but that every eye can see
The same disgrace which they themselves behold;
And therefore would they still in darkness be,
To have their unseen sin remain untold;
For they their guilt with weeping will unfold,
And grave, like water that doth eat in steel,
Upon my cheeks what helpless shame I feel."

Here she exclaims against repose and rest,
And bids her eyes hereafter still be blind.
She wakes her heart by beating on her breast,
And bids it leap from thence, where it may find
Some purer chest to close so pure a mind.
Frantic with grief, thus breathes she forth her spite
Against the unseen secrecy of night.

"O, comfort-killing Night, image of Hell!
Dim register and notary of shame!
Black stage for tragedies and murthers fell!
Vast sin-concealing chaos! nurse of blame!
Blind muffled bawd! dark harbour for defame!
Grim cave of death, whispering conspirator
With close-tongu'd treason and the ravisher!

"O, hateful, vaporous, and foggy Night!
Since thou art guilty of my cureless crime,
Muster thy mists to meet the eastern light,
Make war against proportion'd course of time:
Or if thou wilt permit the sun to climb
His wonted height, yet ere he go to bed,
Knit poisonous clouds about his golden head.

"With rotten damps ravish the morning air;
Let their exhal'd unwholesome breaths make sick
The life of purity, the supreme fair,
Ere he arrive his weary noon-tide prick;
And let thy misty vapours march so thick,
  That in their smoky ranks his smother'd light
  May set at noon, and make perpetual night.

"Were Tarquin Night, (as he is but Night's child)
The silver-shining queen he would distain;
Her twinkling handmaids too, by him defil'd,
Through night's black bosom should not peep again:
So should I have copartners in my pain;
  And fellowship in woe doth woe assuage,
  As palmers' chat makes short their pilgrimage.

"Where, now, I have no one to blush with me,
To cross their arms, and hang their heads with mine,
To mask their brows, and hide their infamy;
But I alone, alone must sit and pine,
Seasoning the earth with showers of silver brine;
  Mingling my talk with tears, my grief with groans,
  Poor wasting monuments of lasting moans.

"O Night! thou furnace of foul-reeking smoke,
Let not the jealous Day behold that face
Which underneath thy black all-hiding cloak
Immodestly lies martyr'd with disgrace:
Keep still possession of thy gloomy place,
  That all the faults which in thy reign are made,
  May likewise be sepulcher'd in thy shade.

"Make me not object to the tell-tale Day!
The light will shew, character'd in my brow,
The story of sweet chastity's decay,
The impions breach of holy wedlock vow:
Yea, the illiterate, that know not how
To cipher what is writ in learned books,
Will quote my loathsome trespass in my looks.

"The nurse to still her child will tell my story,
And fright her crying babe with Tarquin's name;
The orator to deck his oratory
Will couple my reproach to Tarquin's shame;
Feast-finding minstrels, tuning my defame,
Will tie the hearers to attend each line,
How Tarquin wronged me, I Collatine.

"Let my good name, that senseless reputation,
For Collatine's dear love be kept unspotted:
If that be made a theme for disputation,
The branches of another root are rotted,
And undeserv'd reproach to him allotted,
That is as clear from this attaint of mine,
As I ere this was pure to Collatine.

"O unseen shame! invisible disgrace!
O unfelt sore! crest-wounding, private scar!
Reproach is stamp'd in Collatinus' face,
And Tarquin's eye may read the mot afar,
How he in peace is wounded, not in war.
Alas! how many bear such shameful blows,
Which not themselves, but he that gives them, knows.

"If, Collatine, thine honour lay in me,
From me by strong assault it is bereft.
My honey lost, and I, a drone-like bee,
Have no perfection of my summer left,
But robb'd and ransack'd by injurious theft:
  In thy weak hive a wandering wasp hath crept,
  And suck'd the honey which thy chaste bee kept.

"Yet am I guilty of thy honour's wrack;
Yet for thy honour did I entertain him;
Coming from thee, I could not put him back,
For it had been dishonour to disdain him:
Besides, of weariness he did complain him,
  And talk'd of virtue. — O, unlook'd for evil,
  When virtue is profan'd in such a devil!

"Why should the worm intrude the maiden bud,
Or hateful cuckoos hatch in sparrows' nests?
Or toads infect fair founts with venom mud?
Or tyrant folly lurk in gentle breasts?
Or kings be breakers of their own behests?
  But no perfection is so absolute,
  That some impurity doth not pollute.

"The aged man that coffers up his gold,
Is plagu'd with cramps, and gouts, and painful fits,
And scarce hath eyes his treasure to behold,
But like still-pining Tantalus he sits,
And useless barns the harvest of his wits;
  Having no other pleasure of his gain,
  But torment that it cannot cure his pain.

"So, then he hath it, when he cannot use it,
And leaves it to be master'd by his young;
Who in their pride do presently abuse it:
Their father was too weak, and they too strong,
To hold their cursed-blessed fortune long.
  The sweets we wish for turn to loathed sours,
  Even in the moment that we call them ours.

"Unruly blasts wait on the tender spring,
Unwholesome weeds take root with precious flowers,
The adder hisses where the sweet birds sing,
What virtue breeds iniquity devours;
We have no good that we can say is ours,
  But ill annexed opportunity
  Or kills his life, or else his quality.

"O, Opportunity, thy guilt is great:
'Tis thou that execut'st the traitor's treason;
Thou sett'st the wolf where he the lamb may get;
Whoever plots the sin, thou 'point'st the season:
'Tis thou that spurn'st at right, at law, at reason;
  And in thy shady cell, where none may spy him,
  Sits sin to seize the souls that wander by him.

"Thou mak'st the vestal violate her oath;
Thou blow'st the fire, when temperance is thaw'd;
Thou smother'st honesty, thou murther'st troth:
Thou foul abettor! thou notorious bawd!
Thou plantest scandal, and displacest laud:
  Thou ravisher, thou traitor, thou false thief,
  Thy honey turns to gall, thy joy to grief!

"Thy secret pleasure turns to open shame,
Thy private feasting to a public fast:
Thy smoothing titles to a ragged name,
Thy sugar'd tongue to bitter wormwood taste:
Thy violent vanities can never last.
  How comes it then, vile Opportunity,
  Being so bad, such numbers seek for thee?

"When wilt thou be the humble suppliant's friend,
And bring him where his suit may be obtained?
When wilt thou sort an hour great strifes to end,
Or free that soul which wretchedness hath chained?
Give physic to the sick, ease to the pained?
  The poor, lame, blind, halt, creep, cry out for thee,
  But they ne'er meet with Opportunity.

"The patient dies while the physician sleeps;
The orphan pines while the oppressor feeds;
Justice is feasting while the widow weeps;
Advice is sporting while infection breeds:
Thou grant'st no time for charitable deeds.
  Wrath, envy, treason, rape, and murther's rages;
  Thy heinous hours wait on them as their pages.

"When Truth and Virtue have to do with thee,
A thousand crosses keep them from thy aid:
They buy thy help; but Sin ne'er gives a fee;
He gratis comes, and thou art well appay'd,
As well to hear, as grant what he hath said.
  My Collatine would else have come to me,
  When Tarquin did; but he was stay'd by thee.

"Guilty thou art of murther and of theft;
Guilty of perjury and subornation;
Guilty of treason, forgery, and shift;
Guilty of incest, that abomination:
An accessory by thine inclination
  To all sins past, and all that are to come,
  From the creation to the general doom.

"Mis-shapen Time, copesmate of ugly Night,
Swift subtle post, carrier of grisly care;
Eater of youth, false slave to false delight,
Base watch of woes, sin's pack-horse, virtue's snare;
Thou nursest all, and murtherest all that are.
  O hear me, then, injurious, shifting Time!
  Be guilty of my death, since of my crime.

"Why hath thy servant, Opportunity,
Betray'd the hours thou gav'st me to repose?
Cancell'd my fortunes, and enchained me
To endless date of never-ending woes?
Time's office is to fine the hate of foes;
  To eat up errors by opinion bred,
  Not spend the dowry of a lawful bed.

"Time's glory is to calm contending kings,
To unmask falsehood, and bring truth to light,
To stamp the seal of time in aged things,
To wake the morn, and sentinel the night,
To wrong the wronger till he render right,
  To ruinate proud buildings with thy hours,
  And smear with dust their glittering golden towers:

"To fill with worm-holes stately monuments,
To feed oblivion with decay of things,
To blot old books, and alter their contents,
To pluck the quills from ancient ravens' wings,
To dry the old oak's sap, and cherish springs;
  To spoil antiquities of hammer'd steel,
  And turn the giddy round of Fortune's wheel:

"To show the beldame daughters of her daughter,
To make the child a man, the man a child,
To slay the tiger that doth live by slaughter,
To tame the unicorn and lion wild,
To mock the subtle, in themselves beguil'd,
  To cheer the ploughman with increaseful crops,
  And waste huge stones with little water-drops.

"Why work'st thou mischief in thy pilgrimage,
Unless thou could'st return to make amends?
One poor retiring minute in an age
Would purchase thee a thousand thousand friends,
Lending him wit that to bad debtors lends:
  O, this dread night, would'st thou one hour come back,
  I could prevent this storm, and shun thy wrack.

"Thou ceaseless lackey to eternity,
With some mischance cross Tarquin in his flight:
Devise extremes beyond extremity
To make him curse this cursed crimeful night:
Let ghastly shadows his lewd eyes affright,
  And the dire thought of his committed evil
  Shape every bush a hideous shapeless devil.

"Disturb his hours of rest with restless trances,
Afflict him in his bed with bedrid groans;
Let there bechance him pitiful mischances,
To make him moan, but pity not his moans:
Stone him with harden'd hearts, harder than stones;
And let mild women to him lose their mildness,
Wilder to him than tigers in their wildness.

"Let him have time to tear his curled hair,
Let him have time against himself to rave,
Let him have time of time's help to despair,
Let him have time to live a loathed slave;
Let him have time a beggar's orts to crave,
And time to see one that by alms doth live,
Disdain to him disdained scraps to give.

"Let him have time to see his friends his foes,
And merry fools to mock at him resort;
Let him have time to mark how slow time goes
In time of sorrow, and how swift and short
His time of folly, and his time of sport:
And ever let his unrecalling crime
Have time to wail th' abusing of his time.

"O Time, thou tutor both to good and bad,
Teach me to curse him that thou taught'st this ill!
At his own shadow let the thief run mad,
Himself himself seek every hour to kill!
Such wretched hands such wretched blood should spill;
For who so base would such an office have
As slanderous death's-man to so base a slave?

"The baser is he, coming from a king,
To shame his hope with deeds degenerate:
The mightier man, the mightier is the thing
That makes him honour'd, or begets him hate;
For greatest scandal waits on greatest state.
  The moon being clouded presently is miss'd,
  But little stars may hide them when they list.

"The crow may bathe his coal-black wings in mire,
And unperceiv'd fly with the filth away;
But if the like the snow-white swan desire,
The stain upon his silver down will stay.
Poor grooms are sightless night, kings glorious day:
  Gnats are unnoted wheresoe'er they fly,
  But eagles gaz'd upon with every eye.

"Out, idle words! servants to shallow fools,
Unprofitable sounds, weak arbitrators!
Busy yourselves in skill-contending schools;
Debate where leisure serves with dull debaters;
To trembling clients be you mediators:
  For me, I force not argument a straw,
  Since that my case is past the help of law.

"In vain I rail at Opportunity,
At Time, at Tarquin, and uncheerful night;
In vain I cavil with mine infamy,
In vain I spurn at my confirm'd despite:
This helpless smoke of words doth me no right.
  The remedy, indeed, to do me good,
  Is to let forth my foul, defiled blood.

"Poor hand, why quiver'st thou at this decree?
Honour thyself to rid me of this shame;
For if I die, my honour lives in thee;
But if I live, thou liv'st in my defame:
Since thou could'st not defend thy loyal dame,
And wast afear'd to scratch her wicked foe,
Kill both thyself and her for yielding so."

This said, from her be-tumbled couch she starteth,
To find some desperate instrument of death;
But this no slaughter-house no tool imparteth,
To make more vent for passage of her breath,
Which, thronging through her lips, so vanisheth
As smoke from Ætna, that in air consumes,
Or that which from discharged cannon fumes.

"In vain," quoth she, "I live; and seek in vain
Some happy mean to end a hapless life:
I fear'd by Tarquin's falchion to be slain,
Yet for the self-same purpose seek a knife;
But when I fear'd, I was a loyal wife.
So am I now: — O no, that cannot be;
Of that true type hath Tarquin rifled me.

"O, that is gone, for which I sought to live,
And therefore now I need not fear to die.
To clear this spot by death, at least, I give
A badge of fame to slander's livery;
A dying life to living infamy.
Poor helpless help, the treasure stol'n away,
To burn the guiltless casket where it lay!

"Well, well, dear Collatine, thou shalt not know
The stained taste of violated troth;
I will not wrong thy true affection so,
To flatter thee with an infringed oath;
This bastard graff shall never come to growth:
He shall not boast, who did thy stock pollute,
That thou art doting father of his fruit.

"Nor shall he smile at thee in secret thought,
Nor laugh with his companions at thy state;
But thou shalt know thy interest was not bought
Basely with gold, but stolen from forth thy gate.
For me, I am the mistress of my fate,
And with my trespass never will dispense,
Till life to death acquit my forc'd offence.

"I will not poison thee with my attaint,
Nor fold my fault in cleanly coin'd excuses;
My sable ground of sin I will not paint,
To hide the truth of this false night's abuses:
My tongue shall utter all; mine eyes, like sluices,
As from a mountain spring that feeds a dale,
Shall gush pure streams to purge my impure tale."

By this, lamenting Philomel had ended
The well-tun'd warble of her nightly sorrow,
And solemn night with slow, sad gait descended
To ugly Hell; when lo! the blushing morrow
Lends light to all fair eyes that light will borrow:
But cloudy Lucrece shames herself to see,
And therefore still in night would cloister'd be.

Revealing day through every cranny spies,
And seems to point her out where she sits weeping;
To whom she sobbing speaks: "O eye of eyes!
Why pri'st thou through my window? leave thy
peeping;
Mock with thy tickling beams eyes that are sleeping:
Brand not my forehead with thy piercing light,
For day hath naught to do what's done by night."

Thus cavils she with every thing she sees.
True grief is fond and testy as a child,
Who wayward once, his mood with naught agrees:
Old woes, not infant sorrows, bear them mild;
Continuance tames the one; the other wild,
Like an unpractis'd swimmer plunging still,
With too much labour drowns for want of skill.

So she, deep drenched in a sea of care,
Holds disputation with each thing she views,
And to herself all sorrow doth compare:
No object but her passion's strength renews,
And as one shifts, another straight ensues:
Sometime her grief is dumb, and hath no words;
Sometime 'tis mad, and too much talk affords.

The little birds that tune their morning's joy,
Make her moans mad with their sweet melody;
For mirth doth search the bottom of annoy:
Sad souls are slain in merry company;
Grief best is pleas'd with grief's society:
True sorrow then is feelingly suffic'd,
When with like semblance it is sympathiz'd.

'Tis double death to drown in ken of shore;
He ten times pines, that pines beholding food;
To see the salve doth make the wound ache more;
Great grief grieves most at that would do it good:
Deep woes roll forward like a gentle flood,
  Who, being stopp'd, the bounding banks o'erflows:
  Grief dallied with nor law nor limit knows.

"You mocking birds," quoth she, "your tunes entomb
Within your hollow swelling feather'd breasts,
And in my hearing be you mute and dumb:
My restless discord loves no stops nor rests;
A woful hostess brooks not merry guests.
  Relish your nimble notes to pleasing ears;
  Distress likes dumps, when time is kept with tears.

"Come, Philomel, that sing'st of ravishment,
Make thy sad grove in my dishevell'd hair.
As the dank earth weeps at thy languishment,
So I at each sad strain will strain a tear,
And with deep groans the diapason bear:
  For burthen-wise I'll hum on Tarquin still,
  While thou on Tereus descant'st, better skill.

"And whiles against a thorn thou bear'st thy part,
To keep thy sharp woes waking, wretched I,
To imitate thee well, against my heart
Will fix a sharp knife, to affright mine eye,
Who, if it wink, shall thereon fall and die.
  These means, as frets upon an instrument,
  Shall tune our heart-strings to true languishment.

"And for, poor bird, thou sing'st not in the day,
As shaming any eye should thee behold,
Some dark deep desert, seated from the way,
That knows not parching heat nor freezing cold,
Will we find out; and there we will unfold
To creatures stern sad tunes to change their kinds:
Since men prove beasts, let beasts bear gentle minds."

As the poor frighted deer, that stands at gaze,
Wildly determining which way to fly,
Or one encompass'd with a winding maze,
That cannot tread the way out readily;
So with herself is she in mutiny,
To live or die which of the twain were better,
When life is sham'd, and death reproach's debtor.

"To kill myself," quoth she, "alack! what were it,
But with my body my poor soul's pollution?
They that lose half, with greater patience bear it,
Than they whose whole is swallow'd in confusion.
That mother tries a merciless conclusion,
Who having two sweet babes, when death takes one,
Will slay the other, and be nurse to none.

"My body or my soul, which was the dearer,
When the one pure, the other made divine?
Whose love of either to myself was nearer,
When both were kept for Heaven and Collatine?
Ah me! the bark peel'd from the lofty pine,
His leaves will wither, and his sap decay;
So must my soul, her bark being peel'd away.

"Her house is sack'd, her quiet interrupted,
Her mansion batter'd by the enemy;
Her sacred temple spotted, spoil'd, corrupted,
Grossly engirt with daring infamy:
Then, let it not be call'd impiety,
  If in this blemish'd fort I make some hole,
  Through which I may convey this troubled soul.

"Yet die I will not, till my Collatine
Have heard the cause of my untimely death,
That he may vow, in that sad hour of mine,
Revenge on him that made me stop my breath.
My stained blood to Tarquin I'll bequeath,
  Which by him tainted shall for him be spent,
  And as his due writ in my testament.

"My honour I'll bequeath unto the knife
That wounds my body so dishonoured.
'Tis honour to deprive dishonour'd life;
The one will live, the other being dead:
So of shame's ashes shall my fame be bred;
  For in my death I murther shameful scorn:
  My shame so dead, mine honour is new-born.

"Dear lord of that dear jewel I have lost,
What legacy shall I bequeath to thee?
My resolution, love, shall be thy boast,
By whose example thou reveng'd may'st be.
How Tarquin must be us'd, read it in me:
  Myself, thy friend, will kill myself, thy foe,
  And for my sake serve thou false Tarquin so.

"This brief abridgment of my will I make:
My soul and body to the skies and ground;
My resolution, husband, do thou take;
Mine honour be the knife's that makes my wound;
My shame be his that did my fame confound;
And all my fame that lives disbursed be
To those that live, and think no shame of me.

"Thou, Collatine, shalt oversee this will;
How was I overseen that thou shalt see it!
My blood shall wash the slander of mine ill;
My life's foul deed my life's fair end shall free it.
Faint not, faint heart, but stoutly say, 'so be it.'
Yield to my hand; my hand shall conquer thee:
Thou dead, both die, and both shall victors be."

This plot of death when sadly she had laid,
And wip'd the brinish pearl from her bright eyes,
With untun'd tongue she hoarsely calls her maid,
Whose swift obedience to her mistress hies;
For fleet-wing'd duty with thought's feathers flies.
Poor Lucrece' cheeks unto her maid seem so,
As winter meads when sun doth melt their snow.

Her mistress she doth give demure good-morrow,
With soft slow tongue, true mark of modesty,
And sorts a sad look to her lady's sorrow,
For why, her face wore sorrow's livery;
But durst not ask of her audaciously
Why her two suns were cloud-eclipsed so,
Nor why her fair cheeks over-wash'd with woe.

But as the earth doth weep, the sun being set,
Each flower moisten'd like a melting eye,
Even so the maid with swelling drops 'gan wet
Her circled eyne, enforc'd by sympathy
Of those fair suns set in her mistress' sky,
Who in a salt-wav'd ocean quench their light,
Which makes the maid weep like the dewy night.

A pretty while these pretty creatures stand,
Like ivory conduits coral cisterns filling:
One justly weeps, the other takes in hand
No cause but company of her drops spilling:
Their gentle sex to weep are often willing,
Grieving themselves to guess at others' smarts,
And then they drown their eyes, or break their hearts.

For men have marble, women waxen, minds,
And therefore are they form'd as marble will;
The weak oppress'd, th' impression of strange kinds
Is form'd in them by force, by fraud, or skill:
Then, call them not the authors of their ill,
No more than wax shall be accounted evil,
Wherein is stamp'd the semblance of a devil.

Their smoothness, like a goodly champaign plain,
Lays open all the little worms that creep;
In men, as in a rough-grown grove, remain
Cave-keeping evils that obscurely sleep.
Through crystal walls each little mote will peep:
Though men can cover crimes with bold stern looks,
Poor women's faces are their own faults' books.

No man inveigh against the withered flower,
But chide rough winter that the flower hath kill'd.
Not that devour'd, but that which doth devour,
Is worthy blame. O, let it not be hild
Poor women's faults, that they are so fulfill'd
With men's abuses: those proud lords, to blame,
Make weak-made women tenants to their shame.

The precedent whereof in Lucrece' view,
Assail'd by night, with circumstances strong
Of present death, and shame that might ensue
By that her death, to do her husband wrong:
Such danger to resistance did belong,
That dying fear through all her body spread;
And who cannot abuse a body dead?

By this, mild patience bid fair Lucrece speak
To the poor counterfeit of her complaining:
"My girl," quoth she, "on what occasion break
Those tears from thee, that down thy cheeks are raining?
If thou dost weep for grief of my sustaining,
Know, gentle wench, it small avails my mood:
If tears could help, mine own would do me good.

"But tell me, girl, when went" (and there she stay'd
Till after a deep groan) "Tarquin from hence?"
"Madam, ere I was up," replied the maid;
"The more to blame my sluggard negligence:
Yet with the fault I thus far can dispense;
Myself was stirring ere the break of day,
And, ere I rose, was Tarquin gone away.

"But lady, if your maid may be so bold,
She would request to know your heaviness."
"O peace!" quoth Lucrece: "if it should be told,
The repetition cannot make it less;
For more it is than I can well express:
And that deep torture may be call'd a hell,
When more is felt than one hath power to tell.

"Go, get me hither paper, ink, and pen,—
Yet save that labour, for I have them here.
What should I say?—One of my husband's men
Bid thou be ready by and by, to bear
A letter to my lord, my love, my dear:
Bid him with speed prepare to carry it;
The cause craves haste, and it will soon be writ."

Her maid is gone, and she prepares to write,
First hovering o'er the paper with her quill.
Conceit and grief an eager combat fight;
What wit sets down is blotted straight with will;
This is too curious-good, this blunt and ill:
Much like a press of people at a door
Throng her inventions, which shall go before.

At last she thus begins: "Thou worthy lord
Of that unworthy wife that greeteth thee,
Health to thy person: next, vouchsafe t' afford
(If ever, love, thy Lucrece thou wilt see)
Some present speed to come and visit me.
So I commend me from our house in grief:
My woes are tedious, though my words are brief."

Here folds she up the tenour of her woe,
Her certain sorrow writ uncertainly.
By this short schedule Collatine may know
Her grief, but not her grief's true quality:
She dares not thereof make discovery,
  Lest he should hold it her own gross abuse,
  Ere she with blood had stain'd her stain'd excuse.

Besides, the life and feeling of her passion
She hoards, to spend when he is by to hear her;
When sighs and groans and tears may grace the fashion
Of her disgrace, the better so to clear her
From that suspicion which the world might bear her.
  To shun this blot she would not blot the letter
  With words, till action might become them better.

To see sad sights moves more than hear them told,
For then the eye interprets to the ear
The heavy motion that it doth behold,
When every part a part of woe doth bear:
'Tis but a part of sorrow that we hear:
  Deep sounds make lesser noise than shallow fords,
  And sorrow ebbs, being blown with wind of words.

Her letter now is seal'd, and on it writ,
"At Ardea to my lord, with more than haste."
The post attends, and she delivers it,
Charging the sour-fac'd groom to hie as fast
As lagging fowls before the northern blast:
  Speed more than speed but dull and slow she deems;
  Extremity still urgeth such extremes.

The homely villain court'sies to her low,
And blushing on her, with a steadfast eye
Receives the scroll, without or yea or no,
And forth with bashful innocence doth hie:
But they whose guilt within their bosoms lie,
  Imagine every eye beholds their blame,
  For Lucrece thought he blush'd to see her shame;

When, silly groom! God wot, it was defect
Of spirit, life, and bold audacity.
Such harmless creatures have a true respect
To talk in deeds, while others saucily
Promise more speed, but do it leisurely:
  Even so this pattern of the worn-out age
  Pawn'd honest looks, but lay'd no words to gage.

His kindled duty kindled her mistrust,
That two red fires in both their faces blazed;
She thought he blush'd, as knowing Tarquin's lust,
And, blushing with him, wistly on him gazed;
Her earnest eye did make him more amazed:
  The more she saw the blood his cheeks replenish,
  The more she thought he spied in her some blemish.

But long she thinks till he return again,
And yet the duteous vassal scarce is gone.
The weary time she cannot entertain,
For now 'tis stale to sigh, to weep, and groan:
So woe hath wearied woe, moan tired moan,
  That she her plaints a little while doth stay,
  Pausing for means to mourn some newer way.

At last she calls to mind where hangs a piece
Of skilful painting, made for Priam's Troy;
Before the which is drawn the power of Greece,
For Helen's rape the city to destroy,
Threatening cloud-kissing Ilion with annoy;
Which the conceited painter drew so proud,
As heaven it seem'd to kiss the turrets bow'd.

A thousand lamentable objects there,
In scorn of nature, art gave lifeless life.
Many a dry drop seem'd a weeping tear,
Shed for the slaughter'd husband by the wife:
The red blood reek'd to show the painter's strife;
And dying eyes gleam'd forth their ashy lights,
Like dying coals burnt out in tedious nights.

There might you see the labouring pioneer
Begrim'd with sweat, and smeared all with dust;
And from the towers of Troy there would appear
The very eyes of men through loop-holes thrust,
Gazing upon the Greeks with little lust:
Such sweet observance in this work was had,
That one might see those far-off eyes look sad.

In great commanders grace and majesty
You might behold, triumphing in their faces;
In youth quick bearing and dexterity;
And here and there the painter interlaces
Pale cowards, marching on with trembling paces:
Which heartless peasants did so well resemble,
That one would swear he saw them quake and
tremble.

In Ajax and Ulysses, O, what art
Of physiognomy might one behold!
The face of either 'cipher'd either's heart;
Their face their manners most expressly told:
In Ajax' eyes blunt rage and rigour roll'd;
  But the mild glance that sly Ulysses lent,
  Show'd deep regard and smiling government.

There pleading might you see grave Nestor stand,
As 'twere encouraging the Greeks to fight;
Making such sober action with his hand,
That it beguil'd attention, charm'd the sight.
In speech, it seem'd, his beard, all silver white,
  Wagg'd up and down, and from his lips did fly
  Thin winding breath, which purl'd up to the sky.

About him were a press of gaping faces,
Which seem'd to swallow up his sound advice;
All jointly listening, but with several graces,
As if some mermaid did their ears entice:
Some high, some low; the painter was so nice,
  The scalps of many, almost hid behind,
  To jump up higher seem'd, to mock the mind.

Here one man's hand lean'd on another's head,
His nose being shadow'd by his neighbour's ear;
Here one, being throng'd, bears back, all boll'n and red:
Another, smother'd, seems to pelt and swear;
And in their rage such signs of rage they bear,
  As, but for loss of Nestor's golden words,
  It seem'd they would debate with angry swords.

For much imaginary work was there;
Conceit deceitful, so compact, so kind,
That for Achilles' image stood his spear,
Grip'd in an armed hand: himself behind
Was left unseen, save to the eye of mind.
  A hand, a foot, a face, a leg, a head,
  Stood for the whole to be imagined.

And from the walls of strong besieged Troy
When their brave hope, bold Hector, march'd to field,
Stood many Trojan mothers, sharing joy
To see their youthful sons bright weapons wield;
And to their hope they such odd action yield,
  That through their light joy seemed to appear
  (Like bright things stain'd) a kind of heavy fear.

And from the strond of Dardan, where they fought,
To Simois' reedy banks the red blood ran,
Whose waves to imitate the battle sought
With swelling ridges; and their ranks began
To break upon the galled shore, and than
  Retire again, till meeting greater ranks
  They join, and shoot their foam at Simois' banks.

To this well-painted piece is Lucrece come,
To find a face where all distress is steld.
Many she sees, where cares have carved some,
But none where all distress and dolour dwell'd,
Till she despairing Hecuba beheld,
  Staring on Priam's wounds with her old eyes,
  Which bleeding under Pyrrhus' proud foot lies.

In her the painter had anatomiz'd
Time's ruin, beauty's wreck, and grim care's reign:
Her cheeks with chaps and wrinkles were disguis'd,
Of what she was no semblance did remain;
Her blue blood chang'd to black in every vein,
  Wanting the spring that those shrunk pipes had fed,
  Show'd life imprison'd in a body dead.

On this sad shadow Lucrece spends her eyes,
And shapes her sorrow to the beldam's woes,
Who nothing wants to answer her but cries,
And bitter words to ban her cruel foes:
The painter was no God to lend her those;
  And therefore Lucrece swears he did her wrong,
  To give her so much grief, and not a tongue.

"Poor instrument," quoth she, "without a sound,
I'll tune thy woes with my lamenting tongue,
And drop sweet balm in Priam's painted wound,
And rail on Pyrrhus that hath done him wrong,
And with my tears quench Troy, that burns so long,
  And with my knife scratch out the angry eyes
  Of all the Greeks that are thine enemies.

"Shew me the strumpet that began this stir,
That with my nails her beauty I may tear.
Thy heat of lust, fond Paris, did incur
This load of wrath that burning Troy doth bear:
Thine eye kindled the fire that burneth here;
  And here, in Troy, for trespass of thine eye,
  The sire, the son, the dame, and daughter die.

G 2

"Why should the private pleasure of some one
Become the public plague of many mo?
Let sin, alone committed, light alone
Upon his head that hath transgressed so;
Let guiltless souls be freed from guilty woe.
For one's offence why should so many fall,
To plague a private sin in general?

"Lo, here weeps Hecuba, here Priam dies,
Here manly Hector faints, here Troilus swounds;
Here friend by friend in bloody channel lies,
And friend to friend gives unadvised wounds,
And one man's lust these many lives confounds.
Had doting Priam check'd his son's desire,
Troy had been bright with fame, and not with fire."

Here feelingly she weeps Troy's painted woes;
For sorrow, like a heavy-hanging bell,
Once set on ringing, with his own weight goes;
Then little strength rings out the doleful knell:
So Lucrece, set a-work, sad tales doth tell
To pencill'd pensiveness and colour'd sorrow;
She lends them words, and she their looks doth borrow.

She throws her eyes about the painting, round,
And whom she finds forlorn she doth lament:
At last she sees a wretched image bound,
That piteous looks to Phrygian shepherds lent;
His face, though full of cares, yet show'd content.
Onward to Troy with the blunt swains he goes,
So mild, that patience seem'd to scorn his woes.

In him the painter labour'd with his skill
To hide deceit, and give the harmless shew;
An humble gait, calm looks, eyes wailing still,
A brow unbent that seem'd to welcome woe;
Cheeks neither red nor pale, but mingled so
  That blushing red no guilty instance gave,
  Nor ashy pale the fear that false hearts have.

But, like a constant and confirmed devil,
He entertain'd a shew so seeming just,
And therein so ensconc'd his secret evil,
That jealousy itself could not mistrust,
False-creeping craft and perjury should thrust
  Into so bright a day such black-fac'd storms,
  Or blot with hell-born sin such saint-like forms.

The well-skill'd workman this mild image drew
For perjur'd Sinon, whose enchanting story
The credulous old Priam after slew;
Whose words like wild-fire burnt the shining glory
Of rich-built Ilion, that the skies were sorry,
  And little stars shot from their fixed places,
  When their glass fell wherein they view'd their faces.

This picture she advisedly perused,
And chid the painter for his wondrous skill,
Saying, some shape in Sinon's was abused;
So fair a form lodg'd not a mind so ill:
And still on him she gaz'd; and gazing still,
  Such signs of truth in his plain face she spied,
  That she concludes the picture was belied.

"It cannot be," quoth she, "that so much guile"
(She would have said) "can lurk in such a look;"
But Tarquin's shape came in her mind the while,
And from her tongue, 'can lurk' from 'cannot' took;
'It cannot be' she in that sense forsook,
  And turn'd it thus: "It cannot be, I find,
  But such a face should bear a wicked mind:

"For even as subtle Sinon here is painted,
So sober-sad, so weary, and so mild,
(As if with grief or travail he had fainted)
To me came Tarquin armed; so beguil'd
With outward honesty, but yet defil'd
  With inward vice: as Priam him did cherish,
  So did I Tarquin; so my Troy did perish.

"Look, look! how listening Priam wets his eyes,
To see those borrow'd tears that Sinon sheds.
Priam, why art thou old, and yet not wise?
For every tear he falls a Trojan bleeds:
His eye drops fire, no water thence proceeds;
  Those round clear pearls of his, that move thy pity,
  Are balls of quenchless fire to burn thy city.

"Such devils steal effects from lightless hell,
For Sinon in his fire doth quake with cold,
And in that cold, hot-burning fire doth dwell;
These contraries such unity do hold,
Only to flatter fools, and make them bold:
  So Priam's trust false Sinon's tears doth flatter,
  That he finds means to burn his Troy with water."

Here, all enrag'd, such passion her assails,
That patience is quite beaten from her breast.
She tears the senseless Sinon with her nails,
Comparing him to that unhappy guest
Whose deed hath made herself herself detest:
  At last she smilingly with this gives o'er;
  "Fool! fool!" quoth she, "his wounds will not be
    sore."

Thus ebbs and flows the current of her sorrow,
And time doth weary time with her complaining.
She looks for night, and then she longs for morrow,
And both she thinks too long with her remaining.
Short time seems long in sorrow's sharp sustaining:
  Though woe be heavy, yet it seldom sleeps;
  And they that watch see time how slow it creeps.

Which all this time hath overslipp'd her thought,
That she with painted images hath spent,
Being from the feeling of her own grief brought
By deep surmise of others' detriment;
Losing her woes in shows of discontent.
  It easeth some, though none it ever cured,
  To think their dolour others have endured.

But now the mindful messenger, come back;
Brings home his lord and other company,
Who finds his Lucrece clad in mourning black;
And round about her tear-distained eye
Blue circles stream'd, like rainbows in the sky:
  These water-galls in her dim element
  Foretel new storms to those already spent.

Which when her sad-beholding husband saw,
Amazedly in her sad face he stares:
Her eyes, though sod in tears, look'd red and raw;
Her livery colour kill'd with deadly cares.
He hath no power to ask her how she fares;
  Both stood like old acquaintance in a trance,
  Met far from home, wondering each other's chance.

At last he takes her by the bloodless hand,
And thus begins: "What uncouth ill event
Hath thee befall'n, that thou dost trembling stand?
Sweet love, what spire hath thy fair colour spent?
Why art thou thus attir'd in discontent?
  Unmask, dear dear, this moody heaviness,
  And tell thy grief that we may give redress."

Three times with sighs she gives her sorrow fire,
Ere once she can discharge one word of woe:
At length, address'd to answer his desire,
She modestly prepares to let them know
Her honour is ta'en prisoner by the foe;
  While Collatine and his consorted lords
  With sad attention long to hear her words.

And now this pale swan in her watery nest
Begins the sad dirge of her certain ending.
"Few words," quoth she, "shall fit the trespass best,
Where no excuse can give the fault amending:
In me more woes than words are now depending;
  And my laments would be drawn out too long,
  To tell them all with one poor tired tongue.

"Then, be this all the task it hath to say:
Dear husband, in the interest of thy bed
A stranger came, and on that pillow lay
Where thou wast wont to rest thy weary head;
And what wrong else may be imagined
By foul enforcement might be done to me,
From that, alas! thy Lucrece is not free.

"For in the dreadful dead of dark midnight,
With shining falchion in my chamber came
A creeping creature, with a flaming light,
And softly cried, 'Awake, thou Roman dame,
And entertain my love; else lasting shame
On thee and thine this night I will inflict,
If thou my love's desire do contradict.

"'For some hard-favour'd groom of thine,' quoth he,
"Unless thou yoke thy liking to my will,
I'll murther straight, and then I'll slaughter thee,
And swear I found you where you did fulfil
The loathsome act of lust, and so did kill
The lechers in their deed: this act will be
My fame, and thy perpetual infamy.'

"With this I did begin to start and cry,
And then against my heart he set his sword,
Swearing, unless I took all patiently,
I should not live to speak another word;
So should my shame still rest upon record,
And never be forgot in mighty Rome
Th' adulterate death of Lucrece and her groom.

"Mine enemy was strong, my poor self weak,
And far the weaker with so strong a fear:
My bloody judge forbade my tongue to speak;
No rightful plea might plead for justice there:
His scarlet lust came evidence to swear
  That my poor beauty had purloin'd his eyes,
  And when the judge is rob'd, the prisoner dies.

"O, teach me how to make mine own excuse,
Or, at the least, this refuge let me find:
Though my gross blood be stain'd with this abuse,
Immaculate and spotless is my mind;
That was not forc'd; that never was inclin'd
  To accessory yieldings, but still pure
  Doth in her poison'd closet yet endure."

Lo, here the hopeless merchant of this loss,
With head declin'd, and voice damm'd up with woe,
With sad set eyes, and wretched arms across,
From lips new waxen pale begins to blow
The grief away, that stops his answer so;
  But wretched as he is, he strives in vain,
  What he breathes out, his breath drinks up again.

As through an arch the violent roaring tide
Out-runs the eye that doth behold his haste,
Yet in the eddy boundeth in his pride
Back to the strait that forc'd him on so fast,
In rage sent out, recall'd in rage, being past;
  Even so his sighs, his sorrows, make a saw,
  To push grief on, and back the same grief draw.

Which speechless woe of his poor she attendeth,
And his untimely frenzy thus awaketh:
"Dear lord, thy sorrow to my sorrow lendeth
Another power; no flood by raining slaketh.
My woe, too sensible, thy passion maketh
  More feeling painful: let it, then, suffice
  To drown one woe one pair of weeping eyes.

"And for my sake, when I might charm thee so,
For she that was thy Lucrece, now attend me:
Be suddenly revenged on my foe,
Thine, mine, his own: suppose thou dost defend me
From what is past, the help that thou shalt lend me
  Comes all too late, yet let the traitor die;
  For sparing justice feeds iniquity.

"But ere I name him, you fair lords," quoth she,
(Speaking to those that came with Collatine)
"Shall plight your honourable faiths to me,
With swift pursuit to venge this wrong of mine;
For 'tis a meritorious fair design,
  To chase injustice with revengeful arms:
  Knights, by their oaths, should right poor ladies' harms."

At this request, with noble disposition
Each present lord began to promise aid,
As bound in knighthood to her imposition,
Longing to hear the hateful foe bewray'd;
But she, that yet her sad task hath not said,
  The protestation stops. "O, speak," quoth she,
  "How may this forced stain be wip'd from me!

"What is the quality of mine offence,
Being constrain'd with dreadful circumstance?
May my pure mind with the foul act dispense,
My low-declined honour to advance?
May any terms acquit me from this chance?
The poison'd fountain clears itself again,
And why not I from this compelled stain?"

With this, they all at once began to say,
Her body's stain her mind untainted clears;
While with a joyless smile she turns away
The face, that map which deep impression bears
Of hard misfortune, carv'd in it with tears.
"No, no," quoth she; "no dame, hereafter living,
By my excuse shall claim excuse's giving."

Here, with a sigh as if her heart would break,
She throws forth Tarquin's name: "He, he," she says,
But more than "he" her poor tongue could not speak;
Till after many accents and delays,
Untimely breathings, sick and short assays,
She utters this: "He, he, fair lords, 'tis he,
That guides this hand to give this wound to me."

Even here she sheathed in her harmless breast
A harmful knife, that thence her soul unsheathed:
That blow did bail it from the deep unrest
Of that polluted prison where it breathed:
Her contrite sighs unto the clouds bequeathed
Her winged sprite, and through her wounds doth fly
Life's lasting date from cancell'd destiny.

Stone-still, astonish'd with this deadly deed,
Stood Collatine and all his lordly crew;
Till Lucrece' father, that beholds her bleed,
Himself on her self-slaughter'd body threw:
And from the purple fountain Brutus drew
  The murtherous knife, and as it left the place,
  Her blood, in poor revenge, held it in chase;

And bubbling from her breast, it doth divide
In two slow rivers, that the crimson blood
Circles her body in on every side,
Who like a late-sack'd island vastly stood,
Bare and unpeopled, in this fearful flood.
  Some of her blood still pure and red remain'd,
  And some look'd black, and that false Tarquin stain'd.

About the mourning and congealed face
Of that black blood a watery rigol goes,
Which seems to weep upon the tainted place:
And ever since, as pitying Lucrece' woes,
Corrupted blood some watery token shows;
  And blood untainted still doth red abide,
  Blushing at that which is so putrefy'd.

"Daughter, dear daughter!" old Lucretius cries,
"That life was mine, which thou hast here deprived.
If in the child the father's image lies,
Where shall I live, now Lucrece is unlived?
Thou wast not to this end from me derived.
  If children pre-decease progenitors,
  We are their offspring, and they none of ours.

"Poor broken glass, I often did behold
In thy sweet semblance my old age new-born:
But now that fair fresh mirror, dim and old,
Shows me a bare-bon'd death by time out-worn.
O, from thy cheeks my image thou hast torn,
And shiver'd all the beauty of my glass,
That I no more can see what once I was.

"O time, cease thou thy course, and last no longer,
If they surcease to be that should survive.
Shall rotten death make conquest of the stronger,
And leave the faltering feeble souls alive?
The old bees die, the young possess their hive:
Then, live sweet Lucrece; live again, and see
Thy father die, and not thy father thee!"

By this starts Collatine as from a dream,
And bids Lucretius give his sorrow place;
And then in key-cold Lucrece' bleeding stream
He falls, and bathes the pale fear in his face,
And counterfeits to die with her a space;
Till manly shame bids him possess his breath,
And live to be revenged on her death.

The deep vexation of his inward soul
Hath serv'd a dumb arrest upon his tongue;
Who, mad that sorrow should his use control,
Or keep him from heart-easing words so long,
Begins to talk; but through his lips do throng
Weak words, so thick come in his poor heart's aid,
That no man could distinguish what he said.

Yet sometime Tarquin was pronounced plain,
But through his teeth, as if the name he tore.
This windy tempest, till it blow up rain,
Held back his sorrow's tide to make it more;
At last it rains, and busy winds give o'er:
  Then, son and father weep with equal strife,
  Who should weep most, for daughter or for wife.

The one doth call her his, the other his,
Yet neither may possess the claim they lay.
The father says, "She's mine:" "O, mine she is,"
Replies her husband: "Do not take away
My sorrow's interest; let no mourner say
  He weeps for her, for she was only mine,
  And only must be wail'd by Collatine."

"O," quoth Lucretius, "I did give that life,
Which she too early and too late hath spill'd."
"Woe, woe!" quoth Collatine, "she was my wife,
I ow'd her, and 'tis mine that she hath kill'd."
"My daughter" and "my wife" with clamours fill'd
  The dispers'd air, who holding Lucrece' life,
  Answer'd their cries, "my daughter and my wife."

Brutus, who pluck'd the knife from Lucrece' side,
Seeing such emulation in their woe,
Began to clothe his wit in state and pride,
Burying in Lucrece' wound his folly's shew.
He with the Romans was esteemed so
  As silly jeering idiots are with kings,
  For sportive words, and uttering foolish things:

But now he throws that shallow habit by,
Wherein deep policy did him disguise,
And arm'd his long-hid wits advisedly,
To check the tears in Collatinus' eyes.
"Thou wronged lord of Rome," quoth he, "arise :
Let my unsounded self, suppos'd a fool,
Now set thy long-experienc'd wit to school.

"Why, Collatine, is woe the cure for woe?
Do wounds help wounds, or grief help grievous deeds?
Is it revenge to give thyself a blow,
For his foul act by whom thy fair wife bleeds?
Such childish humour from weak minds proceeds;
Thy wretched wife mistook the matter so,
To slay herself that should have slain her foe.

"Courageous Roman, do not steep thy heart
In such relenting dew of lamentations,
But kneel with me, and help to bear thy part,
To rouse our Roman gods with invocations,
That they will suffer these abominations,
Since Rome herself in them doth stand disgraced,
By our strong arms from forth her fair streets chased.

"Now, by the Capitol that we adore,
And by this chaste blood so unjustly stained,
By heaven's fair sun that breeds the fat earth's store,
By all our country rights in Rome maintained,
And by chaste Lucrece' soul, that late complained
Her wrongs to us, and by this bloody knife,
We will revenge the death of this true wife."

This said, he struck his hand upon his breast,
And kiss'd the fatal knife to end his vow;
And to his protestation urg'd the rest,
Who, wondering at him, did his words allow:
Then, jointly to the ground their knees they bow,
  And that deep vow which Brutus made before,
  He doth again repeat, and that they swore.

When they had sworn to this advised doom,
They did conclude to bear dead Lucrece thence;
To shew her bleeding body thorough Rome,
And so to publish Tarquin's foul offence:
Which being done with speedy diligence,
  The Romans plausibly did give consent
  To Tarquin's everlasting banishment.

NOTES ON LUCRECE.

p. 54. "*Suggested* this proud issue," &c.: — i. e., instigated, tempted.

p. 57. "*Intending* weariness": — i. e., pretending weariness.

" "*And every one to rest,*" &c.: — Some copies of the edition of 1594 read in this passage, —

> "And every one to rest *himself betakes,*
> Save thieves, and cares, and troubled minds that wakes."

In either case there is a lack of grammatical accord.

p. 59. "Doth *too-too* oft," &c.: — See the Note on "O that this too, too solid flesh would melt," *Hamlet*, Act I. Sc. 2.

p. 60. "—— soft *fancy's* slave": — i. e., soft love's slave.

p. 61. "Shall by a *painted-cloth*": — i. e., painted hangings. See the Note on "I answer you right painted cloth," *As You Like It*, Act III. Sc. 2.

p. 64. "—— the *needle* his finger pricks": — Here 'needle' is a monosyllable.

p. 65. "And give the *sneaped* birds": — i. e., the nipped birds — birds nipped by the early frosts.

p. 69. "Beating her *bulk*": — i. e., her breast. So in *Hamlet*, Act II. Sc. 1, "a sigh that seemed to shatter all his bulk."

p. 72. "—— under the *gripe's* sharp claws": — i. e., the vulture's sharp claws.

p. 73. "Yet, foul night-*waking* cat": — Surely we have here a slight misprint for "night-*walking*." The author did not mean to accuse Tarquin of caterwauling.

" "*Mend* thy ill aim": — The old copies, "*End* thy ill aim," which has been hitherto accepted without a question; but surely there can be no doubt as to the reading of the text.

p. 73. "—— as thou hast *pretended*": — i. e., as thou hast intended. See the second Note upon this poem.

p. 81. "Ere he *arrive his* weary noon-tide prick": — i. e. arrive at his weary, &c. See a few stanzas below, "Why should the worm intrude the maiden bud?"

" "And let thy *misty* vapours": — The edition of 1594 misprints "*musty* vapours." Subsequent old editions are correct.

p. 82. "Will *quote* my loathsome trespass," &c.: — i. e., will observe.

p. 86. "—— to *fine* the hate of foes": — i. e., to end the hate, &c.

p. 89. "—— I *force* not argument a straw": — i. e., I care not for argument a straw.

p. 93. "While thou on *Tereus* descant'st": — See the Note on "some Tereus hath defloured thee," *Titus Andronicus*, Act II. Sc. 5.

p. 96. "Thou, Collatine, shalt *oversee this will*": — In the time of Shakespeare, says Mr. Collier, it was usual for testators to appoint not only executors, but *overseers* of their wills. Such was the case with our poet, when he named John Hall and his daughter Susanna executors, and Thomas Russell and Francis Collins overseers of his last will and testament.

p. 98. "—— O, let it not be *hild*": — i. e., be held. The old spelling is retained for the sake of the rhyme. The word was spelled both *held* and *hild*, regardless of rhyme.

p. 103. "—— which *purl'd* up to the sky": — Query, which *curl'd* up to the sky.

" "—— all *boll'n* and red": — i. e., all swollen and red. In reading this description, it must be remembered that the poet had in mind the stiff drawing, confused grouping, and perspectiveless composition of old tapestries and illuminations.

p. 104. "—— and *than*": — i. e., and then.

" "—— where all distress is *steld*": — So in the twenty-fourth Sonnet: —

"Mine eye hath play'd the painter, and hath steel'd
Thy beauty's form in table of my heart."

No explanation of these passages has yet been given, except that of Mr. Collier, who supposes that steel'd "meant engraved as with steel." I am inclined to the opinion that in both instances the word is 'stiled' or 'styled' (from *stylus*) = written, drawn. See the Note on "My tables," &c., *Hamlet*, Act I. Sc. 5. 'Stile' seems to have been pronounced *steel* in Shakespeare's early years, if not afterwards.

p. 105. "And with my *knife*" :—It was not uncommon in Shakespeare's time for ladies to carry knives and daggers.

p. 106. "—— of many *mo*" :—'Mo' was a common form of 'more.'

" "Once set *on ringing*" :—i. e., a ringing, or, in the abominable neologism of the day, being rung. In the second line below, "a work" is a mere abbreviation of 'on work.'

p. 108. "—— so beguil'd" :—The old copy, "*to* beguild." The context sustains Malone's supposition that 'f' was misprinted 't.'

p. 115. "—— a watery *rigol* goes" :—A rigol is a ring, a circle.

p. 116. "Weak words, so *thick* come" :—i. e., so rapidly.

p. 119. "The Romans *plausibly* did give consent" :—i. e., they gave consent with applause.

THE PASSIONATE PILGRIM.

"The Passionate Pilgrime By W. Shakespeare. At London Printed for W. Iaggard, and are to be sold by W. Leake, at the Greyhound in Paules Churchyard. 1599." 16mo. 36 leaves.

"The Passionate Pilgrime. Or Certaine Amorous Sonnets betweene Venus and Adonis, newly corrected and augmented. By W. Shakespere. The third Edition. Where-vnto is newly added two Loue-Epistles; the first from Paris to Hellen, and Hellen's answere backe againe to Paris. Printed by W. Iaggard. 1612." [COLLIER.

THE PASSIONATE PILGRIM.

INTRODUCTION.

THE collection of Sonnets and short poems unaccountably entitled *The Passionate Pilgrim*, seems to have been made up in part of rejected passages of a poem upon the subject of *Venus and Adonis*, in the sonnet stanza. It was published in 1599 by William Jaggard, who was a most untrustworthy person, at least in regard to the representations of his title pages. He made up his books out of such miscellaneous material as he could lay his hands on, and attributed them to the author whose name would command the readiest sale. Some of the pieces in the following collection were almost surely not written by Shakespeare; others bear unmistakable marks of his hand. Two Sonnets which made a part of Jaggard's book were also printed in the edition of the Sonnets which appeared in 1609; and as they are of course given in this work in their place in the latter collection (Nos. CXXXVIII. and CXLIV.,) they are omitted from the immediately ensuing pages. Three other pieces, which are found in *Love's Labour's Lost*, are also here omitted. The order of the poems in this edition is that in which they were first published, allowance being made for omissions.

THE PASSIONATE PILGRIM.

I.

SWEET Cytherea, sitting by a brook,
With young Adonis, lovely, fresh, and green,
Did court the lad with many a lovely look,
Such looks as none could look but beauty's queen.
She told him stories to delight his ear;
She shew'd him favours to allure his eye;
To win his heart, she touch'd him here and there:
Touches so soft still conquer chastity.
But whether unripe years did want conceit,
Or he refused to take her figur'd proffer,
The tender nibbler would not touch the bait,
But smile and jest at every gentle offer:
Then fell she on her back, fair queen, and toward;
He rose and ran away; — ah, fool too froward!

II.

Scarce had the sun dried up the dewy morn,
And scarce the herd gone to the hedge for shade,
When Cytherea, all in love forlorn,
A longing tarriance for Adonis made,
Under an osier growing by a brook,
A brook, where Adon us'd to cool his spleen.
Hot was the day; she hotter that did look
For his approach, that often there had been.
Anon he comes, and throws his mantle by,

And stood stark naked on the brook's green brim;
The sun look'd on the world with glorious eye,
Yet not so wistly as this queen on him:
  He, spying her, bounc'd in, whereas he stood;
  "O Jove," quoth she, "why was not I a flood?"

III.

Fair is my love, but not so fair as fickle,
Mild as a dove, but neither true nor trusty;
Brighter than glass, and yet, as glass is, brittle,
Softer than wax, and yet, as iron, rusty:
  A lily pale, with damask dye to grace her,
  None fairer, nor none falser to deface her.

Her lips to mine how often hath she join'd,
Between each kiss her oaths of true love swearing!
How many tales to please me hath she coin'd,
Dreading my love, the loss thereof still fearing!
  Yet in the midst of all her pure protestings,
  Her faith, her oaths, her tears and all were jestings.

She burn'd with love, as straw with fire flameth,
She burn'd out love, as soon as straw out burneth;
She fram'd the love, and yet she foil'd the framing,
She bade love last, and yet she fell a-turning.
  Was this a lover, or a lecher whether?
  Bad in the best, though excellent in neither.

IV.

If music and sweet poetry agree,
As they must needs, the sister and the brother,
Then must the love be great 'twixt thee and me,
Because thou lov'st the one, and I the other.
Dowland to thee is dear, whose heavenly touch
Upon the lute doth ravish human sense;

Spenser to me, whose deep conceit is such,
As passing all conceit, needs no defence.
Thou lov'st to hear the sweet melodious sound,
That Phœbus' lute, the queen of music, makes;
And I in deep delight am chiefly drown'd,
Whenas himself to singing he betakes.
  One god is god of both, as poets feign;
  One knight loves both, and both in thee remain.

V.

Fair was the morn, when the fair queen of love,

. . . . .

Paler for sorrow than her milk-white dove,
For Adon's sake, a youngster proud and wild;
Her stand she takes upon a steep-up hill:
Anon Adonis comes with horn and hounds;
She, silly queen, with more than love's good will,
Forbade the boy he should not pass those grounds;
"Once," quoth she, "did I see a fair sweet youth
Here in these brakes deep-wounded with a boar,
Deep in the thigh, a spectacle of ruth!
See in my thigh," quoth she, "here was the sore:"
  She shewed hers; he saw more wounds than one,
  And blushing fled, and left her all alone.

VI.

Sweet rose, fair flower, untimely pluck'd, soon vaded,
Pluck'd in the bud, and vaded in the spring!
Bright orient pearl, alack! too timely shaded!
Fair creature, kill'd too soon by death's sharp sting!
  Like a green plum that hangs upon a tree,
  And falls, through wind, before the fall should be.

I weep for thee, and yet no cause I have;
For why? thou left'st me nothing in thy will.

And yet thou left'st me more than I did crave;
For why? I craved nothing of thee still:
  O, yes, dear friend, I pardon crave of thee;
  Thy discontent thou didst bequeath to me.

VII.

Venus, with [young] Adonis sitting by her,
Under a myrtle shade, began to woo him;
She told the youngling how god Mars did try her,
And as he fell to her, [so] fell she to him.
"Even thus," quoth she, "the warlike god embrac'd
        me;"
And then she clipp'd Adonis in her arms:
"Even thus," quoth she, "the warlike god unlac'd
        me;"
As if the boy should use like loving charms.
"Even thus," quoth she, "he seiz'd on my lips,"
And with her lips on his did act the seizure;
But as she fetched breath, away he skips,
And would not take her meaning nor her pleasure.
  Ah! that I had my lady at this bay,
  To kiss and clip me till I run away!

VIII.

Crabbed age and youth
  Cannot live together;
Youth is full of pleasance,
  Age is full of care:
Youth like summer morn,
  Age like winter weather;
Youth like summer brave,
  Age like winter bare.
Youth is full of sport,
Age's breath is short;

Youth is nimble, age is lame;
Youth is hot and bold,
Age is weak and cold;
Youth is wild, and age is tame.
Age, I do abhor thee,
Youth, I do adore thee;
O, my love, my love is young!
Age, I do defy thee;
O sweet shepherd, hie thee,
For methinks thou stay'st too long!

IX.

Beauty is but a vain and doubtful good,
A shining gloss, that vadeth suddenly;
A flower that dies, when first it 'gins to bud;
A brittle glass, that's broken presently:
A doubtful good, a gloss, a glass, a flower,
Lost, vaded, broken, dead within an hour.

And as goods lost are seld or never found,
As vaded gloss no rubbing will refresh,
As flowers dead lie wither'd on the ground,
As broken glass no cement can redress,
So beauty blemish'd once for ever's lost,
In spite of physic, painting, pain, and cost.

X.

Good night, good rest. Ah, neither be my share!
She bade good night, that kept my rest away:
And daff'd me to a cabin hang'd with care,
To descant on the doubts of my decay.
"Farewell," quoth she, "and come again to-morrow;"
Fare well I could not, for I supp'd with sorrow.

Yet at my parting sweetly did she smile,
In scorn or friendship, nill I construe whether:
'T may be, she joy'd to jest at my exile,
'T may be, again to make me wander thither:
 'Wander,' a word for shadows like myself,
 As take the pain, but cannot pluck the pelf.

XI.

Lord, how mine eyes throw gazes to the East!
My heart doth charge the watch; the morning rise
Doth cite each moving sense from idle rest.
Not daring trust the office of mine eyes,
 While Philomela sits and sings, I sit and mark,
 And wish her lays were tuned like the lark;

For she doth welcome day-light with her ditty,
And drives away dark dismal-dreaming night:
The night so pack'd, I post unto my pretty;
Heart hath his hope, and eyes their wished sight;
 Sorrow chang'd to solace, solace mix'd with sorrow;
 For why? she sigh'd, and bade me come to-morrow.

Were I with her, the night would post too soon;
But now are minutes added to the hours;
To spite me now, each minute seems a moon;
Yet not for me, shine, sun, to succour flowers.
 Pack, night; peep, day; good day, of night now borrow;
 Short, night, to-night, and length thyself to-morrow.

XII.

It was a lording's daughter, the fairest one of three,
That liked of her master as well as well might be,

Till looking on an Englishman, the fair'st that eye could see,
  Her fancy fell a-turning.
Long was the combat doubtful, that love with love did fight,
To leave the master loveless, or kill the gallant knight:
To put in practice either, alas, it was a spite
  Unto the silly damsel.
But one must be refused, more mickle was the pain,
That nothing could be used, to turn them both to gain,
For of the two the trusty knight was wounded with disdain:
  Alas, she could not help it!
Thus art, with arms contending, was victor of the day,
Which by a gift of learning did bear the maid away;
Then lullaby, the learned man hath got the lady gay;
  For now my song is ended.

XIII.

My flocks feed not,
My ewes breed not,
My rams speed not,
  All is amiss:
Love is dying,
Faith 's defying,
Heart 's denying,
  Causer of this.
All my merry jigs are quite forgot,
All my lady's love is lost, God wot:
Where her faith was firmly fix'd in love,
There a nay is plac'd without remove.

One silly cross
Wrought all my loss;
  O frowning Fortune, cursed, fickle dame!
For now I see,
Inconstancy
  More in women than in men remain.

In black mourn I,
All fears scorn I,
Love hath forlorn me,
  Living in thrall:
Heart is bleeding,
All help needing, —
O cruel speeding,
  Fraughted with gall!
My shepherd's pipe can sound no deal,
My wether's bell rings doleful knell;
My curtal dog that wont to have play'd,
Plays not at all, but seems afraid;
With sighs so deep,
Procures to weep,
  In howling-wise, to see my doleful plight.
How sighs resound
Through heartless ground,
  Like a thousand vanquish'd men in bloody fight!

Clear wells spring not,
Sweet birds sing not,
Green plants bring not
  Forth their dye;
Herds stand weeping,
Flocks all sleeping,
Nymphs back peeping
  Fearfully.

All our pleasure known to us poor swains,
All our merry meetings on the plains,
All our evening sport from us is fled,
All our love is lost, for love is dead.
Farewell, sweet lass,
Thy like ne'er was
  For a sweet content, the cause of all my moan:
Poor Corydon
Must live alone;
  Other help for him I see that there is none.

XIV.

Whenas thine eye hath chose the dame,
And stall'd the deer that thou should'st strike,
Let reason rule things worthy blame,
As well as fancy's partial might:
  Take counsel of some wiser head,
  Neither too young, nor yet unwed.

And when thou com'st thy tale to tell,
Smooth not thy tongue with filed talk,
Lest she some subtle practice smell;
(A cripple soon can find a halt:)
  But plainly say thou lov'st her well,
  And set her person forth to sell.

What though her frowning brows be bent,
Her cloudy looks will calm ere night;
And then too late she will repent,
That thus dissembled her delight;
  And twice desire, ere it be day,
  That which with scorn she put away.

What though she strive to try her strength,
And ban and brawl, and say thee nay,

Her feeble force will yield at length,
When craft hath taught her thus to say:
  "Had women been so strong as men,
  In faith you had not had it then."

And to her will frame all thy ways;
Spare not to spend, — and chiefly there
Where thy desert may merit praise,
By ringing in thy lady's ear:
  The strongest castle, tower, and town,
  The golden bullet beats it down.

Serve always with assured trust,
And in thy suit be humble, true;
Unless thy lady prove unjust,
Press never thou to choose anew:
  When time shall serve, be thou not slack
  To proffer, though she put thee back.

The wiles and guiles that women work,
Dissembled with an outward shew,
The tricks and toys that in them lurk,
The cock that treads them shall not know.
  Have you not heard it said full oft,
  A woman's nay doth stand for naught?

Think women seek to strive with men,
To sin, and never for to saint:
Here is no heaven: be holy then,
When time with age shall thee attaint.
  Were kisses all the joys in bed,
  One woman would another wed.

But soft; enough, — too much I fear,
Lest that my mistress hear my song;

She'll not stick to round me i' th' ear,
To teach my tongue to be so long:
  Yet will she blush, here be it said,
  To hear her secrets so bewray'd.

XV.

As it fell upon a day,
In the merry month of May,
Sitting in a pleasant shade
Which a grove of myrtles made,
Beasts did leap, and birds did sing,
Trees did grow, and plants did spring:
Every thing did banish moan,
Save the nightingale alone:
She, poor bird, as all forlorn,
Lean'd her breast up-till a thorn,
And there sung the dolefull'st ditty,
That to hear it was great pity:
Fie, fie, fie, now would she cry,
Teru, Teru, by and by:
That to hear her so complain,
Scarce I could from tears refrain;
For her griefs, so lively shewn,
Made me think upon mine own.
Ah! (thought I) thou mourn'st in vain;
None take pity on thy pain:
Senseless trees, they cannot hear thee;
Ruthless beasts, they will not cheer thee.
King Pandion, he is dead;
All thy friends are lapp'd in lead:
All thy fellow birds do sing,
Careless of thy sorrowing.
[Even so, poor bird, like thee,
None alive will pity me.]
Whilst as fickle fortune smil'd,

Thou and I were both beguil'd.
Every one that flatters thee,
Is no friend in misery.
Words are easy like the wind;
Faithful friends are hard to find.
Every man will be thy friend,
Whilst thou hast wherewith to spend;
But if store of crowns be scant,
No man will supply thy want.
If that one be prodigal,
Bountiful they will him call:
And with such like flattering,
'Pity but he were a king.'
If he be addict to vice,
Quickly him they will entice;
If to women he be bent,
They have him at commandement;
But if fortune once do frown,
Then farewell his great renown:
They that fawn'd on him before,
Use his company no more.
He that is thy friend indeed,
He will help thee in thy need.
If thou sorrow, he will weep;
If thou wake, he cannot sleep:
Thus of every grief in heart
He with thee doth bear a part.
These are certain signs to know
Faithful friend from flattering foe.

NOTES ON THE PASSIONATE PILGRIM.

III.

p. 130. "—— as glass is, *brittle*" : — Perhaps, for the rhyme, we should read '*brickle*,' which was a common form of 'brittle.' So "While *brickle* houre-glasse," &c., *Arcadia*, Book 2, p. 209, Ed. 1605. But *t* and *k* have a tendency to pass into each other. So for 'letters of marque' we have "letters of *mart*," and for 'mate,' "*make*."

"—— with fire *flameth*" : — Perhaps the author wrote "with fire *flaming*," by which the rhyme would be preserved. But the whole stanza is very imperfect in this respect.

V.

p. 131. The second line of this sonnet is lost.

VII.

p. 132. This sonnet appears, with some important variations, in Griffin's *Fidessa*, &c., published in 1596. I believe it, however, to be Shakespeare's.

" "Venus, with [*young*] Adonis" : — So the text in *Fidessa*. *The Passionate Pilgrim* omits "young."

" "—— *so fell she to him*" : — So in *Fidessa*. *The Passionate Pilgrim* has, "*she fell to him*," which the rhyme shows to be wrong.

" "*But* as she fetched breath" : — The old copy, "*And*, as," &c. — an obvious error, caused by the 'Ands' above and below.

IX.

p. 133. "—— that's broken *presently*" : — i. e., at the present, the instant, instantly.

XI.

p. 134. "—— each minute seems *a moon*":—The old copy, "seems *an hour*." The correction, which is indicated and supported by the rhyme, was made by Steevens.

XIII.

p. 135. This poem was printed in Weelke's *Madrigals*, 1597, and in *England's Helicon*, 1600, with the signature *Ignoto*. It is most probably not Shakespeare.

" "Love is *dying*":—So *The Passionate Pilgrim; England's Helicon*, "Love *is denying*." In the next line but one below, that version has, "Heart's *renying*."

p. 136. "*With* sighs so deep":—In Weelke's *Madrigals*, "*My* sighs," &c.

p. 137. "Farewell, sweet *lass*":—So in Weelke's *Madrigals*; the other versions, "sweet *loue*."

" "—— the cause of all my *moan*":—So in *England's Helicon*; in *The Passionate Pilgrim*, "my *woe*."

XIV.

" "As well as *fancy's partial might*":—In *The Passionate Pilgrim*, "As well as *fancy party all* might." For the change of 'fancy' to 'fancy's' I am responsible. In an old MS. copy of this poem collated by Mr. Collier, this line stands, "As well as *partial fancy like*," which Mr. Dyce prefers. I admit that I cannot understand it. That there is mere assonance, but not rhyme, between the second and fourth lines of this poem, is of small importance.

" "And set *her person forth to sell*":—i. e., praise her person highly, as a salesman praises his wares. So in *Troilus and Cressida*, "Well but commend what we intend to sell," and in Sonnet XXI., "I will not praise that purpose not to sell." All modern editions hitherto have adopted a very absurd reading, "And set *thy* person forth to sell," found by Malone in a MS. copy of the poem.

p. 138. "*Think women seek to strive*," &c.:—The first four lines of this stanza are corrupted in the old copies, which read thus unintelligibly:—

"Think women *still* to striue with men
To sinne and neuer for to saint;
There is no heauen *by* holy then
When time with age shall *them* attaint."

The following is the reading of the MS. version used by Malone: —

"Think women *love* to *match* with men,
And not to live so like a saint:
Here is no heaven; *they* holy then
Begin, when age *doth* them attaint."

This MS. version has no authority; and the reading which it furnishes, at so very great a variation from the old printed text, seems to me far inferior to that which is attained by the comparatively slight correction that I have made.

XV.

p. 139. An imperfect copy of this poem was published in R. Barnefield's *Encomion of Lady Pecunia*, 1598. It also appeared in *England's Helicon*, 1600, signed "Ignoto." Perhaps it was Barnefield's, — hardly Shakespeare's. From "Whilst as fickle Fortune smil'd," &c., is found only in *The Passionate Pilgrim*.

" "Ruthless *beasts*": — The old copy, with manifest error, "ruthlesse *bears*."

" "[*Even so, poor bird*," &c.: — This and the following line close the poem in *England's Helicon*. They are omitted in *The Passionate Pilgrim*.

p. 140. "They have him at *commandement*": — *Commandement* is here a quadrisyllable. See the Note on "Be valued against your wife's commandment," Vol. IV. p. 260.

SONNETS.

"SHAKE-SPEARE'S SONNETS. Neuer before Imprinted. At London By *G. Eld*, for *T. T.* and are to be solde by *William Aspley*. 1609." 4to. 40 leaves.

The same. By the same, "and are to be solde by *Iohn Wright*, dwelling at Christ Church gate. 1609."

"A Louer's complaint. By William Shake-speare," is printed at the end of this volume, of which it makes eleven pages.

SONNETS.

INTRODUCTION.

SHAKESPEARE'S Sonnets were first printed in 1609 in a small quarto volume, the publisher of which dedicated them to a Mr. W. H., whom he styles their "only begetter." They, or some of them, or possibly some others of Shakespeare's writing, are mentioned in Meres's *Palladis Tamia*, (which appeared in 1598,) in company with their author's *Venus and Adonis* and *Lucrece*, as "his sugred sonnets among his private friends." In only three of them, those numbered 111, 135, and 136, is he unmistakably speaking in his own person, though the first of these seems clearly connected in spirit with its predecessor. As to the motives of the rest we have only that kind of internal evidence which addresses itself to the judgment of the individual reader. They may, or they may not, have been the direct and deliberate expressions of his own feeling; and some of them, as, for instance, the first seventeen, with which the succeeding five seem to be intimately connected, are of such a nature that it is difficult to conjecture why they should have been written by any man. This is all that we know about a collection of more than two thousand verses, second only in importance and in interest to the best dramatic productions of their author.

Conjecture has long been busy to discover the purpose of these sonnets, and the person or persons to whom they were addressed. Farmer thought, or, rather, guessed, that they were written to William Hart, the poet's nephew; Tyrwhitt suggested that the line —

"A man in hue, all *Hewes* in his controlling" —

in the twentieth sonnet, indicates William Hughes, or Hews, as their subject; George Chalmers argued that the recipient of the impassioned adulation which pervades so many of them was no other than the virgin Queen Elizabeth herself! Dr. Drake supposed that in "W. H." we have the transposed initials of Henry Wriothesly, Earl of Southampton; and lastly, Mr. Boaden brought forward William Herbert, Earl of Pembroke, as the beautiful youth, the dearly loved false friend, whose reluctance to marry, and whose readiness to love lightly the wanton and alluring woman whom the poet loved so deeply, were the occasion of these mysterious and impressive poems.*

Of these hypotheses, the latter, which alone is worthy of serious consideration, was adopted by Mr. Armitage Brown, and very minutely worked out in his book entitled *Shakespeare's Autobiographical Poems.* Mr. Brown thinks that Shakespeare used the sonnet form merely as a stanza, and that all his sonnets, exclusive of the last two, (which manifestly have no connection with any others,) were written as six consecutive poems. He thus divides them, and designates their subjects: —

First Poem. Sonnets 1 to 26. *To his friend, persuading him to marry.*

Second Poem. Sonnets 27 to 55. *To his friend, forgiving him for having robbed him of his mistress.*

Third Poem. Sonnets 56 to 77. *To his friend, complaining of his coldness, and warning him of life's decay.*

Fourth Poem. Sonnets 78 to 101. *To his friend, complaining that he prefers another poet's praises, and reproving him for faults that may injure his character.*

Fifth Poem. Sonnets 102 to 126. *To his friend, excusing himself for having been some time silent, and disclaiming the charge of inconstancy.*

Sixth Poem. Sonnets 127 to 152. *To his mistress, on her infidelity.*

These divisions are merely arbitrary; and all the author's ingenuity has failed to convince me either that the limits which he has drawn exist otherwise than in his imagination, or that the sonnets within those limits are consecutively interdependent. He himself admits that in the sixth poem or division the order of the stanzas or sonnets is confused in the edition of 1609

* A profound German, Herr Barnstorff, and an acute Frenchman, Monsieur Philarete Chasles, have conceived, and even printed, and men of Shakespeare's race have actually discussed, theories upon this subject which I thus allude to only lest some reader might otherwise suppose that they had escaped my notice.

— the only one of even quasi authority. That many of the sonnets which were printed together are upon the same subject, or have some connection with each other, is clear enough; but, excepting the first seventeen, (all of which urge a very young man to marry,) continuity of purpose is rarely traceable through more than half a dozen of them in the order in which they were first given to the world. In my opinion they were printed in the first edition much in the sequence in which they were gathered together, with little attention to systematic arrangement; and the consequence is a distracting, and, most probably, a remediless confusion after the twenty-second sonnet, even as to those which have manifestly some connection with each other.

The Mr. W. H., to whom these poems are dedicated as their only begetter, could not have been so designated because they were all addressed to him, or because he alone was in any sense their subject or their object. For some of them are addressed to a woman, others to a lad, others to a man; in three Shakespeare speaks unmistakably for himself, and upon subjects purely personal; and the last two are mere fanciful and independent productions. But though it is thus manifest that no one man could have been the only inspirer or occasion of all these sonnets, yet Mr. W. H. could easily have been their only procurer for the purposes of publication, and thus have performed an office which Thomas Thorpe might well have acknowledged by something more substantial than the barren wish which has proved such a riddle to after generations. It is true that two hundred and fifty years ago the word 'beget' was restricted, as it is now, to the expression of the idea of procreation. But this dedication is not written in the common phraseology of its period; it is throughout a piece of affectation and elaborate quaintness, in which the then antiquated prefix 'be' might be expected to occur; 'beget' being used for 'get,' as Wiclif uses 'betook' for 'took' in Mark xv. 1 — "And ledden him and betoken him to Pilat."

Mr. Dyce was the first, I believe, to advance the opinion that most of these sonnets were composed "in an assumed character on different subjects, and at different times." * This supposition is in accordance with the custom of Shakespeare's day for poets to write songs and sonnets for the use of those who could not

* In his Memoir of Shakespeare prefixed to Pickering's edition of the Poems.

write verse themselves. Sometimes this was done for friendship's sake, sometimes for money, and often for the mere pleasure of both parties. That Shakespeare, who had such facility with his pen, and who seems to have been so obliging and so sociable, and whom we know to have been so thrifty, should not have had occasion to conform to this literary custom of his time, would have been hardly credible, even without that singularly phrased testimony of Francis Meres, "his sugred sonnets *among his private friends*." By these words Meres seems to point directly to such an origin for at least some sonnets which Shakespeare had written before 1598. But were the sonnets to which Meres refers those which have come down to us? For unless we can regard the sonnets which were published in 1609, and which are all of Shakespeare's that are known to exist, as mere fanciful exercises in poetry, we must ask, Would Shakespeare, or the man for whom he wrote, have shown about among his friends these evidences of so profound an emotion, these witnesses of an internal struggle that went near to shatter his whole being? I confess that I can neither believe that he would, nor quite accept, as I once did, the alternative. It is, however, to be observed, that Shakespeare, who so carefully published his *Venus and Adonis* and his *Lucrece*, and who looked so sharply after his interests, did not publish his sonnets, although he must have known how eagerly they would have been sought by the public — a fact which favors the supposition that they, like the plays, had been sold, and were not properly under his control. On the other hand, the fact that he for whom the sonnets speak is described as one who knows his "years be past the best," as "beaten and chopped with tanned antiquity," and as having "travelled on to age's sleepy night," which I was once inclined to regard as evidence that Shakespeare could not have written them in his own person, because in 1598 he was but thirty-four years old, and in 1609 but forty-five, has no such significance. There is evidence enough that in those days a man was called old, and even aged, when he had passed the freshness of his first youth. Even in 1641–2 Sir Simonds D'Ewes, the great authority on precedents of the Long Parliament, and who was its manuscript chronicler, was styled "an ancient gentleman," and he was then but thirty-nine years old. In those days men seem to have shown the marks of age sooner than they do now. They lived harder lives, put less restraint upon their passions, gave emotion freer way, drank more alcohol, went through much wear and tear which the experience of the race has taught us to avoid; and even among the wealthy classes they enjoyed less of those daily household comforts which by affording present ease husband the vital energies.

Five of the sonnets — Nos. 80, 83, 85, 86, and 121 — were evidently written to be presented to some lady who had verses addressed to her by at least one other person than the supposed writer of these; for the praises of another poet are explicitly mentioned in them. No. 78 was addressed to one who was the theme of many pens, for it contains these lines:—

> "So oft I have invoked thee for my muse,
> And found such fair assistance in my verse,
> As every alien pen hath got my use,
> And under thee their poetry disperse.
>
> * * * *
>
> In others' works thou dost but mend the style,
> And arts with thy sweet graces graced be."

These are of the number which Mr. Brown classes as part of the Fourth Poem, the chief subject of which is a complaint by Shakespeare that his friend prefers another poet's praises. But making all allowance for a warmth in the expression of friendship, which, admissible then, would seem ridiculous in our day, I cannot but regard many of the sonnets in this supposed Fourth Poem, and the six above mentioned among them, as addressed to a woman.

A singular and striking feature of these sonnets is the poet's reiteration of the immortality which they secure for their subject. These boasts of giving deathless fame to the subjects of his verse seem inconsistent with the notion of Shakespeare's character which we derive from what we know of him, as well as from what little we are told of him by his contemporaries, — with his indifference to fame, with that modesty, and simplicity, and sweetness which made him beloved even by those who thought themselves his rivals. He might have written thus jestingly; but could he have made such an assertion repeatedly in sad and serious earnest, and in his own person? And if his sonnets were merely complimentary, would he not rather have said that immortality was secured for his verses by their subject?

These poems are peculiar in this respect; and the peculiarity adds to our perplexity in considering the question whether their author wrote them in his own person or in another's.

For whom these sonnets were written, if they were indeed vicarious, it is more difficult to discover, than to whom they were addressed. I have, I confess, no opinion upon the subject which is at all satisfactory to me, or perhaps even worthy of the reader's serious attention. But I have thought that the first seventeen may have been written at the request of a doting mother, who wished to persuade a handsome, wayward son into an early marriage. Why should one man beseech another to take a wife with such tender and impassioned importunity? Why should Shakespeare have entreated a youthful friend, whom he loved with a love passing that of woman, to marry "for love of me"? There seems to be no imaginable reason for seventeen such poetical petitions. But that a mother should be thus solicitous, is not strange, or that she should long to see the beautiful children of her own beautiful offspring. The desire for grandchildren, and the love of them, seem sometimes even stronger than parental yearning. But I hazard this conjecture with little confidence. An obscurity which seems impenetrable has fallen upon the origin of these impressive compositions. Mr. Thomas Thorpe appears in his dedication as the Sphinx of literature; and thus far he has not met his Œdipus.

TO. THE. ONLIE. BEGETTER. OF.
THESE. INSVING. SONNETS.
MR. W. H. ALL. HAPPINESSE.
AND. THAT. ETERNITIE.
PROMISED.
BY.
OUR. EVER-LIVING. POET.
WISHETH.
THE. WELL-WISHING.
ADVENTVRER. IN.
SETTING.
FORTH.

T. T.

SONNETS.

I.

FROM fairest creatures we desire increase,
 That thereby beauty's rose might never die,
But as the riper should by time decease,
His tender heir might bear his memory:
But thou, contracted to thine own bright eyes,
Feed'st thy light's flame with self-substantial fuel,
Making a famine where abundance lies,
Thyself thy foe, to thy sweet self too cruel.
Thou that art now the world's fresh ornament,
And only herald to the gaudy spring,
Within thine own bud buriest thy content,
And, tender churl, mak'st waste in niggarding.
 Pity the world, or else this glutton be,
 To eat the world's due, by the grave and thee.

II.

When forty winters shall besiege thy brow,
And dig deep trenches in thy beauty's field,
Thy youth's proud livery, so gaz'd on now,
Will be a tatter'd weed, of small worth held:
Then, being ask'd where all thy beauty lies,
Where all the treasure of thy lusty days,
To say, within thine own deep-sunken eyes,
Were an all-eating shame, and thriftless praise.
How much more praise deserv'd thy beauty's use,
If thou could'st answer — "This fair child of mine
Shall sum my count, and make my old excuse," —
Proving his beauty by succession thine!
  This were to be new made when thou art old,
  And see thy blood warm when thou feel'st it cold.

III.

Look in thy glass, and tell the face thou viewest,
Now is the time that face should form another;
Whose fresh repair if now thou not renewest,
Thou dost beguile the world, unbless some mother.
For where is she so fair, whose un-ear'd womb
Disdains the tillage of thy husbandry?
Or who is he so fond will be the tomb
Of his self-love, to stop posterity?
Thou art thy mother's glass, and she in thee
Calls back the lovely April of her prime:
So thou through windows of thine age shalt see,
Despite of wrinkles, this thy golden time.
  But if thou live, remember'd not to be,
  Die single, and thine image dies with thee.

IV.

Unthrifty loveliness, why dost thou spend
Upon thyself thy beauty's legacy?
Nature's bequest gives nothing, but doth lend;
And being frank, she lends to those are free.
Then, beauteous niggard, why dost thou abuse
The bounteous largess given thee to give?
Profitless usurer, why dost thou use
So great a sum of sums, yet canst not live?
For, having traffic with thyself alone,
Thou of thyself thy sweet self dost deceive.
Then how, when Nature calls thee to be gone,
What acceptable audit canst thou leave?
  Thy unus'd beauty must be tomb'd with thee,
  Which, us'd, lives th' executor to be.

V.

Those hours, that with gentle work did frame
The lovely gaze where every eye doth dwell,
Wili play the tyrants to the very same,
And that unfair, which fairly doth excel:
For never-resting Time leads Summer on
To hideous Winter, and confounds him there;
Sap check'd with frost, and lusty leaves quite gone,
Beautv o'er-snow'd and bareness every where:
Then, were not Summer's distillation left,
A liquid prisoner pent in walls of glass,
Beauty's effect with beauty were bereft,
Nor it, nor no remembrance what it was:
  But flowers distill'd, though they with Winter meet,
  Leese but their shew; their substance still lives
      sweet.

VI.

Then let not Winter's ragged hand deface
In thee thy Summer, ere thou be distill'd:
Make sweet some phial; treasure thou some place
With beauty's treasure, ere it be self-kill'd.
That use is not forbidden usury,
Which happies those that pay the willing loan;
That's for thyself to breed another thee,
Or ten times happier, be it ten for one:
Ten times thyself were happier than thou art,
If ten of thine ten times refigur'd thee.
Then what could death do if thou should'st depart,
Leaving thee living in posterity?
  Be not self-will'd, for thou art much too fair
  To be death's conquest, and make worms thine heir.

VII.

Lo, in the orient when the gracious light
Lifts up his burning head, each under eye
Doth homage to his new-appearing sight,
Serving with looks his sacred majesty;
And having climb'd the steep-up heavenly hill,
Resembling strong youth in his middle age,
Yet mortal looks adore his beauty still,
Attending on his golden pilgrimage:
But when from high-most pitch with weary car,
Like feeble age, he reeleth from the day,
The eyes, 'fore duteous, now converted are
From his low tract, and look another way.
  So thou, thyself out-going in thy noon,
  Unlook'd on di'st, unless thou get a son.

VIII.

Music to hear, why hear'st thou music sadly?
Sweets with sweets war not, joy delights in joy.
Why lov'st thou that which thou receiv'st not gladly
Or else receiv'st with pleasure thine annoy?
If the true concord of well-tuned sounds,
By unions married, do offend thine ear,
They do but sweetly chide thee, who confounds
In singleness the parts that thou should'st bear.
Mark, how one string, sweet husband to another,
Strikes each in each by mutual ordering;
Resembling sire and child and happy mother,
Who all in one one pleasing note do sing:
  Whose speechless song, being many, seeming one,
  Sings this to thee, — Thou single wilt prove none.

IX.

Is it for fear to wet a widow's eye,
That thou consum'st thyself in single life?
Ah! if thou issueless shalt hap to die,
The world will wail thee, like a makeless wife;
The world will be thy widow, and still weep,
That thou no form of thee hast left behind,
When every private widow well may keep,
By children's eyes, her husband's shape in mind.
Look, what an unthrift in the world doth spend,
Shifts but his place, for still the world enjoys it;
But beauty's waste hath in the world an end,
And, kept unus'd, the user so destroys it.
  No love toward others in that bosom sits,
  That on himself such murtherous shame commits.

X.

For shame! deny that thou bear'st love to any,
Who for thyself art so unprovident.
Grant, if thou wilt, thou art belov'd of many,
But that thou none lov'st is most evident;
For thou art so possess'd with murtherous hate,
That 'gainst thyself thou stick'st not to conspire,
Seeking that beauteous roof to ruinate,
Which to repair should be thy chief desire.
O, change thy thought, that I may change my mind!
Shall hate be fairer lodg'd than gentle love?
Be, as thy presence is, gracious and kind,
Or to thyself, at least, kind-hearted prove:
  Make thee another self, for love of me,
  That beauty still may live in thine or thee.

XI.

As fast as thou shalt wane, so fast thou growest
In one of thine, from that which thou departest;
And that fresh blood which youngly thou bestowest,
Thou may'st call thine, when thou from youth convertest.
Herein lives wisdom, beauty, and increase;
Without this, folly, age, and cold decay:
If all were minded so, the times should cease,
And threescore year would make the world away.
Let those whom Nature hath not made for store,
Harsh, featureless, and rude, barrenly perish:
Look, whom she best endow'd she gave the more;
Which bounteous gift thou should'st in bounty cherish.
  She carv'd thee for her seal, and meant thereby
  Thou should'st print more, not let that copy die.

XII.

When I do count the clock that tells the time,
And see the brave day sunk in hideous night;
When I behold the violet past prime,
And sable curls all silver'd o'er with white;
When lofty trees I see barren of leaves,
Which erst from heat did canopy the herd,
And Summer's green all girded up in sheaves,
Borne on the bier with white and bristly beard;
Then, of thy beauty do I question make,
That thou among the wastes of time must go,
Since sweets and beauties do themselves forsake,
And die as fast as they see others grow;
  And nothing 'gainst Time's scythe can make defence,
  Save breed, to brave him when he takes thee hence.

XIII.

O that you were yourself! but, love, you are
No longer yours than you yourself here live:
Against this coming end you should prepare,
And your sweet semblance to some other give:
So should that beauty which you hold in lease
Find no determination: then you were
Yourself again, after yourself's decease,
When your sweet issue your sweet form should bear.
Who lets so fair a house fall to decay,
Which husbandry in honour might uphold
Against the stormy gusts of Winter's day,
And barren rage of death's eternal cold?
  O, none but unthrifts. — Dear my love, you know,
  You had a father: let your son say so.

XIV.

Not from the stars do I my judgment pluck,
And yet, methinks, I have astronomy,
But not to tell of good, or evil luck,
Of plagues, of dearths, or seasons' quality;
Nor can I fortune to brief minutes tell,
Pointing to each his thunder, rain, and wind;
Or say with princes if it shall go well,
By oft predict that I in heaven find:
But from thine eyes my knowledge I derive,
And, constant stars, in them I read such art,
As truth and beauty shall together thrive,
If from thyself to store thou would'st convert;
  Or else of thee this I prognosticate,
  Thy end is truth's and beauty's doom and date.

XV.

When I consider every thing that grows
Holds in perfection but a little moment;
That this huge stage presenteth naught but shews,
Whereon the stars in secret influence comment;
When I perceive that men as plants increase,
Cheered and check'd even by the selfsame sky,
Vaunt in their youthful sap, at height decrease,
And wear their brave state out of memory;
Then the conceit of this inconstant stay
Sets you most rich in youth before my sight,
Where wasteful time debateth with decay,
To change your day of youth to sulli'd night;
  And, all in war with Time, for love of you,
  As he takes from you, I engraft you new.

XVI.

But wherefore do not you a mightier way
Make war upon this bloody tyrant, Time,
And fortify yourself in your decay
With means more blessed than my barren rhyme?
Now stand you on the top of happy hours,
And many maiden gardens yet unset,
With virtuous wish would bear your living flowers,
Much liker than your painted counterfeit:
So should the lines of life that life repair,
Which this, Time's pencil, or my pupil pen,
Neither in inward worth nor outward fair
Can make you live yourself in eyes of men.
  To give away yourself, keeps yourself still,
  And you must live, drawn by your own sweet skill.

XVII.

Who will believe my verse in time to come,
If it were fill'd with your most high deserts?
Though yet, Heaven knows, it is but as a tomb
Which hides your life, and shews not half your parts.
If I could write the beauty of your eyes,
And in fresh numbers number all your graces,
The age to come would say, 'This poet lies;
Such heavenly touches ne'er touch'd earthly faces.'
So should my papers, yellow'd with their age,
Be scorn'd, like old men of less truth than tongue,
And your true rights be term'd a poet's rage,
And stretched metre of an antique song;
  But were some child of yours alive that time,
  You should live twice — in it, and in my rhyme.

XVIII.

Shall I compare thee to a summer's-day?
Thou art more lovely and more temperate:
Rough winds do shake the darling buds of May,
And Summer's lease hath all too short a date.
Sometime too hot the eye of heaven shines,
And often is his gold complexion dimm'd,
And every fair from fair sometime declines,
By chance, or nature's changing course, untrimm'd;
But thy eternal summer shall not fade,
Nor lose possession of that fair thou owest;
Nor shall death brag thou wander'st in his shade,
When in eternal lines to time thou growest.
  So long as men can breathe, or eyes can see,
  So long lives this, and this gives life to thee.

XIX.

Devouring Time, blunt thou the lion's paws,
And make the earth devour her own sweet brood;
Pluck the keen teeth from the fierce tiger's jaws,
And burn the long-liv'd phœnix in her blood:
Make glad and sorry seasons as thou fleets,
And do whate'er thou wilt, swift-footed Time,
To the wide world and all her fading sweets;
But I forbid thee one most heinous crime:
O, carve not with thy hours my love's fair brow,
Nor draw no lines there with thine antique pen;
Him in thy course untainted do allow,
For beauty's pattern to succeeding men.
  Yet do thy worst, old Time: despite thy wrong,
  My love shall in my verse ever live young.

XX.

A woman's face, with Nature's own hand painted,
Hast thou, the master-mistress of my passion;
A woman's gentle heart, but not acquainted
With shifting change, as is false women's fashion:
An eye more bright than theirs, less false in rolling,
Gilding the object whereupon it gazeth;
A man in hue, all hues in his controlling,
Which steals men's eyes, and women's souls amazeth;
And for a woman wert thou first created;
Till Nature, as she wrought thee, fell a-doting,
And by addition me of thee defeated,
By adding one thing to my purpose nothing.
  But since she prick'd thee out for women's pleasure,
  Mine be thy love, and thy love's use their treasure.

XXI.

So is it not with me, as with that Muse
Stirr'd by a painted beauty to his verse,
Who heaven itself for ornament doth use,
And every fair with his fair doth rehearse;
Making a couplement of proud compare,
With sun and moon, with earth and sea's rich gems,
With April's first-born flowers, and all things rare
That heaven's air in this huge rondure hems.
O, let me, true in love, but truly write;
And then, believe me, my love is as fair
As any mother's child, though not so bright
As those gold candles fix'd in heaven's air:
  Let them say more that like of hear-say well;
  I will not praise, that purpose not to sell.

XXII.

My glass shall not persuade me I am old,
So long as youth and thou are of one date;
But when in thee Time's furrows I behold,
Then look I death my days should expirate;
For all that beauty that doth cover thee
Is but the seemly raiment of my heart,
Which in thy breast doth live, as thine in me.
How can I, then, be elder than thou art?
O, therefore, love, be of thyself so wary,
As I, not for myself, but for thee will,
Bearing thy heart, which I will keep so chary
As tender nurse her babe from faring ill.
  Presume not on thy heart when mine is slain;
  Thou gav'st me thine, not to give back again.

XXIII.

As an unperfect actor on the stage,
Who with his fear is put besides his part,
Or some fierce thing replete with too much rage,
Whose strength's abundance weakens his own heart,
So I, for fear of trust, forget to say
The perfect ceremony of love's rite,
And in mine own love's strength seem to decay,
O'er-charg'd with burthen of mine own love's might.
O, let my books be, then, the eloquence
And dumb presagers of my speaking breast,
Who plead for love, and look for recompense,
More than that tongue that more hath more express'd.
  O, learn to read what silent love hath writ:
  To hear with eyes belongs to love's fine wit.

XXIV.

Mine eye hath play'd the painter, and hath steel'd
Thy beauty's form in table of my heart:
My body is the frame wherein 'tis held,
And perspective it is best painter's art.
For through the painter must you see his skill,
To find where your true image pictur'd lies;
Which in my bosom's shop is hanging still,
That hath his windows glazed with thine eyes.
Now see what good turns eyes for eyes have done:
Mine eyes have drawn thy shape, and thine for me
Are windows to my breast, where-through the sun
Delights to peep, to gaze therein on thee;
  Yet eyes this cunning want to grace their art,
  They draw but what they see, know not the heart.

XXV.

Let those who are in favour with their stars
Of public honour and proud titles boast,
Whilst I, whom fortune of such triumph bars,
Unlook'd for joy in that I honour most.
Great princes' favourites their fair leaves spread
But as the marigold at the sun's eye;
And in themselves their pride lies buried,
For at a frown they in their glory die.
The painful warrior, famoused for worth,
After a thousand victories once foil'd,
Is from the book of honour razed forth,
And all the rest forgot for which he toil'd:
  Then happy I, that love and am belov'd,
  Where I may not remove nor be remov'd.

XXVI.

Lord of my love, to whom in vassalage
Thy merit hath my duty strongly knit,
To thee I send this written embassage,
To witness duty, not to shew my wit:
Duty so great, which wit so poor as mine
May make seem bare, in wanting words to shew it,
But that I hope some good conceit of thine
In thy soul's thought, all naked, will bestow it;
Till whatsoever star that guides my moving,
Points on me graciously with fair aspect,
And puts apparel on my tattered loving,
To shew me worthy of thy sweet respect:
  Then may I dare to boast how I do love thee;
  Till then, not shew my head where thou may'st prove me.

XXVII.

Weary with toil I haste me to my bed,
The dear repose for limbs with travel tired;
But then begins a journey in my head,
To work my mind, when body's work 's expired:
For then my thoughts (from far where I abide)
Intend a zealous pilgrimage to thee,
And keep my drooping eyelids open wide,
Looking on darkness which the blind do see:
Save that my soul's imaginary sight
Presents thy shadow to my sightless view,
Which, like a jewel hung in ghastly night,
Makes black night beauteous, and her old face new
  Lo, thus by day my limbs, by night my mind,
  For thee, and for myself, no quiet find.

XXVIII.

How can I, then, return in happy plight,
That am debarr'd the benefit of rest?
When day's oppression is not eas'd by night,
But day by night, and night by day, oppress'd?
And each, though enemies to either's reign,
Do in consent shake hands to torture me;
The one by toil, the other to complain
How far I toil, still farther off from thee.
I tell the day, to please him thou art bright,
And dost him grace when clouds do blot the heaven:
So flatter I the swart-complexion'd night,
When sparkling stars twire not, thou gild'st the even:
  But day doth daily draw my sorrows longer,
  And night doth nightly make grief's strength seem
      stronger.

XXIX.

When in disgrace with fortune and men's eyes,
I all alone beweep my outcast state,
And trouble deaf Heaven with my bootless cries,
And look upon myself, and curse my fate,
Wishing me like to one more rich in hope,
Featur'd like him, like him with friends possess'd,
Desiring this man's art, and that man's scope,
With what I most enjoy contented least;
Yet in these thoughts myself almost despising,
Haply I think on thee, and then my state
(Like to the lark at break of day arising
From sullen earth) sings hymns at heaven's gate:
  For thy sweet love remember'd such wealth brings,
  That then I scorn to change my state with kings.

XXX.

When to the sessions of sweet silent thought
I summon up remembrance of things past,
I sigh the lack of many a thing I sought,
And with old woes new wail my dear time's waste:
Then can I drown an eye, unus'd to flow,
For precious friends hid in death's dateless night,
And weep afresh love's long-since-cancell'd woe,
And moan th' expense of many a vanish'd sight.
Then can I grieve at grievances fore-gone,
And heavily from woe to woe tell o'er
The sad account of fore-bemoaned moan,
Which I new pay, as if not paid before:
  But if the while I think on thee, dear friend,
  All losses are restor'd, and sorrows end.

XXXI.

Thy bosom is endeared with all hearts,
Which I by lacking have supposed dead,
And there reigns love, and all love's loving parts,
And all those friends which I thought buried.
How many a holy and obsequious tear
Hath dear religious love stol'n from mine eye,
As interest of the dead, which now appear
But things remov'd, that hidden in thee lie!
Thou art the grave where buried love doth live,
Hung with the trophies of my lovers gone,
Who all their parts of me to thee did give;
That due of many now is thine alone:
  Their images I lov'd I view in thee,
  And thou (all they) hast all the all of me.

XXXII.

If thou survive my well-contented day,
When that churl death my bones with dust shall cover,
And shalt by fortune once more re-survey
These poor rude lines of thy deceased lover,
Compare them with the bettering of the time;
And though they be out-stripp'd by every pen,
Reserve them for my love, not for their rhyme,
Exceeded by the height of happier men.
O, then vouchsafe me but this loving thought:
'Had my friend's muse grown with this growing age,
A dearer birth than this his love had brought,
To march in ranks of better equipage:
  But since he died, and poets better prove,
  Theirs for their style I'll read, his for his love.'

XXXIII.

Full many a glorious morning have I seen
Flatter the mountain tops with sovereign eye,
Kissing with golden face the meadows green,
Gilding pale streams with heavenly alchymy;
Anon permit the basest clouds to ride
With ugly rack on his celestial face,
And from the forlorn world his visage hide,
Stealing unseen to West with this disgrace.
Even so my sun one early morn did shine,
With all triumphant splendour on my brow;
But out, alack! he was but one hour mine,
The region cloud hath mask'd him from me now.
  Yet him for this my love no whit disdaineth;
  Suns of the world may stain when heaven's sun staineth.

XXXIV.

Why didst thou promise such a beauteous day,
And make me travel forth without my cloak,
To let base clouds o'ertake me in my way,
Hiding thy bravery in their rotten smoke?
'Tis not enough that through the cloud thou break,
To dry the rain on my storm-beaten face,
For no man well of such a salve can speak,
That heals the wound, and cures not the disgrace:
Nor can thy shame give physic to my grief;
Though thou repent, yet I have still the loss:
Th' offender's sorrow lends but weak relief
To him that bears the strong offence's cross.
  Ah, but those tears are pearl, which thy love sheds,
  And they are rich and ransom all ill deeds.

XXXV.

No more be griev'd at that which thou hast done:
Roses have thorns, and silver fountains mud;
Clouds and eclipses stain both moon and sun,
And loathsome canker lives in sweetest bud.
All men make faults, and even I in this,
Authorizing thy trespass with compare;
Myself corrupting, salving thy amiss,
Excusing thy sins more than thy sins are:
For to thy sensual fault I bring in sense, —
Thy adverse party is thy advocate, —
And 'gainst myself a lawful plea commence.
Such civil war is in my love and hate,
  That I an accessary needs must be
  To that sweet thief which sourly robs from me.

XXXVI.

Let me confess that we two must be twain
Although our undivided loves are one:
So shall those blots that do with me remain,
Without thy help by me be borne alone.
In our two loves there is but one respect,
Though in our lives a separable spite,
Which though it alter not love's sole effect,
Yet doth it steal sweet hours from love's delight.
I may not evermore acknowledge thee,
Lest my bewailed guilt should do thee shame;
Nor thou with public kindness honour me,
Unless thou take that honour from thy name:
  But do not so; I love thee in such sort,
  As, thou being mine, mine is thy good report.

XXXVII.

As a decrepit father takes delight
To see his active child do deeds of youth,
So I, made lame by fortune's dearest spite,
Take all my comfort of thy worth and truth;
For whether beauty, birth, or wealth, or wit,
Or any of these all, or all, or more,
Entitled in thy parts do crowned sit,
I make my love engrafted to this store:
So then I am not lame, poor, nor despis'd,
Whilst that this shadow doth such substance give,
That I in thy abundance am suffic'd,
And by a part of all thy glory live.
  Look what is best, that best I wish in thee:
  This wish I have; then, ten times happy me!

XXXVIII.

How can my Muse want subject to invent,
While thou dost breathe, that pour'st into my verse
Thine own sweet argument, too excellent
For every vulgar paper to rehearse?
O, give thyself the thanks, if aught in me
Worthy perusal stand against thy sight;
For who's so dumb that cannot write to thee,
When thou thyself dost give invention light?
Be thou the tenth muse, ten times more in worth
Than those old nine which rhymers invocate;
And he that calls on thee, let him bring forth
Eternal numbers to out-live long date.
  If my slight muse do please these curious days,
  The pain be mine, but thine shall be the praise.

XXXIX.

O, how thy worth with manners may I sing,
When thou art all the better part of me?
What can mine own praise to mine own self bring?
And what is't but mine own, when I praise thee?
Even for this let us divided live,
And our dear love lose name of single one,
That by this separation I may give
That due to thee which thou deserv'st alone.
O absence, what a torment would'st thou prove,
Were it not thy sour leisure gave sweet leave
To entertain the time with thoughts of love,
Which time and thoughts so sweetly doth deceive,
  And that thou teachest how to make one twain,
  By praising him here, who doth hence remain!

XL.

Take all my loves, my love; yea, take them all:
What hast thou then more than thou had'st before?
No love, my love, that thou may'st true love call:
All mine was thine before thou had'st this more.
Then, if for my love thou my love receivest,
I cannot blame thee for my love thou usest;
But yet be blam'd, if thou thyself deceivest
By wilful taste of what thyself refusest.
I do forgive thy robbery, gentle thief,
Although thou steal thee all my poverty;
And yet love knows it is a greater grief
To bear love's wrong, than hate's known injury.
  Lascivious grace, in whom all ill well shews,
  Kill me with spites; yet we must not be foes.

XLI.

Those pretty wrongs that liberty commits,
When I am sometime absent from thy heart,
Thy beauty and thy years full well befits,
For still temptation follows where thou art.
Gentle thou art, and therefore to be won,
Beauteous thou art, therefore to be assailed;
And when a woman woos, what woman's son
Will sourly leave her till she have prevailed?
Ay me! but yet thou might'st my seat forbear,
And chide thy beauty and thy straying youth,
Who lead thee in their riot even there
Where thou art forc'd to break a two-fold truth;
  Hers, by thy beauty tempting her to thee,
  Thine, by thy beauty being false to me.

XLII.

That thou hast her, it is not all my grief,
And yet it may be said, I lov'd her dearly;
That she hath thee, is of my wailing chief,
A loss in love that touches me more nearly.
Loving offenders, thus I will excuse ye: —
Thou dost love her, because thou know'st I love her;
And for my sake even so doth she abuse me,
Suffering my friend for my sake to approve her.
If I lose thee, my loss is my love's gain,
And losing her, my friend hath found that loss;
Both find each other, and I lose both twain,
And both for my sake lay on me this cross:
  But here's the joy; my friend and I are one.
  Sweet flattery! — then, she loves but me alone.

XLIII.

When most I wink, then do mine eyes best see,
For all the day they view things unrespected;
But when I sleep, in dreams they look on thee,
And, darkly bright, are bright in dark directed.
Then thou, whose shadow shadows doth make bright,
How would thy shadow's form, form happy shew
To the clear day with thy much clearer light,
When to unseeing eyes thy shade shines so?
How would, I say, mine eyes be blessed made
By looking on thee in the living day,
When in dead night thy fair imperfect shade
Through heavy sleep on sightless eyes doth stay?
  All days are nights to see, till I see thee,
  And nights bright days, when dreams do shew thee me.

XLIV.

If the dull substance of my flesh were thought,
Injurious distance should not stop my way;
For then, despite of space, I would be brought
From limits far remote where thou dost stay.
No matter then, although my foot did stand
Upon the farthest earth remov'd from thee;
For nimble thought can jump both sea and land,
As soon as think the place where he would be.
But ah! thought kills me, that I am not thought,
To leap large lengths of miles when thou art gone,
But that, so much of earth and water wrought,
I must attend time's leisure with my moan;
  Receiving naught by elements so slow
  But heavy tears, badges of either's woe.

XLV.

The other two, slight air and purging fire,
Are both with thee, wherever I abide;
The first my thought, the other my desire,
These present-absent with swift motion slide:
For when these quicker elements are gone
In tender embassy of love to thee,
My life, being made of four, with two alone
Sinks down to death, oppress'd with melancholy,
Until life's composition be recured
By those swift messengers return'd from thee,
Who even but now come back again, assured
Of thy fair health, recounting it to me:
  This told, I joy; but then, no longer glad,
  I send them back again, and straight grow sad.

XLVI.

Mine eye and heart are at a mortal war,
How to divide the conquest of thy sight;
Mine eye my heart thy picture's sight would bar,
My heart mine eye the freedom of that right.
My heart doth plead, that thou in him dost lie,
(A closet never pierc'd with crystal eyes,)
But the defendant doth that plea deny,
And says in him thy fair appearance lies.
To 'cide this title is impannelled
A quest of thoughts, all tenants to the heart;
And by their verdict is determined
The clear eye's moiety, and the dear heart's part:
  As thus; mine eye's due is thine outward part,
  And my heart's right thine inward love of heart.

XLVII.

Betwixt mine eye and heart a league is took,
And each doth good turns now unto the other.
When that mine eye is famish'd for a look,
Or heart in love with sighs himself doth smother,
With my love's picture then my eye doth feast,
And to the painted banquet bids my heart:
Another time mine eye is my heart's guest,
And in his thoughts of love doth share a part:
So, either by thy picture or my love,
Thyself away art present still with me;
For thou not farther than my thoughts canst move,
And I am still with them, and they with thee;
  Or, if they sleep, thy picture in my sight
  Awakes my heart to heart's and eye's delight.

XLVIII.

How careful was I, when I took my way,
Each trifle under truest bars to thrust,
That to my use it might unused stay
From hands of falsehood, in sure wards of trust!
But thou, to whom my jewels trifles are,
Most worthy comfort, now my greatest grief,
Thou, best of dearest, and mine only care,
Art left the prey of every vulgar thief.
Thee have I not lock'd up in any chest,
Save where thou art not, though I feel thou art,
Within the gentle closure of my breast,
From whence at pleasure thou may'st come and part;
  And even thence thou wilt be stol'n, I fear,
  For truth proves thievish for a prize so dear.

XLIX.

Against that time, if ever that time come,
When I shall see thee frown on my defects,
Whenas thy love hath cast his utmost sum,
Call'd to that audit by advis'd respects;
Against that time, when thou shalt strangely pass,
And scarcely greet me with that sun, thine eye;
When love, converted from the thing it was,
Shall reasons find of settled gravity;
Against that time do I ensconce me here,
Within the knowledge of mine own desert,
And this my hand against myself uprear,
To guard the lawful reasons on thy part:
  To leave poor me thou hast the strength of laws,
  Since why to love I can allege no cause.

L.

How heavy do I journey on the way,
When what I seek (my weary travel's end)
Doth teach that ease and that repose to say,
"Thus far the miles are measur'd from thy friend!"
The beast that bears me, tired with my woe,
Plods dully on to bear that weight in me,
As if by some instinct the wretch did know
His rider lov'd not speed being made from thee.
The bloody spur cannot provoke him on
That sometimes anger thrusts into his hide,
Which heavily he answers with a groan,
More sharp to me than spurring to his side;
  For that same groan doth put this in my mind,
  My grief lies onward, and my joy behind.

LI.

Thus can my love excuse the slow offence
Of my dull bearer, when from thee I speed:
From where thou art why should I haste me thence?
Till I return, of posting is no need.
O, what excuse will my poor beast then find,
When swift extremity can seem but slow?
Then should I spur, though mounted on the wind;
In winged speed no motion shall I know:
Then can no horse with my desire keep pace;
Therefore desire (of perfect love being made)
Shall neigh (no dull flesh) in his fiery race;
But love, for love, thus shall excuse my jade;
  Since from thee going he went wilful-slow,
  Towards thee I'll run, and give him leave to go.

LII.

So am I as the rich, whose blessed key
Can bring him to his sweet up-locked treasure,
The which he will not every hour survey,
For blunting the fine point of seldom pleasure,
Therefore are feasts so solemn and so rare,
Since, seldom coming, in the long year set
Like stones of worth, they thinly placed are,
Or captain jewels in the carcanet.
So is the time that keeps you as my chest,
Or as the wardrobe which the robe doth hide,
To make some special instant special-blest,
By new unfolding his imprison'd pride.
  Blessed are you, whose worthiness gives scope,
  Being had, to triumph, being lack'd, to hope.

LIII.

What is your substance, whereof are you made,
That millions of strange shadows on you tend?
Since every one hath, every one, one shade,
And you, but one, can every shadow lend.
Describe Adonis, and the counterfeit
Is poorly imitated after you;
On Helen's cheek all art of beauty set,
And you in Grecian tires are painted new:
Speak of the spring, and foison of the year,
The one doth shadow of your beauty shew,
The other as your bounty doth appear;
And you in every blessed shape we know.
  In all external grace you have some part,
  But you like none, none you, for constant heart.

LIV.

O, how much more doth beauty beauteous seem,
By that sweet ornament which truth doth give!
The rose looks fair, but fairer we it deem
For that sweet odour which doth in it live.
The canker-blooms have full as deep a dye
As the perfumed tincture of the roses;
Hang on such thorns, and play as wantonly
When Summer's breath their masked buds discloses;
But, for their virtue only is their shew,
They live unwoo'd, and unrespected fade;
Die to themselves. Sweet roses do not so;
Of their sweet deaths are sweetest odours made:
And so of you, beauteous and lovely youth,
When that shall fade, my verse distils your truth.

LV.

Not marble, nor the gilded monuments
Of princes, shall out-live this powerful rhyme;
But you shall shine more bright in these contents
Than unswept stone, besmear'd with sluttish time.
When wasteful war shall statues overturn,
And broils root out the work of masonry,
Nor Mars his sword, nor war's quick fire shall burn
The living record of your memory.
Gainst death and all-oblivious enmity
Shall you pace forth: your praise shall still find room
Even in the eyes of all posterity,
That wear this world out to the ending doom.
So, till the judgment that yourself arise,
You live in this, and dwell in lovers' eyes.

LVI.

Sweet love, renew thy force; be it not said,
Thy edge should blunter be than appetite,
Which but to-day by feeding is allay'd,
To-morrow sharpen'd in his former might:
So, love, be thou; although to-day thou fill
Thy hungry eyes, even till they wink with fulness,
To-morrow see again, and do not kill
The spirit of love with a perpetual dulness.
Let this sad interim like the ocean be
Which parts the shore, where two contracted new
Come daily to the banks, that, when they see
Return of love, more blest may be the view;
Or call it Winter, which being full of care,
Makes Summer's welcome thrice more wish'd, more rare.

LVII.

Being your slave, what should I do but tend
Upon the hours and times of your desire?
I have no precious time at all to spend,
Nor services to do, till you require.
Nor dare I chide the world-without-end hour,
Whilst I, my sovereign, watch the clock for you,
Nor think the bitterness of absence sour,
When you have bid your servant once adieu:
Nor dare I question with my jealous thought,
Where you may be, or your affairs suppose;
But, like a sad slave, stay and think of naught,
Save where you are, how happy you make those.
So true a fool is love, that in your will
(Though you do any thing) he thinks no ill.

LVIII.

That God forbid, that made me first your slave,
I should in thought control your times of pleasure,
Or at your hand th' account of hours to crave,
Being your vassal, bound to stay your leisure!
O, let me suffer (being at your beck)
Th' imprison'd absence of your liberty;
And patience, tame to sufferance, bide each check,
Without accusing you of injury.
Be where you list; your charter is so strong,
That you yourself may privilege your time
To what you will; to you it doth belong
Yourself to pardon of self-doing crime.
I am to wait, though waiting so be hell,
Not blame your pleasure, be it ill or well.

LIX.

If there be nothing new, but that which is
Hath been before, how are our brains beguil'd,
Which, labouring for invention, bear amiss
The second burthen of a former child?
O that record could, with a backward look,
Even of five hundred courses of the sun,
Shew me your image in some antique book,
Since mind at first in character was done;
That I might see what the old world could say
To this composed wonder of your frame;
Whether we are mended, or whe'r better they,
Or whether revolution be the same.
O, sure I am, the wits of former days
To subjects worse have given admiring praise.

LX.

Like as the waves make towards the pebbled shore,
So do our minutes hasten to their end;
Each changing place with that which goes before,
In sequent toil all forwards do contend.
Nativity, once in the main of light,
Crawls to maturity, wherewith being crown'd,
Crooked eclipses 'gainst his glory fight,
And Time that gave doth now his gift confound.
Time doth transfix the flourish set on youth,
And delves the parallels in beauty's brow;
Feeds on the rarities of Nature's truth,
And nothing stands but for his scythe to mow:
  And yet to times in hope my verse shall stand,
  Praising thy worth, despite his cruel hand.

LXI.

Is it thy will thy image should keep open
My heavy eyelids to the weary night?
Dost thou desire my slumbers should be broken,
While shadows, like to thee, do mock my sight?
Is it thy spirit that thou send'st from thee
So far from home, into my deeds to pry;
To find out shames and idle hours in me,
The scope and tenour of thy jealousy?
O no, thy love, though much, is not so great:
It is my love that keeps mine eye awake;
Mine own true love that doth my rest defeat,
To play the watchman ever for thy sake:
  For thee watch I, whilst thou dost wake elsewhere,
  From me far off, with others all too near.

LXII.

Sin of self-love possesseth all mine eye,
And all my soul, and all my every part;
And for this sin there is no remedy,
It is so grounded inward in my heart.
Methinks no face so gracious is as mine,
No shape so true, no truth of such account;
And for myself mine own worth do define,
As I all other in all worths surmount.
But when my glass shews me myself indeed,
Beaten and chapp'd with tann'd antiquity,
Mine own self-love quite contrary I read;
Self so self-loving were iniquity.
'Tis thee myself that for myself I praise,
Painting my age with beauty of thy days.

LXIII.

Against my love shall be, as I am now
With Time's injurious hand crush'd and o'erworn;
When hours have drain'd his blood, and fill'd his brow
With lines and wrinkles; when his youthful morn
Hath travell'd on to age's steepy night;
And all those beauties, whereof now he 's king,
Are vanishing, or vanish'd out of sight,
Stealing away the treasure of his spring;
For such a time do I now fortify
Against confounding age's cruel knife,
That he shall never cut from memory
My sweet love's beauty, though my lover's life:
His beauty shall in these black lines be seen,
And they shall live, and he in them still green.

LXIV.

When I have seen by Time's fell hand defaced
The rich proud cost of out-worn buried age;
When sometime lofty towers I see down-rased,
And brass eternal, slave to mortal rage:
When I have seen the hungry ocean gain
Advantage on the kingdom of the shore,
And the firm soil win of the watery main,
Increasing store with loss, and loss with store:
When I have seen such interchange of state,
Or state itself confounded to decay,
Ruin hath taught me thus to ruminate —
That Time will come and take my love away.
  This thought is as a death, which cannot choose
  But weep to have that which it fears to lose.

LXV.

Since brass, nor stone, nor earth, nor boundless sea,
But sad mortality o'er-sways their power,
How with this rage shall beauty hold a plea,
Whose action is no stronger than a flower?
O, how shall Summer's honey-breath hold out
Against the wreckful siege of battering days,
When rocks impregnable are not so stout,
Nor gates of steel so strong, but time decays?
O fearful meditation! where, alack,
Shall Time's best jewel from Time's chest lie hid?
Or what strong hand can hold his swift foot back?
Or who his spoil of beauty can forbid?
  O, none, unless this miracle have might,
  That in black ink my love may still shine bright.

LXVI.

Tir'd with all these, for restful death I cry;—
As, to behold desert a beggar born,
And needy nothing trimm'd in jollity,
And purest faith unhappily forsworn,
And gilded honour shamefully misplac'd,
And maiden virtue rudely strumpeted,
And right perfection wrongfully disgrac'd,
And strength by limping sway disableëd,
And art made tongue-tied by authority,
And folly (doctor-like) controlling skill,
And simple truth miscall'd simplicity,
And captive good attending captain ill:
  Tir'd with all these, from these would I be gone,
  Save that to die I leave my love alone.

LXVII.

Ah, wherefore with infection should he live,
And with his presence grace impiety,
That sin by him advantage should achieve,
And lace itself with his society?
Why should false painting imitate his cheek,
And steal dead seeing of his living hue?
Why should poor beauty indirectly seek
Roses of shadow, since his rose is true?
Why should he live, now nature bankrupt is,
Beggar'd of blood to blush through lively veins?
For she hath no exchequer now but his,
And, proud of many, lives upon his gains.
  O, him she stores, to show what wealth she had
  In days long since, before these last so bad.

LXVIII.

Thus is his cheek the map of days out-worn,
When beauty liv'd and di'd as flowers do now,
Before these bastard signs of fair were born,
Or durst inhabit on a living brow;
Before the golden tresses of the dead,
The right of sepulchres, were shorn away,
To live a second life on second head;
Ere beauty's dead fleece made another gay.
In him those holy antique hours are seen,
Without all ornament, itself, and true,
Making no summer of another's green,
Robbing no old to dress his beauty new;
  And him as for a map doth Nature store,
  To shew false Art what beauty was of yore.

LXIX.

Those parts of thee that the world's eye doth view,
Want nothing that the thought of hearts can mend;
All tongues (the voice of souls) give thee that due,
Uttering bare truth, even so as foes commend.
Thine outward thus with outward praise is crown'd;
But those same tongues that give thee so thine own,
In other accents do this praise confound,
By seeing farther than the eye hath shewn.
They look into the beauty of thy mind,
And that, in guess, they measure by thy deeds;
Then, churls, their thoughts, although their eyes were kind,
To thy fair flower add the rank smell of weeds;
  But why thy odour matcheth not thy shew,
  The solve is this;—that thou dost common grow.

LXX.

That thou art blam'd shall not be thy defect,
For slander's mark was ever yet the fair;
The ornament of beauty is suspect,
A crow that flies in heaven's sweetest air.
So thou be good, slander doth but approve
Thy worth the greater, being woo'd of time;
For canker vice the sweetest buds doth love,
And thou present'st a pure unstained prime.
Thou hast pass'd by the ambush of young days,
Either not assail'd, or victor being charged;
Yet this thy praise cannot be so thy praise,
To tie up envy, evermore enlarged:
  If some suspect of ill mask'd not thy shew,
  Then thou alone kingdoms of hearts should'st owe.

LXXI.

No longer mourn for me, when I am dead,
Than you shall hear the surly sullen bell
Give warning to the world that I am fled
From this vile world, with vilest worms to dwell:
Nay, if you read this line, remember not
The hand that writ it; for I love you so,
That I in your sweet thoughts would be forgot,
If thinking on me then should make you woe.
O, if (I say) you look upon this verse,
When I perhaps compounded am with clay,
Do not so much as my poor name rehearse,
But let your love even with my life decay;
  Lest the wise world should look into your moan,
  And mock you with me after I am gone.

LXXII.

O, lest the world should task you to recite
What merit liv'd in me, that you should love
After my death, dear love, forget me quite,
For you in me can nothing worthy prove;
Unless you would devise some virtuous lie,
To do more for me than mine own desert,
And hang more praise upon deceased I,
Then niggard truth would willingly impart.
O, lest your true love may seem false in this,
That you for love speak well of me untrue,
My name be buried where my body is,
And live no more to shame nor me nor you.
  For I am sham'd by that which I bring forth,
  And so should you, to love things nothing worth.

LXXIII.

That time of year thou may'st in me behold,
When yellow leaves, or none, or few, do hang
Upon those boughs which shake against the cold,—
Bare ruin'd choirs, where late the sweet birds sang.
In me thou seest the twilight of such day
As after sun-set fadeth in the west,
Which by and by black night doth take away,
Death's second self, that seals up all in rest:
In me thou seest the glowing of such fire,
That on the ashes of his youth doth lie,
As the death-bed whereon it must expire,
Consum'd with that which it was nourish'd by.
  This thou perceiv'st, which makes thy love more strong,
  To love that well which thou must leave ere long:

LXXIV.

But be contented: when that fell arrest
Without all bail shall carry me away,
My life hath in this line some interest,
Which for memorial still with thee shall stay:
When thou reviewest this, thou dost review
The very part was consecrate to thee.
The earth can have but earth, which is his due;
My spirit is thine, the better part of me:
So then thou hast but lost the dregs of life,
The prey of worms, my body being dead;
The coward conquest of a wretch's knife,
Too base of thee to be remembered.
  The worth of that is that which it contains,
  And that is this, and this with thee remains.

LXXV.

So are you to my thoughts, as food to life,
Or as sweet-season'd showers are to the ground;
And for the peace of you I hold such strife
As 'twixt a miser and his wealth is found:
Now proud as an enjoyer, and anon
Doubting the filching age will steal his treasure;
Now counting best to be with you alone,
Then better'd that the world may see my pleasure:
Sometime all full with feasting on your sight,
And by and by clean starved for a look;
Possessing or pursuing no delight,
Save what is had or must from you be took.
  Thus do I pine and surfeit day by day;
  Or gluttoning on all, or all away.

LXXVI.

Why is my verse so barren of new pride,
So far from variation or quick change?
Why, with the time, do I not glance aside
To new-found methods and to compounds strange?
Why write I still all one, ever the same,
And keep invention in a noted weed,
That every word doth almost tell my name,
Shewing their birth, and where they did proceed?
O, know, sweet love, I always write of you,
And you and love are still my argument:
So, all my best is dressing old words new,
Spending again what is already spent:
  For as the sun is daily new and old,
  So is my love, still telling what is told.

LXXVII.

Thy glass will shew thee how thy beauties wear,
Thy dial how thy precious minutes waste;
The vacant leaves thy mind's imprint will bear,
And of this book this learning may'st thou taste:
The wrinkles which thy glass will truly shew,
Of mouthed graves will give thee memory;
Thou by thy dial's shady stealth may'st know
Time's thievish progress to eternity.
Look, what thy memory cannot contain,
Commit to these waste blanks, and thou shalt find
Those children nurs'd, deliver'd from thy brain,
To take a new acquaintance of thy mind.
  These offices, so oft as thou wilt look,
  Shall profit thee, and much enrich thy book.

LXXVIII.

So oft have I invok'd thee for my Muse,
And found such fair assistance in my verse,
As every alien pen hath got my use,
And under thee their poesy disperse.
Thine eyes that taught the dumb on high to sing,
And heavy ignorance aloft to fly,
Have added feathers to the learned's wing,
And given grace a double majesty.
Yet be most proud of that which I compile,
Whose influence is thine, and born of thee:
In others' works thou dost but mend the style,
And arts with thy sweet graces graced be;
  But thou art all my art, and dost advance
  As high as learning my rude ignorance.

LXXIX.

Whilst I alone did call upon thy aid,
My verse alone had all thy gentle grace;
But now my gracious numbers are decay'd,
And my sick Muse doth give another place.
I grant, sweet love, thy lovely argument
Deserves the travail of a worthier pen;
Yet what of thee thy poet doth invent,
He robs thee of, and pays it thee again.
He lends thee virtue, and he stole that word
From thy behaviour; beauty doth he give,
And found it in thy cheek; he can afford
No praise to thee but what in thee doth live.
  Then, thank him not for that which he doth say,
  Since what he owes thee, thou thyself dost pay.

LXXX.

O, how I faint when I of you do write,
Knowing a better spirit doth use your name,
And in the praise thereof spends all his might,
To make me tongue-tied, speaking of your fame:
But since your worth (wide as the ocean is)
The humble as the proudest sail doth bear,
My saucy bark, inferior far to his,
On your broad main doth wilfully appear.
Your shallowest help will hold me up afloat,
Whilst he upon your soundless deep doth ride;
Or, being wreck'd, I am a worthless boat,
He of tall building, and of goodly pride:
  Then, if he thrive, and I be cast away,
  The worst was this — my love was my decay.

LXXXI.

Or I shall live your epitaph to make,
Or you survive when I in earth am rotten:
From hence your memory death cannot take,
Although in me each part will be forgotten.
Your name from hence immortal life shall have,
Though I, once gone, to all the world must die:
The earth can yield me but a common grave,
When you entombed in men's eyes shall lie.
Your monument shall be my gentle verse,
Which eyes not yet created shall o'er-read;
And tongues to be your being shall rehearse,
When all the breathers of this world are dead;
  You still shall live (such virtue hath my pen)
  Where breath most breathes, even in the mouths of men.

LXXXII.

I grant thou wert not married to my Muse,
And, therefore, may'st without attaint o'er-look
The dedicated words which writers use
Of their fair subject, blessing every book.
Thou art as fair in knowledge as in hue,
Finding thy worth a limit past my praise;
And, therefore, art enforc'd to seek anew
Some fresher stamp of the time-bettering days.
And do so, love; yet when they have devis'd
What strained touches rhetoric can lend,
Thou, truly fair, wert truly sympathiz'd
In true plain words, by thy true-telling friend;
  And their gross painting might be better used
  Where cheeks need blood: in thee it is abused.

LXXXIII.

I never saw that you did painting need,
And, therefore, to your fair no painting set;
I found, or thought I found, you did exceed
The barren tender of a poet's debt:
And, therefore, have I slept in your report,
That you yourself, being extant, well might shew
How far a modern quill doth come too short,
Speaking of worth, what worth in you doth grow.
This silence for my sin you did impute,
Which shall be most my glory, being dumb;
For I impair not beauty being mute,
When others would give life, and bring a tomb.
  There lives more life in one of your fair eyes,
  Than both your poets can in praise devise.

LXXXIV.

Who is it that says most? which can say more,
Than this rich praise, that you alone are you?
In whose confine immured is the store,
Which should example where your equal grew.
Lean penury within that pen doth dwell,
That to his subject lends not some small glory;
But he that writes of you, if he can tell
That you are you, so dignifies his story;
Let him but copy what in you is writ,
Not making worse what nature made so clear,
And such a counterpart shall fame his wit,
Making his style admired every where.
  You to your beauteous blessings add a curse,
  Being fond on praise, which makes your praises worse.

LXXXV.

My tongue-tied Muse in manners holds her still,
While comments of your praise, richly compil'd,
Reserve their character with golden quill,
And precious phrase by all the Muses fil'd.
I think good thoughts, whilst other write good words,
And, like unletter'd clerk, still cry "Amen"
To every hymn that able spirit affords,
In polish'd form of well-refined pen.
Hearing you prais'd, I say, ''Tis so, 'tis true,'
And to the most of praise add something more;
But that is in my thought, whose love to you,
Though words come hindmost, holds his rank before:
  Then, others for the breath of words respect,
  Me, for my dumb thoughts, speaking in effect.

LXXXVI.

Was it the proud full sail of his great verse,
Bound for the prize of all too precious you,
That did my ripe thoughts in my brain inherse,
Making their tomb the womb wherein they grew?
Was it his spirit, by spirits taught to write
Above a mortal pitch, that struck me dead?
No, neither he, nor his compeers by night
Giving him aid, my verse astonished:
He, nor that affable familiar ghost,
Which nightly gulls him with intelligence,
As victors of my silence cannot boast.
I was not sick of any fear from thence;
  But when your countenance fil'd up his line,
  Then lack'd I matter; that enfeebled mine.

LXXXVII.

Farewell: thou art too dear for my possessing,
And like enough thou know'st thy estimate:
The charter of thy worth gives thee releasing;
My bonds in thee are all determinate.
For how do I hold thee but by thy granting?
And for that riches where is my deserving?
The cause of this fair gift in me is wanting,
And so my patent back again is swerving.
Thyself thou gav'st, thy own worth then not knowing,
Or me, to whom gav'st it, else mistaking;
So thy great gift, upon misprision growing,
Comes home again, on better judgment making.
  Thus have I had thee, as a dream doth flatter,
  In sleep a king, but waking, no such matter.

LXXXVIII.

When thou shalt be dispos'd to set me light,
And place my merit in the eye of scorn,
Upon thy side against myself I'll fight,
And prove thee virtuous, though thou art forsworn:
With mine own weakness being best acquainted,
Upon thy part I can set down a story
Of faults conceal'd, wherein I am attainted,
That thou, in losing me, shalt win much glory:
And I by this will be a gainer too;
For bending all my loving thoughts on thee,
The injuries that to myself I do,
Doing thee vantage, double vantage me.
  Such is my love, to thee I so belong,
  That for thy right myself will bear all wrong.

LXXXIX.

Say that thou did'st forsake me for some fault,
And I will comment upon that offence:
Speak of my lameness, and I straight will halt,
Against thy reasons making no defence.
Thou canst not, love, disgrace me half so ill,
To set a form upon desired change,
As I'll myself disgrace: knowing thy will,
I will acquaintance strangle, and look strange;
Be absent from thy walks; and in my tongue
Thy sweet beloved name no more shall dwell,
Lest I (too much profane) should do it wrong,
And haply of our old acquaintance tell.
  For thee, against myself I'll vow debate,
  For I must ne'er love him whom thou dost hate.

XC.

Then hate me when thou wilt; if ever, now:
Now, while the world is bent my deeds to cross,
Join with the spite of fortune, make me bow,
And do not drop in for an after loss.
Ah, do not, when my heart hath scap'd this sorrow,
Come in the rearward of a conquered woe;
Give not a windy night a rainy morrow,
To linger out a purpos'd overthrow.
If thou wilt leave me, do not leave me last,
When other petty griefs have done their spite,
But in the onset come: so shall I taste
At first the very worst of fortune's might;
  And other strains of woe, which now seem woe,
  Compar'd with loss of thee, will not seem so.

XCI.

Some glory in their birth, some in their skill,
Some in their wealth, some in their body's force;
Some in their garments, though new-fangled ill;
Some in their hawks and hounds, some in their horse;
And every humour hath his adjunct pleasure,
Wherein it finds a joy above the rest;
But these particulars are not my measure:
All these I better in one general best.
Thy love is better than high birth to me,
Richer than wealth, prouder than garments' cost,
Of more delight than hawks or horses be;
And having thee, of all men's pride I boast:
  Wretched in this alone, that thou may'st take
  All this away, and me most wretched make.

XCII.

But do thy worst to steal thyself away;
For term of life thou art assured mine;
And life no longer than thy love will stay,
For it depends upon that love of thine:
Then need I not to fear the worst of wrongs,
When in the least of them my life hath end.
I see a better state to me belongs
Than that which on thy humour doth depend.
Thou canst not vex me with inconstant mind,
Since that my life on thy revolt doth lie.
O, what a happy title do I find,
Happy to have thy love, happy to die!
  But what's so blessed fair that fears no blot?
  Thou may'st be false, and yet I know it not.

XCIII.

So shall I live, supposing thou art true,
Like a deceived husband; so love's face
May still seem love to me, though alter'd new;
Thy looks with me, thy heart in other place:
For there can live no hatred in thine eye;
Therefore in that I cannot know thy change.
In many's looks the false heart's history
Is writ in moods, and frowns, and wrinkles strange;
But Heaven in thy creation did decree,
That in thy face sweet love should ever dwell;
Whate'er thy thoughts or thy heart's workings be,
Thy looks should nothing thence but sweetness tell.
  How like Eve's apple doth thy beauty grow,
  If thy sweet virtue answer not thy shew!

XCIV.

They that have power to hurt, and will do none,
That do not do the thing they most do shew,
Who, moving others, are themselves as stone,
Unmoved, cold, and to temptation slow;
They rightly do inherit Heaven's graces,
And husband nature's riches from expense;
They are the lords and owners of their faces,
Others but stewards of their excellence.
The summer's flower is to the summer sweet,
Though to itself it only live and die;
But if that flower with base infection meet,
The basest weed outbraves his dignity;
For sweetest things turn sourest by their deeds:
Lilies that fester smell far worse than weeds.

XCV.

How sweet and lovely dost thou make the shame,
Which, like a canker in the fragrant rose,
Doth spot the beauty of thy budding name!
O, in what sweets dost thou thy sins enclose!
That tongue that tells the story of thy days
(Making lascivious comments on thy sport)
Cannot dispraise but in a kind of praise;
Naming thy name blesses an ill report.
O, what a mansion have those vices got,
Which for their habitation chose out thee,
Where beauty's veil doth cover every blot,
And all things turn to fair that eyes can see!
Take heed, dear heart, of this large privilege;
The hardest knife ill us'd doth lose his edge.

XCVI.

Some say, thy fault is youth, some wantonness;
Some say, thy grace is youth, and gentle sport;
Both grace and faults are lov'd of more and less:
Thou mak'st faults graces that to thee resort.
As on the finger of a throned queen
The basest jewel will be well esteem'd,
So are those errors that in thee are seen
To truths translated, and for true things deem'd.
How many lambs might the stern wolf betray,
If like a lamb he could his looks translate!
How many gazers might'st thou lead away,
If thou would'st use the strength of all thy state!
  But do not so; I love thee in such sort,
  As thou being mine, mine is thy good report.

XCVII.

How like a winter hath my absence been
From thee, the pleasure of the fleeting year!
What freezings have I felt, what dark days seen,
What old December's bareness every where!
And yet this time remov'd was summer's time;
The teeming Autumn, big with rich increase,
Bearing the wanton burthen of the prime,
Like widow'd wombs after their lords' decease:
Yet this abundant issue seem'd to me
But hope of orphans, and unfather'd fruit;
For Summer and his pleasures wait on thee,
And, thou away, the very birds are mute;
  Or, if they sing, 'tis with so dull a cheer,
  That leaves look pale, dreading the winter 's near.

XCVIII.

From you have I been absent in the spring,
When proud-pied April, dress'd in all his trim,
Hath put a spirit of youth in every thing,
That heavy Saturn laugh'd and leap'd with him:
Yet nor the lays of birds, nor the sweet smell
Of different flowers in odour and in hue,
Could make me any summer's story tell,
Or from their proud lap pluck them where they grew:
Nor did I wonder at the lily's white,
Nor praise the deep vermilion in the rose;
They were but sweet, but figures of delight,
Drawn after you; you pattern of all those.
  Yet seem'd it winter still, and, you away,
  As with your shadow I with these did play:

XCIX.

The forward violet thus did I chide: —
Sweet thief, whence did'st thou steal thy sweet that smells,
If not from my love's breath? the purple pride
Which on thy soft cheek for complexion dwells,
In my love's veins thou hast too grossly dy'd.
The lily I condemned for thy hand,
And buds of marjoram had stol'n thy hair:
The roses fearfully on thorns did stand,
One blushing shame, another white despair;
A third, nor red nor white, had stol'n of both,
And to this robbery had annex'd thy breath;
But, for his theft, in pride of all his growth
A vengeful canker eat him up to death.
  More flowers I noted, yet I none could see,
  But sweet or colour it had stol'n from thee.

C.

Where art thou, Muse, that thou forgett'st so long
To speak of that which gives thee all thy might?
Spend'st thou thy fury on some worthless song,
Darkening thy power to lend base subjects light?
Return, forgetful Muse, and straight redeem
In gentle numbers time so idly spent:
Sing to the ear that doth thy lays esteem,
And gives thy pen both skill and argument.
Rise, resty Muse, my love's sweet face survey,
If Time have any wrinkle graven there;
If any, be a satire to decay,
And make Time's spoils despised every where.
  Give my love fame faster than Time wastes life;
  So thou prevent'st his scythe and crooked knife.

CI.

O truant Muse! What shall be thy amends,
For thy neglect of truth in beauty dyed?
Both truth and beauty on my love depends;
So dost thou too, and therein dignified.
Make answer, Muse: wilt thou not haply say,
"Truth needs no colour, with his colour fix'd;
Beauty no pencil, beauty's truth to lay;
But best is best, if never intermix'd?"
Because he needs no praise, wilt thou be dumb?
Excuse not silence so; for 't lies in thee
To make him much out-live a gilded tomb,
And to be prais'd of ages yet to be.
  Then do thy office, Muse: I teach thee how
  To make him seem long hence as he shews now.

CII.

My love is strengthen'd, though more weak in seeming;
I love not less, though less the shew appear:
That love is merchandis'd, whose rich esteeming
The owner's tongue doth publish every where.
Our love was new, and then but in the spring,
When I was wont to greet it with my lays;
As Philomel in Summer's front doth sing,
And stops his pipe in growth of riper days:
Not that the Summer is less pleasant now,
Than when her mournful hymns did hush the night,
But that wild music burthens every bough,
And sweets grown common lose their dear delight.
  Therefore, like her, I sometime hold my tongue,
  Because I would not dull you with my song.

CIII.

Alack, what poverty my Muse brings forth,
That having such a scope to shew her pride,
The argument, all bare, is of more worth
Than when it hath my added praise beside.
O, blame me not, if I no more can write:
Look in your glass, and there appears a face,
That over-goes my blunt invention quite,
Dulling my lines, and doing me disgrace.
Were it not sinful, then, striving to mend,
To mar the subject that before was well?
For to no other pass my verses tend,
Than of your graces and your gifts to tell;
  And more, much more, than in my verse can sit,
  Your own glass shews you, when you look in it.

CIV.

To me, fair friend, you never can be old,
For as you were, when first your eye I ey'd,
Such seems your beauty still. Three winters cold
Have from the forests shook three summers' pride;
Three beauteous springs to yellow autumn turn'd,
In process of the seasons have I seen;
Three April perfumes in three hot Junes burn'd,
Since first I saw you fresh, which yet are green.
Ah, yet doth beauty, like a dial hand,
Steal from his figure, and no pace perceived;
So your sweet hue, which methinks still doth stand,
Hath motion, and mine eye may be deceived:
  For fear of which, hear this, thou age unbred,—
  Ere you were born was beauty's summer dead.

CV.

Let not my love be call'd idolatry,
Nor my beloved as an idol shew,
Since all alike my songs and praises be,
To one, of one, still such, and ever so.
Kind is my love to-day, to-morrow kind,
Still constant in a wondrous excellence;
Therefore my verse to constancy confin'd,
One thing expressing, leaves out difference.
Fair, kind, and true, is all my argument,
Fair, kind, and true, varying to other words;
And in this change is my invention spent,
Three themes in one, which wondrous scope affords.
  Fair, kind, and true, have often liv'd alone,
  Which three, till now, never kept seat in one.

CVI.

When in the chronicle of wasted time
I see descriptions of the fairest wights,
And beauty making beautiful old rhyme
In praise of ladies dead and lovely knights,
Then, in the blazon of sweet beauty's best,
Of hand, of foot, of lip, of eye, of brow,
I see their antique pen would have express'd
Even such a beauty as you master now.
So all their praises are but prophecies
Of this our time, all you prefiguring;
And for they look'd but with divining eyes,
They had not skill enough your worth to sing:
  For we, which now behold these present days,
  Have eyes to wonder, but lack tongues to praise.

CVII.

Not mine own fears, nor the prophetic soul
Of the wide world, dreaming on things to come,
Can yet the lease of my true love control,
Suppos'd as forfeit to a confin'd doom.
The mortal moon hath her eclipse endur'd,
And the sad augurs mock their own presage;
Incertainties now crown themselves assur'd,
And peace proclaims olives of endless age.
Now, with the drops of this most balmy time
My love looks fresh, and death to me subscribes,
Since, spite of him, I'll live in this poor rhyme,
While he insults o'er dull and speechless tribes:
  And thou in this shalt find thy monument,
  When tyrants' crests and tombs of brass are spent.

CVIII.

What's in the brain that ink may character,
Which hath not figur'd to thee my true spirit?
What's new to speak, what new to register,
That may express my love, or thy dear merit?
Nothing, sweet boy; but yet, like prayers divine,
I must each day say o'er the very same,
Counting no old thing old, thou mine, I thine,
Even as when first I hallow'd thy fair name.
So that eternal love, in love's fresh case,
Weighs not the dust and injury of age;
Nor gives to necessary wrinkles place,
But makes antiquity for aye his page;
  Finding the first conceit of love there bred,
  Where time and outward form would show it dead.

CIX.

O, never say that I was false of heart,
Though absence seem'd my flame to qualify
As easy might I from myself depart,
As from my soul, which in thy breast doth lie.
That is my home of love: if I have ranged,
Like him that travels, I return again,
Just to the time, not with the time exchanged;
So that myself bring water for my stain.
Never believe, though in my nature reign'd
All frailties that besiege all kinds of blood,
That it could so preposterously be stain'd,
To leave for nothing all thy sum of good;
  For nothing this wide universe I call,
  Save thou, my rose; in it thou art my all.

CX.

Alas, 'tis true I have gone here and there,
And made myself a motley to the view;
Gor'd mine own thoughts, sold cheap what is most
dear,
Made old offences of affections new:
Most true it is, that I have look'd on truth
Askance and strangely; but, by all above,
These blenches gave my heart another youth,
And worse essays prov'd thee my best of love.
Now all is done, save what shall have no end:
Mine appetite I never more will grind
On newer proof, to try an older friend,
A god in love, to whom I am confin'd.
Then give me welcome, next my heaven the best
Even to thy pure and most most loving breast.

CXI.

O, for my sake do you with Fortune chide,
The guilty goddess of my harmful deeds,
That did not better for my life provide
Than public means, which public manners breeds:
Thence comes it that my name receives a brand;
And almost thence my nature is subdu'd
To what it works in, like the dyer's hand.
Pity me, then, and wish I were renew'd,
Whilst, like a willing patient, I will drink
Potions of eysel 'gainst my strong infection;
No bitterness that I will bitter think,
Nor double penance, to correct correction.
Pity me, then, dear friend, and I assure ye,
Even that your pity is enough to cure me.

CXII.

Your love and pity doth th' impression fill
Which vulgar scandal stamp'd upon my brow;
For what care I who calls me well or ill,
So you o'er-green my bad, my good allow?
You are my all-the-world, and I must strive
To know my shames and praises from your tongue;
None else to me, nor I to none alive,
That my steel'd sense or changes, right or wrong.
In so profound abysm I throw all care
Of others' voices, that my adder's sense
To critic and to flatterer stopped are.
Mark how with my neglect I do dispense:—
  You are so strongly in my purpose bred,
  That all the world besides methinks they are dead.

CXIII.

Since I left you mine eye is in my mind;
And that which governs me to go about
Doth part his function, and is partly blind,
Seems seeing, but effectually is out;
For it no form delivers to the heart
Of bird, of flower, or shape, which it doth latch:
Of his quick objects hath the mind no part,
Nor his own vision holds what it doth catch;
For if it see the rud'st or gentlest sight,
The most sweet favour, or deformed'st creature,
The mountain or the sea, the day or night,
The crow or dove, it shapes them to your feature:
  Incapable of more, replete with you,
  My most true mind thus maketh mine untrue.

CXIV.

Or whether doth my mind, being crown'd with you,
Drink up the monarch's plague, this flattery?
Or whether shall I say, mine eye saith true,
And that your love taught it this alchymy,
To make of monsters and things indigest,
Such cherubins as your sweet self resemble,
Creating every bad a perfect best,
As fast as objects to his beams assemble?
O, 'tis the first: 'tis flattery in my seeing,
And my great mind most kingly drinks it up:
Mine eye well knows what with his gust is 'greeing,
And to his palate doth prepare the cup:
  If it be poison'd, 'tis the lesser sin
  That mine eye loves it, and doth first begin.

CXV.

Those lines that I before have writ do lie,
Even those that said I could not love you dearer;
Yet then my judgment knew no reason why
My most full flame should afterwards burn clearer.
But reckoning time, whose million'd accidents
Creep in 'twixt vows, and change decrees of kings,
Tan sacred beauty, blunt the sharp'st intents,
Divert strong minds t' the course of altering things;
Alas! why, fearing of time's tyranny,
Might I not then say, 'Now I love you best,'
When I was certain o'er incertainty,
Crowning the present, doubting of the rest?
  Love is a babe; then might I not say so,
  To give full growth to that which still doth grow?

CXVI.

Let me not to the marriage of true minds
Admit impediments: love is not love
Which alters when it alteration finds,
Or bends with the remover to remove:
O no; it is an ever-fixed mark,
That looks on tempests, and is never shaken;
It is the star to every wandering bark,
Whose worth 's unknown, although his height be taken.
Love's not Time's Fool, though rosy lips and cheeks
Within his bending sickle's compass come;
Love alters not with his brief hours and weeks,
But bears it out even to the edge of doom.
  If this be error, and upon me proved,
  I never writ, nor no man ever loved.

CXVII.

Accuse me thus: that I have scanted all
Wherein I should your great deserts repay;
Forgot upon your dearest love to call,
Whereto all bonds do tie me day by day;
That I have frequent been with unknown minds,
And given to time your own dear-purchas'd right;
That I have hoisted sail to all the winds
Which should transport me farthest from your sight:
Book both my wilfulness and errors down,
And on just proof surmise accumulate;
Bring me within the level of your frown,
But shoot not at me in your waken'd hate,
  Since my appeal says, I did strive to prove
  The constancy and virtue of your love.

CXVIII.

Like as, to make our appetites more keen,
With eager compounds we our palate urge;
As, to prevent our maladies unseen,
We sicken to shun sickness when we purge;
Even so, being full of your ne'er-cloying sweetness,
To bitter sauces did I frame my feeding;
And, sick of welfare, found a kind of meetness
To be diseas'd, ere that there was true needing.
Thus policy in love, t' anticipate
The ills that were not, grew to faults assured,
And brought to medicine a healthful state,
Which, rank of goodness, would by ill be cured;
But thence I learn, and find the lesson true,
Drugs poison him that so fell sick of you.

CXIX.

What potions have I drunk of siren tears,
Distill'd from limbecks foul as Hell within,
Applying fears to hopes, and hopes to fears,
Still losing when I saw myself to win!
What wretched errors hath my heart committed,
Whilst it hath thought itself so blessed never!
How have mine eyes out of their spheres been fitted,
In the distraction of this madding fever!
O benefit of ill! now I find true,
That better is by evil still made better;
And ruin'd love, when it is built anew,
Grows fairer than at first, more strong, far greater.
So I return rebuk'd to my content,
And gain by ill thrice more than I have spent.

CXX.

That you were once unkind befriends me now,
And for that sorrow which I then did feel,
Needs must I under my transgression bow,
Unless my nerves were brass or hammer'd steel.
For if you were by my unkindness shaken,
As I by yours, you have pass'd a hell of time;
And I, a tyrant, have no leisure taken
To weigh how once I suffer'd in your crime.
O that our night of woe might have remember'd
My deepest sense, how hard true sorrow hits;
And soon to you, as you to me, then tender'd
The humble salve which wounded bosoms fits!
  But that your trespass now becomes a fee;
  Mine ransoms yours, and yours must ransom me.

CXXI.

'Tis better to be vile than vile esteemed,
When not to be receives reproach of being;
And the just pleasure lost, which is so deemed,
Not by our feeling, but by others' seeing:
For why should others' false adulterate eyes
Give salutation to my sportive blood?
Or on my frailties why are frailer spies,
Which in their wills count bad what I think good?
No, I am that I am; and they that level
At my abuses, reckon up their own:
I may be straight, though they themselves be bevel.
By their rank thoughts my deeds must not be shewn;
  Unless this general evil they maintain, —
  All men are bad, and in their badness reign

CXXII.

Thy gift, thy tables, are within my brain
Full character'd with lasting memory,
Which shall above that idle rank remain,
Beyond all date, even to eternity;
Or, at the least, so long as brain and heart
Have faculty by nature to subsist;
Till each to ras'd oblivion yield his part
Of thee, thy record never can be miss'd.
That poor retention could not so much hold,
Nor need I tallies thy dear love to score;
Therefore to give them from me was I bold,
To trust those tables that receive thee more:
  To keep an adjunct to remember thee,
  Were to import forgetfulness in me.

CXXIII.

No, Time, thou shalt not boast that I do change:
Thy pyramids, built up with newer might,
To me are nothing novel, nothing strange;
They are but dressings of a former sight.
Our dates are brief, and therefore we admire
What thou dost foist upon us that is old,
And rather make them born to our desire,
Than think that we before have heard them told.
Thy registers and thee I both defy,
Not wondering at the present nor the past;
For thy records and what we see do lie,
Made more or less by thy continual haste.
  This I do vow, and this shall ever be,
  I will be true, despite thy scythe and thee.

CXXIV.

If my dear love were but the child of state,
It might for fortune's bastard be unfathered,
As subject to time's love, or to time's hate,
Weeds among weeds, or flowers with flowers gathered.
No, it was builded far from accident;
It suffers not in smiling pomp, nor falls
Under the blow of thralled discontent,
Whereto th' inviting time our fashion calls:
It fears not policy, that heretic,
Which works on leases of short number'd hours,
But all alone stands hugely politic,
That it nor grows with heat, nor drowns with showers.
To this I witness call the fools of time,
Which die for goodness, who have liv'd for crime.

CXXV.

Were 't aught to me I bore the canopy,
With my extern the outward honouring,
Or laid great bases for eternity,
Which prove more short than waste or ruining?
Have I not seen dwellers on form and favour
Lose all, and more, by paying too much rent;
For compound sweet foregoing simple savour,
Pitiful thrivers, in their gazing spent?
No; let me be obsequious in thy heart,
And take thou my oblation, poor but free,
Which is not mix'd with seconds, knows no art,
But mutual render, only me for thee.
Hence, thou suborn'd informer! a true soul,
When most impeach'd, stands least in thy control.

CXXVI.

O thou, my lovely boy, who in thy power
Dost hold Time's fickle glass, his sickle, hour;
Who hast by waning grown, and therein shew'st
Thy lovers withering, as thy sweet self grow'st;
If Nature, sovereign mistress over wrack,
As thou go'st onwards still will pluck thee back,
She keeps thee to this purpose, that her skill
May time disgrace, and wretched minutes kill.
Yet fear her, O thou minion of her pleasure!
She may detain, but not still keep her treasure:
Her audit, though delay'd, answer'd must be,
And her quietus is to render thee.

CXXVII.

In the old age black was not counted fair,
Or if it were, it bore not beauty's name;
But now is black beauty's successive heir,
And beauty slander'd with a bastard shame;
For since each hand hath put on nature's power,
Fairing the foul with art's false borrow'd face,
Sweet beauty hath no name, no holy bower,
But is profan'd, if not lives in disgrace.
Therefore my mistress' eyes are raven black,
Her eyes so suited; and they mourners seem
At such, who, not born fair, no beauty lack,
Slandering creation with a false esteem:
  Yet so they mourn, becoming of their woe,
  That every tongue says, beauty should look so.

CXXVIII.

How oft, when thou, my music, music playest,
Upon that blessed wood, whose motion sounds
With thy sweet fingers, when thou gently swayest
The wiry concord that mine ear confounds,
Do I envy those jacks, that nimble leap
To kiss the tender inward of thy hand,
Whilst my poor lips, which should that harvest reap,
At the wood's boldness by thee blushing stand.
To be so tickled, they would change their state
And situation with those dancing chips,
O'er whom thy fingers walk with gentle gait,
Making dead wood more bless'd than living lips.
  Since saucy jacks so happy are in this,
  Give them thy fingers, me thy lips to kiss.

CXXIX.

Th' expense of spirit in a waste of shame
Is lust in action; and till action, lust
Is perjur'd, murtherous, bloody, full of blame,
Savage, extreme, rude, cruel, not to trust;
Enjoy'd no sooner but despised straight;
Past reason hunted, and no sooner had,
Past reason hated, as a swallow'd bait,
On purpose laid to make the taker mad;
Mad in pursuit, and in possession so;
Had, having, and in quest to have, extreme;
A bliss in proof, — and prov'd, a very woe;
Before, a joy propos'd; behind, a dream.
  All this the world well knows, yet none knows well
  To shun the heaven that leads men to this hell.

CXXX.

My mistress' eyes are nothing like the sun;
Coral is far more red than her lips' red:
If snow be white, why then her breasts are dun;
If hairs be wires, black wires grow on her head.
I have seen roses damask'd, red and white,
But no such roses see I in her cheeks;
And in some perfumes is there more delight
Than in the breath that from my mistress reeks.
I love to hear her speak; yet well I know
That music hath a far more pleasing sound:
I grant I never saw a goddess go;
My mistress, when she walks, treads on the ground.
  And yet, by heaven, I think my love as rare
  As any she belied with false compare.

CXXXI.

Thou art as tyrannous, so as thou art,
As those whose beauties proudly make them cruel;
For well thou know'st, to my dear doting heart
Thou art the fairest and most precious jewel.
Yet, in good faith, some say, that thee behold,
Thy face hath not the power to make love groan:
To say they err I dare not be so bold,
Although I swear it to myself alone.
And, to be sure that is not false I swear,
A thousand groans, but thinking on thy face,
One on another's neck, do witness bear,
Thy black is fairest in my judgment's place.
  In nothing art thou black, save in thy deeds,
  And thence this slander, as I think, proceeds.

CXXXII.

Thine eyes I love, and they, as pitying me,
Knowing thy heart torments me with disdain,
Have put on black, and loving mourners be,
Looking with pretty ruth upon my pain.
And, truly, not the morning sun of heaven
Better becomes the grey cheeks of the East,
Nor that full star that ushers in the even
Doth half that glory to the sober West,
As those two mourning eyes become thy face.
O, let it, then, as well beseem thy heart
To mourn for me, since mourning doth thee grace,
And suit thy pity like in every part:
  Then will I swear, beauty herself is black,
  And all they foul that thy complexion lack.

CXXXIII.

Beshrew that heart, that makes my heart to groan
For that deep wound it gives my friend and me!
Is't not enough to torture me alone,
But slave to slavery my sweet'st friend must be?
Me from myself thy cruel eye hath taken,
And my next self thou harder hast engrossed:
Of him, myself, and thee, I am forsaken;
A torment thrice threefold thus to be crossed.
Prison my heart in thy steel bosom's ward,
But, then, my friend's heart let my poor heart bail;
Whoe'er keeps me, let my heart be his guard;
Thou canst not then use rigour in my jail:
  And yet thou wilt; for I being pent in thee,
  Perforce am thine, and all that is in me.

CXXXIV.

So, now I have confess'd that he is thine,
And I myself am mortgag'd to thy will;
Myself I'll forfeit, so that other mine
Thou wilt restore, to be my comfort still:
But thou wilt not, nor he will not be free,
For thou art covetous, and he is kind;
He learn'd but, surety-like, to write for me,
Under that bond that him as fast doth bind.
The statute of thy beauty thou wilt take,
Thou usurer, that putt'st forth all to use,
And sue a friend came debtor for my sake;
So him I lose through my unkind abuse.
  Him have I lost; thou hast both him and me:
  He pays the whole, and yet am I not free.

CXXXV.

Whoever hath her wish, thou hast thy will,
And *Will* to boot, and will in over-plus;
More than enough am I, that vex thee still,
To thy sweet will making addition thus.
Wilt thou, whose will is large and spacious,
Not once vouchsafe to hide my will in thine?
Shall will in others seem right gracious,
And in my will no fair acceptance shine?
The sea, all water, yet receives rain still,
And in abundance addeth to his store;
So thou, being rich in will, add to thy will
One will of mine, to make thy large will more.
  Let no unkind, no fair beseechers kill;
  Think all but one, and me in that one *Will*.

CXXXVI.

If thy soul check thee that I come so near,
Swear to thy blind soul that I was thy *Will*,
And will, thy soul knows, is admitted there;
Thus far for love, my love-suit, sweet, fulfil.
Will will fulfil the treasure of thy love,
Ay, fill it full with wills, and my will one.
In things of great receipt with ease we prove,
Among a number one is reckon'd none:
Then in the number let me pass untold,
Though in thy stores' account I one must be;
For nothing hold me, so it please thee hold
That nothing me, a something sweet to thee:
  Make but my name thy love, and love that still,
  And then thou lov'st me, — for my name is *Will*.

CXXXVII.

Thou blind fool, Love, what dost thou to mine eyes,
That they behold, and see not what they see?
They know what beauty is, see where it lies,
Yet what the best is, take the worst to be.
If eyes, corrupt by over-partial looks,
Be anchor'd in the bay where all men ride,
Why of eyes' falsehood hast thou forged hooks,
Whereto the judgment of my heart is tied?
Why should my heart think that a several plot,
Which my heart knows the wide world's common place?
Or mine eyes, seeing this, say, this is not,
To put fair truth upon so foul a face?
  In things right true my heart and eyes have erred,
  And to this false plague are they now transferred.

CXXXVIII.

When my love swears that she is made of truth,
I do believe her, though I know she lies,
That she might think me some untutor'd youth,
Unlearned in the world's false subtleties.
Thus vainly thinking that she thinks me young,
Although she knows my days are past the best,
Simply I credit her false-speaking tongue:
On both sides thus is simple truth supprest.
But wherefore says she not, she is unjust?
And wherefore say not I, that I am old?
O, love's best habit is in seeming trust,
And age in love loves not to have years told:
  Therefore I lie with her, and she with me,
  And in our faults by lies we flatter'd be.

CXXXIX.

O, call not me to justify the wrong,
That thy unkindness lays upon my heart;
Wound me not with thine eye, but with thy tongue,
Use power with power, and slay me not by art.
Tell me thou lov'st elsewhere; but in my sight,
Dear heart, forbear to glance thine eye aside:
What need'st thou wound with cunning, when thy might
Is more than my o'er-press'd defence can 'bide?
Let me excuse thee: ah! my love well knows
Her pretty looks have been mine enemies,
And therefore from my face she turns my foes,
That they elsewhere might dart their injuries.
  Yet do not so; but since I am near slain,
  Kill me out-right with looks, and rid my pain.

CXL.

Be wise as thou art cruel; do not press
My tongue-tied patience with too much disdain;
Lest sorrow lend me words, and words express
The manner of my pity-wanting pain.
If I might teach thee wit, better it were,
Though not to love, yet, love, to tell me so;
As testy sick men, when their deaths be near,
No news but health from their physicians know:
For, if I should despair, I should grow mad,
And in my madness might speak ill of thee;
Now this ill-wresting world is grown so bad,
Mad slanderers by mad ears believed be.
  That I may not be so, nor thou belied,
  Bear thine eyes straight, though thy proud heart go wide.

CXLI.

In faith I do not love thee with mine eyes,
For they in thee a thousand errors note;
But 'tis my heart that loves what they despise,
Who in despite of view is pleas'd to dote.
Nor are mine ears with thy tongue's tune delighted;
Nor tender feeling, to base touches prone,
Nor taste, nor smell, desire to be invited
To any sensual feast with thee alone:
But my five wits, nor my five senses can
Dissuade one foolish heart from serving thee,
Who leave unsway'd the likeness of a man,
Thy proud heart's slave and vassal wretch to be:
  Only my plague thus far I count my gain,
  That she that makes me sin awards me pain.

CXLII.

Love is my sin, and thy dear virtue hate,
Hate of my sin, grounded on sinful loving.
O, but with mine compare thou thine own state,
And thou shalt find it merits not reproving;
Or, if it do, not from those lips of thine,
That have profan'd their scarlet ornaments,
And seal'd false bonds of love as oft as mine,
Robb'd others' beds revenues of their rents.
Be it lawful I love thee, as thou lov'st those
Whom thine eyes woo as mine importune thee:
Root pity in thy heart, that when it grows,
Thy pity may deserve to pitied be.
  If thou dost seek to have what thou dost hide,
  By self-example may'st thou be deni'd!

CXLIII.

Lo, as a careful housewife runs to catch
One of her feather'd creatures broke away,
Sets down her babe, and makes all swift dispatch
In pursuit of the thing she would have stay;
Whilst her neglected child holds her in chase,
Cries to catch her whose busy care is bent
To follow that which flies before her face,
Not prizing her poor infant's discontent:
So run'st thou after that which flies from thee,
Whilst I, thy babe, chase thee afar behind;
But if thou catch thy hope, turn back to me,
And play the mother's part, kiss me, be kind:
  So will I pray that thou may'st have thy *Will*,
  If thou turn back, and my loud crying still.

CXLIV.

Two loves I have of comfort and despair,
Which like two spirits do suggest me still:
The better angel is a man, right fair,
The worser spirit a woman, colour'd ill.
To win me soon to hell, my female evil
Tempteth my better angel from my side,
And would corrupt my saint to be a devil,
Wooing his purity with her foul pride.
And whether that my angel be turn'd fiend,
Suspect I may, yet not directly tell;
But being both from me, both to each friend,
I guess one angel in another's hell:
  Yet this shall I ne'er know, but live in doubt,
  Till my bad angel fire my good one out.

CXLV.

Those lips that Love's own hand did make,
Breath'd forth the sound that said, "I hate,"
To me that languish'd for her sake;
But when she saw my woeful state,
Straight in her heart did mercy come,
Chiding that tongue, that ever sweet
Was us'd in giving gentle doom,
And taught it thus anew to greet.
"I hate," she alter'd with an end,
That follow'd it as gentle day
Doth follow night, who, like a fiend,
From Heaven to Hell is flown away:
  "I hate" from hate away she threw,
  And sav'd my life, saying—"Not you."

CXLVI.

Poor soul, the centre of my sinful earth,
[Fool'd by] these rebel pow'rs that thee array,
Why dost thou pine within, and suffer dearth,
Painting thy outward walls so costly gay?
Why so large cost, having so short a lease,
Dost thou upon thy fading mansion spend?
Shall worms, inheritors of this excess,
Eat up thy charge? is this thy body's end?
Then, soul, live thou upon thy servant's loss,
And let that pine to aggravate thy store;
Buy terms divine in selling hours of dross;
Within be fed, without be rich no more:
  So shalt thou feed on death, that feeds on men,
  And, death once dead, there's no more dying then.

CXLVII.

My love is as a fever, longing still
For that which longer nurseth the disease;
Feeding on that which doth preserve the ill,
Th' uncertain sickly appetite to please.
My reason, the physician to my love,
Angry that his prescriptions are not kept,
Hath left me, and I desperate now approve,
Desire is death, which physic did except.
Past cure I am, now reason is past care,
And frantic mad with ever-more unrest:
My thoughts and my discourse as madmen's are,
At random from the truth vainly express'd;
  For I have sworn thee fair, and thought thee bright,
  Who art as black as Hell, as dark as night

CXLVIII.

O me, what eyes hath Love put in my head,
Which have no correspondence with true sight!
Or, if they have, where is my judgment fled,
That censures falsely what they see aright?
If that be fair whereon my false eyes dote,
What means the world to say it is not so?
If it be not, then love doth well denote
Love's eye is not so true as all men's: no,
How can it? O, how can love's eye be true,
That is so vex'd with watching and with tears?
No marvel, then, though I mistake my view;
The sun itself sees not, till heaven clears.
  O cunning Love, with tears thou keep'st me blind,
  Lest eyes well-seeing thy foul faults should find.

CXLIX.

Canst thou, O cruel! say, I love thee not,
When I, against myself, with thee partake?
Do I not think on thee, when I forgot
Am of myself, all tyrant, for thy sake?
Who hateth thee that I do call my friend?
On whom frown'st thou that I do fawn upon?
Nay, if thou low'r'st on me, do I not spend
Revenge upon myself with present moan?
What merit do I in myself respect,
That is so proud thy service to despise,
When all my best doth worship thy defect,
Commanded by the motion of thine eyes?
  But, love, hate on, for now I know thy mind:
  Those that can see thou lov'st, and I am blind

CL.

O, from what power hast thou this powerful might,
With insufficiency my heart to sway?
To make me give the lie to my true sight,
And swear that brightness doth not grace the day?
Whence hast thou this becoming of things ill,
That in the very refuse of thy deeds
There is such strength and warrantise of skill,
That in my mind thy worst all best exceeds?
Who taught thee how to make me love thee more,
The more I hear and see just cause of hate?
O, though I love what others do abhor,
With others thou should'st not abhor my state:
  If thy unworthiness rais'd love in me,
  More worthy I to be belov'd of thee.

CLI.

Love is too young to know what conscience is;
Yet who knows not conscience is born of love?
Then, gentle cheater, urge not my amiss,
Lest guilty of my faults thy sweet self prove:
For, thou betraying me, I do betray
My nobler part to my gross body's treason;
My soul doth tell my body that he may
Triumph in love; flesh stays no farther reason,
But rising at thy name, doth point out thee
As his triumphant prize. Proud of this pride,
He is contented thy poor drudge to be,
To stand in thy affairs, fall by thy side.
  No want of conscience hold it, that I call
  Her love, for whose dear love I rise and fall.

CLII.

In loving thee thou know'st I am forsworn,
But thou art twice forsworn, to me love swearing;
In act thy bed-vow broke, and new faith torn,
In vowing new hate after new love bearing.
But why of two oaths' breach do I accuse thee,
When I break twenty? I am perjur'd most;
For all my vows are oaths but to misuse thee,
And all my honest faith in thee is lost:
For I have sworn deep oaths of thy deep kindness,
Oaths of thy love, thy truth, thy constancy;
And to enlighten thee, gave eyes to blindness,
Or made them swear against the thing they see;
For I have sworn thee fair: more perjur'd I,
To swear against the truth so foul a lie!

CLIII.

Cupid laid by his brand, and fell asleep:
A maid of Dian's this advantage found,
And his love-kindling fire did quickly steep
In a cold valley-fountain of that ground;
Which borrow'd from this holy fire of love
A dateless lively heat, still to endure,
And grew a seething bath, which yet men prove,
Against strange maladies a sovereign cure.
But at my mistress' eye love's brand new-fired,
The boy for trial needs would touch my breast;
I sick withal, the help of bath desired,
And thither hied a sad distemper'd guest,
But found no cure: the bath for my help lies
Where Cupid got new fire, my mistress' eyes.

CLIV.

The little Love-god lying once asleep,
Laid by his side his heart-inflaming brand,
Whilst many nymphs, that vow'd chaste life to keep,
Came tripping by; but in her maiden hand
The fairest votary took up that fire
Which many legions of true hearts had warm'd:
And so the General of hot desire
Was, sleeping, by a virgin hand disarm'd.
This brand she quenched in a cool well by,
Which from love's fire took heat perpetual,
Growing a bath, and healthful remedy
For men diseas'd; but I, my mistress' thrall,
  Came there for cure, and this by that I prove,
  Love's fire heats water, water cools not love.

NOTES ON THE SONNETS.

III.

p. 154. "—— whose *un-ear'd* womb": — i. e., unploughed; the converse of the common metaphor 'virgin soil.'

V.

p. 155. "*Leese* but their shew": — 'Leese' is an old form of 'lose.'

IX.

p. 157. "—— like a *makeless* wife": — i. e., a widow, a woman who has lost her mate. 'Make' and 'mate' were used interchangeably.

XII.

p. 159. "And sable curls *all* silver'd": — The first edition, "*or* silver'd," which Malone corrected. Tyrwhitt suggested, "*are* silver'd."

XIV.

p. 160. "—— I have *astronomy*": — i. e., astrology. All knowledge of the stars was commonly supposed to have divination for its object; and hence, until a comparatively recent period, there was not a distinction drawn between astronomy and astrology.

XIX.

p. 162. "—— as thou *fleets*": the 4to., "as thou *fleet'st*," which, as the rhyme is lost, may be safely regarded as a misprint. See in Sonnet VIII. for the rhyme, "They do but sweetly chide thee who *confounds*."

XXI.

p. 163. "—— in this huge *rondure* hems": — i. e., this huge sphere. So in *King John*, Act II. Sc. 1, "'Tis not the rondure of your old fac'd walls."

XXII.

p. 164. "Then look I death my days should *expirate*":—The first edition, "should *expiate*." See the Note on "the hour of death is *expirate*," *King Richard the Third*, Act III. Sc. 3. And see the last line of *Titus Andronicus*, "That like events may ne'er it ruinate," and *King Henry the Sixth*, Part III. Act V. Sc. 1, "I will not ruinate my father's house." In the Note on *Richard III.*, by a slip of memory, 'conspirate' is mentioned as one of the verbs which Shakespeare uses in this form.

XXIII.

"—— is put *besides* his part":—See the Note on "and besides myself," *The Comedy of Errors*, Act III. Sc. 2.

XXIV.

p. 165. "—— and hath steel'd":—See the Note on "when all distress is steld," in *Lucrece*, p. 122.

XXV.

" "—— famoused for *worth*":—i. e., for prowess, martial honor. Valiant knights were said to gain great worship (worth-ship) in battle. See *King Arthur*, *passim*.

" "Is from the book of honour razed *forth*":—The old copies, "razed *quite*," which is clearly corrupt. I had supposed this reading to be peculiar to myself, but find that it was suggested by Theobald. He also proposed, as a relief from the difficulty of the old text, the change of 'worth' to 'fight,' at the end of the second line above, which has been adopted universally, although, in my judgment, much the inferior reading.

XXVI.

p. 166. "—— of *thy* sweet respect":—The old copy, "of *their* sweet respect." In that volume 'they,' 'their,' 'thee,' 'them,' and 'thy' are very frequently misprinted for each other.

XXVII.

" "Presents *thy* shadow":—The 4to., "*their* shadow."

XXVIII.

p. 167. "When sparkling stars *twire* not":—The meaning of 'twire' is not determined. It is used variously, in passages in which it would seem to mean to twitter, to twinkle, and to leer. Richardson gives "to swerve from a straight line," as its radical thought.

p. 167. "—— grief's *strength* seem stronger": — The old copy, "grief's *length*," &c. — an error due to the last word of the preceding line.

XXXI.

p. 168. "—— and *obsequious* tear": — i. e., tear at obsequies, like "obsequious sorrow," in *Hamlet*, Act I. Sc. 2.

" "—— that hidden in *thee* lie": — The old copy has, "*there*" for 'thee.'

XXXIV.

p. 170. "—— the strong offence's *cross*": — The old copy has "offences *loss*." Malone made the necessary change.

XXXV.

" "Excusing *thy* sins," &c.: — In the 4to., 'thy' is twice misprinted "*their*," in this line.

" "For to thy *sensual* fault": — i. e., thy fault of sense, as opposed to a mental or moral error. We should now use 'sensuous.' See the same word similarly used in Sonnet CXLI.

XXXVII.

p. 171. "Entitled in *thy* parts": — The old copy, "*their* parts."

XXXIX.

p. 172. "—— so sweetly *doth* deceive": — The 4to., "*dost* deceive;" and perhaps so the author wrote.

XL.

p. 173. "—— if thou *thyself* deceivest": — The 4to., "*this* selfe deceavest."

XLI.

" "—— till *she* have prevailed": — The 4to., "*he* have," &c.

" "—— thou might'st *my seat* forbear": — So in *Othello*, Act II. Sc. 1: —

"For that I do suspect the lusty Moor
Hath leap'd into my seat."

XLIII.

p. 174. "—— *thy* fair imperfect shade": — The 4to., "*their* faire," &c.

XLV.

p. 175. "Of *thy* fair health": — The 4to., "Of *their* faire," &c.; and in the third line of the next Sonnet, "Mine eye, my heart *their* pictures," &c.; in the eighth line, "*their* faire appearance;" and in the thirteenth and fourteenth lines, "*their*" for 'thine.'

L.

p. 178. "Plods *dully* on": — The 4to., "Plods *duly* on" — a misprint hardly worth notice.

LIV.

p. 180. "But, *for* their virtue": — i. e., but because their virtue.

LIX.

p. 182. "—— or *whe'r* better they": — i. e., or whether, &c.

LXII.

p. 184. "*Beaten* and chapp'd": — The old copy, "*Beated* and chopt," which has been followed hitherto, although a manifest misprint.

LXV.

p. 185. "Or who his spoil *of* beauty": — The old copy, "his spoil *or* beauty."

LXVI.

p. 186. "—— by limping sway *disablèd*": — The old copy, "*disabled;*" but rhythm and rhyme show that the word is to be pronounced in four syllables, in the uncontracted participial form.

LXIX.

p. 187. "—— give thee that *due*": — The 4to., "that *end*," which Tyrwhitt corrected.

" "*Thine* outward": — The 4to., "*Their* outward."

" "The *solve* is this": — The 4to. has the easy misprint, "The *solye*."

LXXIII.

p. 189. "Bare *ruin d* choirs": — The edition of 1609, "*rn'wd* quiers;" that of 1640, "ruin'd" — a variation hardly worth notice.

LXXVI.

p. 191. "—— and *where* they did proceed": — Not improbably a misprint of 'and *whence*,' &c.

LXXVII.

" "Commit to these waste *blanks*": — The old copy, "these waste *blacks*."

LXXXV.

p. 195. "—— that able *spirit* affords": — Another of the many instances of the use of 'spirit' as a monosyllable.

LXXXVI.

p. 196. "—— fil'd up his line": — So Ben Jonson, in his verses on Shakespeare, —

"In his well torned and true filed lines."

And in the preceding Sonnet, —

"And precious phrase by all the Muses fil'd."

XCIX.

p. 202. "*One* blushing shame": — In the 4to., "*Our* blushing shame."

CVI.

p. 206. "They had not *skill* enough": — The 4to., "*still* enough."

CVIII.

p. 207. "—— what *new* to register": — The 4to., "what *now*," &c. Malone made the manifestly proper change.

CX.

p. 208. "Now all is done, *save*," &c.: — The 4to., "*have*," which Tyrwhitt corrected.

CXI.

" "—— *with* Fortune chide": — The old copy, "*wish* fortune," &c.

" "Potions of *eysel*": — Vinegar was called eysel.

CXII.

p. 209. "That my steel'd *sense*": — Here, and in the next line but one, 'sense' is plural.

" "—— methinks *they* are dead": — The 4to., "methinks *y'* are dead."

CXIII.

" "—— which it doth *latch*": — i. e., catch. See the Note on "Where hearing should not latch them," *Macbeth*, Act IV. Sc. 3.

" "—— thus maketh *mine untrue*": — i. e., maketh the semblance, the fictitious (and so the false or untrue) object which is constantly before me: 'untrue' used substantively.

CXXV.

p. 215. "Which is not mix'd with *seconds*": — The second quality of flour was, and, I believe, still is, called seconds.

CXXVI.

p. 216. "Dost hold Time's *fickle glass*, his sickle, *hour*:" — I do not know that this line has elicited any comment; but it presents a most remarkable instance of inversion for "Dost hold Time's fickle *hour-glass*, his sickle."

CXXVII.

" "*In the old age black was not counted fair*": — This is an allusion to the remarkable fact that during the chivalric ages brunettes were not acknowledged as beauties any where in Christendom. In all the old *contes*, *fabliaux*, and romances that I am acquainted with, the heroines are blondes. And more, the possession of dark eyes and hair, and the complexion that accompanies them, is referred to by the troubadours as a misfortune. But the brunettes have changed the fashion since that day. Is it partly so because, as the naturalists inform us, the blond type is disappearing, and taste conforms to necessity?

CXXVIII.

p. 217. "Do I envy those *jacks*": — i. e., those keys.

" "O'er whom *thy* fingers walk": — The 4to., "*their* fingers," &c., and so again in the last line of this sonnet.

CXXIX.

p. 217. "—— and *prov'd, a* very woe": — Malone's correction of the 4to. reading, "and *proud and* very wo."

CXXXII.

p. 219. "Knowing thy heart *torments* me": — The 4to., "*torment* me" — the mere omission of the final *s* so often mentioned in these Notes.

CXLI.

p. 223. "To any *sensual* feast": — i. e., sensuous feast. See the Note above on Sonnet XXXV.

CXLIV.

p. 225. "—— from my *side*": — The 4to., "my sight," with obvious error.

CXLVI.

p. 226. "[*Fool'd by*] these rebel pow'rs": — In the old copy the last words of the preceding line are accidentally repeated at the beginning of this: —

"*My sinfull earth* these rebell powres that thee array."

Some change being necessary, that made by Malone may be well accepted.

CLII.

p. 229. "—— more perjur'd *I*": — The 4to., "more perjur'd *eye*" — a mere phonographic error.

A LOVER'S COMPLAINT.

A Lover's Complaint was first printed in 1609, at the end of the first edition of Shakespeare's Sonnets. Its style furnishes us our only means of conjecturing the date of its composition; which hence appears to have been later than that of any other of his poems, except, perhaps, a few of his sonnets.

A LOVER'S COMPLAINT.

FROM off a hill whose concave womb re-worded
A plaintful story from a sist'ring vale,
My spirits t' attend this double voice accorded,
And down I lay to list the sad-tun'd tale:
Ere long espy'd a fickle maid full pale,
Tearing of papers, breaking rings a-twain,
Storming her world with sorrow's wind and rain.

Upon her head, a platted hive of straw,
Which fortified her visage from the sun,
Whereon the thought might think sometime it saw
The carcass of a beauty spent and done.
Time had not scythed all that youth begun,
Nor youth all quit; but, spite of Heaven's fell rage,
Some beauty peep'd through lattice of sear'd age.

Oft did she heave her napkin to her eyne,
Which on it had conceited characters,
Laund'ring the silken figures in the brine
That seasoned woe had pelleted in tears,
And often reading what contents it bears;
As often shrieking undistinguish'd woe,
In clamours of all size, both high and low.

Sometimes her levell'd eyes their carriage ride,
As they did batt'ry to the spheres intend;
Sometime diverted their poor balls are ti'd
To th' orbed Earth: sometimes they do extend
Their view right on; anon their gazes lend
To every place at once, and nowhere fix'd,
The mind and sight distractedly commix'd.

Her hair, nor loose, nor ti'd in formal plat,
Proclaim'd in her a careless hand of pride:
For some, untuck'd, descended her sheav'd hat,
Hanging her pale and pined cheek beside;
Some in her threaden fillet still did bide,
And, true to bondage, would not break from thence,
Though slackly braided in loose negligence.

A thousand favours from a maund she drew
Of amber, crystal, and of beaded jet,
Which one by one she in a river threw,
Upon whose weeping margent she was set;
Like usury, applying wet to wet,
Or monarch's hands, that let not bounty fall
Where want cries 'some,' but where excess begs all.

Of folded schedules had she many a one,
Which she perus'd, sigh'd, tore, and gave the flood;
Crack'd many a ring of posi'd gold and bone,
Bidding them find their sepulchres in mud;
Found yet more letters sadly penn'd in blood,
With sleided silk feat and affectedly
Enswath'd, and seal'd to curious secrecy.

These often bath'd she in her fluxive eyes,
And often kiss'd, and often 'gan to tear;
Cried, "O false blood! thou register of lies,
What unapproved witness dost thou bear!
Ink would have seem'd more black and damned here!"
This said, in top of rage the lines she rents,
Big discontent so breaking their contents.

A reverend man that graz'd his cattle nigh,
Sometime a blusterer, that the ruffle knew
Of court, of city, and had let go by
The swiftest hours, observed as they flew;
Towards this afflicted fancy fastly drew;
And, privileg'd by age, desires to know
In brief, the grounds and motives of her woe.

So slides he down upon his grained bat,
And comely-distant sits he by her side;
When he again desires her, being sat,
Her grievance with his hearing to divide:
If that from him there may be aught appli'd
Which may her suffering ecstasy assuage,
'Tis promis'd in the charity of age.

"Father," she says, "though in me you behold
The injury of many a blasting hour,
Let it not tell your judgment I am old;
Not age, but sorrow, over me hath power;
I might as yet have been a spreading flower,
Fresh to myself, if I had self-appli'd
Love to myself, and to no love beside.

"But woe is me! too early I attended
A youthful suit (it was to gain my grace)
Of one by nature's outwards so commended,
That maiden's eyes stuck over all his face:
Love lack'd a dwelling, and made him her place;
And when in his fair parts she did abide,
She was new lodg'd, and newly deified.

"His browny locks did hang in crooked curls;
And every light occasion of the wind
Upon his lips their silken parcels hurls.
What's sweet to do, to do will aptly find:
Each eye that saw him did enchant the mind;
For on his visage was, in little, drawn
What largeness thinks in paradise was sawn.

"Small shew of man was yet upon his chin;
His phœnix down began but to appear,
Like unshorn velvet, on that termless skin,
Whose bare out-bragg'd the web it seem'd to wear;
Yet shew'd his visage by that cost most dear;
And nice affections wavering stood in doubt
If best 'twere as it was, or best without.

"His qualities were beauteous as his form,
For maiden-tongu'd he was, and thereof free;
Yet, if men mov'd him, was he such a storm
As oft 'twixt May and April is to see,
When winds breathe sweet, unruly though they be.
His rudeness so with his authoriz'd youth,
Did livery falseness in a pride of truth.

"Well could he ride, and often men would say
'That horse his mettle from his rider takes:
Proud of subjection, noble by the sway,
What rounds, what bounds, what course, what stop
he makes!'
And controversy hence a question takes,
Whether the horse by him became his deed,
Or he his manage by th' well-doing steed.

"But quickly on this side the verdict went;
His real habitude gave life and grace
To appertainings and to ornament,
Accomplish'd in himself, not in his case:
All aids, themselves made fairer by their place,
Came for additions; yet their purpos'd trim
Piec'd not his grace, but were all grac'd by him.

"So on the tip of his subduing tongue
All kind of arguments and question deep,
All replication prompt, and reason strong,
For his advantage still did wake and sleep:
To make the weeper laugh, the laugher weep,
He had the dialect and different skill,
Catching all passions in his craft of will;

"That he did in the general bosom reign
Of young, of old; and sexes both enchanted,
To dwell with him in thoughts, or to remain
In personal duty, following where he haunted:
Consents bewitch'd, ere he desire, have granted;
And dialogu'd for him what he would say,
Ask'd their own wills, and made their wills obey.

"Many there were that did his picture get,
To serve their eyes, and in it put their mind;
Like fools that in th' imagination set
The goodly objects which abroad they find
Of lands and mansions, theirs in thought assign'd;
And labouring in more pleasures to bestow them,
Than the true gouty landlord which doth owe them:

"So many have, that never touch'd his hand,
Sweetly suppos'd them mistress of his heart.
My woeful self, that did in freedom stand,
And was my own fee-simple, (not in part,)
What with his art in youth, and youth in art,
Threw my affections in his charmed power,
Reserv'd the stalk, and gave him all my flower.

"Yet did I not, as some my equals did,
Demand of him, nor being desired, yielded;
Finding myself in honour so forbid,
With safest distance I mine honour shielded:
Experience for me many bulwarks builded
Of proofs new-bleeding, which remain'd the foil
Of this false jewel, and his amorous spoil.

"But ah, who ever shunn'd by precedent
The destin'd ill she must herself assay!
Or forc'd examples, 'gainst her own content,
To put the by-pass'd perils in her way!
Counsel may stop a while what will not stay;
For when we rage, advice is often seen
By blunting us to make our wits more keen.

"Nor gives it satisfaction to our blood,
That we must curb it upon others' proof,
To be forbid the sweets that seem so good,
For fear of harms that preach in our behoof.
O appetite, from judgment stand aloof!
The one a palate hath that needs will taste,
Though reason weep, and cry, 'It is thy last.'

"For further I could say, 'This man 's untrue,'
And knew the patterns of his foul beguiling;
Heard where his plants in others' orchards grew,
Saw how deceits were gilded in his smiling;
Knew vows were ever brokers to defiling;
Thought, characters, and words, merely but art,
And bastards of his foul adulterate heart.

"And long upon these terms I held my city,
Till thus he 'gan besiege me: 'Gentle maid,
Have of my suffering youth some feeling pity,
And be not of my holy vows afraid:
That's to you sworn, to none was ever said;
For feasts of love I have been call'd unto,
Till now did ne'er invite, nor never vow.

"'All my offences that abroad you see,
Are errors of the blood, none of the mind;
Love made them not; with acture they may be,
Where neither party is nor true nor kind:
They sought their shame that so their shame did find;
And so much less of shame in me remains,
By how much of me their reproach contains.

"'Among the many that mine eyes have seen,
Not one whose flame my heart so much as warmed,
Or my affection put to th' smallest teen,
Or any of my leisures ever charmed:
Harm have I done to them, but ne'er was harmed;
Kept hearts in liveries, but mine own was free,
And reign'd, commanding in his monarchy.

"'Look here what tributes wounded fancies sent me,
Of paled pearls, and rubies red as blood;
Figuring that they their passions likewise lent me
Of grief and blushes, aptly understood
In bloodless white and the encrimson'd mood;
Effects of terror and dear modesty,
Encamp'd in hearts, but fighting outwardly.

"'And lo, behold these talents of their hair,
With twisted metal amorously impleach'd,
I have receiv'd from many a several fair,
(Their kind acceptance weepingly beseech'd,)
With the annexions of fair gems enrich'd,
And deep-brain'd sonnets that did amplify
Each stone's dear nature, worth, and quality.

"'The diamond?—why, 'twas beautiful and hard,
Whereto his invis'd properties did tend;
The deep-green em'rald, in whose fresh regard
Weak sights their sickly radiance do amend;
The heaven-hued sapphire and the opal blend
With objects manifold; each several stone,
With wit well blazon'd, smil'd or made some moan.

"'Lo, all these trophies of affections hot,
Of pensiv'd and subdu'd desires the tender,
Nature hath charg'd me that I hoard them not,
But yield them up where I myself must render,
That is, to you, my origin and ender:
For these, of force, must your oblations be,
Since I their altar, you enpatron me.

"'O then advance of yours that phraseless hand,
Whose white weighs down the airy scale of praise;
Take all these similes to your own command,
Hallow'd with sighs that burning lungs did raise;
What me your minister, for you obeys,
Works under you; and to your audit comes
Their distract parcels in combined sums.

"'Lo, this device was sent me from a nun,
Or sister sanctifi'd of holiest note;
Which late her noble suit in court did shun,
Whose rarest havings made the blossoms dote;
For she was sought by spirits of richest coat,
But kept cold distance, and did thence remove,
To spend her living in eternal love.

"'But O, my sweet, what labour is't to leave
The thing we have not, mast'ring what not strives,—
Paling the place which did no form receive,
Playing patient sports in unconstrained gyves!
She that her fame so to herself contrives,
The scars of battle 'scapeth by the flight,
And makes her absence valiant, not her might.

"'O, pardon me, in that my boast is true;
The accident which brought me to her eye,
Upon the moment did her force subdue,
And now she would the caged cloister fly:
Religious love put out religion's eye:
Not to be tempted, would she be immur'd,
And now, to tempt all, liberty procur'd.

"'How mighty then you are, O, hear me tell!
The broken bosoms that to me belong
Have emptied all their fountains in my well,
And mine I pour your ocean all among:
I strong o'er them, and you o'er me being strong,
Must for your victory us all congest,
As compound love to physic your cold breast.

"'My parts had power to charm a sacred nun,
Who disciplin'd and dieted in grace,
Believ'd her eyes when they t' assail begun,
All vows and consecrations giving place.
O most potential love! vow, bond, nor space,
In thee hath neither sting, knot, nor confine,
For thou art all, and all things else are thine.

"'When thou impressest, what are precepts worth
Of stale example? When thou wilt inflame,
How coldly those impediments stand forth
Of wealth, of filial fear, law, kindred, fame?
Love's arms are proof, 'gainst rule, 'gainst sense, 'gainst shame,
And sweetens, in the suff'ring pangs it bears,
The aloes of all forces, shocks, and fears.

"'Now all these hearts that do on mine depend,
Feeling it break, with bleeding groans they pine,
And supplicant their sighs to you extend,
To leave the battery that you make 'gainst mine,
Lending soft audience to my sweet design,
And credent soul to that strong-bonded oath,
That shall prefer and undertake my troth.'

"This said, his watery eyes he did dismount,
Whose sights till then were levell'd on my face;
Each cheek a river running from a fount
With brinish current downward flow'd apace:
O, how the channel to the stream gave grace!
Who glaz'd with crystal gate the glowing roses
That flame through water which their hue incloses.

"O father, what a hell of witchcraft lies
In the small orb of one particular tear!
But with the inundation of the eyes
What rocky heart to water will not wear!
What breast so cold that is not warmed here!
O cleft effect! cold modesty, hot wrath,
Both fire from hence and chill extincture hath.

"For, lo, his passion, but an art of craft,
Even there resolv'd my reason into tears;
There my white stole of chastity I daff'd,
Shook off my sober guards, and civil fears;
Appear to him, as he to me appears,
All melting; though our drops this difference bore,
His poison'd me, and mine did him restore.

" In him a plenitude of subtle matter,
Applied to cautels, all strange forms receives,
Of burning blushes, or of weeping water,
Or swooning paleness ; and he takes and leaves,
In either's aptness, as it best deceives,
To blush at speeches rank, to weep at woes,
Or to turn white and swoon at tragic shews;

" That not a heart which in his level came,
Could scape the hail of his all-hurting aim,
Shewing fair nature is both kind and tame;
And veil'd in them, did win whom he would maim:
Against the thing he sought he would exclaim;
When he most burn'd in heart-wish'd luxury,
He preach'd pure maid, and prais'd cold chastity.

" Thus merely with the garment of a Grace
The naked and concealed fiend he cover'd,
That th' unexperienc'd gave the tempter place,
Which, like a cherubin, above them hover'd.
Who, young and simple, would not be so lover'd?
Ay me! I fell; and yet do question make
What I should do again for such a sake.

" O, that infected moisture of his eye,
O, that false fire which in his cheek so glowed,
O, that forc'd thunder from his heart did fly,
O, that sad breath his spongy lungs bestowed,
O, all that borrowed motion, seeming owed,
Would yet again betray the fore-betray'd,
And new pervert a reconciled maid!"

NOTES ON A LOVER'S COMPLAINT.

---

p. 242. "—— her *sheav'd* hat" : — i. e., her straw hat.

" "—— from *a maund*" : — i. e., a basket.

" "—— and of *beaded* jet" : — The 4to., "of *bedded* iet."

" "With *sleided* silk *feat*," &c. : — i. e., With floss silk neatly, &c.

p. 243. "—— *gan* to tear" : — The old copy, "*gaue* to teare" — a manifest misprint.

" "Towards this afflicted *fancy*" : — i. e., this afflicted love, or loved one.

p. 244. "*Of* one by nature's" : — The 4to., "*O* one," &c. The correction is Mr. Dyce's.

p. 245. "*Came* for additions" : — The 4to., "*can* for additions."

p. 248. "—— these *talents of their hair*" : — i. e., these lockets, or hair set in gold.

" "—— amorously *impleached*" : — i. e., interwoven.

" "Whereto his *invis'd* properties" : — i. e., invisible properties.

p. 249. "*Or* sister sanctified" : — Mr. Dyce suggests, with much reason, that we should read, "*A* sister," &c.

" "—— by *spirits of richest coat*" : — A plain allusion, I think, to Elizabeth's gorgeously arrayed band of gentlemen pensioners. See the Note on "nay, which is more, pensioners," *Merry Wives of Windsor*, Act II. Sc. 2. Here 'spirits' is a monosyllable.

" "*Paling* the place" : — The old copy, "*Playing*," &c.

p. 250. "—— would she be *immur'd*": — The 4to., "*enur'd.*"

" "—— to charm a sacred *nun*": — The 4to., "a sacred *sunne*" — a slight and obvious misprint.

" "—— and *dieted* in grace": — The old copies, "and I *died,*" &c., which Malone corrected on the suggestion of an anonymous correspondent.

" "Love's arms are *proof* 'gainst rule," &c.: — The 4to., "Love's armes are *peace,* gainst rule," &c., which is clearly corrupt. The reading of the text is Malone's. Mr. Dyce suggests, "*Love* arms *our* peace," &c.

p. 251. "—— his watery eyes he did *dismount*": — An allusion to the rest from which small fire arms used to be levelled.

" "*O* cleft effect": — The 4to., "*Or* cleft effect."

p. 252. "Applied to cautels": — i. e., deceits.

ATTRIBUTED VERSES.

THE PHŒNIX AND TURTLE.

FROM THE ADDITIONAL POEMS TO CHESTER'S "LOVE'S MARTYR,
1601.

LET the bird of loudest lay,
On the sole Arabian tree,
Herald sad and trumpet be,
To whose sound chaste wings obey.

But thou shrieking harbinger,
Foul precurrer of the fiend,
Augur of the fever's end,
To this troop come thou not near.

From this session interdict
Every fowl of tyrant wing,
Save the eagle, feather'd king:
Keep the obsequy so strict.

Let the priest in surplice white,
That defunctive music can,
Be the death-divining swan,
Lest the requiem lack his right.

And thou, treble-dated crow,
That thy sable gender mak'st
With the breath thou giv'st and tak'st,
'Mongst our mourners shalt thou go.

Here the anthem doth commence:
Love and constancy is dead;
Phœnix and the turtle fled
In a mutual flame from hence.

So they lov'd, as love in twain
Had the essence but in one;
Two distincts, division none:
Number there in love was slain.

Hearts remote, yet not asunder;
Distance, and no space was seen
'Twixt the turtle and his queen:
But in them it were a wonder.

So between them love did shine,
That the turtle saw his right
Flaming in the phœnix' sight:
Either was the other's mine.

Property was thus appall'd,
That the self was not the same;
Single nature's double name
Neither two nor one was call'd.

Reason. in itself confounded,
Saw division grow together;
To themselves yet either-neither,
Simple were so well compounded:

That it cried, How true a twain
Seemeth this concordant one!
Love hath reason, reason none,
If what parts can so remain.

Whereupon it made this threne
To the phœnix and the dove,
Co-supremes and stars of love;
As chorus to their tragic scene.

THRENOS.

Beauty, truth, and rarity,
Grace in all simplicity,
Here enclos'd in cinders lie.

Death is now the phœnix' nest;
And the turtle's loyal breast
To eternity doth rest,

Leaving no posterity: —
'Twas not their infirmity,
It was married chastity.

Truth may seem, but cannot be;
Beauty brag, but 'tis not she;
Truth and beauty buried be.

To this urn let those repair,
That are either true or fair;
For these dead birds sigh a prayer.

Wm. Shakespeare.

ON THE KING.

Crowns have their compass, length of days their date,
Triumphs their tomb, Felicity her fate:
Of naught but earth can Earth make us partaker,
But knowledge makes a king most like his Maker.

NOTES ON THE ATTRIBUTED VERSES.

---

p. 257. THE PHŒNIX AND TURTLE, &c.:—There is no other external evidence that these verses are Shakespeare's than their appearance with his signature in a collection of poems published in London while he was living there in the height of his reputation. The style, however, is at least a happy imitation of his, especially in the bold and original use of epithet.

" "That *defunctive* music *can*":—i. e., that is capable of, that understands, funereal music.

p. 259. "—— made this *threne*":—i. e., this funeral ode.

" ON THE KING.—This epigrammatic quatrain was first made public in Mr. Collier's Life of Shakespeare. (p. cciii. Ed. 1844.) He printed it "from a coeval manuscript," which, he says, "seems to have belonged to a curious accumulator of matters of the kind, and which also contains an unknown production by Dekker, as well as various other pieces by dramatists and poets of the time." Its thought is not unworthy of Shakespeare; and in its compactness of expression, and its felicitous alliteration, it presents strong resemblances to the work of his hands.

www.ingramcontent.com/pod-product-compliance
Lightning Source LLC
LaVergne TN
LVHW021104110826
845150LV00001B/170

* 9 7 8 1 4 2 5 5 6 5 3 7 4 *